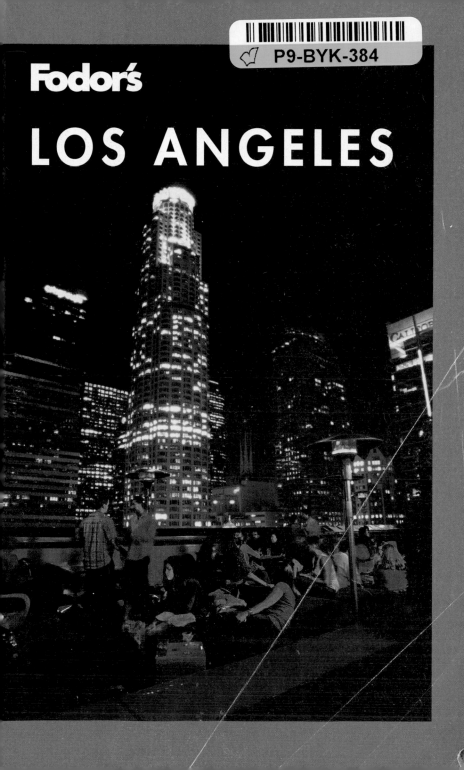

Fodor's

LOS ANGELES

WELCOME TO LOS ANGELES

One of the glitziest places on the planet, the City of Angels combines the people-watching of Rodeo Drive, the nonstop nightlife of the Sunset Strip, and the star quality of the Hollywood Walk of Fame. World-class art museums like the Getty and such jaw-dropping architectural gems as the Walt Disney Concert Hall turn heads. In this top dining destination, the taco stands and celebrity-filled eateries win equal acclaim. The weather in Los Angeles is ideal year-round, so bust out your sunglasses and cruise with the top down to the beach or even to Disneyland.

TOP REASONS TO GO

★ **Star Gazing:** No telescope required at the Hollywood Bowl or Beverly Hills.

★ **Eating:** From food trucks to fine dining to famous markets, you'll find a new fave.

★ **Sun and Fun:** Beaches and boardwalks beckon in Santa Monica, Venice, and Malibu.

★ **Shopping:** Melrose and Robertson will have you knee-deep in shopping bags.

★ **Architecture:** Two Franks—Gehry and Lloyd Wright—top the list of masters.

★ **Great drives:** You can glide down Laurel Canyon Boulevard or the Pacific Coast Highway.

Fodor's LOS ANGELES

Publisher: Amanda D'Acierno, *Senior Vice President*

Editorial: Arabella Bowen, *Editor in Chief*; Linda Cabasin, *Editorial Director*

Design: Fabrizio La Rocca, *Vice President, Creative Director*; Tina Malaney, *Associate Art Director*; Chie Ushio, *Senior Designer*; Ann McBride, *Production Designer*

Photography: Melanie Marin, *Associate Director of Photography*; Jessica Parkhill and Jennifer Romains, *Researchers*

Maps: Rebecca Baer, *Senior Map Editor*; Mark Stroud (Moon Street Cartography) and David Lindroth, *Cartographers*

Production: Linda Schmidt, *Managing Editor*; Evangelos Vasilakis, *Associate Managing Editor*; Angela L. McLean, *Senior Production Manager*

Sales: Jacqueline Lebow, *Sales Director*

Marketing & Publicity: Heather Dalton, *Marketing Director*; Katherine Punia, *Senior Publicist*

Business & Operations: Susan Livingston, *Vice President, Strategic Business Planning*; Sue Daulton, *Vice President, Operations*

Fodors.com: Megan Bell, *Executive Director, Revenue & Business Development*; Yasmin Marinaro, *Senior Director, Marketing & Partnerships*

Editor: Mark Sullivan, Debbie Harmsen

Writers: Sarah Amandalore, Jim Arnold, Cindy Arora, Michele Bigley, Alene Dawson, Dianne de Guzman, Kathy McDonald, Clarissa Wei

Production Editor: Jennifer DePrima

26th Edition

ISBN 978-0-8041-4219-9

ISSN 1095-3914

SPECIAL SALES

This book is available at special discounts for bulk purchases for sales promotions or premiums. For more information, e-mail specialmarkets@randomhouse.com

PRINTED IN THE UNITED STATES OF AMERICA

10 9 8 7 6 5 4 3 2 1

CONTENTS

1 **EXPERIENCE LOS ANGELES. . . . 9**
   Los Angeles Today 10
   What's Where 12
   Los Angeles Planner 14
   Los Angeles Top Attractions. 16
   Top Experiences. 18
   If You Like. 20
   Great Itineraries. 22
   Free and Almost Free 25
   Top Museums 26
   Los Angeles with Kids 27
   Great Architecture. 28
   L.A. Sports Action 29

2 **DOWNTOWN
   LOS ANGELES 35**

3 **HOLLYWOOD AND
   THE STUDIOS 53**
   A Day at Griffith Park. 56
   Hollywood 61
   Studio City 72
   Universal City 72
   Burbank. 72
   North Hollywood 74
   Los Feliz. 74
   Silver Lake 76
   Echo Park. 76

4 **BEVERLY HILLS,
   WEST HOLLYWOOD,
   AND THE WESTSIDE 77**
   Beverly Hills 80
   Century City 86
   Westwood 86
   Brentwood 88
   Bel Air. 90
   West Hollywood. 90

Fodor's Features

Cruising the Sunset Strip 30
Along the Strand 106
L.A.'s Historic Bars. 145

5 **SANTA MONICA AND
   THE BEACHES 97**
   Santa Monica. 100
   Pacific Palisades. 103
   Venice. 105
   Playa del Rey 111
   Malibu. 111
   Manhattan Beach 114
   Hermosa Beach 115
   Redondo Beach 115

6 **PASADENA 117**

7 **NIGHTLIFE 131**
   Planning. 134
   Downtown 135
   Hollywood 137
   West Hollywood. 143
   Santa Monica and
   the Beaches 151

8 **PERFORMING ARTS. 153**
   Performing Arts Planner. 155

CONTENTS

9 SHOPPING 167
   Downtown 170
   Hollywood and the Studios 172
   Beverly Hills and the Westside. . . 176
   Santa Monica and the Beaches . . 191
   Pasadena 194
10 WHERE TO EAT 195
   Best Bets for
   Los Angeles Dining 198
   South-of-the-Border Flavor 200
   Planning. 202
   Restaurant Reviews. 203
11 WHERE TO STAY 239
   Planning. 242
   Hotel Reviews 243
   Best Bets for
   Los Angeles Lodging 244
12 ORANGE COUNTY
   AND CATALINA ISLAND. 269
   Welcome to Orange County
   and Catalina Island. 270
   Planning. 272
   Disneyland Resort. 274
   Knott's Berry Farm 286
   The Coast 288
   Catalina Island. 305

   TRAVEL SMART
   LOS ANGELES 311
   INDEX. 320
   ABOUT OUR WRITERS. 336

MAPS

   Downtown Los Angeles 36
   Hollywood and the Studios 54

   Hollywood 60
   Beverly Hills and the Westside. . . .78
   Santa Monica and the Beaches . . .98
   Pasadena and Environs 118
   Los Angeles Nightlife. 133
   Shopping in L.A. 169
   Dining in Los Angeles 197
   Where to Eat in
   Downtown Los Angeles 204
   Where to Eat in Beverly Hills,
   Los Feliz, Hollywood,
   and West Hollywood 208–209
   Where to Eat in Burbank,
   North Hollywood,
   and Studio City 212
   Where to Eat in Bel Air,
   Brentwood, Century City,
   Malibu, Santa Monica,
   and Venice 230–231
   Where to Eat in Pasadena. 236
   Where to Stay in
   Downtown Los Angeles 246
   Where to Stay in Burbank,
   North Hollywood, Pasadena,
   and Studio City 250
   Where to Stay in Beverly Hills,
   Century City, Los Feliz, Hollywood,
   and West Hollywood 254–255
   Where to Stay in Santa Monica,
   Venice, the Westside, and
   Westwood 262–263
   Disneyland 277
   Where to Eat and Stay
   in Anaheim 284
   The Orange County Coast. 289
   Catalina Island. 306

ABOUT THIS GUIDE

Fodor's Recommendations

Everything in this guide is worth doing—we don't cover what isn't—but exceptional sights, hotels, and restaurants are recognized with additional accolades. Fodor'sChoice★ indicates our top recommendations; and **Best Bets** call attention to notable hotels and restaurants in various categories. Care to nominate a new place? Visit Fodors.com/contact-us.

Trip Costs

We list prices wherever possible to help you budget well. Hotel and restaurant price categories from **$** to **$$$$** are noted alongside each recommendation. For hotels, we include the lowest cost of a standard double room in high season. For restaurants, we cite the average price of a main course at dinner or, if dinner isn't served, at lunch. For attractions, we always list adult admission fees; discounts are usually available for children, students, and senior citizens.

Hotels

Our local writers vet every hotel to recommend the best overnights in each price category, from budget to expensive. Unless otherwise specified, you can expect private bath, phone, and TV in your room. For expanded hotel reviews, facilities, and deals, visit Fodors.com.

Top Picks
★ Fodor'sChoice

Listings
- ✉ Address
- ✉ Branch address
- ☎ Telephone
- 🖷 Fax
- ⊕ Website
- ✉ E-mail
- 🎫 Admission fee
- ⊙ Open/closed times
- Ⓜ Subway
- ✛ Directions or Map coordinates

Hotels & Restaurants
- 🏨 Hotel
- ⤴ Number of rooms
- ❗⚬❗ Meal plans
- ✕ Restaurant
- ⟋ Reservations
- 🏛 Dress code
- ▭ No credit cards
- Ⓢ Price

Other
- ⇨ See also
- ☞ Take note
- 🏌 Golf facilities

Restaurants

Unless we state otherwise, restaurants are open for lunch and dinner daily. We mention dress code only when there's a specific requirement and reservations only when they're essential or not accepted. To make restaurant reservations, visit Fodors.com.

Credit Cards

The hotels and restaurants in this guide typically accept credit cards. If not, we'll say so.

EXPERIENCE
LOS ANGELES

1

LOS ANGELES TODAY

Starstruck . . . excessive . . . smoggy . . . superficial. . . . There's a modicum of truth to each of the adjectives regularly applied to L.A. But Angelenos—and most objective visitors—dismiss their prevalence as signs of envy from people who hail from places less blessed with fun and sun. Pop culture, for instance, *does* permeate life in LaLaLand: a massive economy employing millions of Southern Californians is built around it.

Nevertheless, this city also boasts highbrow appeal, having amassed an impressive array of world-class museums and arts venues. America's second-largest city has more depth than paparazzi shutters can ever capture. So set aside your preconceived notions and take a look at L.A. today.

Downtown's Upswing

Los Angeles has been archly described as "72 suburbs in search of a city." Hence the renaissance its once-desolate Downtown is experiencing may come as something of a surprise. Long-neglected neighborhoods here have been spruced up, and streets even the police deemed irredeemable have been revitalized.

The Broad Foundation's 120,000-square-foot, three-story contemporary art museum, simply called "the Broad," created quite a buzz when it announced it would open in late 2014. Across the street from Walt Disney Concert Hall and the Los Angeles Museum of Contemporary Art, the honeycomb-shape structure holds more than 2,000 art objects, which will include pieces by heavy hitters in the art world like Cindy Sherman and Andy Warhol.

Even taking an ailing economy into account, in the last decade Downtown saw a remarkable development boom—most notably L.A. LIVE: a 27-acre, $2.5-billion entertainment complex, which includes the Nokia Theatre and the innovative Grammy Museum. Restaurants, boutiques, and art studios are opening all the time, more people are moving in, and public spaces are finally being put to good use.

And that's not all: the $20-million makeover of the galleries at the Huntington Library, Art Collections, and Botanical Gardens have made it a "must-see" for lovers of European art.

Access Hollywood

Hollywood may disappoint tourists looking to overdose on glitz: after all, most of its moviemakers departed for the San Fernando Valley decades ago, leaving the

WHAT'S NEW

Downtown Los Angeles is undergoing a major makeover. Longtime residents who once would never have considered venturing into the center of the city are finding lots of reasons to linger. In 2014, the city hosted its first New Year's celebration, attracting more than 25,000 people to Grand Park in the Civic Center.

The super-stylish Ace Hotel opened in 2014, adding to the luster of Downtown. It's in the old United Artists building, one of the city's architectural gems. Downtown's Grand Central Market underwent a major makeover in 2013, bringing in eateries that cater to a hip crowd. Around for a century, the atmospheric market is now attracting an upscale crowd noshing on Texas barbecue and Thai sticky rice. Don't worry, it's still a great place to pick up

area to languish. Even after the much-hyped debut of the Hollywood & Highland Center, the area remained more gritty than glamorous.

Yet new life continues to be pumped in. In the last few years, Vintage venues such as the Hollywood Palladium have been refurbished; the popular Madame Tussauds constructed a movie-theme museum adjacent to TCL Chinese Theatre, and Cirque du Soleil began a show with a decade-long run at the Kodak Theatre.

New Lights on the Coast

Having fun in the sun isn't relegated to the beaches and other outdoor activities alone in L.A., when you consider the number of amusement parks close to the city.

One of the first sites you see driving into Santa Monica is a tremendous Ferris wheel at Pacific Park out on the Santa Monica Pier—and now it stands out even more. The wheel was recently replaced, and the new one is covered with about 160,000 dazzling LED lights that shine much brighter than the 5,000 or so red, white, and blue bulbs on the old one.

Food for Thought

Star chefs continue to flock from across the country to make their mark on Los Angeles. Recent big openings have included Bestia, a hot seasonal Italian restaurant in Downtown, and all-star team Ludo Lefebvre, Jon Shook, and Vinny Dotolo's Trois Mec. Both restaurants have hard-to-score seats, so plan months in advance. For house-made pasta, try Evan Funke's Bucato. The rustic Italian fare is unlike any other in Los Angeles, but note that there's a strict no-photo policy. Seafood is aplenty, so nosh over at Michael Cimarusti's Connie and Ted's Seafood or David LeFevre's newest outpost, Fishing with Dynamite.

Eats in L.A. remain relatively egalitarian. Even posh places seldom require jackets, so the dress code is casual. Ditto for the menu. (In the city that invented fast food, it's no coincidence that Govind Armstrong flips gourmet burgers or that Wolfgang Puck built his reputation on pizza.) Of course, if you want to go budget, you can easily justify chowing down at McDonald's, Carl's Jr., and In-N-Out Burger because all, having started in the Five-County Area, qualify as "indigenous cuisine."

freshly ground spices and other kitchen staples.

The next addition to Hollywood will be the Academy Museum of Motion Pictures, which will highlight how film and the moviemaking business has woven its way into pop culture over

the course of time since its creation. The 290,000-square-foot museum, estimated to cost around $400 million, is due to open in 2017.

Getting to the L.A. area is easier than ever. Long Beach Airport dazzled passengers with a $140 million renovation

in 2013. The airport's 3 million annual visitors can enjoy more efficient gates and a garden atrium, upgraded lounges, and upscale dining options that include a wine bar with outdoor fire pits.

WHAT'S WHERE

Numbers refer to chapters.

2 Downtown Los Angeles. Downtown L.A. shows off spectacular modern architecture with the swooping Walt Disney Concert Hall and the stark Cathedral of Our Lady of the Angels. The Music Center and the Museum of Contemporary Art anchor a world-class arts scene, while El Pueblo de Los Angeles, Chinatown, and Little Tokyo reflect the city's history and diversity.

3 Hollywood and the Studios. Glitzy and tarnished, good and bad—Hollywood is just like the entertainment business itself. The Walk of Fame, TCL Chinese Theatre, Paramount Pictures studio, and the Hollywood Bowl keep the neighborhood's romantic past alive. Universal Studios Hollywood and Warner Bros. are in the Valley.

4 Beverly Hills and the Westside. Go for the glamour, the restaurants, and the scene. Rodeo Drive is particularly good for a look at wretched or ravishing excess. But don't forget the Westside's cultural attractions—especially the dazzling Getty Center. West Hollywood's an area for urban indulgences—shopping, restaurants, nightspots—rather than sightseeing. Its

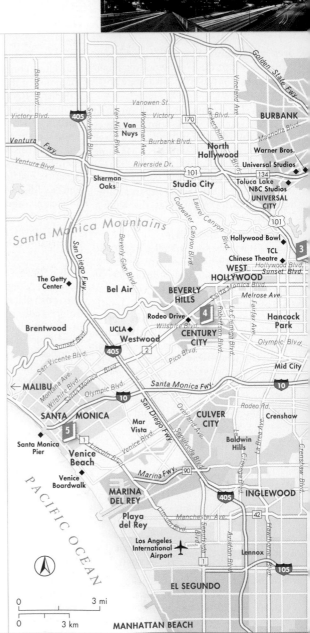

main arteries are the Sunset Strip (Sunset Boulevard), and Melrose Avenue, lined with shops ranging from punk to postmodern.

5 Santa Monica and the Beaches. In Santa Monica, a lively beach scene plays out every day. Venice, just south of Santa Monica, is a more raffish mix of artists, beach punks, and yuppies, most of whom you can see on the Venice Boardwalk. Drive up the Pacific Coast Highway to Malibu, where the rich and famous reside. An extravagant residence of a different kind, the Getty Villa Malibu is filled with exquisite antiquities.

6 Pasadena. Like Santa Monica, Pasadena may appear to be an extension of L.A. but it's actually a separate city with a strong sense of community. It's a quiet, genteel area to visit, with outstanding Arts and Crafts homes, good dining, and a pair of exceptional museums: the Norton Simon and the Huntington Library, Art Collections, and Botanical Gardens in adjoining San Marino.

LOS ANGELES PLANNER

When to Go

Any time of the year is the right time to visit Los Angeles. From November to May, you can find crisp, sunny, unusually smog-free days. December to April is the rainy season, but storms are usually brief, followed by brilliant skies. Dining alfresco, sailing, and catching a concert under the stars—these are reserved for L.A. summers, which are virtually rainless (with an occasional air-quality alert).

Prices skyrocket and reservations are essential when tourism peaks July through September.

Southern California is a temperate area, moderated by the Pacific Ocean. In addition, mountains along the north and east sides of the Los Angeles coastal basin act as buffers against the extreme summer heat and winter cold of the surrounding desert and plateau regions.

Pasadena and the San Fernando Valley are significantly hotter than Beverly Hills or Hollywood, while coastal areas can be dramatically cooler. Late spring brings "June gloom," when skies tend to be overcast until afternoon.

Getting Around

In L.A., where the automobile is worshipped—and will be, no matter how high gas prices go—the freeways are the best way for you to get around town.

Renting a Car. Definitely plan to do it at the airport. And if you want to cruise around in a convertible—a quintessential L.A. experience that allows you to catch some sun while sitting in traffic—reserve well in advance. It's also a good idea to spring for a GPS system.

Parking. With the exception of Downtown high-rises, where parking costs can be exorbitant—parking in L.A. is not inexpensive and plentiful. Avoid rush hour (before 10 am and between 5 and 7 pm) if at all possible, and remember that even-numbered freeways run east–west, and odd-numbered ones run north–south.

Taking Taxis. There are, however, ways to get around Los Angeles without a car. Taxis are not as plentiful as in New York or San Francisco, but you can always find them at major hotels. From LAX to Downtown, a cab ride runs about $42, and shuttle vans cost about $16 per person. Ride-sharing services like Uber, Sidecar, and Lyft are other options.

Dining and Lodging

Chefs in L.A. are frontrunners in the farm-to-fork mentality, and scour the city's many farmers' markets for the freshest of locally grown ingredients. For lodging, there's everything from ultraluxe, swanky hotels in Beverly Hills to quiet beachfront resorts along the coast in Santa Monica, with a wide range of prices in every area.

Tips for the Freeway

Pick a lane. The car-pool lane, the "fast lane," the truck lane, the merge lane—this isn't your typical freeway. First of all, keep out of the two far right lanes, which buses and trucks are restricted to. To drive the speed limit, pick the middle lane; the fourth lane moves about 5 miles over the speed limit. Newbies should stay out of the far left lane. Speeds here range from 75 to 90 mph and you've got to deal with car-pool-lane mergers. And what about that car-pool lane—also known as the diamond lane? Use it if you have two or more people in your car and it's moving along at a good clip.

Signaling is a must. You might be able to get away with a quick lane-change in other cities, but don't try it in L.A. Drivers may try to merge into the same spot as you from three lanes away.

Get a freeway map. The small, laminated maps that just cover the jumble of freeways are indispensable if you merge onto the wrong freeway, get lost, or get stuck in traffic and want to find an alternative route. Nearly every gas station sells them; you can get a decent one for a few bucks. ■TIP→ You can also find one on the inside back cover of this guide.

Don't pull over. Short of a real emergency, never, ever, pull over and stop on a freeway. So you took the wrong ramp and need to huddle with your map? Take the next exit and find a safe, well-lighted public space to stop your car and get your bearings.

L.A. DRIVING TIMES	
From LAX to Downtown L.A.	30–75 min/19 miles
From LAX to Beverly Hills	30–75 min/15 miles
From LAX to Santa Monica	20–60 min/18 miles
From Downtown L.A. to Beverly Hills	20–45 min/11 miles
From Downtown L.A. to Pasadena	15–25 min/11 miles
From Downtown L.A. to Burbank	18–30 min/12 miles
From Downtown L.A. to Universal City	15–40 min/10 miles
From Santa Monica to Redondo Beach	25–55 min/15 miles
From Santa Monica to West Hollywood	25–50 min/10 miles
From Santa Monica to Malibu	32–75 min/25 miles

For a Guided Tour

The **Los Angeles Conservancy** (☎ 213/623–2489 ⊕ www.laconservancy.org) regularly conducts Saturday-morning walking tours of Downtown architectural landmarks and districts.

Tours begin at 10 am, last about 2½ hours, and are offered rain or shine. Call for schedule and fees.

Starline Tours (☎ 323/463–3333 ⊕ www.starlinetours. com/los-angeles-tours.asp) offers a wide range of sight-seeing tours around town. It's an ideal way to get a taste of Los Angeles without the hassle of figuring out transportation.

City and State Contacts

California Office of Tourism ☎ 916/444–4429, 800/862–2543 ⊕ visitcalifornia.com.

Los Angeles Tourism & Convention Board ☎ 213/624–7300, 800/228–2452 ⊕ discoverlosangeles. com.

LOS ANGELES TOP ATTRACTIONS

Disneyland

(A) "The Happiest Place on Earth" continues to delight children and all but the most cynical adults. A visit here can be enchanting, exciting, romantic, or nostalgic, depending on your age. Disneyland, the original vision of Walt Disney, is now paired with Disney's California Adventure, showcasing more recent Disney characters and Hollywood-oriented attractions. Outside these popular theme parks, Downtown Disney supports a wide range of restaurants, bars, and clubs that appeal to the whole family.

Walt Disney Concert Hall

(B) Designed by Frank Gehry, the voluptuous curves of this stainless steel–clad masterpiece located in Downtown is a signature of the modern metropolis. One of several venues of the Music Center, the 2,265-seat Disney Hall is home to the Los Angeles Philharmonic. It features unrivaled acoustics and a stunning pipe organ, which is as much a work of art as a musical instrument. For a truly opulent evening, pair a concert with dinner at Patina, located inside the building. Afterward there are plenty of nightlife options within easy reach.

TCL Chinese Theatre and the Hollywood Walk of Fame

(C) An iconic metaphor for Hollywood, the elaborate Grauman's Chinese Theatre opened in 1927 with the premier of Cecil B. DeMille's *King of Kings*. That's when the tradition of stars imprinting their hands or feet into the cement began with an "accidental" footprint by Norma Talmadge. More than 160 stars have contributed, and among the more unique prints are the nose of Jimmy Durante and hoofs of Trigger. The theater is adjacent to the Hollywood & Highland Center. Then, of course there's the Walk of Fame that runs a mile along Hollywood Boulevard, with the handprints of more than 1,600 stars.

Getty Center

(D) On a hillside above Brentwood, the $1-billion-plus Getty Center is not only a museum, but a statement that L.A. has taken its place in the art world. The Richard Meier–designed complex has a skin of travertine marble and natural light floods galleries filled with impressionist canvases, Greek antiquities, and jaw-dropping exhibits of furniture and decorative arts from French monarchy. Pedestrian plazas and gardens abound, and a sunset dinner at the restaurant, with its panoramic views, is the stuff of memories.

Rodeo Drive

(E) Dominated by the exclusive names of Gucci, Versace, and Cartier, Rodeo Drive is a shoppers' paradise. Along the cobblestoned Via Rodeo, you can drop a thousand dollars on python pumps or nosh on a $500 sushi dinner. Fortunately, Rodeo Drive doesn't cater exclusively to the rich and famous, and more moderate shops and restaurants are interspersed with the iconic boutiques.

Santa Monica Pier

(F) Spend a sunny day beside the Pacific Ocean riding the Ferris wheel and playing dozens of games for prizes at this popular family destination. Cotton candy and other hard-to-resist treats are within easy reach. Drop by in the late afternoon to experience the dazzling sunsets.

Venice Beach Boardwalk

(G) The bohemian lifestyle of this famous boardwalk is constantly threatened by the rapid gentrification of Venice. Still, the magicians, fortune-tellers, and Muscle Beach weight lifters still survive. Struggling artists sell their paintings, infiltrated by tackier purveyors of cheap watches and sunglasses. Rent a bicycle or in-line skates, grab a hot dog, and enjoy the sights and the sunset.

TOP EXPERIENCES

Hordes of tourists descend on Los Angeles each year with visions of seeing stars—of the Hollywood Boulevard and celebrity variety that is—but before you purchase that star map there are a few things you should know about how to live like a local.

For starters, never bat an eye when you encounter a movie star. Remember they are real people, too (albeit real people who live like royalty). Here are a few activities to help you fit in with the natives.

Bike the Strand

Despite urban myths that claim otherwise, Angelenos do abandon their cars every now and then—especially if it's to rent an old-school beach cruiser and bike down the 22-mile-long Strand, which stretches from Will Rogers State Beach in Santa Monica to Torrance County Beach in Redondo.

The Strand runs parallel to the Pacific Ocean through Santa Monica and Venice. Don't miss one-of-a-kind sights, including the oversize Ferris wheel on the Santa Monica Pier, the greased up bodybuilders of Muscle Beach, and the roller dancers (think disco on roller skates) of Venice Beach. And if biking isn't your thing, there are plenty of rollerbladers and walkers as well.

Drive-Through In-N-Out

It's no secret that the people of Los Angeles love their cars. In fact, they're famous for driving convertibles, scoffing at the idea of public transportation, and spending an inordinate amount of time on freeways.

But what the casual observer may not know is that Angelenos have another passion—for the local burger chain In-N-Out—that, thankfully, is perfectly car-friendly. Of course, Angelenos don't get out of their cars to make this magical moment happen. Easy directions: Drive up to an In-N-Out window, order from the secret menu (available online), and enjoy your "Animal Style" in the car.

Eat at the Farmers Market

At 3rd and Fairfax, the Farmers Market is pretty much Los Angeles's version of a community center. Everyone comes here to eat, drink, and, most important, people-watch. Founded by a collective of farmers in 1934, the Farmers Market now houses more than 85 shops and restaurants—you can find everything from a Brazilian grill to a French *crêperie* to a Lebanese kebab stand—in an open-air bazaar ringed by stalls and stands.

The Farmers Market and the adjacent shopping area, The Grove, are also low-key places to spot celebrities going about their everyday business.

Try a Taco Truck

It seems that everyone in Los Angeles has a taco truck that they swear by. Typically, these taco stands on wheels have a regular corner and semi-regular hours. The only reliable way to find a good one is to ask a local—or do some research on a foodie website.

Not all taco trucks are created equal and it pays to know the specialty of the house—or truck, that is. A few things that most taco trucks share in common: tasty tacos, cheap prices, and a locals-only peek into L.A.'s hometown cuisine.

See a Show at the Hollywood Bowl

No doubt you've seen the iconic dome in movies, but nothing compares to spending a summer evening in a bleacher seat (or, better yet, one of the coveted boxes) at the Hollywood Bowl. To really get your local on, pack a picnic complete

with bottle of wine and wicker basket and don't be afraid to share goodies with your neighbors.

Performances run the gamut from reggae night to rock concerts to Los Angeles Philharmonic performances. But as most Angelenos would agree, the experience is as much about sitting outside under the night sky as it is about the music.

Hike in Griffith Park

The park, extremely accessible from the city, offers a 53-mile network of trails, roads, and bridle paths. One of the most popular routes is up Mount Hollywood, which boasts panoramic views of the Los Angeles basin, the Griffith Observatory, and the Hollywood Sign along the way.

Don't feel like working up a sweat? Although riders must stay on specially marked trails, much of the park can be seen on horseback. Private stables are located in the park's northwest and southwest boundaries.

Stop at a Seafood Shack

There may be nothing that epitomizes Los Angeles more than a drive down the scenic Pacific Coast Highway, or PCH, as locals call it. After taking in the sweeping views and turquoise waters, stop at a seafood shack, such as Malibu Seafood or the Reel Inn, for some ahi burgers or fish-and-chips.

Afterward, check out one of Malibu's most beautiful beaches: Topanga State Beach, Zuma Beach, or the small and secluded La Piedra, El Pescador, and El Matador beaches.

Go to a Dodger or Lakers Game—or Both

One way to blend in with the locals is to surround yourself with them—literally.

Get out to Dodger Stadium for a baseball game, and don't forget to dress in all blue and eat a Dodger Dog while you're there. Unless it's a big game, Dodger tickets are easy to come by—especially if you're willing to sit in the cheap bleacher seats. You can also spend a bit more to sit in one of the special sections such as the All-You-Can-Eat Pavilion.

It's much harder to procure Lakers tickets when they play at Staples Center, but if you plan ahead, a Lakers game is a sure-fire way to see big celebrities and even bigger feats of aerodynamics.

Catch a Movie at the ArcLight

It would be an understatement to say that Angelenos take their movies seriously. Considering that the entertainment industry is many locals' bread and butter, it's no surprise that moviegoing ups the ante here, too. Look no further than the ArcLight in Hollywood for a signature L.A. moviegoing experience. The ArcLight has all the fixin's: stadium seating, gourmet food, and authentic costumes from favorite films on display in the lobby.

But what sets the ArcLight above the rest is that each movie is introduced by a live announcer schooled in movie trivia. If you're super lucky, you might catch the directors as they frequently make appearances here to discuss their work.

If you want to *really* do it like a local, catch a flick in the middle of the day—remember, Angelenos have sunny days to burn.

IF YOU LIKE

Hitting the Road

Considering that the greater L.A. area sprawls over more square mileage than some small countries, it comes as no surprise that residents clock a lot of road time. Contrary to popular belief, however, standstill freeway traffic is only part of the picture. In Los Angeles, the popular 1950s-era pastime of cruising is still alive and well.

One of the premier ways to see the L.A. hot spots so often captured on the silver screen is to take a drive down **Sunset Boulevard.** The famed thoroughfare runs from the **Pacific Coast Highway** in Malibu to Downtown Los Angeles, but the most well-known stretch is the **Sunset Strip,** in West Hollywood.

Heading east on **Sunset Boulevard,** pass by legendary music venues including the Roxy, the Whisky-A-Go-Go, and the Viper Room. Continue a little father to glimpse movie star magnet of yesteryear the Sunset Tower Hotel (formerly the Argyle Hotel) and current celebrity hangout the Chateau Marmont.

The famous roadway, **Mulholland Drive,** snakes along the ridge separating L.A. from its suburban neighbor, the San Fernando Valley. Like Sunset Boulevard, Mulholland Drive starts at the ocean and extends all the way into Hollywood, but unlike its urban counterpart, Mulholland forgoes street scenes for mountain views and traffic lights for unpaved stretches of road.

Another not-to-be-missed scenic stretch is the winding road that climbs through Laurel Canyon, a nexus of the 1960s music scene and former home to rockers Joni Mitchell and Neil Young among many others. At its apex, **Laurel Canyon Boulevard** meets up with Mulholland Drive, so be sure to fuel up before you start the climb.

Outdoor Pursuits

Although Los Angeles's car culture is well-publicized, its bike culture is a little more under-the-radar, but that is not to say there isn't a healthy cycling scene. With seemingly endless days of summer, Angelenos love to spend time outdoors.

One of the quintessential L.A. activities is to rent an old-school beach cruiser and bike along the 22-mile-long **Strand,** which stretches from Santa Monica's **Will Rogers State Beach** to **Torrance County Beach** in Venice.

If you are an outdoor enthusiast, don't forget to pack your hiking boots alongside your stiletto heels so that you can hike the **Santa Monica Mountains.** Popular routes include the Backbone Trail, a 43-mile-stretch of chaparral-covered hillsides, oak woodlands, and creeks that links Will Rogers State Historic Park to Point Mugu, anchored in the middle by **Malibu Creek State Park** and **Topanga State Park.** The highly accessible **Griffith Park,** just north of Hollywood, is technically part of this mountain chain as well.

For some solitude and rural terrain, visit **Angeles National Forest,** in the northern reaches of L.A. County. The mostly flat and shaded Gabrielino Trail along the upper Arroyo Seco is a favorite of mountain bikers, runners, birders, and horseback riders. To get there, exit the 210 Freeway at Arroyo Boulevard–Windsor Avenue in Altadena. Drive three-quarters of a mile north and look for the small parking lot just before you reach Ventura Avenue.

Seeing Stars

A surefire way to see stars (or at least the constellation they call home) is by **purchasing a star map** from vendors on street corners around the city. If you keep up with celeb gossip, check the places they eat and shop, and the playgrounds they take their kids to, to increase chances of a star sighting. Save yourself a lot of pavement-pounding by signing up to be a part of a live audience and **watch a TV show being taped.** If you haven't planned in advance, you can always **take a studio tour.**

In Los Angeles, moviegoing is elevated to an art form. Instead of seeing a flick at the multiplex, catch what's showing at the **Hollywood Forever Cemetery** (aka "Resting Place of Hollywood's Immortals"), surrounded by the graves of Cecil B. DeMille, Jayne Mansfield, Rudolph Valentino, Douglas Fairbanks, and hundreds of other screen legends.

Eye-Popping Views

Perch yourself high above Hollywood Hills and have a picnic at the **Hollywood Bowl.** Choose your soundtrack from a lineup of rock concerts sponsored by local radio station KCRW or time it with a Los Angeles Philharmonic concert.

Top off any trip to Los Angeles—literally—by taking in the view from the **Griffith Observatory.** Located on the southern slope of Mount Hollywood in Griffith Park, the 75-year-old icon offers stellar views of the heavens thanks to the observatory's original 12-inch Zeiss refracting telescope as well as a trio of solar telescopes.

Griffith Observatory is one of the best vantage points to see the **Hollywood Sign.** For a view of the sign from the ground, walk, run, or bike around **Hollywood Reservoir Trail.** The 4-mile walk around also offers great views of hillside mansions. The reservoir was built by the god of Los Angeles water, William Mulholland; its dam has a memorable movie cameo in Roman Polanski's *Chinatown*.

Seemingly floating above Downtown Los Angeles like a Jetsons-age oasis, the rooftop bar at the **Standard Hotel** attracts everyone from buttoned-up office workers, who flock to the space for happy hour drinks, to the swanked-out, late-night crowd. It's a great place to take in the surrounding scenery.

Get a bird's-eye view of the city from the **Getty Center,** in Brentwood. Wander among the stunning, travertine marble-clad pavilions and explore the gardens. And then there's the art, including exceptional European paintings and antique French furniture. But it's hard to tear your eyes from the view, especially at sunset. Dine in nearby Brentwood, West Hollywood, or back in Beverly Hills—Spago, anyone?

GODZILLA

GREAT ITINERARIES

The trick to having a decent quality of life in Los Angeles, claims one longtime Angeleno, is to live near where you work. The same adage holds true for visitors in that staying put in a single area of the city—being in a car for as short a time as possible—is a good rule of thumb. The best way to explore is one neighborhood at a time. Here are a few of our favorite itineraries to try.

Downtown Los Angeles

■TIP➜ Best for fans of modern architecture and ethnic cuisine lovers.

If you have a half day: Formerly an unwelcoming neighborhood dominated by the glass-and-steel office buildings of Bunker Hill on one side and the poverty and despair of Skid Row on the other, Downtown Los Angeles has staged a major comeback in recent years.

While the skyscrapers and tent cities still exist, there is also a middle ground that lures visitors with the promise of high art and historic architecture.

Don't miss the gems of Grand Avenue the Walt Disney Concert Hall and the Museum of Contemporary Art. At the concert hall, be sure to take the hour-long self-guided audio tour, which includes a walk through the venue's second-story hidden garden.

If you have a whole day: After checking out MOCA and Disney Hall, see the art deco icon Union Station to admire the heavy wood-beam ceilings, leather upholstered chairs, and inlaid marble floors.

Then, walk across Alameda Street to stroll past the shops and restaurants of L.A.'s historic Olvera Street, where you'll find traditional Mexican fare. Other ethnic eats can be found venturing into Little Tokyo for a wide variety of Japanese cuisine or to Chinatown, especially for dim sum.

Hollywood

■TIP➜ Best for first-timers to L.A., as well as film and music history buffs.

If you have a half day: Tourists flock to Hollywood Boulevard to see old movie palaces such as TCL Chinese Theatre, where movie stars have left their mark, literally, in the concrete courtyard of the theater since 1927.

These days the theater's entrance is also graced by dozens of impersonators—from Marilyn Monroe to Spiderman—who are more than happy to pose for photos with visitors.

Go to Hollywood & Highland Center for lunch, followed by a tour of the Kodak Theatre, which hosts the annual Academy Awards ceremony.

Wander the Walk of Fame, a 5-acre stretch of bronze stars embedded in pink terrazzo that lines Hollywood Boulevard to pay homage to your favorite movie stars. Or visit the independent record store Amoeba Records for just about everything a music lover could want.

If you have a whole day: Some of the historic movie palaces, including TCL, still show films, but the real movie buffs should opt to see a movie at the ArcLight, a state-of-the-art theater on Sunset Boulevard that features gourmet food and reserved seating. The ArcLight also boasts an in-house café bar that is perfect for a quick meal before a film or an après-show martini.

West Hollywood

■TIP➜ Best for trend-savvy shoppers, farmers' market foodies, and parents pushing strollers.

If you have a half day: Thanks to its central location, West Hollywood is the ideal place to spend a couple of hours without

committing an entire day—not that there isn't a day's worth of things to do in this neighborhood.

A shopping hub in its own right, visitors can choose to stroll around the outdoor pedestrian area, The Grove, or at the mammoth indoor Beverly Center. There are also countless small boutiques and specialty shops lining Beverly Boulevard, 3rd Street, and Melrose Avenue.

For lunch, grab a corned beef sandwich or some matzo ball soup at Canter's Delicatessen, a Los Angeles landmark since 1931, or to the Farmers Market for a collection of ethnic food stalls and local products.

If you have a whole day: Tack Robertson Boulevard onto your shopping agenda to find boutiques ranging from the local favorite American Apparel to the celebrity magnet Kitson.

West Hollywood is known for its buzzing nightlife, so afterward choose from hundreds of small restaurants for dinner, then follow up with a drink from one of the area's many bars.

Beverly Hills and the Westside
■ TIP➔ Best for high-end shoppers, ladies who lunch, and contemporary art museum-goers.

If you have a half day: Depending on how hardcore of a shopper you are, you can easily check out the boutiques of Beverly Hills in a couple of hours. In fact, with all of the designer flagships and tony department stores, it might be dangerous to spend too much time (translation: too much money) in this ritzy neighborhood.

Hit Rodeo Drive for all the runway names, such as Chanel, Christian Dior, Dolce & Gabbana, Fendi, Gucci, Prada, Valentino, and Versace.

Of course, not all the action is on Rodeo; don't forget to wander the side streets for more high fashion. The department stores—Barneys New York, Neiman Marcus, and Saks Fifth Avenue—are located nearby on Wilshire Boulevard. After you finish shopping, refuel with a dose of sugar at local dessert favorite Sprinkles Cupcakes.

If you have a whole day: After all that shopping, jump in the car to get some culture by heading east to the Miracle Mile, a stretch of Wilshire Boulevard that's home to the mammoth Los Angeles County Museum of Art as well as smaller museums, such as the Craft and Folk Art Museum.

Santa Monica and the Beaches
■ TIP➔ Best for families with kids of all ages, sun worshippers and surfers, and anyone who likes cruising in a convertible.

If you have a half day: With a couple of hours on your hands, it's a quick trip (if there's no traffic) to the beaches of Santa Monica or Venice. While they may not offer quite as much in the natural beauty department as their Malibu counterparts, they have plenty of sights of a different variety.

Don't miss the boardwalk vendors who hang out on Venice Beach or the street performers who frequent the Santa Monica Pier. Grab a snack at one of the beach-theme restaurants on the Strand such as divey Big Dean's Oceanfront Café or dressy Shutters on the Beach.

If you have a whole day: The ideal way to see Los Angeles's most beautiful beaches is to set aside an entire day for Malibu. Driving down the scenic Pacific Coast Highway is a treat in and of itself with sheer cliffs on one side of the road and ocean views on the other.

Topanga State Beach, Malibu Lagoon State Beach, and Malibu Surfrider Beach are all beautiful and popular spots to pass the day, but it's worth the extra drive time to see Point Dume State Beach, which is nestled away from the hustle and bustle of the highway.

Be sure to seek out the single-track trail that winds its way up a nearby coastal bluff revealing breathtaking views of Santa Monica Bay, the Malibu Coast, and Catalina Island. Stop for lunch at any of the seafood shacks that line PCH.

Pasadena
■TIP→ Best for multigenerational groups, as well as art and architecture aficionados.

If you have a half day: Aside from spending time pouring over the massive collection of rare manuscripts and books at the Huntington Library, be sure to set aside a couple of hours for the Botanical Gardens to explore the more than a dozen themed areas, including authentic examples of both Japanese and Chinese gardens.

The Huntington has a beautiful outdoor café, as well as the Rose Garden Tea Room, where you can grab a tasty treat.

Another must-see museum is the Norton Simon Museum, with a collection that includes everything from ancient Asian art to 20th-century works.

If you have a whole day: Take a tour of Charles and Henry Greene's 1908 masterpiece the Gamble House, followed by a trip to the Castle Green, the architects' Moorish Colonial– and Spanish-style building.

Then, walk around into Old Town Pasadena, a revitalized shopping area with boutiques and eateries housed in historic buildings.

If you happen to be here during the once-a-month, massive Rose Bowl Flea Market, which takes over the Rose Bowl parking lot, you can browse around roughly 2,500 vendors' stalls.

Orange County and Catalina Island
■TIP→ Best for families traveling with young children and those who yearn for the great outdoors.

If you have a half day: Head to one of the seemingly endless string of beaches along this stretch of shoreline, extending from Long Beach to San Juan Capistrano. There's plenty to do besides sit in the sand: head to one of the fascinating aquariums, explore a nature preserve, or take in some impressive art at the area's surprisingly good museums.

Finding somewhere to eat won't be a problem, as this area is a major foodie destination. There are also plenty of reasonably priced family eateries.

If you have a whole day: If you're traveling with kids, you're going to end up at one of the classic theme parks, either Disneyland or Knott's Berry Farm. Grown-ups will be drawn to the natural beauty of Catalina Island. There's a tiny town with its fair share of attractions, but make sure you see the unspoiled coastline.

FREE AND ALMOST FREE

Even in this town—where money seems to ooze from every hill and corner—there are plenty of fun things to do that are free and appeal to everyone from kids to art lovers to movie and film buffs. These are some of our top picks.

Check Out Freebies at Museums. Though high-profile Angelenos have elevated conspicuous consumption to an art, you can still spend time here without dropping a dime. Visiting culture vultures will be relieved to learn the Getty Center and Getty Villa offer complimentary admission. Just about all the other major museums in Los Angeles have free days, including the Geffen Contemporary and the Museum of Contemporary Art. Also, several museums stay open as late as 9 pm some nights.

Be Part of the Audience. Watching one of your favorite television or awards shows being filmed is an exciting experience that will make you feel as if you're part of the entertainment industry. **Audiences Unlimited** (✉ *100 Universal City Plaza, Bldg. 153, Universal City* ☎ *818/260–0041* ⊕ *www.tvtickets.com*) helps fill seats for television programs (and sometimes for televised award shows). The free tickets are distributed on a first-come, first-served basis to those 16 and older.

See the Great Grunion Runs. The most popular and most unusual form of fishing in the L.A. area involves no hooks, bait, or poles, and is absolutely free. The grunion runs, which take place from March through July, occur when hundreds of thousands of small silver fish called grunion wash up on Southern California beaches to lay their eggs in the sand. The fish can be picked up by hand while they are briefly stranded on the beach. All that's required is a fishing license and a willingness to get your toes wet.

Spend the Evening on the Griffith Observatory's Rooftop Observation Deck. Known for stunning and famous views of Los Angeles, this rooftop deck is open until 10 pm every night except Monday.

Watch Rehearsals at the Hollywood Bowl. There's no charge to visit the Hollywood Bowl and the grounds that surround it, but an even better tip is that in the summer, from 9 am to noon on Tuesday, Thursday, and Friday, it's possible to watch rehearsals for free. Take a snack and enjoy the view. If you can't make a rehearsal, seeing the stark-white amphitheater with the Hollywood sign set against the mountains in the background is worth the trip alone.

Walk in Famous Footsteps. Frugal movie fans can get reel on Hollywood Boulevard's star-paved Walk of Fame or in the forecourt of TCL Chinese Theatre where celebs have been pressing hands, feet, and other body parts into cement since 1927 (time it right and you may catch a premiere, too). Music buffs can view memorabilia from past headliners at the free Hollywood Bowl Museum.

Visit the Hollywood Forever Cemetery. Inside the Hollywood Memorial Park right in the center of Hollywood, the Hollywood Forever Cemetery is where several of the film industry's famous are buried. Pick up a free map just inside for a self-guided tour.

TOP MUSEUMS

Despite its long-standing reputation as a second-rate art capital after New York, Los Angeles easily vies for the top spot when it comes to its museum exhibitions and gallery shows. Unlike in many other cultural capitals, the museums here aren't concentrated in one area of the city. No matter where you are, there's likely to be a top-notch museum within easy driving distance.

On the gallery front, the scene is no less colorful. Four major epicenters—Chinatown, Culver City, Santa Monica, and West Hollywood—boast hundreds of art spaces. In Downtown, the largest concentration of galleries is in the area called Gallery Row. Approximately 30 galleries and museums are within a short walk of one another.

Must-See Museums
On a busy stretch of Wilshire Boulevard in Westwood, the **UCLA Hammer Museum** (✉ *10899 Wilshire Blvd., Westwood* ☎ *310/443–7000* ⊕ *www.hammer.ucla. edu*) is known for cutting-edge exhibitions with a special emphasis on "the art of our time," as they put it. The Hammer is also known for its extensive library dedicated to the study of video art.

In a modernist compound of rough-hewn Italian travertine on a hilltop in the Santa Monica Mountains, the Richard Meier–designed **Getty Center** (✉ *1200 Getty Center Dr., Los Angeles* ☎ *310/440–7300* ⊕ *www.getty.edu*) has fabulous views of the Pacific Ocean and the San Gabriel Mountains, as well as an extensive garden designed by Robert Irwin. The permanent collection includes works from the 19th century to the present.

Claiming the crown of the largest art museum in the western United States, the **Los Angeles County Museum of Art** (✉ *5905 Wilshire Blvd., Miracle Mile* ☎ *323/857–6000* ⊕ *www.lacma.org*) is a complex of seven buildings with more than 100,000 objects dating from ancient times to the present.

The LACMA may be the biggest museum in the West, but the **Museum of Contemporary Art** is certainly in the running in the best category, and is *the* place to go to see blockbuster exhibits. It has three buildings: the MOCA Grand Avenue (✉ *250 S. Grand Ave., Downtown* ☎ *213/626–6222* ⊕ *www.moca.org*) and the Geffen Contemporary (✉ *152 N. Central Ave., Little Tokyo* ☎ *213/626–6222* ⊕ *www.moca.org*) are located in Downtown, while the Pacific Design Center (✉ *8687 Melrose Ave., West Hollywood* ☎ *213/626–6222* ⊕ *www.moca.org*) is in West Hollywood.

Other Great Museums
Don't miss the **Getty Villa** (✉ *17985 Pacific Coast Hwy., Pacific Palisades* ☎ *310/440–7300* ⊕ *www.getty.edu*) in Pacific Palisades for Greek, Roman, and Etruscan antiquities. The gorgeous grounds are well worth a stroll.

If you're traveling with kids, check out the **California Science Center** (✉ *700 State Dr., Exposition Park* ☎ *213/744–7400* ⊕ *www.casciencectr.org*). The young crowd can explore space or take a journey into the workings of the human body. Another favorite with younger people is the **Natural History Museum of Los Angeles County** (✉ *900 Exposition Blvd.* ☎ *213/763–3466* ⊕ *www.nhm.org*), with its stunning Dinosaur Hall.

LOS ANGELES WITH KIDS

With seemingly endless sunny days, Angeleno kids almost never have to play indoors. There are a few things to keep in mind, however, when navigating the City of Angeles with your pint-size angel: If possible, avoid the freeways by exploring no more than one neighborhood each day; and you can never have too much sunscreen (L.A. moms don't leave home without the stuff).

Of course, the top reason many families comes to the L.A. area is to visit Disneyland. Experience all the classic attractions that you may recall from your own childhood visit, such as the "It's a Small World" ride, a meet-and-greet with Tinkerbell, or a Mickey Mouse home tour, who, unlike less amenable celebrities, makes a daily appearance for fans. But there's plenty more to see and do.

Head Under the Sea

A huge tank with shimmering schools of fish and swaying kelp forest? Check. Shark lagoon featuring more than 150 varieties, including gray nurse, sand tiger, and whitetip? Check. Tropical reef habitat filled with zebra sharks, porcupine puffers, and a large blue Napoleon wrasse? Check. Head down to the Long Beach–based **Aquarium of the Pacific** to learn tons of interesting facts about the Pacific Ocean.

Commune with Nature

Don't miss your chance to test ride a high-wire bicycle or catch a film on the seven-story IMAX theater at the **California Science Center**. Then, just down the road is the **Natural History Museum**, where kids can explore everything from diamonds to its new dinosaur hall. In spring, don't miss the outdoor butterfly habitat, fittingly named the Pavilion of Wings, which makes way for the Spider Pavilion come fall.

Walk in the Park

Griffith Park is the largest municipal park and urban wilderness area in the United States, and the kids will go wild for the pony rides and the classic 1926 merry-go-round. But the pièce de résistance is the Griffith Park and Southern Railroad, a circa-1940s miniature train that travels through an old Western town and a Native American village. Other highlights are the Los Angeles Zoo and the Griffith Observatory, an L.A. icon in its own right.

Learn By Doing

Little ones can pan for gold in a small creek, play Spider-Man on a weblike climber, or race around a trike track at the **Kidspace Children's Museum**. Indoor activities include a walk-through kaleidoscope, two climbing towers—one mimicking raindrops, the other modeled after a wisteria vine—a bug diner (think: banana worm bread and roasted cricket pizza), and a contraption that lets kids generate their very own earthquake.

Hit the Beach

The best way to check out **Santa Monica Beach** is by renting bikes or roller skates at any one of the shacks on the Strand (a stretch of concrete boardwalk that snakes along the beach toward Venice). Some must-sees along the way: The roller dancers of Venice Beach, the body builders of Muscle Beach, and the Santa Monica Pier, a 100-year-old structure that's home to a vintage 1920s carousel, an oversize Ferris wheel, and old-time amusement park games. After hitting the beach, drive over to the pedestrian-only Third Street Promenade to grab a bite and do some shopping.

GREAT ARCHITECTURE

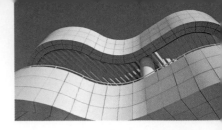

Sorry, New York, you may offer the best of the best in other categories, but when it comes to groundbreaking new architecture, Los Angeles takes the prize (the Pritzker, that is).

Amid the patchwork of California bungalows and stucco Caliterraneans that dot the cityscape dwell some of the last century's most notable architectural feats, many of them carefully restored and lovingly tended.

Here are a few examples that no architecture buff should miss.

Classic Architecture

A stone's throw from the blaring ranchero music of South Broadway, the circa 1880s **Bradbury Building** (⊠ *304 S. Broadway, Downtown*) designed by George H. Wyman lays testament to Downtown's halcyon days. This Victorian-style office building, best known for the intricate cast iron metalwork that details its soaring, light-filled atrium, is a mecca for architecture students. Don't be surprised if you see a few artsy types soaking up the ambience.

A fine example of Frank Lloyd Wright's work, the '20s-era **Hollyhock House** (⊠ *4800 Hollywood Blvd., Los Feliz* ☎ *323/644–6269* ⊕ *www.hollyhockhouse.net*) can be found in scenic Barnsdall Art Park. Make sure to see the interior, which has some of the master's lovely stained-glass windows and a huge stone fireplace.

Home to countless examples of the California Craftsman, Pasadena lays claim to the quintessential example, Charles and Henry Greene's **Gamble House** (⊠ *4 Westmoreland Pl., Pasadena* ☎ *626/793–3334* ⊕ *www.gamblehouse.org*). Built in 1908, the house is heavy on stained glass and teak woodwork.

If the Gamble House doesn't satiate your appetite for all things Greene and Greene, check out the **Castle Green** (⊠ *99 S. Raymond Ave., Pasadena* ☎ *626/793–0359* ⊕ *www.castlegreen.com*), a seven-story Moorish Colonial and Spanish-style building on a palm tree–lined site in Old Town Pasadena.

Modern Masterpieces

Join the horde of photographers snapping photos on Grand Avenue. No, it's not a celebrity-fueled paparazzi gathering, just the day's crew of people snapping photos of Frank Gehry's **Walt Disney Concert Hall** (⊠ *111 S. Grand Ave., Downtown* ☎ *323/850–2000* ⊕ *www.laphil.com*). Wrapped in curving stainless steel, the music hall possesses a clothlike quality reminiscent of a ship's sails billowing in the wind.

And then there's L.A.'s other major Gehry favorite, the **Geffen Contemporary** (⊠ *152 N. Central Ave., Downtown* ☎ *213/626–6222* ⊕ *www.moca.org*), which opened in the early 1980s as a temporary space for works housed inside the Museum of Contemporary Art.

In South Central Los Angeles, Simon Rodia's **Watts Towers** (⊠ *1761–1765 E. 107th St., Watts* ⊕ *www.wattstowers.us*) consist of 17 sculptures constructed of steel and covered with a mosaic of broken glass, seashells, and pieces of 20th-century American ceramics.

L.A. SPORTS ACTION

Los Angeles is a serious sports city, with many of its professional and college teams in playoffs. It's a great way to hang with the locals—if you can score tickets to games, that is.

Baseball

Dodgers. You can watch the Dodgers take on its National League rivals while munching on pizza, tacos, or foot-long "Dodger dogs" at one of the game's most comfortable ballparks, Dodger Stadium. ⊠ *Dodger Stadium, 1000 Elysian Park Ave., exit off I-110, Pasadena Fwy.* ☎ *323/224–1507* ⊕ *www.dodgers.com.*

Los Angeles Angels of Anaheim. The Los Angeles Angels of Anaheim made headlines after acquiring home-run hitter Josh Hamilton from the Texas Rangers for $125 million in late 2012. ⊠ *Angel Stadium of Anaheim, 2000 E. Gene Autry Way, Anaheim* ☎ *714/940–2000* ⊕ *www.angelsbaseball.com.*

Basketball

Clippers. It's often easier and cheaper to score tickets for L.A.'s "other" basketball team, the Clippers. ⊠ *Staples Center, 1111 S. Figueroa St.* ☎ *213/742–7100* ⊕ *www.nba.com/clippers.*

Los Angeles Lakers. See where Magic Johnson once strutted his stuff. It's not easy to get tickets, but if you can, don't miss the chance to see this championship-winning team—especially if the Lakers are playing their rivals, the Celtics, Clippers, or Spurs. ⊠ *Staples Center, 1111 S. Figueroa St., Downtown* ☎ *310/426–6000* ⊕ *www.nba.com/lakers.*

Los Angeles Sparks. After the 2010 retirement of WNBA superstar Lisa Leslie, the Los Angeles Sparks have put the spotlight on forward Candace Parker, who was named MVP in an all-star game in 2013. ⊠ *Staples Center, 1111 S Figueroa St.* ☎ *310/426–6031* ⊕ *www.wnba.com/sparks.*

University of California at Los Angeles. The University of California at Los Angeles Bruins play at Pauley Pavilion on the UCLA campus. ⊠ *Pauley Pavilion, 405 Hilgard Ave.* ☎ *310/825–2101* ⊕ *uclabruins.collegesports.com.*

University of Southern California. The Trojans of the University of Southern California play at the Galen Center. ⊠ *Galen Center, 3400 S. Figueroa St.* ☎ *213/740–4672* ⊕ *www.usctrojans.com.*

Football

UCLA Bruins. The UCLA Bruins pack 'em in at the **Rose Bowl.** ⊠ *Rose Bowl, 1010 Rose Bowl, Pasadena* ☎ *626/577–3100* ⊕ *uclabruins.collegesports.com.*

USC Trojans. The USC Trojans play at the **L.A. Memorial Coliseum,** both a state and federal historic landmark. ⊠ *L.A. Memorial Coliseum, 3939 S. Figueroa St., Downtown* ☎ *213/740–4672* ⊕ *usctrojans.collegesports.com.*

Hockey

Anaheim Ducks. The Anaheim Ducks push the puck at **Honda Center** (⊠ *2695 E. Katella Ave., Anaheim* ☎ *714/704–2500*). Long an underdog team, it became the first Southern California team to win the Stanley Cup in 2007. ⊠ *Honda Center, 2695 E. Katella Ave.* ☎ *877/945–3946* ⊕ *ducks.nhl.com.*

L.A. Kings. The National Hockey League's L.A. Kings was the first professional hockey team to make California its home. The team made a name for itself nationally when it cinched the Stanley Cup for the first time in 2012. ⊠ *Staples Center, 1111 S. Figueroa St.* ☎ *213/742–7100* ⊕ *www.lakings.com.*

CRUISING THE SUNSET STRIP

For more than half a century, Hollywood's night owls have headed for the 1 ¾-mile stretch of Sunset Boulevard between Crescent Heights Boulevard on the east and Doheny Drive on the west, known as the Sunset Strip. The experience of driving it from end to end gives you a sampling of everything that makes L.A. what it is, with all its glamour and grit, and its history of those who rose fast and fell faster.

Left and top right, two views of Sunset Boulevard. Bottom right, Mel's Drive-in Diner.

In the 1930s and '40s, stars such as Errol Flynn and Rita Hayworth came for wild evenings of dancing and drinking at nightclubs like Trocadero, Ciro's, and Mocambo.

The Strip's image as Tinseltown's glamorous nighttime playground began to die in the '50s, and by the mid-'60s it was the center of L.A.'s raucous music-and-nightlife scene. Bands like the Doors and the Byrds played the Whisky a Go Go, and the city's counterculture clashed with police in the famous Sunset Strip curfew riots in the summer of 1966.

In the '70s, the Strip was all about glam rock, with David Bowie, T. Rex, and Queen hitting the venues. But this was when it began a decline that would last almost two decades, until it became a seedy section of the city where hookers hung out on every corner.

It's only been in the last decade that the Strip has seen a true revitalization, with new hotels, restaurants, and bars opening that have become haunts for celebs and A-listers. It retains its rough-and-tumble image in some sections but overall is a much classier spot to spend a night out.

A CLASSIC DRIVE THROUGH L.A.

Depending on the time of day, driving the Strip is a different experience. In the afternoon grab lunch at a hotel and hobnob with industry types. At night, drive with the top down and come to hear music, hit a club, or have cocktails at a rooftop bar. Either way, it's good to park the car and walk (yes, walk!).

WHERE TO EAT & DRINK

See and be seen at **Sky-bar at the Mondrian Hotel** (✉ 8440 Sunset Blvd. ☎ 323/848–6025), the luxe outdoor lounge and pool deck. The bar opens to the public at 8 pm daily. Come early to enjoy sweeping views of the city before turning your gaze inward to the beautiful people milling around.

Gordon Ramsay at the London Hotel (✉ 1020 N. San Vicente Blvd. ☎ 310/358-7788) is one of the more glamorous dining experiences in town. Jeans and sandals are replaced by stilettos and sparkly dresses. For a more casual vibe, head to the bar or the adjacent Boxwood Café.

TIPS FOR PARKING

Parking and traffic around the Strip can be tough on weekends. Although there's some parking on side streets, it may be worth it to park in a lot and pay $10-$25. Most of the hotels have garages as well.

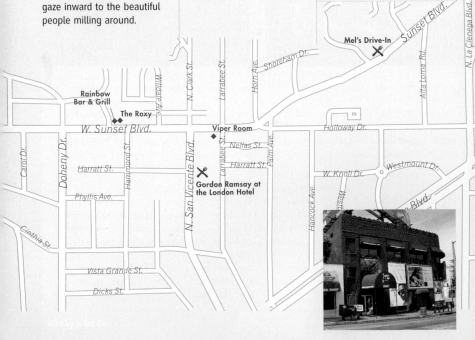

Whisky a Go Go

The Roxy

The Key Club

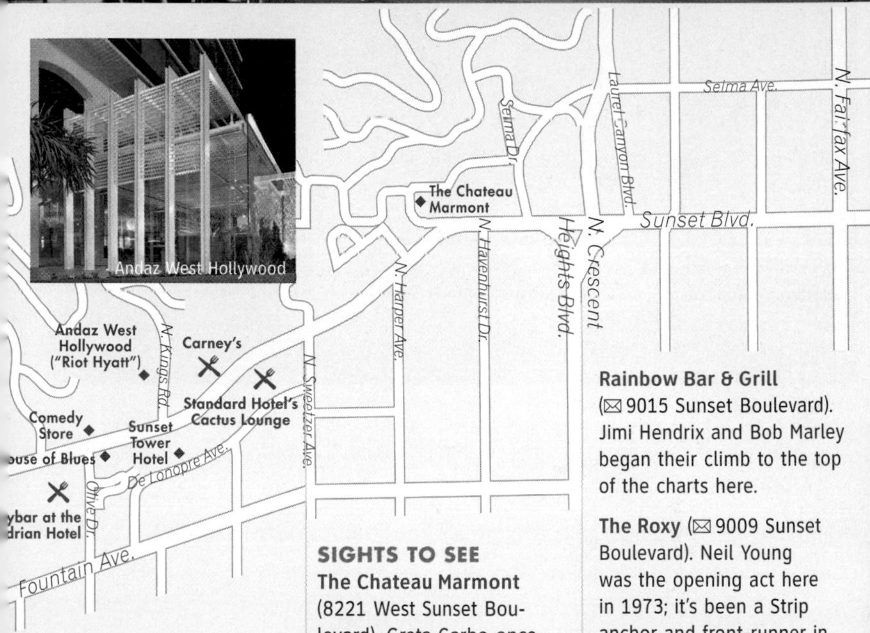

Andaz West Hollywood

Andaz West
Hollywood
("Riot Hyatt")

Carney's

Comedy
Store

Standard Hotel's
Cactus Lounge

Sunset
Tower
Hotel

ouse of Blues

De Longpre Ave.

ybar at the
drian Hotel

Fountain Ave.

N. Kings Rd.

N. Sweetzer Ave.

Other Dr.

The Chateau
Marmont

Serena Dr.

N. Harper Ave.

N. Havenhurst Dr.

Heights Blvd.

N. Crescent

Selma Ave.

Laurel Canyon Blvd.

Sunset Blvd.

N. Fairfax Ave.

Stop in for a burger and shake at Mel's Drive-In (✉ 8585 Sunset Blvd. ☎ 310/854–7201), open 24 hours a day. The iconic 1950s-inspired diner in the heart of the Strip is a fun place to people-watch, day or night.

For the city's best hot dogs, chili fries, and frozen chocolate-dipped bananas, head to Carney's (✉ 8351 Sunset Blvd. ☎ 310/654–8300), a popular spot for a quick bite. You can't miss it—look for the yellow railcar.

SIGHTS TO SEE

The Chateau Marmont (8221 West Sunset Boulevard). Greta Garbo once called this castle-like hotel home. It's also where John Belushi died.

Comedy Store (✉ 8433 Sunset Boulevard). David Letterman and Robin Williams rose to fame here.

Andaz West Hollywood ("Riot Hyatt") (✉ 8401 Sunset Boulevard). Led Zeppelin, the Rolling Stones, and the Who stayed and played here when they hit town.

Rainbow Bar & Grill (✉ 9015 Sunset Boulevard). Jimi Hendrix and Bob Marley began their climb to the top of the charts here.

The Roxy (✉ 9009 Sunset Boulevard). Neil Young was the opening act here in 1973; it's been a Strip anchor and front-runner in revitalization.

The Viper Room (✉ 8852 Sunset Blvd.) This always popular, always booked venue was where River Phoenix OD'd in 1993.

The House of Blues (✉ 8430 Sunset Boulevard). This relative newcomer has hosted top acts such as Tupac Shakur and Prince with Maceo Parker.

A DRIVE BEYOND THE STRIP

California's Pacific Coast Highway at dusk

There's more to see along Sunset Boulevard than the Strip. If you have time and want to take another classic L.A. drive, you'll understand how Sunset Boulevard got its name if just before dusk you continue west until it ends at the ocean, where it hits the Pacific Coast Highway (PCH) in Pacific Palisades.

WHEN TO GO

If you time it right, you can catch that famous L.A. sunset. If that's not possible, late morning after rush hour is good as well. Arrive just in time for lunch at a waterfront restaurant or a picnic on the beach.

The PCH is also known for its fresh seafood shacks along the roadside. For a cocktail with a great view, try **Gladstone's 4 Fish** (✉ *17300 Pacific Coast Hwy.*), where Sunset Boulevard hits the PCH.

TRIP TIPS

While it's hard to tear your eyes away from sites along the way, there are hairpin turns on the Boulevard, and driving is challenging. Also stop-and-go traffic—especially along the Strip—means lots of fender benders. Be careful and keep a safe distance.

Sunset view from Gladstone's

DOWNTOWN
LOS ANGELES

GETTING ORIENTED

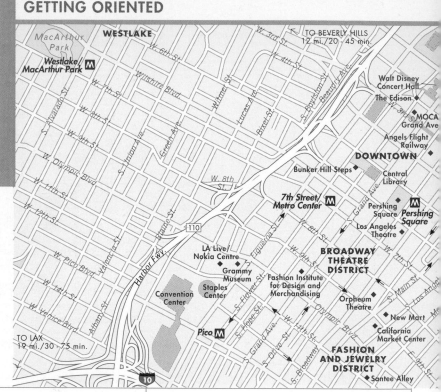

DRIVING TIMES AND DISTANCES

Minimum times represent little to no traffic; maximum times assume the worst. Adjust accordingly taking rush hour and peak weekend travel time into account.

■ **From LAX:** 30–75 min/ 19 miles

■ **From Hollywood:** 15–30 min/7 miles

■ **From Beverly Hills:** 20–45 min/12 miles

■ **From Pasadena:** 15–25 min/12 miles

■ **From Santa Monica:** 22–45 min/15 miles

GETTING HERE

Driving Strategy

The good news is that freeways 5, 101, 110, and 10 all get you there—but the bad news is that the traffic can be horrendous. If you're coming from the Hollywood area, skip the freeways altogether and take Sunset Boulevard, which turns into César Chávez Boulevard. Make a right on South Grand Avenue, and after a few blocks you'll be in the heart of Downtown. If you're coming directly from LAX, take the 105 E to the 110 N exit to the 6th Street/9th Street exit toward Downtown/Convention Center/Figueroa Street.

Parking

If staying at a hotel in Downtown with a garage, keeping your car there and getting around by foot, cab, or even the Metro is a better option than driving. If you must take your car, there are several options including lots and street parking, the latter being less convenient and ideal.

2

PLANNING YOUR TIME

Visit weekdays during the day, when the area is bustling and restaurants are open for lunch. It's easy to find street parking on weekends, but with the exception of Chinatown, L.A. Live, Olvera Street, and destination bars such as the Edison, at night the area shuts down.

Seeing everything in one day is possible, but it's best to spread it out over two. For art lovers, the Museum of Contemporary Art, MOCA at the Geffen Contemporary, the African American Museum, the Japanese American Museum, and the Chinese American Museum are worthy of more than just a pass-through.

Plan your visits around specific areas you can walk to in one circuit. Parking lots run $4 to $12, so if you're on a budget you don't want to be moving your car around too much.

The entertainment industry loves to use Downtown for movie backdrops, so when film crews take over entire blocks for shooting, traffic jams up in every direction.

Downtown

TOP REASONS TO GO

Visit Frank Gehry's Walt Disney Concert Hall. Be wowed by the genius architecture and grab tickets for a Los Angeles Philharmonic performance led by passionate conductor Gustavo Dudamel.

See a Lakers or Clippers Game. Catch the action at the Staples Center and possibly rub elbows with stars such as Jack Nicholson, Billy Crystal, and Leonardo DiCaprio.

Get Interactive at the Grammy Museum. Set your inner rock god free, playing virtual drums, or learn about folk music from Bob Dylan at this highly interactive museum.

Take a Historic Walking Tour. The L.A. Conservancy offers several tours, such as of Olvera Street, where you can see traditional Mexican culture and shop for crafts.

Dine in at the Grand Central Market. Check out the newly revitalized Grand Central Market, where you can grab bites from artisanal food vendors.

Sightseeing
★★★★★
Nightlife
★★★
Dining
★★★
Lodging
★★
Shopping
★★★

If there's one thing Angelenos love, it's a makeover, and city planners have put the wheels in motion for a dramatic revitalization. Downtown is both glamorous and gritty and is an example of Los Angeles's complexity as a whole. There's a dizzying variety of experiences not to be missed here if you're curious about the artistic, historic, ethnic, or sports-loving sides of L.A.

Updated by
Clarissa Wei

Downtown Los Angeles isn't just one neighborhood: it's a cluster of pedestrian-friendly enclaves where you can sample an eclectic mix of flavors, wander through world-class museums, and enjoy great live performances or sports events.

As you venture into the different neighborhoods of Downtown—**Chinatown, Little Tokyo,** and **El Pueblo de Los Angeles**—take advantage of the tastes, sounds, and sights. Eat roasted duck in Chinatown, red bean cakes in Little Tokyo, or pickled cactus on Olvera Street. Spend time browsing at the **Grand Central Market,** where stalls are filled with colorful locally grown produce and homemade treats such as tamales and olive bread. The market recently received a makeover, and is now offering everything from Texan barbecue to Thai-style chicken over rice. For art lovers, the **Geffen Contemporary at MOCA** has one of the most important modern and contemporary art collections, and those who are fans of architecture should make a point to see another Gehry creation, the **Walt Disney Concert Hall,** or the massive, geometrically designed **Cathedral of Our Lady for the Angels.**

To see the glory of Broadway's golden years, look "up," above the storefront signs, to see the marvelous architecture and theater marquees of the majestic buildings they reside in. From the late 19th century to the 1950s—before malls and freeways—**Broadway** glittered with the finest shops and the highest number of luxurious theaters in the world, making it a rich, cultural haven. Though it remains the main road through Downtown's Historic District, the area has changed dramatically over the years. Currently bustling with businesses catering to mostly Mexican

The Cathedral of Our Lady of the Angels, one of Downtown's must-sees, is a 21st-century architectural landmark.

and Central American immigrants, between 1st and 9th streets you can find mariachi and *banda* music blaring from electronics-store speakers, street-food vendors hawking sliced papaya sprinkled with chili powder, and fancy dresses for a girl's *quinceañera* (15th birthday).

Glance in every direction and you'll see construction crews building luxury lofts and retail space aimed at making Downtown a one-stop destination to work, live, and play.

Two massive entertainment complexes are further transforming the area: The long-awaited Frank Gehry–designed Grand Avenue Project is in the works, to be built around the **Music Center** performance complex, and the **L.A. Live/Nokia Theatre** project, anchored around the **Staples Center** sports arena.

TOP ATTRACTIONS

FAMILY **California Science Center.** You're bound to see excited kids running up to the dozens of interactive exhibits here that illustrate the relevance of science to everyday life. Clustered in different "worlds," this center keeps them busy for hours. They can design their own building and learn how to make it earthquake-proof, or watch Tess, the 50-foot animatronic star of the exhibit "Body Works," dramatically demonstrate how the body's organs work together. Air and Space Exhibits show what it takes to go to outer space with Gemini 11, a real capsule flown into space by Pete Conrad and Dick Gordon in 1966. The museum is also home to NASA's Space Shuttle Endeavor. ■**TIP→** A timed ticket is needed to visit the massive spacecraft. An IMAX theater shows large-format releases. ✉ *700 Exposition Park Dr., Exposition Park* ☎ *213/744–7400, 323/724–3623* ⊕ *www. californiasciencecenter.org* ☞ *Free; IMAX ticket prices vary* ☉ *Daily 10–5.*

Fodor's Choice

★ **Cathedral of Our Lady of the Angels.** A half-block from Frank Gehry's curvaceous Walt Disney Concert Hall sits the austere Cathedral of Our Lady of the Angels—a spiritual draw as well as an architectural attraction. Controversy surrounded Spanish architect José Rafael Moneo's unconventional design for the seat of the Archdiocese of Los Angeles. But judging from the

DOWNTOWN WITH KIDS

Downtown is a very kid-friendly neighborhood. If you're traveling with kids, check out the **California Science Center** as well as the extremely popular Dinosaur Hall at the **Natural History Museum of Los Angeles County.**

swarms of visitors and the standing-room-only holiday masses, the church has carved out a niche for itself in Downtown L.A.

The plaza in front is glaringly bright on sunny days; a children's play garden with bronze animals relieves the stark space. Imposing bronze doors, designed by local artist Robert Graham, are decorated with multicultural icons. The canyonlike interior is spare, polished, and airy. By day, sunlight illuminates the sanctuary through translucent curtain walls of thin Spanish alabaster, a departure from the usual stained glass. Artist John Nava used residents from his hometown of Ojai, California, as models for some of the 135 figures in the tapestries that line the nave walls. Make sure to head underground to wander the bright, mazelike white-marble corridors of the mausoleum. Free guided tours start at the entrance fountain at 1 pm on weekdays. Ask about free concerts on Wednesdays at 12:45 pm. There's plenty of underground visitor parking; the vehicle entrance is on Hill Street. ⊠ *555 W. Temple St., Downtown* ☎ *213/680–5200* ⊕ *www. olacathedral.org* ⊡ *Free, parking $4 every 15 min, $18 maximum* ⊗ *Weekdays 6–6, Sat. 9–6, Sun. 7–6.*

El Pueblo de Los Angeles. The oldest section of the city, known as El Pueblo de Los Angeles, represents the rich Mexican heritage of L.A. It had a close shave with disintegration in the early 20th century, until the socialite Christine Sterling walked through in 1926. Jolted by the historic area's decay, Sterling fought to preserve key buildings and led the transformation of Olvera Street into a Mexican-American marketplace. Today this character remains; vendors sell puppets, leather goods, sandals, and woolen shawls from stalls that line the center of the narrow street. You can find everything from donkey-shape salt and pepper shakers to gorgeous glassware and pottery.

At the beginning of Olvera Street is the Plaza, a wonderful Mexican-style park with plenty of benches and walkways shaded by a huge Moreton Bay fig tree. On weekends, mariachi bands and folkloric dance groups perform. Not to be missed is one of city's top sites—Cathedral of Our Lady of the Angels, designed by architect José Rafael Moneo.

Two annual events particularly worth seeing: the Blessing of the Animals and Las Posadas. On the Saturday before Easter, Angelenos bring their pets (not just dogs and cats, but horses, pigs, cows, birds, hamsters) to be blessed by a priest. For Las Posadas (every night between December 16 and 24), merchants and visitors parade up and down the

Olvera Street, at the heart of the city's oldest neighborhood, is the place to experience many aspects of L.A.'s Mexican American culture.

street, led by children dressed as angels, to commemorate Mary and Joseph's search for shelter on Christmas Eve. For information, stop by the Olvera Street Visitors Center at 622 N. Main Street, a Victorian built in 1887 as a hotel and boardinghouse. The center is open weekdays and weekends 9 to 4. Free hour-long walking tours leave here at 10, 11, and noon Tuesday to Saturday. ⊠ *125 Paseo De La Plaza, Downtown* ☎ *213/628–1274* ⊕ *elpueblo.lacity.org.*

Grammy Museum. For a unique experience, head to the wildly entertaining interactive Grammy Museum—a space that brings the music industry's history to life. The museum, which has 30,000 square feet of space, has four floors of films and interactive exhibits on performers ranging from pop stars to opera divas. ⊠ *800 W. Olympic Blvd., Downtown* ☎ *213/765–6800* ⊕ *www.grammymuseum.org* ☞ *$12.95* ⊙ *Weekdays 11:30–7:30, weekends 10–7:30.*

Geffen Contemporary at MOCA. A Frank Gehry creation, the Geffen Contemporary is one of the architect's boldest pieces. The space used to be a police car warehouse in Little Tokyo. This location, the largest of the three MOCA branches, boasts more than 40,000 square feet of exhibition space and features enterprising pieces that are typically larger in size and more recent. ⊠ *152 N. Central Ave., Downtown* ☎ *213/626–6222* ⊕ *www.moca.org/museum/moca_geffen.php* ☞ *$12* ⊙ *Mon. and Fri. 11–5, Thurs. 11–8, weekends 11–6.*

Grand Central Market. Handmade white-corn tamales, warm olive bread, dried figs, Mexican fruit drinks. Hungry yet? This mouthwatering gathering place is the city's largest and most active food market. The market, which was treated to a makeover in 2013, is now the home to various

BEST SPOTS FOR STAR-SIGHTING

■ **Courtside seats at a Lakers game during the playoffs.** Best way to see Kobe up close? Be a celebrity, know a celebrity, or be a celebrity's agent. Having an in at one of the big Downtown law firms that often buy season tickets is also a winning strategy. Otherwise, hire a private concierge service and be prepared to pay—a lot. Whatever you do, don't buy tickets off the street.

■ **Opening night galas.** Try for the Walt Disney Concert Hall or preview opening parties at the Museum of Contemporary Art. Celebrities support their fellow artists in Los Angeles and often entry to these fêtes is as easy as paying for the ticket to get in.

■ **The rooftop bar at the Standard.** The place still has enough buzz to attract the occasional celebrity. Booking a room is the surest way to gain access to the rooftop bar and pool. Word of advice: Never name-drop in Los Angeles. People who are truly connected here don't have to.

artisanal food vendors. The spot bustles nonstop with locals and visitors surveying the butcher shop's display of everything from lambs' heads to pigs' tails. Produce stalls are piled high with locally grown avocados and heirloom tomatoes. Stop by **Del Rey**, at stall A7, for a remarkable selection of rare chilis and spices or **Sticky Rice**, at stall C-4-5, for a fantastic Thai-style chicken. Even if you don't plan on buying anything, the market is a great place to browse and people-watch. ⊠ *317 S. Broadway, Downtown* ☎ *213/624–2378* ⊕ *www.grandcentralmarket. com* ⊜ *Free* ☉ *Daily 8–6.*

L.A. Live. Filling the void that was a no-man's-land except for the legendary Staples Center sports arena, enter the mammoth L.A. Live to enjoy an evening of entertainment without driving all over town—a rare occurrence in Los Angeles. The first thing that you'll notice as you emerge from the parking lots is the giant LED screens and sparkling lights. But there's also a happy buzz here as people head out to dinner before or after a sporting event, award ceremony, or concert at the Nokia Theatre. There are dozens of restaurants and eateries here including Los Angeles favorite Katsuya, the spot for sizzling Kobe beef platters and sushi so good it's addictive (the crab rolls are not to be missed). ⊠ *800 W. Olympic Blvd., Downtown* ☎ *213/763–6030* ⊕ *www.nokiatheatrelalive.com.*

MOCA Grand Avenue. The main branch of the Museum of Contemporary Art Grand Avenue, MOCA Grand Avenue features underground galleries and elegant exhibitions. With thousands of pieces dating back to 1940, the galleries are inundated with works by groundbreakers like Jean-Michel Basquiat and Cindy Sherman. Take advantage of the free audio tour. ⊠ *250 S. Grand Ave., Downtown* ☎ *213/626-6222* ⊕ *www. moca.org/museum/moca_grandave.php* ⊜ *$12* ☉ *Mon. and Fri. 11–5, Thurs. 11–8, weekends 11–6.*

Fodor's Choice ★ **Walt Disney Concert Hall.** One of the architectural wonders of Los Angeles, the 2,265-seat Walt Disney Concert Hall is a sculptural monument of gleaming, curved steel designed by master architect Frank Gehry.

Frank Gehry's Walt Disney Concert Hall was an instant L.A. icon.

It's part of a complex that includes a public park, gardens, and shops, as well as two outdoor amphitheaters. This is the home of Los Angeles Master Chorale as well as Los Angeles Philharmonic, under the baton of Music Director Gustavo Dudamel, an international celebrity in his own right. Audio tours and guided tours are available. The complimentary walking tours, which start at noon, take an hour and begin in the lobby. ⊠ *111 S. Grand Ave., Downtown* ☎ *323/850–2000* ⊕ *www.laphil.org.*

WORTH NOTING

Angels Flight Railway. The turn-of-the-20th-century funicular, dubbed "the shortest railway in the world," operated between 1901 and 1969, when it was dismantled to make room for an urban renewal project. Almost 30 years later, Angels Flight returned with its original orange-and-black wooden cable cars hauling travelers up a 298-foot incline from Hill Street to the fountain-filled Watercourt at California Plaza. Your reward is a stellar view of the neighborhood. ⊠ *351 S. Hill St., between 3rd and 4th Sts., Downtown* ☎ *213/626–1901* ⊕ *www. angelsflight.com* ⊗ *Daily 6:45 am–10 pm.*

Avila Adobe. Built as private home for cattle rancher Francisco Avila in 1818, this museum preserves seven of what were originally 18 rooms in the city's oldest standing residence. This graceful structure features 3-foot-thick walls made of adobe brick over cottonwood timbers, a traditional interior courtyard, and 1840s-era furnishings that bring to life an era when the city was still part of Mexico. The museum is open daily from 9 to 4. ⊠ *E-10 Olvera St., Downtown* ☎ *213/485–6855* ⊕ *elpueblo.lacity.org/index.htm* ⊗ *Daily 9–4.*

Bradbury Building. Stunning wrought-iron railings, ornate plaster moldings, pink marble staircases, a birdcage elevator, and a skylighted atrium that rises almost 50 feet: it's easy to see why the iconic Bradbury Building leaves visitors awestruck. Designed in 1893 by a novice architect who drew his inspiration from a science-fiction story and a conversation with his dead brother via a Ouija board, the office building was originally the site of turn-of-the-20th-century sweatshops, but now houses a variety of businesses that try to keep normal working conditions despite the barrage of picture-snappers. *Blade Runner* and *Chinatown* were filmed here. Visits are limited to the lobby and the first-floor landing. ✉ *304 S. Broadway, at 3rd St., Downtown* ☎ *213/626–1893* ◷ *Weekdays 9–5.*

Bunker Hill Steps. Threading a peaceful path through Downtown's urban towers, a fountain stream spills down the center of this monumental staircase designed by Lawrence Halprin. Its quiet beauty is reminiscent of Rome's Spanish Steps. The stream originates at the top of the stairs, where Robert Graham's nude female sculpture *Source Figure* stands atop a cylindrical base. If you're not inclined to walk up the 294 steps, hop aboard the escalator parallel to the stairs. Halfway up there's a coffee shop where you can fortify yourself before tackling the remaining climb. ✉ *633 W. 5th St., Downtown* ⊕ *www.laconservancy. org/locations/bunker-hill-steps.*

California African American Museum. With more than 3,500 historical artifacts, this museum is dedicated to showcasing the contemporary art of 20th-century African diaspora. The museum has a research library with more than 20,000 books available for public use. Try visiting on a Sunday—there's almost always a diverse lineup of speakers and performances. ✉ *600 State Dr., Exposition Park* ☎ *213/744–7432* ⊕ *www.caamuseum.org* 🎟 *Free* ◷ *Tues.–Sat. 10–5, Sun. 11–5.*

Chinatown. Smaller than San Francisco's Chinatown, this neighborhood near Union Station still represents a slice of Southeast Asian life. Sidewalks are usually jammed with tourists, locals, and, of course, Asian residents hustling from shop to shop picking up goods, spices, and trinkets from small shops and mini-plazas that line the street. Although some longtime establishments have closed in recent years, the area still pulses with its founding culture. During Chinese New Year, giant dragons snake down the street. And, of course, there are the many restaurants and quick-bite cafés specializing in Chinese feasts.

An influx of local artists has added a spark to the neighborhood by taking up empty spaces and opening galleries along Chung King Road, a faded pedestrian passage behind the West Plaza shopping center between Hill and Yale. Also look for galleries along a little side street called Gin Ling Way on the east side of Broadway. Chinatown has its main action on North Broadway. There are several garages available for parking here that range $3–$8 per day. ✉ *Bordered by Yale, Bernard, Ord, and Alameda Sts.* ⊕ *www.chinatownla.com.*

DID YOU KNOW?

It wasn't always the case, but over the last decade Downtown L.A. has become a hot spot for nightlife, with hotel rooftop bars and new, notable restaurants opening.

Chinese American Museum. Since it's in El Pueblo Plaza, you might assume that this museum features Mexican-American art. It's actually the last surviving structure of L.A.'s original Chinatown. Three floors of exhibits reveal the different cultures that have called this area home, as well as how the original residents paved the way for what is now a vibrant and varied Chinatown. Rotating exhibits feature the work of Chinese-American artists. ⊠ *425 N. Los Angeles St., Downtown* ☏ *213/485–8567* ⊕ *www.camla.org* ⊡ *$3* ☉ *Tues.–Sun. 10–3.*

City Hall of Los Angeles. This gorgeous 1928 landmark building is a TV star—it was in the opening scenes of *Dragnet* and served as the Daily Planet building in the original *Adventures of Superman*. During extensive renovations, the original Lindburg Beacon was put back in action atop the hall's 13th-story tower. The revolving spotlight, inaugurated by President Calvin Coolidge from the White House via a telegraph key, was used from 1928 to 1941 to guide pilots into the Los Angeles airport. Free tours of the beautifully detailed building are available weekdays 9 to noon, and sometimes include a visit to the observation deck. You can also opt for a self-guided tour. ⊠ *200 N. Spring St., Downtown* ☏ *213/485–2121* ⊕ *www.lacity.org/index.htm* ☉ *Weekdays 9–5.*

Exposition Park. Originally developed in 1880 as an open-air farmers' market, this 114-acre park has a lovely sunken rose garden and three museums—the California African-American Museum, the California Science Center, and the Natural History Museum of Los Angeles County—as well as an IMAX theater. There's also the Los Angeles Memorial Coliseum and Sports Arena, where Olympic festivities were held in 1932 and 1984 and where USC games are now played. Good news for commuters: The Metro Expo Line, which connects the Westside to Downtown Los Angeles, has a stop at Exposition Park. ⚠ Note that the park and neighborhood are sketchy at night. ⊠ *Between Exposition and Martin Luther King Jr. Blvds., Exposition Park* ⊕ *www.expositionpark.org.*

Italian Hall Building. This landmark is noteworthy because its south wall bears an infamous mural. Famed Mexican muralist David Alfaro Siqueiros shocked his patrons in the 1930s by depicting an oppressed worker of Latin America being crucified on a cross topped by a menacing American eagle. The anti-imperialist mural was promptly whitewashed but was later restored by the Getty Museum. It can be seen on the Italian Hall building today. An on-site museum is slated to open in 2014. ⊠ *650 N. Main St., Downtown* ☏ *213/485–8432* ⊕ *www.italianhall.org.*

Japanese American Cultural and Community Center. Plenty of traditional and contemporary cultural events make this center well worth the trip. Founded in 1980, JACCC is home to a number of civic and arts organizations. Through the center's basement you reach the James Irvine Garden, a serene sunken space where local plants mix with bamboo, Japanese wisteria, and Japanese maples. The main floor of the museum houses the George J. Doizaki Gallery, which has 2,000 square feet of exhibition space and has housed everything from national treasures of Japan to the Bugaku costumes from the Kasuga Grand Shrine in Nara. ⊠ *244 S. San Pedro St., Downtown* ☏ *213/628–2725* ⊕ *www.jaccc.org* ☉ *George J. Doizaki Gallery Tues.–Fri. noon–5, weekends 11–4. James Irvine Japanese Garden Tues.–Fri. 10–5.*

DID YOU KNOW?

L.A.'s Chinatown has its share of Chinese restaurants, shops, and cultural institutions, but you'll also find a growing community of artists and galleries.

THE LOS ANGELES METRO

Once upon a time, Los Angeles had an enviable public transportation system known as the Pacific Electric Red Cars, trolleys that made it possible to get around this sprawling city without an automobile. In the mid-1900s, the last of the Red Cars disappeared, and Los Angeles lost itself in the car culture. Make no mistake, the car culture is here to stay; an afternoon in rush-hour traffic will drive that point home.

But for the last few years, a sleek new rail system has emerged. You can now take a subway through parts of Downtown Los Angeles, Hollywood, Pasadena, and North Hollywood. The Metro Red Line subway, which is the most useful for exploring parts of the city, starts at Downtown's Union Station, then curves northwest to Hollywood and on to Universal City and North Hollywood. The Blue and Green light rail lines are geared for commuters. The latest addition, the Gold Line, goes from Union Station up to Pasadena.

It takes some planning, but using the Metro can spare you time you might otherwise spend stuck in traffic—if the stations are convenient. If you're worried about being caught in the subway during an earthquake, keep in mind that stations and tunnels were built with reinforced steel and were engineered to withstand a magnitude-8 earthquake.

The Metro Rail stations are worth exploring themselves, and you can sign up for a free docent-led **MTA Art Moves** (☎ 213/922–2738 ⊕ www.metro.net/about/art), which departs from the entrances to the Hollywood & Highland and Union stations. You'll receive a free day pass to ride the rails as you visit the colorful murals, sculptures, and architectural elements that illustrate themes of Los Angeles history.

The Universal City station is next to the site of the Campo de Caheunga, where Mexico relinquished control of California to the United States in 1847, and the station features a timeline of the area's past done in the traditional style of colorful Mexican folk art.

The North Hollywood station also celebrates local history: native Gabrielino culture, many immigrant communities, Amelia Earhart (a local), Western wear designer Nudie, and the history of transportation in Los Angeles County.

They are recycled film reels on the ceiling of the Hollywood and Vine station as well as original Paramount Pictures film projectors from the 1930s, and floor paving that looks like the yellow brick road from *The Wizard of Oz*. Imposing, glass-clad columns juxtaposed with rock formations can be seen at the Vermont and Beverly station. The old Red Car trolley makes a guest appearance in the Hollywood and Western station.

Japanese American National Museum. What was it like to grow up on a sugar plantation in Hawaii? How difficult was life for Japanese Americans interned in concentration camps during World War II? These questions are addressed by changing exhibits at this museum in Little Tokyo. Insightful volunteer docents are on hand to share their own stories and experiences. The museum occupies an 85,000-square-foot adjacent pavilion as well as its original site in a renovated 1925

The Palace Theatre, which opened in 1911.

Buddhist temple. ⊠ *100 North Central Ave., off E. 1st St., Downtown* 📠 *213/625–0414* ⊕ *www.janm.org* 🖃 *$9* ☼ *Tues.–Wed., and Fri.–Sun. 11–5; Thurs. noon–8.*

Little Tokyo. One of three official Japantowns in the country—all of which are in California—Little Tokyo is blossoming again thanks to the next generation of Japanese-Americans setting up small businesses. Besides dozens of sushi bars, tempura restaurants, and karaoke bars, there's a lovely garden at the Japanese American Cultural and Community Center and a renovated 1925 Buddhist temple with an ornate entrance at the Japanese American National Museum.

On 1st Street you'll find a strip of buildings from the early 1900s. Look down when you get near San Pedro Street to see the art installation called *Omoide no Shotokyo* ("Remembering Old Little Tokyo"). Embedded in the sidewalk are brass inscriptions naming the original businesses, quoted reminiscences from residents, and steel timelines of Japanese-American history up to World War II. Nisei Week (a *nisei* is a second-generation Japanese American) is celebrated every August with traditional drums, dancing, a carnival, and a huge parade. ⊠ *Bounded by 1st, San Pedro, 3rd, and Central Sts., Downtown* ⊕ *www.visitlittletokyo.com.*

Los Angeles Theatre. Built in 1931, the Los Angeles Theatre opened with the premiere of Charlie Chaplin's classic *City Lights*. Full of glorious French baroque–inspired details, the six-story lobby is awe-inspiring with its dramatic staircase, enormous fountain, grandiose chandeliers, and ornate gold detailing. You can occasionally witness the old Hollywood glamour by catching a special movie screening. ⊠ *615 Broadway, Downtown* 📠 *213/629–2939* ⊕ *www.losangelestheatre.com.*

Million Dollar Theatre. The Million Dollar Theatre opened in 1918 as part of Sid Grauman's famed chain of movie theaters. This Spanish baroque–style venue had the special feature of having its own organ. Film stars such as Gloria Swanson, Rudolph Valentino, and a young Judy Garland frequently made appearances. In the '40s, the venue swung with jazz and big band performers including Billie Holiday. The theater is open for special events and is worth a stop if you're walking past to inspect the lavish exterior with entertainment figures carved into the molding. ⊠ *307 S. Broadway, Downtown* ☎ *213/617–3600* ⊕ *www. milliondollartheater.la.*

FAMILY   **Natural History Museum of Los Angeles County.** This 1913-built Beaux-Arts museum has the usual dioramas of animals in their natural habitats, but it keeps kids interested with interactive displays. The Discovery Center lets them touch real animal pelts, and the Insect Zoo allows them to get up close and personal with the white-eyed assassin bug and other creepy crawlers. Dinosaur Hall features more than 300 fossils, including the adult, juvenile, and baby skeletons of the fearsome *Tyrannosaurus rex.* Also look for pre-Columbian artifacts and a display of crafts from the South Pacific. The 3.5-acre Nature Gardens, which debuted in 2013, features native plant and insect species and an expansive edible garden. ⊠ *900 Exposition Blvd., Exposition Park* ☎ *213/763–3466* ⊕ *www. nhm.org* 🎫 *$12* ⊘ *Daily 9:30–5.*

Orpheum Theatre. Opened in 1926, the opulent Orpheum Theatre played host to live attractions including classic comedians, burlesque dancers, jazz greats like Lena Horne, Ella Fitzgerald, and Duke Ellington, and later on rock-and-roll performers such as Little Richard. After extensive restorations, the Orpheum once again reveals a stunning white-marble lobby, majestic auditorium with fleur-de-lis panels, and two dazzling chandeliers. A thick red-velvet and golden-trimmed curtain opens at showtime, and a white Wurlitzer pipe organ (one of the last remaining organs of its kind from the silent-movie era) is at the ready. The original 1926 rooftop neon sign again shines brightly over a new era for this theater. ⊠ *842 S. Broadway, Downtown* ☎ *877/677–4386* ⊕ *www.laorpheum.com.*

Pershing Square. The city's cultures come together in one of the oldest parks, named in honor of World War I General John J. Pershing. Opened in 1866, the park was renovated in the 1990s by architect Ricardo Legorreta and landscape architect Laurie Olin with colorful walls, fountains, and towers. Although the massive block-and-sphere architecture looks somewhat dated, Pershing remains an icon of Downtown L.A. Nearby office workers utilize the area for a stroll or lunch break. From mid-November to mid-January, the place attracts ice-skaters to an outdoor rink. ⊠ *Bordered by 5th, 6th, Hill, and Olive Sts.* ☎ *213/847–4970* 🎫 *Free* ⊘ *Daily.*

Richard J. Riordan Central Library. The nation's third-largest public library, the Richard J. Riordan Central Library is centered on the handsome original building, designed in 1926 by Bertram Goodhue. Restored to their pristine condition, a pyramid tower and a torch symbolizing the "light of learning" crown the building. The Cook rotunda on the second floor features murals by Dean Cornwell depicting the history of California, and the Tom Bradley Wing, named for another mayor, has a soaring eight-story atrium.

DID YOU KNOW?

The Geffen Contemporary, a branch of the Museum of Contemporary Art in Little Tokyo, is one of L.A.'s top museums.

The library offers frequent special exhibits, plus a small café where you can refuel. Don't ignore the gift shop, which is loaded with unique items for readers and writers. Hour-long walking tours are offered Tuesday to Friday at 12:30, Saturday at 11 and 2, and Sunday at 2. A self-guided tour map is also available on the library's website. ⊠ *630 W. 5th St., at Flower St., Downtown* ☎ *213/228–7000* ⊕ *www.lapl.org* 🎦 *Free* ⊙ *Mon. and Thurs. 10–8, Wed., Fri., and Sat. 10–5:30, Sun. 1–5.*

Staples Center. Home to the Lakers, the Clippers, the Sparks, and the ice hockey team the Los Angeles Kings, the Staples Center is Downtown's top sports destination. It's also the preferred venue for superstars like Bruce Springsteen, Madonna, and Justin Timberlake. Though not open for visits except for events, the saucer-shape building is an eye-catcher. ⊠ *1111 S. Figueroa St., Downtown* ☎ *213/742–7100* ⊕ *www.staplescenter.com.*

Union Station. Even if you don't plan on going anywhere, head to Union Station to soak up the ambience of one of the country's last great rail stations. Envisioned by John and Donald Parkinson, the architects who also designed the grand City Hall, the 1939 masterpiece combines Spanish Colonial Revival and art deco elements that have retained their classic warmth and quality. The waiting hall's commanding scale and enormous chandeliers have provided the setting for countless films, TV shows, and music videos. ⊠ *800 N. Alameda St., Downtown.*

WATTS

Watts Towers. This trio of delicately wrought spires is the legacy of Simon Rodia, a tile setter who emigrated from Italy to California and erected one of the world's greatest folk-art structures. From 1921 until 1954, without any help, this eccentric man built the three main towers using pipes, bed frames, and anything else he could find. He embellished them with bits of colorful glass, broken pottery, and more than 70,000 seashells.

After a much-needed restoration, it is now maintained by the Los Angeles County Museum of Art. The towers are the centerpiece of a state historic park and cultural center, part of an effort by neighborhood leaders to overcome the area's rough history ⊠ *1727 E. 107th St., take I-110 to I-105 east; exit north at S. Central Ave., turn right onto 108th St., left onto Willowbrook Ave., Watts* ☎ *213/847–4646* ⊕ *www.wattstowers. us* 🎦 *$7, includes tour* ⊙ *Gallery Wed.–Sat. 10–4, Sun. noon–4; tours Thurs. and Fri. 11–3, Sat. 10:30–3, Sun. 12:30–3.*

HOLLYWOOD AND THE STUDIOS

with Los Feliz, Silver Lake, and Echo Park

GETTING ORIENTED

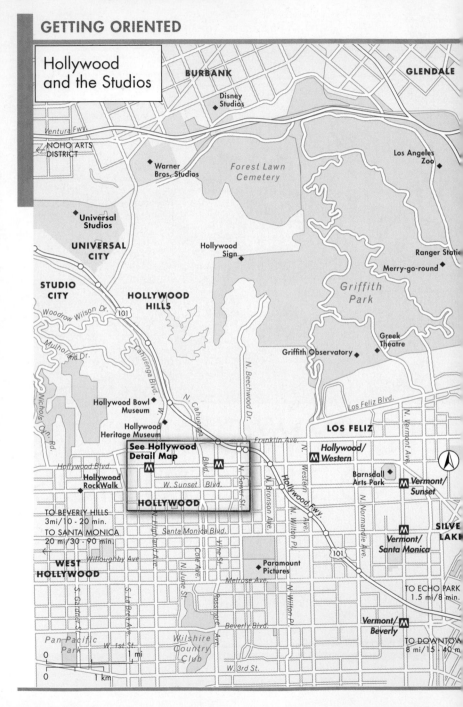

Hollywood
and the Studios

BURBANK

GLENDALE

Disney
Studios

Ventura Fwy.

NOHO ARTS
DISTRICT

Los Angeles
Zoo

Warner
Bros. Studios

Forest Lawn
Cemetery

Universal
Studios

UNIVERSAL
CITY

Hollywood
Sign

Ranger Station

Merry-go-round

STUDIO
CITY

HOLLYWOOD
HILLS

Woodrow Wilson Dr.   101

Griffith
Park

Mulholland Dr.

Cahuenga Blvd.

Greek
Theatre

Griffith Observatory

Nichols Cyn. Rd.

Hollywood Bowl
Museum

N. Cahuenga

N. Beechwood Dr.

Los Feliz Blvd.

N. Vermont Ave.

Hollywood
Heritage Museum

Franklin Ave.

LOS FELIZ

**See Hollywood
Detail Map**

Blvd.

Hollywood/
Western

Hollywood Blvd.

N. Gower St.

Barnsdall
Arts Park

Hollywood
RockWalk

W. Sunset   Blvd.

N. Bronson Ave.

Vermont/
Sunset

HOLLYWOOD

Hollywood Fwy.

Western Ave.

N. Witton Ave.

TO BEVERLY HILLS
3 mi / 10 - 20 min.
TO SANTA MONICA
20 mi / 30 - 90 min.

High Ave.

Santa Monica Blvd.

N. Normandie Ave.

SILVER
LAKE

Vermont/
Santa Monica

**WEST
HOLLYWOOD**

Willoughby Ave.

S. Gardner St.

S. La Brea Ave.

Cole Ave.

Vine St.

N. June St.

Crossroads Ave.

Paramount
Pictures

Melrose Ave.

N. Witton Pl.

101

TO ECHO PARK
1.5 mi / 8 min.

Beverly Blvd.

Vermont/
Beverly

TO DOWNTOWN
8 mi / 15 - 40 m.

Pan Pacific
Park

W. 1st St.

Wilshire
Country
Club

0   1 mi

W. 3rd St.

0   1 km

TOP REASONS TO GO

See the Studios. Catch a glimpse of where the stars work—Paramount Pictures, Warner Bros. Studios, Universal Studios Hollywood, and NBC Television Studios.

Walk in Famous Footsteps. There's the TCL Chinese Theatre, displaying the footprints of more than 200 of the silver screen's biggest stars, and the Hollywood Walk of Fame, with sidewalk stars honoring more than 2,500 of the entertainment industry's most famous.

Picnic at the Hollywood Bowl. Even if you don't get tickets for a show, stop at this L.A. landmark just north of Hollywood Boulevard for a great outdoor meal.

Get Up to Griffith Park. The largest municipal park and urban wilderness in the country has a zoo, miles of trails to hike, an observatory, and one of L.A.'s best views.

Check Out the Best Hollywood Memorabilia. The Hollywood Museum has an incredible collection of Tinseltown's most glamorous costumes, photos, and more.

GETTING HERE

Driving Strategy. During rush hour, traffic jams on the Hollywood Freeway (U.S. 101/Highway 170), San Diego Freeway (I-405), and Ventura Freeway (U.S. 101/Highway 134) can be brutal, so avoid trips to or from the Valley at those times.

In fact, the best way to get from Hollywood to Burbank is to skip the freeways all together and take Hollywood Boulevard to Cahuenga Boulevard heading north, taking a right on Barham Boulevard straight into Burbank.

Los Angeles Metro's Red Line subway makes two stops in the heart of Hollywood: the Hollywood/Vine Station and the Hollywood/Highland Station. This is by far the easiest way to get to the Valley or to Downtown Los Angeles.

PLANNING YOUR TIME

Plan to spend the better part of a morning or afternoon taking in central Hollywood, including seeing Grauman's Chinese Theatre and the Hollywood Walk of Fame.

Hollywood Boulevard sometimes attracts a rough collection of homeless people and runaways; if you've got children in tow, stick to a daytime walk.

Later in the evening, you can return to Hollywood for a movie at the El Capitan or the fabulous ArcLight, or a summertime concert at the Hollywood Bowl.

Expect to spend most of a day at Universal Studios Hollywood and CityWalk; studio tours at Paramount and Warner Bros. last up to two hours.

DRIVING TIMES AND DISTANCES

Minimum times listed below represent little to no traffic; maximum times assume the worst. Adjust accordingly, taking rush hour and peak weekend travel time into account.

■ **LAX to Hollywood:** 30–60 min/25 miles

■ **Beverly Hills to Hollywood:** 15–45 min/5 miles

■ **Hollywood to Burbank:** 20–40 min/7 miles

■ **Santa Monica to Hollywood:** 30–90 min/20 miles

3

A DAY AT GRIFFITH PARK

With so much of Los Angeles paved in cement and asphalt, 4,100-acre Griffith Park stands out as a special place. It's the largest municipal park and urban wilderness area in the United States.

(above) On the trail in Griffith Park (lower right) A resident of the park's zoo (upper right) The Griffith Observatory

On warm weekends, there are parties, barbecues, mariachi bands, and strolling vendors selling fresh fruit. Joggers, cyclists, and walkers course its roadways. There are also top attractions within the park, including the Griffith Observatory and the Los Angeles Zoo.

The park was named after Col. Griffith J. Griffith, a mining tycoon who donated 3,000 acres of land to the city for the park in 1896. It has been used as a film and television location since the early days of motion pictures. One early Hollywood producer advised, "A tree is a tree, a rock is a rock, shoot it in Griffith Park."

GETTING HERE

The park has several entrances: off Los Feliz Boulevard at Western Canyon Avenue, Vermont Avenue, Crystal Springs Drive, and Riverside Drive; from the Ventura/134 Freeway at Victory Boulevard, Zoo Drive, or Forest Lawn Drive; from the Golden State Freeway (I-5) at Los Feliz Boulevard and Zoo Drive. The park is open from 5 am to 10 pm.

TOP EXPERIENCES

VISIT THE GRIFFITH OBSERVATORY

The view from the front of the Griffith Observatory is absolutely breathtaking, and since its recent massive makeover what's inside is equally impressive. Visit during a scheduled talk or show at the Leonard Nimoy Event Horizon Theater, look through the Zeiss Telescope on a clear night, or check out the Samuel Oschin Planetarium and its incredible dome.

It's also fun—and free—to tour the expansive grounds, which include a monument dedicated to James Dean; several scenes from *Rebel Without a Cause* were filmed here. And to see the lights of the city twinkle at night from above, stay late and head up to the Observatory Deck, open until 10 pm every evening except Monday.

CLIMB MOUNT HOLLYWOOD

There's plenty of fabulous hiking to do in this park, but the best is to the top of Mount Hollywood. Park for free at the Griffith Observatory lot and pick up the trail, which begins there. It's an easy half-hour hike to the top. On super clear days you'll be able to see all the way to the Pacific Ocean and Catalina Island. About two-thirds of the way up is Dante's View, an area with benches to stop for a break or snack.

An up-close view of the Hollywood sign from just below means hiking a little more than 6 miles round-trip from the parking lot.

CHECK OUT THE LOS ANGELES ZOO AND BOTANICAL GARDENS

In the northeast corner of the park, the zoo's highlights include a gorilla reserve, a Sumatran tiger, a snow leopard, and an acre dedicated to one of the largest troops of chimpanzees in the United States. In addition, the zoo claims to have more flamingoes than any other zoo worldwide.

OTHER FUN THINGS TO DO

ENJOY A BIKE TOUR

There's a flat, family-friendly 4.7-mile path that runs along Crystal Springs Drive and Zoo Drive. Rentals are available inside the park at **Spokes n' Stuff Bike Shop** (✉ *4730 Crystal Springs Dr., at Ranger Station Parking Lot* ☎ *323/653–4099* ⊕ *www.spokes-n-stuff.com*).

CATCH A CONCERT AT THE GREEK THEATRE

This 6,100-seat **Greek Theatre** (☎ *323/665–1927* ⊕ *www.greektheatrela.com*) is an outdoor venue where top artists such as Elton John and Paul Simon have performed.

Sightseeing
★★★★★
Nightlife
★★★★
Dining
★★★
Lodging
★★
Shopping
★★

The Tinseltown mythology of Los Angeles was born in Hollywood, still one of the city's largest and most vibrant neighborhoods. In the Hollywood Hills to the north of Franklin Avenue sit some of the most marvelous mansions the moguls ever built; in the flats below Sunset and Santa Monica Boulevards are the classic Hollywood bungalows where studio workers once resided. Reputation aside, though, it's mostly a workaday neighborhood without the glitz and glamour of places like Beverly Hills. The only major studio still located in Hollywood is Paramount; Warner Bros., Disney, and Universal Studios Hollywood are to the north, in Burbank and Universal City.

Updated by
Jim Arnold

Of course, the "idea" of Hollywood as a center of the entertainment industry encompasses more than just that one neighborhood: to the north there's Studio City, a thriving strip at the base of the Hollywood Hills that's home to many smaller film companies; Universal City, where you'll find Universal Studios Hollywood; and bustling Burbank, home of several of the major studios. North Hollywood, a suburban enclave that's actually in the San Fernando Valley, has its own thriving arts district. Los Feliz, to the east, where you'll find Griffith Park and the hip and trendy Vermont Avenue area. Beyond that you'll find Silver Lake and Echo Park.

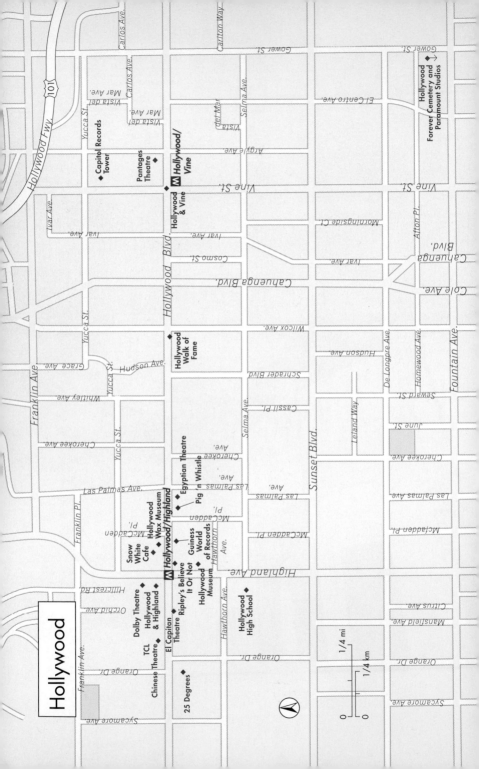

Hollywood

Hollywood Fwy.
101

Carlos Ave.

Carlos Ave.

Vista del Mar Ave.

Vista del Mar Ave.

Vista del Mar Ave.

Yucca St.

Gower St.

Gower St.

Selma Ave.

El Centro Ave.

Argyle Ave.

Hollywood Forever Cemetery and Paramount Studios

Capitol Records Tower ◆

Pantages Theatre ◆

Ⓜ **Hollywood/ Vine**

◆ **Hollywood & Vine**

Vine St.

Vine St.

Ivar Ave.

Ivar Ave.

Ivar Ave.

Cosmo St.

Hollywood Blvd.

Morningside Ct.

Afton Pl.

Cahuenga Blvd.

Cahuenga Blvd.

Cahuenga Blvd.

Cole Ave.

Ivar Ave.

Wilcox Ave.

Franklin Ave.

Grace Ave.

Hudson Ave.

Yucca St.

Whitley Ave.

◆ **Hollywood Walk of Fame**

Schrader Blvd.

Hudson Ave.

De Longpre Ave.

Homewood Ave.

Fountain Ave.

Cherokee Ave.

Yucca St.

Cassil Pl.

Selma Ave.

Seward St.

June St.

Teland Way

Cherokee Ave.

Sunset Blvd.

◆ **Egyptian Theatre**

Cherokee Ave.

Cherokee Ave.

Las Palmas Ave.

◆ **Pig 'n Whistle**

Las Palmas Ave.

Las Palmas Ave.

Las Palmas Ave.

Franklin Pl.

McCadden Pl.

McCadden Pl.

McCadden Pl.

Snow White Cafe ◆

Hollywood Wax Museum ◆

Ⓜ **Hollywood/Highland**

◆ **Guiness World of Records**

Hawthorn Ave.

Dolby Theatre ◆

Hollywood & Highland ◆

Hillcrest Rd.

Orchid Ave.

◆ **Ripley's Believe It Or Not**

◆ **Hollywood Museum**

Highland Ave.

Citrus Ave.

Mansfield Ave.

TCL Chinese Theatre ◆

El Capitan Theatre ◆

Hawthorn Ave.

◆ **Hollywood High School**

Orange Dr.

Orange Dr.

Franklin Ave.

◆ **25 Degrees**

Sycamore Ave.

Sycamore Ave.

Orange Dr.

1/4 mi

1/4 km

0

0

There are more than 2,500 stars honored on the Hollywood Walk of Fame.

HOLLYWOOD

Sure, Hollywood's top attractions are a bit touristy—but if it's your first time, you should at least make a brief stop here. Be sure to check out the Hollywood Walk of Fame and catch a movie in one of the neighborhood's opulent movie palaces, such as the TCL Chinese Theatre or El Capitan.

Like Downtown L.A., Hollywood continues to undergo a transformation designed to lure a hip, younger crowd and big money back into the fold. New sleek clubs and restaurants seem to pop up every month drawing in celebrities, scenesters, and starry-eyed newcomers to create a colorful nighttime landscape (and some parking headaches).

Many daytime attractions can be found on foot around the home of the Academy Awards at the **Dolby Theatre,** part of the Hollywood & Highland entertainment complex. The adjacent **Grauman's Chinese Theatre** delivers silver screen magic with its iconic facade and ornate interiors from a bygone era. A shining example of a successful Hollywood revival can be seen and experienced just across Hollywood Boulevard at the 1926 **El Capitan Theatre,** which offers live stage shows and a Wurlitzer organ concert before selected movie engagements.

Walk the renowned **Hollywood Walk of Fame** to find your favorite celebrities and you can encounter derelict diversions literally screaming for your attention (and dollar), numerous panhandlers, and an occasional costumed superhero not sanctioned by Marvel Comics. At Sunset and Vine, a developer-interpreted revival with sushi, stars, and swank condos promises to continue the ongoing renovations of the area.

In summer, visit the crown jewel of Hollywood, the **Hollywood Bowl,** which features shows by the Los Angeles Philharmonic and many guest stars.

The San Fernando Valley is only a couple of miles north of the Hollywood Bowl, yet some say it's worlds away. Over the hill from the notably "cooler" areas of Downtown and Hollywood, "The Valley" gets a bad rap. But all snickering aside, the Valley is home to many of the places that have made Los Angeles famous: **Disney Studios, Warner Bros. Studios,** and **Universal Studios Hollywood.**

If you've never been to L.A.—or if you have, and are coming back with your kids—it's hard to resist the allure of the soundstages and backlots of Tinseltown's studios. Studio tours are the best way for mere mortals to get close to where celebs work. Most tours last at least a couple of hours, and allow you to see where hit television shows are filmed, spot actors on the lot, and visit movie soundstages—some directors even permit visitors on the set while shooting.

TOP ATTRACTIONS

Dolby Theatre. Formerly the Kodak Theatre, the Dolby's interior design was inspired by European opera houses, but underneath all the trimmings, the space has one of the finest technical systems in the world. The half-hour tour of this theater that hosts the Academy Awards is a worthwhile expense for movie buffs who just can't get enough insider information. Tour guides share plenty of behind-the-scenes tidbits about Oscar ceremonies as they take you through the theater. You'll get to step into the VIP lounge where celebrities mingle on the big night and get a bird's-eye view from the balcony seating. ■**TIP→ If you have the Hollywood CityPass, the tour is included.** ⊠ *6801 Hollywood Blvd., Hollywood* ☎ *323/308–6300* ⊕ *www.dolbytheatre.com* 🎫 *Tours $17* ⊙ *Daily 10:30–4.*

El Capitan Theatre. This theater—where Orson Welles debuted *Citizen Kane*—originally opened in 1926 as a playhouse and was remodeled in the 1940s into a movie palace. Restored to its former grandeur by the Walt Disney Company, the palatial venue features soaring ceilings and a lavish East Indian motif. Movies are often preceded by live stage or music events. ⊠ *6838 Hollywood Blvd., Hollywood* ☎ *323/467–7674* ⊕ *www.elcapitan.go.com.*

Hollywood Forever Cemetery. Leave it to Hollywood to have a graveyard that feels more V.I.P. than R.I.P. With its revived grounds and mediagenic approach, this celebrity-filled cemetery (formerly the Hollywood Memorial Park) is well worth a visit. The lush gardens, lovely lakes, and spectacular views of the Hollywood sign and Griffith Observatory (whose founder, Griffith J. Griffith, is buried here) make it a good spot for an afternoon walk; you can pick up a map of the grounds in the gift shop. Among the graves are those of Cecil B. DeMille, Douglas Fairbanks Sr., and Mel Blanc, voice of many Warner Bros. cartoon characters, whose headstone reads, "That's all, folks!"

Film and music fans flock here to find their dearly departed idols, including King Kong's love, Fay Wray, and punk rockers Johnny Ramone and Dee Dee Ramone (buried under his given name Douglas Glenn Colvin).

The facade of the TCL Chinese Theatre

The large Grecian tomb in the center of the lake belongs to philanthropist William A. Clark Jr., founder of the Los Angeles Philharmonic. Inside the Cathedral Mausoleum is Rudolph Valentino's crypt, stained red from many lipstick kisses. For years, a mysterious "Lady in Black" visited Valentino's tomb on the anniversary of his death.

In summer, the cemetery hosts events including film screenings starring Valentino and other interred residents on the mausoleum's outer wall, and the grounds become quite a party scene. At Halloween-time the cemetery hosts Dia De Los Muertos, a Mexican festival celebrating the dead with colorful costumes, art, and music. When planning a visit, even for a festive event, maintain a respectful attitude. The cemetery still performs burials and proper etiquette is expected. ⊠ *6000 Santa Monica Blvd., Hollywood* ☎ *323/469–1181* ⊕ *www.hollywoodforever. com* ⊡ *Free; $10 for film screenings* ☉ *Daily 8–5.*

Fodor's Choice **Hollywood Museum.** Lovers of Hollywood's glamorous past will be sing-
★ ing "Hooray for Hollywood" when they stop by this gem of cinema history. It's inside the Max Factor Building, purchased in 1928. Factor's famous makeup was made on the top floors and on the ground floor was a salon. After its renovation, this art deco landmark now holds more than 10,000 bits of film memorabilia.

The extensive exhibits inside include those dedicated to Marilyn Monroe and Bob Hope and to costumes and set props from such films as *Moulin Rouge, The Silence of the Lambs,* and *Planet of the Apes.* There's an impressive gallery of photos showing movie stars frolicking at such venues as the Brown Derby, Ciro's, the Trocadero, and the Mocambo.

DID YOU KNOW?

The glamorous El Capitan Theatre on Hollywood Boulevard is where Orson Welles held the world premiere of *Citizen Kane*.

Hallway walls are covered with the stunning autograph collection of ultimate fan Joe Ackerman; aspiring filmmakers will want to check out an exhibit of early film equipment. The museum's showpiece, however, is the Max Factor exhibit, where separate dressing rooms are dedicated to Factor's "color harmony," which created distinct looks for "brownettes" (Factor's term), redheads, and of course, bombshell blondes. You can practically smell the peroxide of Marilyn Monroe getting her trademark platinum look here, and see makeup cases owned by Lucille Ball, Lana Turner, Ginger Rogers, Bette Davis, Rita Hayworth, and others who made the makeup as popular as the starlets who wore it. ⊠ *1660 N. Highland Ave., Hollywood* ☎ *323/464–7776* ⊕ *www.thehollywoodmuseum.com* 🎬 *$15* ⊗ *Wed.–Sun. 10–5.*

Hollywood Walk of Fame. Along Hollywood Boulevard (and part of Vine Street) runs a trail of affirmations for entertainment-industry overachievers. On this mile-long stretch of sidewalk, inspired by the concrete handprints in front of the TCL Chinese Theatre, names are embossed in brass, each at the center of a pink star embedded in dark-gray terrazzo. They're not all screen deities; many stars commemorate people who worked in a technical field, such as sound or lighting. The first eight stars were unveiled in 1960 at the northwest corner of Highland Avenue and Hollywood Boulevard: Olive Borden, Ronald Colman, Louise Fazenda, Preston Foster, Burt Lancaster, Edward Sedgwick, Ernest Torrence, and Joanne Woodward (some of these names have stood the test of time better than others). Since then, more than 2,000 others have been immortalized, though that honor doesn't come cheap—upon selection by a special committee, the personality in question (or more likely his or her movie studio or record company) pays about $30,000 for the privilege. To aid you in spotting celebrities you're looking for, stars are identified by one of five icons: a motion-picture camera, a radio microphone, a television set, a record, or a theatrical mask. ⊠ *Hollywood Blvd. and Vine St., Hollywood* ☎ *323/469–8311* ⊕ *www.walkoffame.com.*

Fodor's Choice ★ Paramount Pictures. With a history dating to the early 1920s, this studio lot was home to some of Hollywood's most luminous stars, including Rudolph Valentino, Mae West, Mary Pickford, and Lucille Ball, who filmed episodes of *I Love Lucy* here. Paramount is probably the most authentic studio tour you can take, giving you a real sense of the film industry's history. It's also the only studio left in Hollywood—all the others are in Burbank, Universal City, or Culver City. The lot still churns out memorable movies and TV shows, such as *Transformers* and *The Wolf of Wall Street*. You can take a two-hour studio tour or a 4½-hour VIP tour, led by guides who walk and trolley you around the back lots. As well as gleaning some gossipy history (see the lawn where Lucy and Desi broke up), you'll spot the sets of TV and film shoots in progress. Reserve ahead for tours, which are for those ages 10 and up. You can also be part of the audience for live TV tapings. Show tickets are free; you must reserve ahead of time. ⊠ *5555 Melrose Ave., Hollywood* ☎ *323/956–1777* ⊕ *www.paramountstudiotour.com* 🎬 *$48 regular tour, $165 VIP tour* ⊗ *Tours daily 9:30–2.*

DID YOU KNOW?

Don't worry about trying to figure out the best seats on the Universal Studios tram—you'll be scared out of it no matter where you sit!

TCL Chinese Theatre. A place that inspires the phrase "only in Hollywood," these stylized Chinese pagodas and temples have become a shrine to stardom. Although you have to buy a movie ticket to appreciate the interior trappings, the courtyard is open to the public. The main theater itself is worth visiting, if only to see a film in the same seats as hundreds of celebrities who have attended big premieres here.

And then, of course, outside in front are the oh-so-famous cement hand- and footprints. This tradition is said to have begun at the theater's opening in 1927, with the premiere of Cecil B. DeMille's *King of Kings,* when actress Norma Talmadge just happened to step in wet cement. Now more than 160 celebrities have contributed imprints for posterity, including some oddball specimens, such as ones of Whoopi Goldberg's dreadlocks. ⊠ *6925 Hollywood Blvd., Hollywood* ☎ *323/461–3331* ⊕ *www.tclchinesetheatres.com.*

WORTH NOTING

Capitol Records Tower. According to legend, singer Nat King Cole and songwriter Johnny Mercer suggested that the record company's headquarters should be shaped to look like a stack of 45s, and their comment produced this lasting symbol of '50s chic. Or so the story goes. Architect Welton Becket claimed he just wanted to design a structure that economized space, and in so doing, he created the world's first cylindrical office building.

On its south wall, L.A. artist Richard Wyatt's mural *Hollywood Jazz, 1945–1972* immortalizes musical greats Duke Ellington, Billie Holiday, Ella Fitzgerald, and Miles Davis. Of course, pop icons the Beatles, who are on display in stunning photos near the Vine Street entrance, are Capitol's most treasured offering. John Lennon's star on the Hollywood Walk of Fame is in the sidewalk out front and is often the scene of gatherings on his birthday.

The recording studios are beneath the parking lot; all kinds of major artists, including Frank Sinatra, the Beatles, and Radiohead, have filled the echo chambers with sound. At the top of the tower, a blinking light spells out "Hollywood" in Morse code. The building is not open to the public. ⊠ *1750 N. Vine St., Hollywood.*

OFF THE BEATEN PATH

Chemosphere House. Shaped like a flying saucer from a 1960s film, the Chemosphere House sits perched high up off Mulholland Drive overlooking the Valley. Designed by the late architect John Lautner, a student of Frank Lloyd Wright, this house is held together with special glues used at the request of the original owner, who worked with a chemical company. It's an awesome sight for architecture fans of the mod era. To get here, head north up Laurel Canyon, right on Mulholland, and right on Torreyson Place. Turn left up the narrow unmarked road where the private home sits at the top. ⊠ *7776 Torreyson Dr., Hollywood.*

Egyptian Theatre. Hieroglyphics in Hollywood? Why not? Impresario Sid Grauman built Hollywood's first movie palace in 1922; the Egyptian-theme theater hosted many premieres in its early heyday. In 1992 it closed—with an uncertain future. Six years later it reopened with its Tinseltown shine restored.

The nonprofit American Cinematheque now hosts special screenings and discussions with notable filmmakers, and on weekends you can watch a documentary called *Forever Hollywood* ($7). Walk past giant palm trees to the theater's forecourt and entrance. Backstage tours, which detail the theater's Old Hollywood legacy, take place once a month. Films, primarily classics and independents, are shown in the evening. ⊠ *6712 Hollywood Blvd., Hollywood* ☎ *323/466–3456* ⊕ *www. egyptiantheatre.com* ⊠ *$10.*

QUICK
BITES **Pig 'n Whistle.** During Hollywood's heyday, the Pig 'n Whistle was the place to stop for a bite before or after seeing a movie in the neighboring Egyptian Theatre. You can expect overstuffed booths, dramatic paneled ceilings, and attentive service. ⊠ *6714 Hollywood Blvd., Hollywood* ☎ *323/463–0000* ⊕ *www.pignwhistlehollywood.com* ☉ *Weekdays noon–2 am, weekends 11:30–2 am.*

Guinness World of Records. Saluting those who have gone the extra mile to earn a place in the world-famous book, this museum exhibits replicas and photographs of endearing record breakers that include such oddities as the most-tattooed person and the world's heaviest man. An interactive theater lets you sit in moving, vibrating seats while viewing a film so you can "experience" the force of a record being broken. This place is mainly for world-record buffs and freak show fans. ⊠ *6764 Hollywood Blvd., Hollywood* ☎ *323/463–6433* ⊕ *www.guinnessmuseumhollywood.com* ⊠ *$16.99* ☉ *Mon.–Sun. 10 am–midnight.*

QUICK
BITES **25 Degrees.** Proudly serving its signature burgers, fries, and shakes, 25 Degrees has won awards for having one of the best burgers in town. At street level, the around-the-clock eatery exudes a bit of the old Hollywood glamour while putting a modern spin on the classic burger joint. ⊠ *Hollywood Roosevelt Hotel, 7000 Hollywood Blvd., Hollywood* ☎ *323/466–7000* ⊕ *www.25degreesrestaurant.com/los-angeles.*

Hollywood and Vine. The mere mention of this intersection inspires images of a street corner bustling with movie stars, hopefuls, and moguls arriving on foot or in Duesenbergs and Rolls-Royces. In the old days this was the hub of the radio and movie industry: film stars like Gable and Garbo hustled in and out of their agents' office buildings (some now converted to luxury condos) at these fabled cross streets. Even the Red Line Metro station here keeps up the Hollywood theme, with a *Wizard of Oz*–style yellow brick road, vintage movie projectors, and old film reels on permanent display. Sights visible from this intersection include the Capitol Records Building, the Avalon Theater, the Pantages Theatre, and the W Hollywood Hotel. ⊠ *Hollywood Ave. and Vine St.*

　　Pantages Theatre. Just steps from the fabled intersection of Hollywood and Vine, this Hollywood Boulevard landmark is an art deco palace originally built as a vaudeville showcase in 1930. Once host of the Academy Awards, it's now home to such Broadway shows as *The Lion King, Hairspray, Wicked,* and *The Book of Mormon.* ⊠ *6233 Hollywood Blvd., Hollywood* ☎ *323/468–1770* ⊕ *www.hollywoodpantages.com.*

DOLBY THEATRE

Hollywood Heritage Museum. A must for Cecil B. DeMille fans, this unassuming building across from the Hollywood Bowl is a treasure trove of memorabilia from the earliest days of Hollywood filmmaking, including a thorough history of the mogul's starry career. Large sections of the original stone statues from *The Ten Commandments* lay like fallen giants among smaller items in glass cases around the perimeter of this modest museum. A documentary tracking Hollywood's golden era is worth taking in.

The building itself is the restored Lasky–DeMille Barn, designated a California State Historic Landmark in 1956. Early birds can catch the museum's 3½-hour walking tour of Hollywood Boulevard on Saturday morning at 9 ($10). Make sure to reserve a spot in advance. ⊠ *2100 N. Highland Ave., Hollywood* ☎ *323/874–2276* ⊕ *www. hollywoodheritage.org* ▣ *$7* ◯ *Wed.–Sun. noon–4.*

Hollywood High School. This mid-century modern building has seen a who's who of Hollywood royalty in its classrooms, and many productions have been shot in its halls. Surely no other high school has such a shining alumni list—such names as Carol Burnett, Carole Lombard, John Ritter, Lana Turner, and Sarah Jessica Parker call HHS their alma mater. You can't enter the school grounds, but take a look at the star-studded mural *Portrait of Hollywood*, by famed local painter Eloy Torrez, on the auditorium exterior on the Highland Avenue side. ⊠ *1521 N. Highland Ave., Hollywood* ⊕ *www. hollywoodhighschool.net.*

Hollywood RockWalk. A place that has provided equipment for virtually every band to have come out of Los Angeles since the 1960s, Guitar Center pays tribute to its rock-star clientele with a Hollywood RockWalk, out front. The concrete slabs are imprinted with the talented hands of Van Halen, Bonnie Raitt, Chuck Berry, Dick Dale, Def Leppard, Carlos Santana, KISS, and others. Two standouts are Joey Ramone's upside-down hand and Lemmy of Motörhead's "middle finger salute." The store's mini-museum displays signed sheet music and memorabilia like Bob Dylan's hat and harmonica. ⊠ *Guitar Center, 7425 Sunset Blvd., Hollywood* ☎ *323/874–1060* ⊕ *www.rockwalk. com* ▣ *Free* ◯ *Museum Sun. and Mon. 9–10, Tues. 9–6, Thurs. 9–9, Fri. and Sat. 10–9.*

Hollywood Sign. With letters 50 feet tall, Hollywood's trademark sign can be spotted from miles away. The icon, which originally read "Hollywoodland," was erected in the Hollywood Hills in 1923 to promote a real-estate development. In 1949 the "land" portion of the sign was taken down. By 1973, the sign had earned landmark status, but since the letters were made of wood, its longevity came into question. A makeover project was launched and the letters were auctioned off (rocker Alice Cooper bought the "o" and singing cowboy Gene Autry sponsored an "l") to make way for a new sign made of sheet metal. Inevitably, the sign has drawn pranksters who have altered it over the years, albeit temporarily, to spell out "Hollyweed" (in the 1970s, to push for more lenient marijuana laws), "Go Navy" (before a Rose Bowl game), and "Perotwood" (during Ross Perot's failed

1992 presidential election). A fence and surveillance equipment have since been installed to deter intruders. ■TIP➜ Use caution if driving up to the sign on residential streets, because many cars speed around the blind corners. ✉ *Griffith Park, Mt. Lee Dr., Hollywood* ⊕ *www. hollywoodsign.org.*

Hollywood Wax Museum. If a walk through Hollywood hasn't yielded any star-spotting, head over to this venerable icon of a museum, which has been open continuously since 1965. Get up close and personal with Drew Barrymore, Cameron Diaz, and Lucy Liu, or pose with a dapper, lifelike Samuel L. Jackson. Vignettes from classic films re-create well-known scenes, such as Katharine Hepburn and Humphrey Bogart in *The African Queen* or Tom Hanks in *Forrest Gump*, as well as the figures from the *Wizard of Oz*. There's an homage to Heath Ledger in *The Dark Knight,* alongside older icons such as John Wayne and Charlie Chaplin. Be sure to walk the red carpet with the latest Oscar stars and, if you're so inclined, creep along the dimly lit "horror chamber" where scenes from popular films of fright are reconstructed. The effect is heightened at night when fewer visitors are around. ✉ *6767 Hollywood Blvd., Hollywood* ☎ *323/462–5991* ⊕ *www.hollywoodwaxmuseum.com/hollywood* 🎫 *$16.99* ⊙ *Daily 10 am–midnight.*

QUICK
BITES

Snow White Cafe. Opened in 1946, the Snow White Cafe was supposedly created by some of the original Disney animators and is filled with murals of the film's characters. It's a good place for a quick bite. ✉ *6769 Hollywood Blvd., Hollywood* ☎ *323/465–4444* ⊕ *www.snowwhitecafe.com.*

FAMILY **Los Angeles Zoo.** A short drive from Downtown Los Angeles at the junction of the Ventura Freeway (Highway 134) and the Golden State Freeway (I-5) is the 80-acre Los Angeles Zoo. You'll need good walking shoes, as distances are compounded by plenty of construction detours. You'll see tigers, lions, and bears, along with a few endangered species such as the California condor and Sumatran tigers. "Elephants of Asia" opened to great acclaim with elaborate enclosure of sand, grassy hills, and waterfalls. New attractions include the Indian Rhino Encounter and a Rainforest of the Americas exhibit. ✉ *5333 Zoo Dr., Griffith Park* ☎ *323/644–4200* ⊕ *www.lazoo.org* 🎫 *$18* ⊙ *Daily 10–5.*

Ripley's Believe It or Not. The ticket prices may be a bit steep for these slighted faded relics of the bizarre and sometimes creepy, but where else can you see a bikini made of human hair, a sculpture of Marilyn Monroe made of shredded money, and animal freaks of nature? You're asked to "believe it or not," and many of the curiosities may fail a strict authenticity test, but the oddball place still offers some goofy fun. ✉ *6780 Hollywood Blvd., Hollywood* ☎ *323/466–6335* ⊕ *www. ripleys.com/hollywood* 🎫 *$16.99* ⊙ *Daily 10 am–midnight.*

STUDIO CITY

Ventura Boulevard, the famed commercial strip, cuts through the lively neighborhood of Studio City. This area, located west of Universal City, is home to several smaller film and TV studios.

UNIVERSAL CITY

Although it has its own zip code and subway station, Universal City is just the name for the unincorporated area of Los Angeles where Universal Studios Hollywood and CityWalk are located. The hill that provides the backdrop for Universal City is the back side of the one where you'll find the famous Hollywood Sign.

TOP ATTRACTIONS

FAMILY **Universal Studios Hollywood.** This studio is more a theme park with lots of roller coasters and thrill rides than a backstage pass, though its studio tour does provide a good firsthand look at familiar TV and movie sets. Despite the amusement park clichés, many first-timers consider this studio a must-see. The favorite attraction is the tram tour, during which you can experience the parting of the Red Sea; duck from dinosaurs in Jurassic Park; visit Dr. Seuss's Whoville; see the airplane wreckage of *War of the Worlds* and the still-creepy house from *Psycho;* and be attacked by the killer shark of *Jaws* fame. Monitors play video clips as you pass. ■TIP➔ This tram ride is usually the best place to begin your visit, since lines get long in the afternoon. If you get here when the park opens, you'll likely save yourself from long waits.

Most attractions are designed to give you a thrill in one form or another, including the spine-tingling Transformers: The Ride 3-D ride or the bone-rattling roller coaster Revenge of the Mummy. The House of Horrors is guaranteed to provide screams, while the Animal Actors show offers milder entertainment courtesy of some talented furry friends. The Simpsons Ride takes on a hair-raising animated journey through their hometown of Springfield. Looking for something for grown-ups? CityWalk is a separate venue run by Universal Studios where you'll find shops, restaurants, nightclubs, and movie theaters. ✉ *100 Universal City Pl., Universal City* ☎ *818/622–3801* ⊕ *www. universalstudioshollywood.com* 🎟 *$84, parking $15 ($10 after 3)* ⊗ *Contact park for seasonal hrs.*

BURBANK

Johnny Carson, host of *The Tonight Show,* used to joke about beautiful downtown Burbank, yet the area has become one of the area's most desirable suburbs. It's also home to Warner Bros. Studios, Disney Studios, and NBC Studios. It's also home to Bob Hope Airport (BUR), one of the two major airports serving L.A.

Go to Universal Studios for a big-bang theme park experience of moviemaking.

TOP ATTRACTIONS

Disney Studios. Although tours of this film studio are not available, a peek from Riverside Drive shows you that Disney's innovations go beyond the big and small screens to fanciful touches of architecture (note the little Mickey Mouse heads mounted on the surrounding fence). On the Michael Eisner Building, designed by architect Michael Graves, giant figures of the Seven Dwarfs support the roof's gable. The cartoonish Animation Building is topped with an 85-foot-tall *Sorcerer's Apprentice* hat. You can see the colorful complex from the Ventura Freeway (Highway 134). ⊠ *500 S. Buena Vista, Burbank* ⊕ *www. waltdisneystudios.com.*

QUICK BITES **Bob's Big Boy.** Only in L.A. could a Bob's Big Boy be classified a historical landmark. Built in 1949, this Big Boy stands as the city's best example of streamlined coffee-shop architecture. The best time to come is on Friday between 3 and 10, when the parking lot is flooded with restored hot rods. On weekends evenings, waitresses head out to your car to serve your burger and malt on 1950s-style window trays. ⊠ *4211 W. Riverside Dr., at W. Alameda Ave., Burbank* ☎ *818/843–9334* ⊕ *www.bobs.net.*

Warner Bros. Studios. If you're looking for an authentic behind-the-scenes look at how films and TV shows are made, head to this major studio center, one of the world's busiest. After a short film on the studio's movies and TV shows, hop aboard a tram for a ride through the sets and soundstages of such favorites as *Casablanca* and *Rebel Without A Cause.* You'll see the bungalows where such icons as Marlon Brando and Bette Davis relaxed between shots, and the current production offices for Clint Eastwood and George Clooney. You might even spot a celeb or see a shoot in action—tours change from day to day depending on the productions taking place on the lot.

Tours are given at least every hour, more frequently from May to September, and last 2 hours and 25 minutes. Reservations are required, and advance notice is needed for people with mobility issues. Children under eight are not admitted. A five-hour deluxe tour costing $250 includes lunch and lets you spend more time on the sets, with more ops for behind-the-scenes peeks and star spotting. ⊠ *3400 W. Riverside Dr., Burbank* ☎ *877/492–8687* ⊕ *vipstudiotour.warnerbros.com* ⊠ *$52, $250 for deluxe tour* ☉ *Mon.–Sat. 8:15–5:30; hrs vary on Sun.*

NORTH HOLLYWOOD

Originally called Lankershim after the family of ranchers and farmers who first settled here, this area took the name North Hollywood in the 1920s to capitalize on the popularity of the city just over the hill to the south. Today, the large and bustling neighborhood serves as the terminus of the Metro Red Line subway, around which the NoHo Arts District thrives.

WORTH NOTING

NoHo Arts District. Don't let the name fool you—this West Coast enclave bears little resemblance to its New York namesake. In fact, the name *NoHo* was spawned when the city, desperate to reinvent this depressed area, abbreviated the region's North Hollywood name. A square mile at the intersection of Lankershim and Magnolia in North Hollywood, the NoHo Arts District has slowly tried to transform itself into a cultural hot spot that includes several theaters showcasing aspiring young actors, a comedy club, galleries, boutiques, and restaurants. ⊠ *Lankershim and Magnolia Blvds., North Hollywood* ⊕ *www. nohoartsdistrict.com.*

LOS FELIZ

In the rolling hills below the stunning Griffith Observatory, Los Feliz is one of L.A.'s most affluent neighborhoods. With Hollywood just a few miles west, its winding streets are lined with mansions belonging to some of the biggest celebrities. In recent years, both Vermont and Hillhurst avenues have come alive with hip restaurants, boutiques, and theaters.

TOP ATTRACTIONS

Griffith Observatory. High on a hillside overlooking the city, Griffith Observatory is one of the area's most celebrated landmarks. Its interior is just as impressive as its exterior, thanks to a massive expansion and cosmic makeover. Highlights of the building include the Foucoult's pendulum hanging in the main lobby, the planet exhibitions on the lower level, and the playful wall display of galaxy-themed jewelry along the twisty indoor ramp.

Laurel Canyon and Mulholland Drive

The hills that separate Hollywood from the Valley are more than a symbolic dividing line between the city slickers and the suburbanites; the hills have a community in their own right and a reputation as a bohemian artists' hideaway for those who have been fortunate enough to make a living at their creative pursuits.

The 2002 movie *Laurel Canyon* provided one view of the lifestyle of one kind of Canyon dweller—freethinking entertainment-industry movers and shakers who seek a peaceful refuge in their tree-shaded homes. By day they're churning out business deals and working on projects; by night they're living it up with private parties high above the bustle of the city streets.

Though you may not get to see all the goings-on inside these homes, you can use your imagination as you take a drive through Laurel Canyon and pass estates and party pads dating back to the silent film era. If you have time to cruise Mulholland Drive, you'll get breathtaking views that can help take you away from the city's relentless pulse.

In true L.A. style, the Leonard Nimoy Event Horizon Theater presents guest speakers and shows on space-related topics and discoveries. The Samuel Oschin Planetarium features an impressive dome, digital projection system, theatrical lighting, and a stellar sound system. Shows are $7.

Grab a meal at the Café at the End of the Universe, which serves up dishes created by celebrity chef Wolfgang Puck. For a fantastic view, come at sunset to watch the sky turn fiery shades of red with the city's skyline silhouetted. ⊠ *2800 E. Observatory Ave., Griffith Park* ☎ *213/473–0800* ⊕ *www.griffithobservatory.org* ☉ *Tues.–Fri. noon–10, weekends 10–10.*

Griffith Park. The country's largest municipal park, the 4,210-acre Griffith Park is a must for nature lovers. It's the perfect spot for quiet respite from the hustle and bustle of the surrounding urban areas. Bronson Canyon (where the Batcave from the classic Batman TV series is located) and Crystal Springs are favorite picnic spots. A variety of plants and animals native to Southern California can be found within the park's borders, including deer, coyotes, and even a reclusive mountain lion.

The park is named after Colonel Griffith J. Griffith, a mining tycoon who donated 3,000 acres to the city in 1896. As you might expect, the park has been used as a film and television location since the industry's early days. Here you'll find the Griffith Observatory, the Los Angeles Zoo, the Greek Theater, two golf courses, hiking and bridle trails, a swimming pool, a merry-go-round, and an outdoor train museum. ⊠ *4730 Crystal Springs Dr., Griffith Park* ☎ *323/913–4688* ⊕ *www. laparks.org/dos/parks/griffithpk* ☒ *Free; attractions inside park have separate admission fees* ☉ *Daily 5 am–10:30 pm. Mountain roads close at sunset.*

WORTH NOTING

Barnsdall Art Park. The panoramic view of Hollywood alone is worth a trip to this hilltop cultural center. On the grounds you'll find the 1921 **Hollyhock House,** a masterpiece of modern design by architect Frank Lloyd Wright. It was commissioned by philanthropist Aline Barnsdall to be the centerpiece of an arts community. While Barnsdall's project didn't turn out the way she planned, the park now hosts the L.A. Municipal Art Gallery and Theatre, which provides exhibition space for visual and performance artists.

A film chronicling the history of Hollyhock House is screened in the gallery's lobby—but better yet, join a docent-led tour of the building. Wright dubbed this style "California Romanza" (*romanza* is a musical term meaning "to make one's own form"). Stylized depictions of Barnsdall's favorite flower, the hollyhock, appear throughout the house in its cement columns, roofline, and furnishings. The leaded-glass windows are expertly placed to make the most of both the surrounding gardens and the city views. On summer weekends, there are wildly popular wine tastings and outdoor movie screenings. A small farmers' market is held every Wednesday afternoon in the parking lot near the entrance. ⊠ *4800 Hollywood Blvd., Los Feliz* ☎ *323/644–6269* ⊕ *www.barnsdall.org* ⊠ *Free; house tours $7* ⊙ *Thurs.–Sun. noon–5.*

SILVER LAKE

East of Hollywood, this hilly, mostly residential neighborhood sits southeast of Los Feliz and northwest of Echo Park. Regarded as a bohemian enclave since the 1930s, it was the site of the first large film studio built by Walt Disney. With its thriving gay community, Silver Lake has hip stores and happening restaurants along its stretch of Sunset Boulevard.

ECHO PARK

Centered on a beautifully restored lakefront park, Echo Park is the first residential neighborhood northwest of Downtown Los Angeles. It's seen less gentrification than nearby Silver Lake, and is known for its edgier bars and music clubs. For film buffs, it was one of the principal locations of Roman Polanski's masterpiece film *Chinatown.*

BEVERLY HILLS, WEST HOLLYWOOD, AND THE WESTSIDE

GETTING ORIENTED

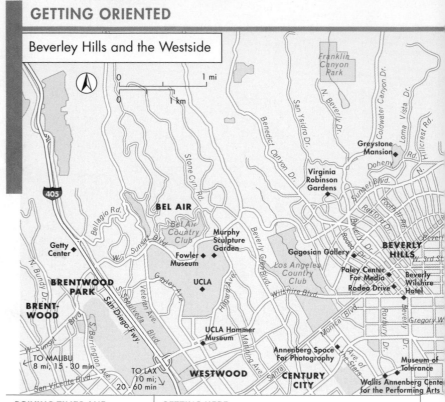

Beverley Hills and the Westside

DRIVING TIMES AND DISTANCES

Minimum times listed *below* represent little to no traffic; maximum times assume the worst.

Adjust accordingly taking rush hour and peak weekend travel time into account.

■ **From LAX:** 30–75 min/ 15 miles

■ **From Downtown:** 20–45 min/12 miles

■ **From Hollywood:** 20–25 min/7 miles

■ **From Malibu:** 15–30 min/ 8 miles

GETTING HERE

Driving Strategy

If Santa Monica is jammed up, try Pico or Olympic Boulevard, which run roughly parallel a bit farther south. Westwood Village and Brentwood's commercial district on San Vicente Boulevard come alive at night and on weekends, and the afternoon rush hour can be maddening—another good reason to plan museum trips early in the day or on Sunday.

Parking

Our advice? In Beverly Hills, park your car in one of several municipal lots (the first one or two hours are free at most of them), and spend as long as you like strolling along Rodeo Drive.

For street parking, bring plenty of quarters (although many meters in the area now also accept credit cards). Parking on residential streets is by permit only.

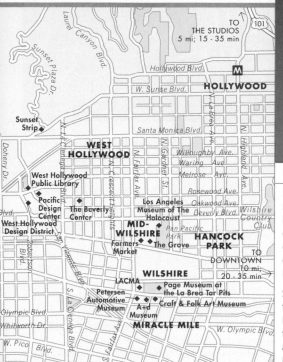

4

PLANNING YOUR TIME

Museums open between 10 and noon. LACMA is open Monday but closed Wednesday and has extended hours into the evening, closing at 8 (9 on Friday). The other museums are closed on Monday (except the Page).

Set aside a day to do this entire tour: an hour or two for the Farmers Market and The Grove, four hours for the museums, and an hour for the Wilshire Boulevard sights.

After a drive along Sunset Boulevard and a foray into the hills to see opulent homes, plan to arrive in the Golden Triangle of Beverly Hills at midday. Most stores open by 10 or 11, with limited hours on Sunday. (Some close on Sunday or Monday.)

Advance reservations are not essential but are recommended for visits to the Museum of Tolerance, closed Saturday, and the Getty Center, closed Monday—so plan accordingly. Each museum merits at least a half day.

TOP REASONS TO GO

Shop on Rodeo. Even if it's window-shopping, it's a one-of-a-kind experience to watch the parade of diamonds, couture gowns, and Ferraris being fetishized.

Explore the Grounds and Gallery at the Getty. The galleries are fantastic, but go to enjoy the view, Richard Meier's architecture, and the Central Garden.

Get Artsy at LACMA. With the addition of the Eli Broad Museum of Contemporary Art as well as the Lynda and Stewart Resnick Exhibition Pavilion, there is a breadth of artistic expression to be enjoyed.

Feast at the Farmers Market. Visit for a shopping respite or to take in and appreciate the Farmers Market's 75-year-old history and atmosphere.

Cruise down Sunset Boulevard to the Ocean. The quintessential Los Angeles experience; it's best to start at La Cienega headed west on Sunset so that you get to see the Sunset Strip. Now's a good time to test drive that convertible.

Sightseeing
★★★★

Nightlife
★★★

Dining
★★★★

Lodging
★★★★

Shopping
★★★★★

If you only have a day to see L.A., see Beverly Hills. Love it or hate it, it delivers on a dramatic, cinematic scale of wealth and excess. Beverly Hills is the town's biggest movie star, and she always lets those willing to part with a few bills into her year-round party. Just remember to bring your sunscreen, sunglasses, and money for parking.

BEVERLY HILLS

Updated by
Alene Dawson

When visiting Beverly Hills for the first time, many people head for the boutiques and restaurants that line the palm tree–fringed sidewalks of **Rodeo Drive.** People tend to stroll, not rush. Shopping ranges from the accessible and familiar (Pottery Barn) to the unique, expensive, and architecturally stunning (Prada). It's hard not to imagine yourself in a film, since this locale has basically become a backlot itself.

TOP ATTRACTIONS

Gagosian Gallery. This contemporary art gallery, owned and directed by the legendary Larry Gagosian, has its roots in Los Angeles and branches in New York and around the world. Previous exhibitions here include works by Damien Hirst, Richard Avedon, Richard Serra, Jeff Koons, and Frank Gehry. During Oscar season the gallery is known for its celeb-filled openings. ⊠ *456 N. Camden Dr., Beverly Hill* ☎ *310/271–9400* ⊕ *www.gagosian.com* ⊙ *Mon.–Sat. 10–6.*

Melrose Avenue. Once a hangout for rebellious types scouring the shelves at vintage clothing shops and record stores, Melrose Avenue has gone more mainstream with the addition of chain stores like Urban Outfitters. The farther west you go on Melrose, the tonier the selection. Here you can get your designer fix at such high-end shops as Marc Jacobs, Helmut Lang, Hérve Léger, Alexander McQueen, Agent Provocateur, Fred Segal, Paul Smith, Diane von Furstenberg, Vera Wang, and Vivienne Westwood. Nearby Melrose Place (a small street that's only a few blocks long) houses Carolina Herrera, Monique Lhuillier, and other upscale shops. ⊠ *Melrose Ave.*

Beverly Hills is a separate city from Los Angeles, with its own beautiful city hall.

QUICK BITES

Nate 'n' Al's. A longtime refuge from California's lean cuisine, Nate 'n' Al's serves up steaming pastrami, matzo ball soup, and potato latkes. Media and entertainment insiders like newsman Larry King have been seen kibbitzing at this old-time establishment getting an East Coast fix. ■TIP→ There can be a bit of a wait, so plan accordingly. ⊠ *414 N. Beverly Dr., at Brighton Way, Beverly Hills* ☎ *310/274–0101* ⊕ *www.natenal.com.*

Urth Café. If the buzz of L.A. slows you down, step into Urth Café. It's full of beautiful people refueling on organic coffee and tea with a range of health-conscious sandwiches, salads, and juices. The outdoor patio is a great place to take in the scene or spot celebrities. ⊠ *8565 Melrose Ave., West Hollywood* ☎ *310/659–0628.*

FAMILY **Museum of Tolerance.** This museum unflinchingly confronts bigotry and racism. One of the most affecting sections covers the Holocaust, with film footage of deportations and concentration camps. As you enter you're issued a "passport" bearing the name of a child whose life was dramatically changed by the Nazis; as you go through the exhibit, you learn the fate of that child. An exhibit called "Anne: The Life and Legacy of Anne Frank," brings her story to life through immersive environments, multimedia presentations, and interesting artifacts. Simon Wiesenthal's Vienna office is set exactly as the famous "Nazi hunter" had it while performing his research that brought more than 1,000 war criminals to justice.

Interactive exhibits include the Millennium Machine, which engages visitors in finding solutions to human rights abuses around the world; Globalhate.com, which examines hate on the Internet by exposing problematic sites via touch-screen computer terminals; and the Point of View Diner, a re-creation of a 1950s diner, red booths and all, that "serves" a menu of controversial topics on video jukeboxes.

Make reservations in advance (especially for Friday, Sunday, and holidays) and plan to spend at least three hours. Although every exhibit may not be appropriate for children, school tours regularly visit the museum. ⊠ *9786 W. Pico Blvd., south of Beverly Hills* ☎ *310/553–8403* ⊕ *www. museumoftolerance.com* ✉ *$15.50* ⊙ *Apr.–Oct., weekdays 10–5, Sun. 11–5; Nov.–Mar., weekdays 10–3, Sun. 11–5.*

Rodeo Drive. The ultimate shopping indulgence, Rodeo Drive is one of Southern California's bona fide tourist attractions. The art of window-shopping is prime among the retail elite: Tiffany & Co., Gucci, Jimmy Choo, Valentino, Harry Winston, Prada—you get the picture. Several nearby restaurants have patios where you can sip a drink while watching shoppers saunter by with shopping bags stuffed with superfluous delights. Near the southern end of Rodeo Drive is Via Rodeo, a curvy cobblestone street designed to resemble a European shopping area, which makes the perfect backdrop to strike a pose for that glamour shot. To give your feet a rest, $5 trolley tours depart on the hour from 11 to 4 at the southeast corner of Rodeo Drive and Dayton Way. They're a terrific way to get an overview of the neighborhood. ⊠ *Beverly Hills* ⊕ *www.rodeodrive-bh.com.*

Wallis Annenberg Center for the Performing Arts. Located in the heart of Beverly Hills, the Wallis Annenberg Center for the Performing Arts opened its doors in 2014. A breath of fresh air, this complex is centered on the 1934 Italianate-style Beverly Hills Post Office. The interior is gorgeous, with six Depression-era murals painted by California artist Charles Kassler depicting laborers and artisans. There's a new building holding the 500-seat Bram Goldsmith Theater and the 150-seat Lovelace Studio Theater. We love the inexpensive public parking right underneath the space—a great deal in L.A.! ⊠ *9390 N. Santa Monica Blvd., Beverly Hill* ☎ *310/246–3800* ⊕ *www.thewallis.org.*

QUICK BITES

Susina Bakery. Pair a shopping high with a sugar rush at Susina Bakery, a Paris-influenced pastry place offering mouthwatering tarts, tiny cookies, decadent cakes, and candied gifts. Don't miss the berry blossom cake. ⊠ *7122 Beverly Blvd.* ☎ *323/934–7900* ⊕ *www.susinabakery.com.*

MILK. This place is so popular that lines often extend outside the door. The "Warm Ooey Gooey Chocolate Sundae" and "Milky Way Malted Milk Shakes" are few of the homemade treats to tempt your sweet tooth. ⊠ *7290 Beverly Blvd.* ☎ *323/939–6455* ⊕ *www.themilkshop.com/contact.*

Sprinkles Cupcakes. The haute cupcake craze has remained so popular here that lines frequently extend out of the door and down the block. If you need an after-hours fix, not to worry. In 2012, Sprinkles debuted the world's

A classic Beverly Hills mansion

first Cupcake ATM, open around the clock. The most popular flavor? Red Velvet, of course. ⊠ *9635 S. Santa Monica Blvd., Beverly Hills* ☎ *310/274–8765* ⊕ *www.sprinkles.com.*

WORTH NOTING

Beverly Gardens Park. This nearly 2-mile-long park takes you from Wilshire Boulevard to North Doheny Drive along Santa Monica Boulevard. Go for an early-morning drive or an afternoon stroll, stopping for a photo op at the famous Beverly Hills sign. Art shows take place here in May and October. ⊠ *Santa Monica Blvd., between Wilshire and Doheny, Beverly Hills* ⊕ *www.beverlyhills.org/exploring/cityparks/beverlygardenspark.*

Greystone Mansion. Once owned by oilman Edward Doheny (Doheny Drive is named after him), this 1927 neo-Gothic mansion sits on 18½ landscaped acres and has been used in such films as *The Witches of Eastwick*, *Indecent Proposal*, and *There Will Be Blood.* Guided tours of the mansion are available, and the gardens are open for self-guided tours where you peek at the exquisite interior through the windows. ⊠ *905 Loma Vista Dr., Beverly Hills* ☎ *310/285–6830* ⊕ *www.greystonemansion.org* ⊠ *Free* ☉ *Daily 10–5.*

> **QUICK BITES**
>
> For the white glove treatment, take in a spot of tea at the **Greystone Mansion.** Afternoon tea on the terrace is served one Saturday a month May–August. The fee is $43 per person for nonresidents. Reservations are highly recommended by calling ☎ *310/550–4753.* Tea starts promptly at 4 pm. What could be more civilized?

Paley Center for Media. This sleek stone-and-glass building, designed by Getty architect Richard Meier, holds a world-class collection of television and radio, You can search for more than 150,000 programs spanning eight decades on easy-to-use computers, then watch them on monitors with comfortable seating. A visit here is a blissful way to while away the hours. Craving a disco-infused, late-'70s episode of Sesame Street? It's here, along with award shows, radio serials, and literally hundreds of sit-coms. The library plays snippets of a variety of programs from a roast of Dean Martin to an interview with John Lennon. Free parking is available in the lot off Santa Monica Boulevard. ⊠ *465 N. Beverly Dr., Beverly Hills* ☎ *310/786–1000* ⊕ *www.paleycenter.org* ☯ *Wed.–Sun. noon–5.*

CENTURY CITY

Just a few blocks west on **Santa Monica Boulevard** is Beverly Hills' buttoned-down brother, **Century City.** If Beverly Hills is about spending money, Century City is about making it. This district of glass office towers is home to entertainment companies—including two of Hollywood's key talent agencies, CAA and ICM, law firms, and investment corporations. It's a particularly precise place, with angular fountains, master-planned boulevards, and pedestrian bridges making it worth a drive down its famous "Avenue of the Stars" if only to imagine yourself amongst them.

TOP ATTRACTIONS

Annenberg Space for Photography. This gallery exhibits award-winning digital and print photography in a sleek, modern space in Century City. Its striking and culturally significant exhibitions include "Beauty Culture" and "Who Shot Rock & Roll: A Photographic History 1955–Present." It's a must-see for photography lovers. ⊠ *2000 Ave. of the Stars* ☎ *213/403–3000* ⊕ *www.annenbergspaceforphotography.org* ▧ *Free* ☯ *Wed.–Sun. 11–6.*

WORTH NOTING

Century City. A 280-acre swath of contemporary urban architecture, this complex was built in the 1960s on what used to be the backlot of Twentieth Century Fox.

WESTWOOD

Tucked between Century City and Brentwood, Westwood is known primary as the home of the University of California.

TOP ATTRACTIONS

Fowler Museum at UCLA. Many visitors head straight to the Fowler Museum at UCLA, which presents exhibits on the world's diverse cultures and visual arts, especially those of Africa, Asia, the Pacific, and Native and Latin American. Enter UCLA campus Lot 4 from Sunset Boulevard at Westwood Plaza and turn left into the lot. ⊠ *308 Charles E. Young Dr. N., Westwood* ☎ *310/825–4361* ⊕ *www.fowler.ucla.edu* ▧ *Free. The parking fee maximum $12 for whole day. 1-hour parking $3, use Lot 4 off Sunset Blvd.* ☯ *Wed. noon–5, Thurs. noon–8, Fri.–Sun noon–5.*

Cobblestone Via Rodeo, off Rodeo Drive, was designed to resemble a European shopping street.

UCLA Hammer Museum. The bold murals and installations at this museum have been known to bring traffic on Wilshire Boulevard to a crawl. In the heart of Westwood, the Hammer emphasizes the here and now, luring in new museumgoers with splashy, eye-catching displays in the museum's glass entryway. Focused on art and artists of our time, the museum forms a bridge between the city's artistic expression and the forward educational spirit of adjacent UCLA. Selections from Armand Hammer's permanent collection include works by Claude Monet, Vincent van Gogh, and John Singer Sargent. The 295-seat Billy Wilder Theater features selections from UCLA's Film and Television Archive. ⊠ *10899 Wilshire Blvd., Westwood* ☎ *310/443–7000* ⊕ *www.hammer.ucla.edu* ⊠ *Free* ☉ *Tues.–Fri. 11–7, Thurs. 11–9, weekends 11–5.*

University of California, Los Angeles (UCLA). With spectacular buildings such as a Romanesque library, the parklike campus of UCLA makes for a fine stroll through one of California's most prestigious universities. In the heart of the north campus, the **Franklin Murphy Sculpture Garden** contains more than 70 works by artists such as Henry Moore and Gaston Lachaise. The **Mildred E. Mathias Botanic Garden,** which contains some 5,000 species of plants from all over the world in a 7-acre outdoor garden, is in the southeast section of the campus and is accessible from Tiverton Avenue. West of the main-campus bookstore, the **J.D. Morgan Center and Athletic Hall of Fame** displays the sports memorabilia and trophies of the university's athletic departments and championship teams.

Campus maps and information are available daily at kiosks at major entrances, and free two-hour walking tours of the campus are given most weekdays at 10:15 and 2:15 and Saturday at 10:15. The main-entrance gate is on Westwood Boulevard. Campus parking costs $12 but there's also a lot at UCLA Parking Structure 4 off Sunset Boulevard that only charges you according to the time you stay—starting at as little as $1 for about 20 minutes. ⊠ *Bordered by Le Conte, Hilgard, and Gayley Aves. and Sunset Blvd., Westwood* ☎ *310/825–8764* ⊕ *www.ucla.edu.*

BRENTWOOD

A wealthy residential enclave west of Beverly Hills, Brentwood is home to the world-class Getty Center.

TOP ATTRACTIONS

FAMILY
Fodor's Choice
★

The Getty Center. With its curving walls and isolated hilltop perch, the Getty Center resembles a pristine fortified city of its own. You may have been lured here by the beautiful views of L.A. (on a clear day stretching all the way to the Pacific Ocean), but the amazing architecture, uncommon gardens, and fascinating art collections will be more than enough to capture and hold your attention. When the sun is out, the complex's rough-cut travertine marble skin seems to soak up the light.

Getting to the center involves a bit of anticipatory lead-up. At the base of the hill, a pavilion disguises the underground parking structure. From there you either walk or take a smooth, computer-driven tram up the steep slope, checking out the Bel Air estates across the humming 405 freeway. The five pavilions that house the museum surround a central courtyard and are bridged by walkways. From the courtyard, plazas, and walkways, you can survey the city from the San Gabriel Mountains to the ocean.

In a ravine separating the museum and the Getty Research Institute, conceptual artist Robert Irwin created the playful Central Garden in stark contrast to Meier's mathematical architectural geometry. The garden's design is what Hollywood feuds are made of: Meier couldn't control Irwin's vision, and the two men sniped at each other during construction, with Irwin stirring the pot with every loose twist his garden path took. The result is a refreshing garden walk whose focal point is an azalea maze (some insist the Mickey Mouse shape is on purpose) in a reflecting pool.

Inside the pavilions are the galleries for the permanent collections of European paintings, drawings, sculpture, illuminated manuscripts, and decorative arts, as well as American and European photographs. The Getty's collection of French furniture and decorative arts, especially from the early years of Louis XIV (1643–1715) to the end of the reign of Louis XVI (1774–92), is renowned for its quality and condition; you can see a pair of completely reconstructed salons. In the paintings galleries, a computerized system of louvered skylights allows natural light to filter in, creating a closer approximation of the conditions in which the artists painted. Notable among the paintings are Rembrandt's *The Abduction of Europa*, Van Gogh's *Irises*, Monet's *Wheatstack, Snow Effects*, and *Morning*, and James Ensor's *Christ's Entry into Brussels*.

If you want to start with a quick overview, pick up the brochure in the entrance hall that guides you to 15 highlights of the collection. There's also an instructive audio tour (free but you have to leave ID) with commentaries by art historians. Art information rooms with multimedia computer stations contain more details about the collections. The Getty also presents an array of lectures, films, concerts, and special programs for kids, families, and all-around culture lovers. The complex includes an upscale restaurant and downstairs cafeteria with panoramic window views, and outdoor coffee bar cafés. ■TIP➔ On-site parking is subject to availability and can fill up by late afternoon on holidays and summer weekends, so try to come early in the day. You may also take public transportation (MTA Bus 761). ⊠ *1200 Getty Center Dr., Brentwood* ☎ *310/440–7300* ⊕ *www.getty.edu* ▧ *Free* ☉ *Tues.–Fri. 10–5:30, Sat. 10–9, Sun. 10–5:30.*

WORTH NOTING

Skirball Cultural Center. The mission of this Jewish cultural institution in the beautiful Santa Monica Mountains is to explore the connections "between 4,000 years of Jewish heritage and the vitality of American democratic ideals." The extraordinary museum, featuring exhibits like "Visions and Values: Jewish Life from Antiquity to America," has a massive collection of Judaica—the third largest in the world. A big draw is the Noah's Ark interactive exhibition, where children are invited to recreate the famous tale using their own imagination. ⊠ *2701 N. Sepulveda Blvd., north of Brentwood* ☎ *310/440–4500* ⊕ *www.skirball.org* ▧ *$10, Thurs. free* ☉ *Tues.–Fri. noon–5, weekends 10–5.*

BEL AIR

Minutes from Beverly Hills, Bel Air is a well-to-do residential neighborhood that draws many people in the film and television industry because of its close-to-it-all location and tucked-away feel.

WEST HOLLYWOOD

West Hollywood is not a place to see things (like museums or movie studios) as much as it is a place to do things—like go to a nightclub, eat at a world-famous restaurant, or attend an art gallery opening. Since the end of Prohibition, the **Sunset Strip** has been Hollywood's nighttime playground, where stars headed to such glamorous nightclubs as the Trocadero, the Mocambo, and Ciro's. It's still going strong, with clubgoers lining up outside well-established spots like the House of Blues and paparazzi staking out the member-only Soho House. But hedonism isn't all that drives West Hollywood. Also thriving is an important interior-design and art-gallery trade exemplified by the Cesar Pelli-designed **Pacific Design Center.**

West Hollywood has emerged as one of the most progressive cities in Southern California. It's also one of the most gay-friendly cities anywhere, with a third of its population estimated to be either gay or lesbian. Its annual Gay Pride Parade is one of the largest in the nation, drawing tens of thousands of participants each June.

BEST SPOTS FOR STAR SIGHTING

■ **Hit Hotel Bars and Spas.** Waiting for your car at the valet stand at any of the big, insider hotels during Award Season most likely at the Beverly Wilshire Beverly Hills (a Four Seasons Hotel), Chateau Marmont, and Sunset Tower. You don't have to book a room in the hotel to valet your car here, you can stop in for a meal or cocktail, as all three hotels have restaurants and bars.

■ **Stroll Along Robertson Boulevard.** The paparazzi-filled street of Robertson in West Hollywood especially coming in and out of the boutique Kitson or iconic restaurant the Ivy.

■ **Eat at Industry Restaurants.** There are those certain places filmmakers and celebs love—whether it's for the special treatment there or simply the food—such as Mr. Chow in Beverly Hills and Dan Tana's on Sunset in West Hollywood.

The three-block stretch of **Wilshire Boulevard** known as Museum Row, east of Fairfax Avenue, racks up five intriguing museums and a prehistoric tar pit to boot. Only a few blocks away are the historic **Farmers Market** and **The Grove** shopping mall, a great place to people-watch over breakfast.

TOP ATTRACTIONS

Pacific Design Center. World-renowned architect Cesar Pelli's original vision for the Pacific Design Center was three buildings that together housed designer showrooms, office buildings, parking, and more—a virtual multibuilding shrine to design. These architecturally intriguing buildings were built years apart: the building sheathed in blue glass (known as the Blue Whale) opened in 1975; the green building opened in 1988. The final "Red" building opened in 2013, completing Pelli's grand vision all of these many years later. All together the 1.2 million-square-foot vast complex covers more than 14 acres, housing more than 120 design showrooms as well as 2,100 interior product lines; it's the largest interior design complex in the western United States. You'll also find restaurants such as Red Seven by Wolfgang Puck, the Silverscreen movie theater, and an outpost of the Museum of Contemporary Art. ⊠ *8687 Melrose Ave., West Hollywood* ☎ *310/657–0800* ⊕ *www.pacificdesigncenter.com* ☽ *Weekdays 9–5.*

MOCA **Pacific Design Center.** Located in the heart of West Hollywood, MOCA Pacific Design Center features rotating exhibitions of architecture, design, and contemporary art. Don't miss the MOCA Store. ⊠ *8687 Melrose Ave., West Hollywood* ☎ *310/657–0800* ⊕ *www. moca.org* ☽ *Tues.–Fri 11–5, weekends 11–6.*

Fodor'sChoice
★ **Los Angeles County Museum of Art (LACMA).** Without a doubt, this is the focal point of the museum district that runs along Wilshire Boulevard. Chris Burden's *Urban Light* sculpture, composed of more than 220 restored cast-iron antique street lamps, elegantly marks the location. Inside you'll find one of the country's most comprehensive art collections, with more than 120,000 objects dating from ancient times to the present. Since opening in 1965, the museum now includes numerous buildings that cover more than 20 acres.

The Farmers Market is a great place to pick up prepared food, baked goods, and more, making it a popular place for a quick meal.

Works from the museum's rotating permanent collection include Latin American artists such as Diego Rivera and Frida Kahlo, prominent Southern California artists, collections of Islamic and European art, and paintings by Henri Matisse, Rene Magritte, Paul Klee, and Wassily Kandinsky. There's also a solid collection of art representing the ancient civilizations of Egypt, the Near East, Greece, and Rome, plus a vast costume and textiles collection dating back to the 16th century.

The Broad Contemporary Art Museum, designed by Renzo Piano, opened in 2008 and impresses with three vast floors. BCAM presents contemporary art from LACMA's collection in addition to temporary exhibitions that explore the interplay of the present and the past. In 2010, the Lynda and Stewart Resnick Exhibition Pavilion, a stunning, light-filled space also designed by Renzo Piano, added more exhibit space.

LACMA's other spaces include the Ahmanson Building, which features Art of the Pacific, European, Middle Eastern, South and Southeast Asian collections; the Robert Gore Rifkind Center for German Expressionist Studies; the Art of the Americas Building; the Pavilion for Japanese Art, featuring scrolls, screens, drawings, paintings, textiles, and decorative arts from Japan; the Bing Center, a research library, resource center, and theater; and the Boone's Children's Gallery, located in the Hammer Building, where story time and art lessons are just some of the activities offered. The museum wows visitors with special exhibitions and hosted major traveling shows, including the recent, vast Stanley Kubrick exhibit and the visually stunning James Turrell retrospective. Look for additional special programming as LACMA celebrates its 50th birthday in 2015.

■TIP➔ Note that LACMA's resident outdoor Stark Bar, is not only eye-catching with its bright red chairs, but has become quite the gathering spot for handcrafted, seasonal cocktails.

■TIP➔ Temporary exhibits sometimes require tickets purchased in advance, so check the calendar ahead of time. ⊠ *5905 Wilshire Blvd., Miracle Mile* ☎ *323/857–6000* ⊕ *www.lacma.org* ⊠ *$15* ⊘ *Mon., Tues., and Thurs. 11–5, Fri. 11–8, weekends 10–7.*

FAMILY **Page Museum at the La Brea Tar Pits.** Do your children have prehistoric animals on the brain? Show them where Ice Age fossils come from by taking them to the stickiest park in town. The area formed when deposits of oil rose to the earth's surface, collected in shallow pools, and coagulated into asphalt. In the early 20th century, geologists discovered that all that goo contained the largest collection of Pleistocene, or Ice Age, fossils ever found at one location: more than 600 species of birds, mammals, plants, reptiles, and insects. Roughly 100 tons of fossil bones have been removed in excavations during the last 100 years, making this one of the world's most famous fossil sites. You can see most of the pits through chain-link fences. (La Brea Tar Pits can be a little smelly, but your kids are sure to love it.)

Pit 91 and Project 23 are ongoing excavation projects; tours are available, and you can volunteer to help with the excavations in summer. There are several pits scattered around Hancock Park and the surrounding neighborhood; construction in the area has often had to accommodate them, and in nearby streets and along sidewalks, little bits of tar occasionally ooze up, unstoppable. The museum displays fossils from the tar pits and has a glass-walled laboratory that allows visitors a rare look at where paleontologists and volunteers work on specimens. ⊠ *5801 Wilshire Blvd., Miracle Mile* ☎ *323/857–6300* ⊕ *www.tarpits. org* ⊠ *$12* ⊘ *Daily 9:30–5.*

Santa Monica Boulevard. From La Cienega Boulevard in the east to Doheny in the west, Santa Monica Boulevard is the commercial core of West Hollywood's gay community, with restaurants and cafés, bars and clubs, bookstores and galleries, and other establishments catering largely to gays and lesbians. Twice a year—during June's L.A.Pride and on Halloween, in October, the boulevard becomes an open-air festival. ⊠ *Santa Monica Blvd., between La Cienega and Doheny* ⊕ *weho.org/.*

Sunset Boulevard. One of the most fabled avenues in the world, Sunset Boulevard began humbly enough in the 18th century as a route from El Pueblo de Los Angeles to the Pacific Ocean. Today, as it passes through West Hollywood it becomes the sexy and seductive Sunset Strip where rock and roll had its heyday and cocktail bars charge a premium for the views. It slips quietly into the tony environs of Beverly Hills and Bel Air, twisting and winding past gated estates and undulating vistas. ⊠ *Sunset Blvd., West Hollywood.*

West Hollywood Library. Across from the Pacific Design Center, this library, designed by architects Steve Johnson and James Favaro in 2011, is a welcome addition to the city. Replete with floor-to-ceiling glass, a modern and airy interior, a huge mural by Shepard Fairey, and other art by Kenny Scharf and Retna, this three-story building and the adjoining

The collection at the Los Angeles County Museum of Art includes more than 100,000 objects, dating from ancient times to the present.

park are a great place to take a break from your tour of the city. The collection of gay-themed books is hard to beat. There's inexpensive parking and a café below. ⊠ *625 N. San Vicente Blvd., West Hollywood* ☎ *310/652–5340* ⊕ *www.colapublib.org/libs/whollywood/index.php* ⊙ *Mon.–Thurs. 11–7, Fri. and Sat- 10–6.*

WORTH NOTING

Architecture and Design Museum. Unique buildings are part of what make Los Angeles such a captivating city, so it's no wonder there's a museum dedicated to design. On Museum Row, it has permanent exhibits examining residential and commercial structures, interior landscaping, and product design. Rotating exhibits in this one-room, exposed-ceiling, warehouse-style space are sure to inspire flights of architectural fancy. ⊠ *6032 Wilshire Blvd., Miracle Mile* ☎ *323/932–9393* ⊕ *www.aplusd. org* ▭ *$7* ⊙ *Tues.–Fri. 11–5, weekends noon–6.*

West Hollywood Design District. More than 200 businesses—art galleries, antiques shops, fashion outlets (including Rag & Bone and Christian Louboutin), and interior design stores—are found in the West Hollywood Design District. There are also about 40 restaurants, including the famous paparazzi magnet, the Ivy. They are all clustered within walking distance of each other—a rare L.A. treat. ⊠ *Melrose Ave. and Robertson and Beverly Blvds.* ☎ *310/289–2534* ⊕ *wehodesigndistrict.com.*

Craft and Folk Art Museum. This small but important cultural landmark pioneered support for traditional folk arts. The two-story space has a global outlook, embracing social movements and long-established trends. It mounts rotating exhibitions where you might see anything from costumes of carnival celebrations around the world to handmade quilts. The courtyard area is a tranquil space often used for opening receptions. The ground-level gift shop stocks a unique collection of handcrafts, jewelry, ceramics, books, and textiles. ⊠ *5814 Wilshire Blvd., Miracle Mile* ☎ *323/937–4230* ⊕ *www.cafam. org* ⊠ *$7* ⊗ *Tues.–Fri. 11–5, weekends noon–6.*

Los Angeles Museum of the Holocaust. A museum dedicated solely to the Holocaust, it uses its extensive collections of photos and artifacts as

well as award-winning audio tours and interactive tools to evoke European Jewish life in the 20th century. The mission is to commemorate the lives of those who perished and those who survived the Holocaust. The building is itself a marvel, having won two awards from the American Institute of Architects. ⊠ *100 S. The Grove Dr.* ☎ *323/651–3704* ⊕ *www.lamoth.org* ⊠ *Free.* ⊗ *Mon.–Thurs. 10–5, Fri. 10–2, weekends 10–5.*

Miracle Mile. The strip of Wilshire Boulevard between La Brea and Fairfax avenues was bought up by developers in the 1920s, and they created a commercial district that catered to automobile traffic. Nobody thought the venture could be successful, so the burgeoning strip became known as Miracle Mile. It was the world's first linear downtown, with building designs incorporating wide store windows to attract attention from passing cars. ⊠ *Wilshire Blvd., Beverly Hills.*

FAMILY **Petersen Automotive Museum.** L.A. is a mecca for car lovers, which explains the popularity of this museum featuring 300 amazing automobiles. But you don't have to be a gearhead to appreciate this building full of antique and unusual vehicles. You can learn how Los Angeles grew up around its freeways, how cars go from the page to the production line, and what role automobiles have played in Hollywood. See a Popemobile, a Batmobile, hot rods, and motorcycles from around the world. Take a 90-minute tour of the basement-level Vault and see how the vehicles are preserved and maintained. Young kids aren't allowed in the Vault, but can enjoy the rest of the museum. ⊠ *6060 Wilshire Blvd., Miracle Mile* ☎ *323/930–2277* ⊕ *www.petersen.org* ⊠ *$10* ⊗ *Tues.–Sun. 10–6.*

Sunset Plaza. With a profusion of sidewalk cafés, Sunset Plaza is one of the best people-watching spots in town. Sunny weekends reach the highest pitch, when people flock to this stretch of Sunset Boulevard for brunch or lunch and to browse in the trendy shops that offer a range of price points. There's free parking in the lot behind the shops. ⊠ *8600 block of Sunset Blvd., a few blocks west of La Cienega Blvd., West Hollywood.*

SANTA MONICA
AND THE BEACHES

GETTING ORIENTED

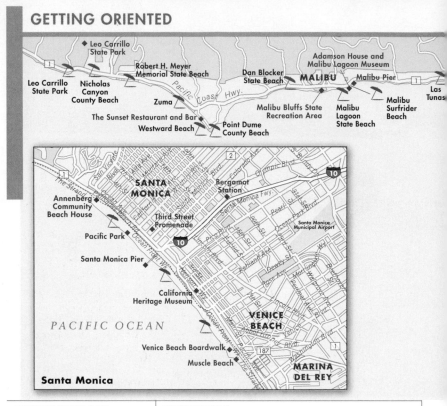

DRIVING TIMES AND DISTANCES

Minimum times listed represent little to no traffic; maximum times assume the worst. Adjust accordingly taking rush hour and peak weekend travel time into account.

■ **LAX to Santa Monica:** 20–60 min/18 miles

■ **Santa Monica to Malibu:** 30–75 min/22 miles

■ **Santa Monica to Venice Beach:** 10–15 min/3 miles

■ **Venice Beach to Redondo Beach:** 25–40 min/13 miles

GETTING HERE

Driving Strategy

From Downtown, the easiest way to hit the coast is by taking the Santa Monica Freeway (I-10) due west. Once you reach the end of the freeway, I-10 runs into the famous Highway 1. Better known as the Pacific Coast Highway, or PCH, Highway 1 continues north to Sonoma County and south to San Diego. MTA buses run from Downtown along Pico, Olympic, Santa Monica, Sunset, and Wilshire boulevards westward to the coast. Driving along the coast is a quintessential L.A. experience—so is sitting in beach traffic. Avoid driving to Malibu during rush hour, when traffic along PCH moves at a snail's pace.

Parking

Public parking is usually available at beaches, though fees can range anywhere from $8 to $20; in some areas, it's possible to find free street and highway parking.

PLANNING YOUR TIME

5

If you've got the time, break your coastal visit into two excursions: Santa Monica and Venice on one excursion, and Malibu on the other.

The best way to "do" L.A.'s coastal communities is to park your car and walk, cycle, or skate along the bike path, known as "The Strand."

For this, of course, a sunny day is best; on all but the hottest days, when literally millions of Angelenos flock to the beaches, get started in the morning, either before or after rush hour.

Places like Santa Monica Pier, Main Street, and the Venice Boardwalk are more interesting to observe as the day progresses.

Try to avoid the boardwalk, beach, and backstreets of Santa Monica and Venice at night, when the crowds dissipate.

Santa Monica and the Beaches

TOP REASONS TO GO

Bike Along the Strand. Spend the day on this 22-mile paved path, also known as the South Bay Bike Trail, which stretches from Santa Monica to Redondo Beach.

Watch the Sun Set over the Pacific in Malibu. Whether you watch it cliffside or parked on beach blanket, the view will stay fixed in your mind as a trip highlight.

Spend the Day at Santa Monica Pier. A fun family day or a night out, the pier's appeal is its Ferris wheel, carousel, fair food, and games galore.

Catch the Mellow Vibe in Venice Beach. Stroll along the canals, shop, and grab an all-organic lunch on Albert Kinney, or watch tanned locals in tie-dye toting longboards.

Take a Surfing Lesson. The sport is said to have started on Redondo Beach in the early 1900s—learn how to hang ten from several great schools along the coast.

Sightseeing
★★★
Nightlife
★★★
Dining
★★★★
Lodging
★★★
Shopping
★★★★

L.A.'s beaches are an iconic and integral part of Southern California, and getting some sand on the floor of your car is practically a requirement. Hugging the Santa Monica Bay in an arch, the desirable communities of Malibu, Santa Monica, and Venice move from ultrarich to ultracasual to bohemian. Continuing south to L.A.'s three beach cities, Manhattan Beach, Hermosa, and Redondo, the scene shifts from posh to working class, but the sand remains the center of the action. What they have in common, however, is cleaner air, mild temperatures, horrific traffic, and an emphasis on the fun-in-the-sun beach-focused lifestyle.

SANTA MONICA

Updated
by Sarah
Amandolare

This pedestrian-friendly little city, about 8.3 square miles, has a dynamic population of artists and writers, entertainment folks, educators, and retired people; its left-wing politics have earned it the nickname of the People's Republic of Santa Monica (just like Berkeley in Northern California). Mature trees, Mediterranean-style architecture, and strict zoning have helped create a sense of place often missing from L.A.'s residential neighborhoods, and its cooler, sometimes-foggy climate is another draw. These surroundings come with a price: real estate costs are astronomical.

TOP ATTRACTIONS

FAMILY **Main Street.** This thoroughfare is a great spot for star sighting and also for anyone who enjoys strolling along a street where a laid-back California crowd pops in and out of old-fashioned, colorful, and cozy boutiques that stock everything from high-end fashion to bohemian favorites. There's also a standard crop of shopping mall outposts plus a good selection of casual restaurants and cafés. ⊠ *Between Pacific St. and Rose Ave., and Santa Monica and Venice Blvds., Santa Monica.*

Marisol Cocina Mexican. Soak up the atmosphere inside this fun-loving eatery at the very end of Santa Monica Pier. Sip oversize margaritas and devour nacho platters before rejoining the crowds outside. ⊠ *401 Santa Monica Pier, Santa Monica* ☎ *310/917–5050.*

Shutters on the Beach. Escape busy Santa Monica State Beach at this unfussy oceanfront hotel and its casual café and bar, Coach, where white wood walls and blue-stripe seating offset wood and wicker furnishings. Head here at sunset for sophisticated, fruity cocktails and fresh seafood, like oysters and Dungeness crab, one block from Santa Monica Pier. ⊠ *1 Pico Blvd., Santa Monica* ☎ *310/458–0030.*

Santa Monica Aquarium. Run by beach conservation group Heal the Bay, this live marine life menagerie contains more than 100 species of marine animals and plants, all found in Santa Monica Bay. The remodeled Dorothy Green Room is the educational hub, featuring live and interactive exhibits about local watersheds, and short films covering ocean issues on weekends. The Kid's Corner provides books, games, and a puppet show. Don't miss this chance to learn about the area's ecology and staggering evidence of how pollution is affecting the ocean and the animals and plants that live there. The Aquarium can be tricky to find—look for it tucked under the eastern end of the Santa Monica Pier bridge along Ocean Front Walk. Follow the colorful seascape murals that cover the outside walls. ⊠ *1600 Ocean Front Walk, Santa Monica* ☎ *310/393–6149* ⊕ *www.healthebay.org/smpa* ⊠ *$5* ⊗ *Tues.–Fri. 2–5, weekends 12:30–5.*

FAMILY **Santa Monica Pier.** Souvenir shops, carnival games, arcades, eateries, an outdoor trapeze school, **Pacific Park,** and more are all part of the festive atmosphere of this truncated pier at the foot of Colorado Boulevard below Palisades Park. The pier's indoor trademark 46-horse Looff Carousel, built in 1922, has appeared in several films, including *The Sting.* Free concerts are held on the pier in summer. ⊠ *Colorado Ave. and the ocean, Santa Monica* ☎ *310/458–8900* ⊕ *www.santamonicapier.org* ⊗ *Hrs. vary by season; check website before visiting.*

Third Street Promenade. Stretch your legs along this pedestrians-only three-block stretch of 3rd Street, just a whiff away from the Pacific, lined with jacaranda trees, ivy-topiary dinosaur fountains, strings of lights, and branches of nearly every major U.S. retail chain. Outdoor cafés, street vendors, movie theaters, and a rich nightlife make this a main gathering spot for both locals and visitors, as well as street musicians and performance artists. Plan a night just to take it all in or take an afternoon for a long people-watching stroll. There's plenty of parking in city structures on the streets flanking the promenade. **Santa Monica Place** reopened in 2010 at the south end of the promenade as a sleek outdoor mall and foodie haven. Its three stories are home to Bloomingdale's, Burberry, Coach, and other upscale retailers. Don't miss the ocean views from the rooftop food court. ⊠ *Third St., between Colorado and Wilshire Blvds., Santa Monica* ⊕ *www.thirdstreetpromenade.com.*

5

WORTH NOTING

Annenberg Community Beach House. This beachfront property was originally developed in the 1920s by William Randolph Hearst as a palatial private residence and a gathering spot for Hollywood's megastars. In 1947 it was converted into a members-only beach club; the state of California bought and renamed the club in 1959, but it took the earthquake of 2004 for the state to reconceive of the property as a public place. With the help of the Annenberg Foundation, it reopened as a community beach house in 2009. Feel like a millionaire lounging by the pool on one of the beachside chairs, or lunch at the café while enjoying uninterrupted ocean views. The house's Beach–Culture events series includes a variety of classes (yoga, beach volleyball), readings, and exhibits; check the website for the calendar. ⊠ *415 Pacific Coast Hwy., Santa Monica* ☎ *310/458–4904* ⊕ *www.beachhouse.smgov.net* ⊠ *Free; pool $10* ⊗ *Daily 8:30–5:30; Event House Gallery open Sat.–Mon. 9–4; Marion Davies Guest House open weekends 11–2; pool open 7 days June–Aug.*

Bergamot Station. Named after a stop on the Red Trolley line that once shuttled between Downtown and the Santa Monica Pier, Bergamot Station is now a depot for intriguing art. The industrial facades house more than 30 art galleries, shops, a café, and a museum. The galleries cover many kinds of media: photography, jewelry, and paintings from somber to lurid. ⊠ *2525 Michigan Ave., Santa Monica* ☎ *310/453–7535* ⊕ *www.bergamotstation.com* ⊗ *Galleries generally Tues.–Fri. 10–6, Sat. 11–5:30.*

Santa Monica Museum of Art. Inside one of the many cavernous, steel-beamed warehouses that make up this unique area, the Santa Monica Museum of Art showcases exhibits of emerging artists. The museum also presents evening salons with artists, performers, and speakers. ⊠ *Bergamot Station G1, 2525 Michigan Ave., Santa Monica* ☎ *310/586–6488* ⊕ *www.smmoa.org* ⊠ *$5 suggested donation* ⊗ *Tues.–Sat. 11–6.*

California Heritage Museum. The real star of the collection here is the 1894 Victorian house the museum occupies. The interior has been beautifully restored to represent four decades of design. Rotating exhibits focused on California decorative and folk art include paintings, furniture, photography, sculpture, and a solid collection of California tiles and pottery. ⊠ *2612 Main St., Santa Monica* ☎ *310/392–8537* ⊕ *www.californiaheritagemuseum.org* ⊠ *$5* ⊗ *Wed.–Sun. 11–4.*

Pacific Park. Built on Santa Monica Pier, extending over the bay, this small amusement area harkens back to the days of the grand Pacific Ocean Park (1957–67). Its attractions include a tame coaster, a large Ferris wheel, and a handful of rides that wildly satisfy the under-6 crowd. ■**TIP→** This isn't squeaky-clean Disneyland, so expect some litter and watch your personal belongings. Since the pier is riddled with nails and splinters, opt for sneakers over flip-flops. ⊠ *380 Santa Monica Pier, Santa Monica* ☎ *310/260–8744* ⊕ *www.pacpark.com* ⊠ *Rides $3–$5, all-day pass $22.95* ⊗ *Hrs. vary, weather permitting. Call or check website for schedule.*

The boardwalk of Venice Beach.

Santa Monica State Beach. It's the first beach you'll hit after the Santa Monica Freeway (I-10) runs into the PCH, and it's one of L.A.'s best known. Wide and sandy, Santa Monica is *the* place for sunning and socializing: be prepared for a mob scene on summer weekends, when parking becomes an expensive ordeal. Swimming is fine (with the usual post-storm pollution caveat); for surfing, go elsewhere. For a memorable view, climb up the stairway over the PCH to Palisades Park, at the top of the bluffs. Free summer-evening concerts are held Thursday nights on the pier. **Amenities:** food and drink; lifeguards; parking; showers; toilets; water sports. **Best for:** sunset; surfing; swimming; walking. ⊠ *1642 Promenade, PCH at California Incline, Santa Monica* ☎ *310/458–8573* ⊕ *www.smgov.net/Portals/Beach* ⊠ *$10 parking* ⊄ *Parking, lifeguard (year-round), restrooms, showers.*

PACIFIC PALISADES

Stunning ocean views, glamorous homes, and dusty canyons define this affluent area, snug between Santa Monica and Malibu. Although there is a downtown village of sorts, south of Sunset Boulevard, natural terrain is the main draw here, luring visitors to hiking trails or along the Palisades' winding roads.

TOP ATTRACTIONS

Fodor's Choice ★ **Getty Villa Malibu.** Feeding off the cultures of ancient Rome, Greece, and Etruria, the remodeled Getty Villa opened in 2006 with much fanfare—and some controversy concerning the acquisition and rightful ownership of some of the Italian artifacts on display. The antiquities

FUN IN THE SUN

Legends Bike Tours. Those who like a little history with their vacations should take a guided tour with Legends, part of Perry's Café and Rentals. A tour takes you through the unique enclaves of Santa Monica and Venice Beach, and you can learn their role in the history of surf and skate in Southern California. Bike tours are offered daily at 11 am from June through September, last two hours (plus one hour of free riding), and cost $45. ⊠ *930 Palisades Beach Rd., Santa Monica* ☎ *310/939–0000* ⊕ *www.perryscafe.com.*

Trapeze School of New York. Get a different view of the energetic scene by taking a trapeze class right on the Santa Monica Pier. Launch off from a platform 23-feet high and sail above the crowds and waves. Beginners are welcome. Classes are held daily, but class times vary, so check the website and make reservations in advance. ⊠ *Santa Monica Pier, Santa Monica* ☎ *310/394–5800* ⊕ *www.trapezeschool.com.*

Venice Beach Skate Plaza. Watch skateboarders displaying a wide range of ability levels as they careen around this concrete park, situated between the beach and the boardwalk in Venice. There's also an impressive crew of disco roller skaters, and drum circles that gravitate toward the middle of the boardwalk. ⊠ *Venice Beach, off E. Market St., Venice.*

are astounding, but on a first visit even they take a backseat to their environment. This megamansion sits on some of the most valuable coastal property in the world. Modeled after an Italian country home, the Villa dei Papiri in Herculaneum, the Getty Villa includes beautifully manicured gardens, reflecting pools, and statuary. The largest and most lovely garden, the Outer Peristyle, gives you glorious views over a rectangular reflecting pool and geometric hedges to the Pacific. The new structures blend thoughtfully into the rolling terrain and significantly improve the public spaces, such as the new outdoor amphitheater, gift store, café, and entry arcade. Talks and educational programs are offered at an indoor theater. ■ **TIP→ An advance timed entry ticket is required for admission. Tickets are free and may be ordered from the website or by phone.** ⊠ *17985 Pacific Coast Hwy., Pacific Palisades* ☎ *310/440–7300* ⊕ *www.getty.edu* ⌑ *Free, tickets required. Parking $15, cash or credit card* ☉ *Wed.–Mon. 10–5.*

Will Rogers State Historic Park and Museum. The humorist, actor, and rambling cowboy, Will Rogers lived on this site in the 1920s and 1930s. His ranch house, a folksy blend of Navajo rugs and Mission-style furniture, has become a museum featuring Rogers' memorabilia. A short film presented in the visitor center highlights Rogers' roping technique and homey words of wisdom. Open for docent-led tours, the ranch house features Rogers' stuffed practice calf and the high ceiling he raised so he could practice his famed roping style indoors.

Rogers was a polo enthusiast, and in the 1930s, his front-yard polo field attracted such friends as Douglas Fairbanks Sr. for weekend games. Today, the park's broad lawns are excellent for picnicking, and there are miles of eucalyptus-lined trails for hiking. Free weekend games are scheduled April through October, weather permitting.

Also part of the park is **Inspiration Point Trail.** Who knows how many of Will Rogers' famed witticisms came to him while he and his wife hiked or rode horses along this trail from their ranch. The point is on a detour off the lovely 2-mile loop, which you pick up right by the riding stables beyond the parking lot ($12 per car). On a clear (or even just semiclear) day, the panorama is one of L.A.'s widest and most "wow" inducing, from the peaks of the San Gabriel Mountains in the distant east to the Oz-like cluster of Downtown L.A. skyscrapers to Catalina Island looming off the coast to the southwest. If you're looking for a longer trip, the top of the loop meets up with the 65-mile Backbone Trail, which connects to Topanga State Park.

A new visitor center with displays of the park's history, and a giftshop with books and DVDs on Rogers' life recently opened. ✉ *1501 Will Rogers State Park Rd., Pacific Palisades* ☎ *310/454–8212* 🖱 *Free; parking $12* ⊘ *Parking daily 8–dusk, house tours Thurs. and Fri. hourly 11–3, weekends, hourly 10–4.*

WORTH NOTING

Will Rogers State Beach. This clean, sandy, 3-mile beach, with a dozen volleyball nets, gymnastics equipment, and playground equipment for kids, is an all-around favorite. The surf is gentle, perfect for swimmers and beginning surfers. Nevertheless, it's best to avoid the place after a storm, when untreated water flows from storm drains into the sea. **Amenities:** food and drink; lifeguards; parking; showers; toilets. **Best for:** sunset; swimming; walking. ✉ *17700 PCH, 2 miles north of Santa Monica Pier, Pacific Palisades* ☎ *310/305–9503* ⊕ *www.parks.ca.gov* 🖱 *$12 parking.*

VENICE

From the resident musicians and roving hippies of the boardwalk, to the hipster boutiques and farm-to-table cafés of Abbot Kinney Boulevard, Venice is not easily defined—which is what makes this creative-minded neighborhood so fun to explore.

Considering all of the dreamers who flock here today, it makes sense that Venice was a turn-of-the-20th-century fantasy that never quite came true. Abbot Kinney, a wealthy Los Angeles businessman, envisioned this little piece of real estate as a romantic replica of Venice, Italy. He developed an incredible 16 miles of canals, floated gondolas on them, and built scaled-down versions of the Doge's Palace and other Venetian landmarks. Some canals were rebuilt in 1996, but they don't reflect the old-world connection quite as well as they could.

Ever since Kinney first planned his project, it was plagued by ongoing engineering problems and drifted into disrepair. Today only a few small canals and bridges remain. On nearby **Abbot Kinney Boulevard** there's a wealth of design and home decor shops and chic cafés—plus great people-watching.

Continued on page 109

ALONG
THE STRAND
L.A.'S COASTAL
BIKE PATH

Cycling along the Strand

Venice Beach graffiti

Santa Monica Beach

Venice Beach café

When L.A. wants to get out and play by the water, people hit the Strand for the afternoon. This paved 22-mile path hugs the coastline and loops through tourist-packed stretches and sleepy beach towns. Quirky cafés, loads of souvenir stands, a family-packed amusement park on a pier, and spots for gazing at the Pacific are just a few things to see along the way.

The path extends from Santa Monica's Will Rogers State Beach to Torrance County Beach in South Redondo. It's primarily flat—aside from a few hills you encounter as you head toward Playa del Rey—and it's a terrific way for people of all fitness levels to experience L.A.'s beaches not far from Hollywood or Beverly Hills. You can explore at your own pace.

The hardest part of the journey isn't tackling the path itself—it's trying to get through it all without being distracted by the surrounding activity. With colorful graffitied murals, surfers and sailboats, weightlifters and tattoo par-

lors, local characters in carnivalesque costumes, volleyball games and skateboarders, there are almost too many things to busy youself with.

Santa Monica amusement park

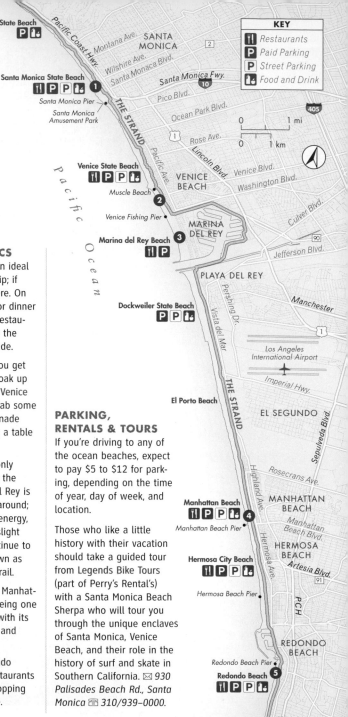

GETTING HERE AND AROUND

ITINERARY BASICS

1 Santa Monica is an ideal place to start your trip; if you're biking, rent here. On the way back, stop for dinner at one of the many restaurants along and near the Third Street Promenade.

Take a break when you get to Venice Beach to soak up the scene on the **2** Venice Ocean Boardwalk. Grab some fresh-squeezed lemonade from a stand or snag a table at a café.

If you're dedicating only a half-day to explore the Strand, **3** Marina del Rey is a good spot to turn around; with more time and energy, follow signs for the slight detour here and continue to the second half, known as the South Bay Bike Trail.

4 Manhattan Beach Manhattan Beach wins for being one of the best for kids, with its wide stretch of sand and good swimming.

The pier at **5** Redondo Beach, lined with restaurants and shops, makes stopping here well worthwhile.

PARKING, RENTALS & TOURS

If you're driving to any of the ocean beaches, expect to pay $5 to $12 for parking, depending on the time of year, day of week, and location.

Those who like a little history with their vacation should take a guided tour from Legends Bike Tours (part of Perry's Rental's) with a Santa Monica Beach Sherpa who will tour you through the unique enclaves of Santa Monica, Venice Beach, and their role in the history of surf and skate in Southern California. ✉ 930 Palisades Beach Rd., Santa Monica ☎ 310/939–0000.

TOP ATTRACTIONS

Venice Beach Boardwalk. The surf and sand of Venice are fine, but the main attraction here is the boardwalk scene, which is a cosmos all its own. Go on weekend afternoons for the best people-watching experience. There are also swimming, fishing, surfing, skateboarding, racquetball, handball, shuffleboard, and basketball (it's the site of some of L.A.'s most hotly contested pickup games). You can rent a bike or some in-line skates and hit the Strand bike path. ⊠ *1800 Ocean Front Walk, west of Pacific Ave., Venice* ☎ *310/392–4687* ⊕ *www. westland.net/venice.*

NEED A BREAK?

The Cow's End Cafe. Stop at this two-story locals' favorite for coffee and pastries. If you want something more filling, partake from the stellar selection of deli sandwiches. Sit out front and watch the crowds drifting in off the beach, or get cozy upstairs in one of the comfortable reading chairs. ⊠ *34 Washington Blvd., Venice* ☎ *310/574–1080* ⊕ *www.thecowsendcafe.com.*

Venice Whaler. This beachfront bar boasts an amazing view and serves tasty pub food with a basic selection of beers. Be prepared for rowdy crowds of sports fans and beachgoers at happy hour and on weekends. ⊠ *10 W. Washington Blvd., Venice* ☎ *310/821–8737* ⊕ *www.venicewhaler.com.*

WORTH NOTING

Marina del Rey. Just south of Venice, this condo-laden, chain restaurant–lined development is a good place to grab brunch (but watch for price gougers), take a stroll, or ride bikes along the waterfront. A number of places, such as **Hornblower Cruises and Events** (⊠ *13755 Fiji Way* ☎ *888/467–6256* ⊕ *www.hornblower.com*) in Fisherman's Village, rent boats for romantic dinner or party cruises around the marina. There are a few man-made beaches, but you're better off hitting the larger (and cleaner) beaches up the coast. ⊠ *Fisherman's Village, 1375 Fiji Way.*

Muscle Beach. Bronzed young men bench-pressing five girls at once, weight lifters doing tricks on the sand—the Muscle Beach facility fired up the country's imagination from the get-go. There are actually two spots known as Muscle Beach. The original Muscle Beach, just south of the Santa Monica Pier, is where bodybuilders Jack LaLanne and Vic and Armand Tanny used to work out in the 1950s. When it was closed in 1959, the bodybuilders moved south along the beach to Venice, to a city-run facility known as "the Pen," and the Venice Beach spot inherited the Muscle Beach moniker. The spot is probably best known now as a place where a young Arnold Schwarzenegger first came to flex his muscles in the late '60s and began his rise to fame. The area now hosts a variety of sports and gymnastic events and the occasional "beach babe" beauty contests that always draws a crowd. ⊠ *1800 Ocean Front Walk, Venice.*

DID YOU KNOW?

Venice Beach is part of skateboarding's Dogtown, where the Zephyr Team (or Z-Boys) created the modern version of the sport.

PLAYA DEL REY

Hills built by ancient sand dunes run parallel to the ocean, lending a secluded feeling to this easygoing coastal community. When night falls, the hillside homes sparkle high above the water, and the cluster of dive bars on Culver Boulevard fill with local characters. Jetties have dulled the waves that drew surfers here in the 1950s and '60s, leaving the neighborhood with a slightly romantic, forgotten vibe.

TOP ATTRACTIONS

FAMILY **Dockweiler State Beach.** The longest (4-mile) strip of beach in the county, Dockweiler has almost all the makings of a perfect beach: RV park, playground, separate bike trail, bonfire pits, mild surf, nice sand. If only the planes from LAX weren't taking off directly overhead and factories weren't puffing out fumes right behind you. But if you don't mind that, you'll find plenty of room to spread out. Bike and skate rentals are also available at the beach. **Amenities:** food and drink; lifeguards; parking (fee); toilets; showers. **Best for:** swimming; walking. ☒ *12000 Vista del Mar, west end of Imperial Hwy., Playa del Rey* ☎ *310/372–2166, 310/322–4951* ☞ *Parking $10.*

5

MALIBU

North of Santa Monica, up the Pacific Coast Highway, past rock slides, rollerbladers, and cliffside estates, is Malibu. Home to blockbuster names like Spielberg, Hanks, and Streisand, this ecologically fragile 23-mile stretch of coastline can feel like a world of its own, with its slopes slipping dramatically into the ocean.

In the public imagination Malibu is synonymous with beaches and wealth—but in the past couple of years there's been some friction between these two signature elements. Some property owners, such as billionaire music producer David Geffen, have come under attack for blocking public access to the beaches in front of their homes. All beaches are technically public, though; if you stay below the mean high-tide mark you're in the clear.

TOP ATTRACTIONS

Adamson House and Malibu Lagoon Museum. With spectacular views of Surfrider Beach and lush garden grounds, this Moorish Spanish–style house epitomizes all the reasons to live in Malibu. It was built in 1929 by the Rindge family, who owned much of the Malibu area in the early part of the 20th century. The Rindges had an enviable Malibu lifestyle, decades before the area was trendy. In the 1920s, Malibu was quite isolated; in fact all visitors and supplies arrived by boat at the nearby Malibu Pier. (The town again becomes isolated today whenever rock slides close the highway.) The house, covered with magnificent tile work in rich blues, greens, yellows, and oranges from the now-defunct Malibu Potteries, is right on the beach—high chain-link fences keep out curious beachgoers. Even an outside dog shower, near the servants' door, is a tiled delight. Docent-led tours provide insights on family life here as well as the history of Malibu and its real estate. Signs posted around the grounds outside direct you on a self-guided tour, but you can't go inside the house without a guide. Garden tours take place on Friday at 10 am. There's pay parking in the adjacent county lot or in the lot at PCH and Cross Creek Road. ⊠ *23200 Pacific Coast Hwy., Malibu* ☎ *310/456–8432* ⊕ *www.adamsonhouse.org* ⊠ *$7* ☉ *Wed.–Sat. 11–3; last tour departs at 2.*

Malibu Lagoon State Beach. Bird-watchers, take note: in this 5-acre marshy area near Malibu Beach Inn you can spot egrets, blue herons, avocets, and gulls. (You need to stay on the boardwalks so as not to disturb their habitats.) The path leads out to a rocky stretch of Surfrider Beach, and makes for a pleasant stroll. The sand is soft, clean, and white, and you're also likely to spot a variety of marine life. Look for the signs to help identify these sometimes exotic-looking creatures. The lagoon is particularly enjoyable in the early morning and at sunset—and even more so now, thanks to a restoration effort that improved the lagoon's smell. The parking lot has limited hours, but street-side parking is usually available at off-peak times. It's near shops and a theater. **Amenities:** lifeguards; parking (fee); showers; toilets. **Best for:** sunset; walking. ⊠ *23200 Pacific Coast Hwy., Malibu* ☎ *310/457–8143* ⊕ *www.parks.ca.gov* ⊠ *$12 parking.*

Malibu Pier. This 780-foot fishing dock is a great place to drink in the sunset, take in some coastal views, or to watch local fishermen reel up a catch. Some tours also leave from here. A pier has jutted out here since the early 1900s; storms destroyed the last one in 1995, and it was rebuilt in 2001. The pier's landing was damaged in 2011 and is undergoing repair. Over the years, private developers have worked with the state to refurbish the pier, which now yields a gift shop, water-sport rentals, burger joint, and restaurant. A surfing museum is in the works. ⊠ *Pacific Coast Hwy. at Cross Creek Rd.* ⊕ *www.malibupier.com.*

Fodor'sChoice
★
Robert H. Meyer Memorial State Beach. Part of Malibu's most beautiful coastal area, this beach is made up of three minibeaches: El Pescador, La Piedra, and El Matador—all with the same spectacular view. Scramble down the steps to the rocky coves via steep, steep stairways; all food and water needs to be toted in as there are no services. Portable toilets at the trailhead are the only restrooms. "El Mat" has a series of caves, Piedra some nifty rock formations, and Pescador a secluded feel; but they're all picturesque and fairly private. **Amenities:** parking (fee); toilets. **Best for:** solitude; sunset; surfing; walking. ⚠ One warning: watch the incoming tide and don't get trapped between those otherwise scenic boulders. ⊠ *32350, 32700, and 32900 PCH, Malibu* ☎ *818/880–0363* ⊕ *www. parks.ca.gov* ⊠ *Parking $8.*

Topanga State Park. This is another way into Santa Monica via the Trippet Ranch entrance, which gives you several options: a ½-mile nature loop, a 7-mile round-trip excursion to the Parker Mesa Overlook (breathtaking on a clear day), or a 10-mile trek to the Will Rogers Park. Parking is $10 per vehicle. (Exit U.S. 101 onto Topanga Canyon Boulevard in Woodland Hills and head south until you can turn left onto Entrada; if going north on PCH, turn onto Topanga Canyon Boulevard—a bit past Sunset Boulevard—and go north until you can turn right onto Entrada.) ⊠ *20829 Entrada Rd., Malibu* ☎ *310/455–2465.*

The Getty Villa: a gorgeous setting for a spectacular collection of ancient art.

Zuma Beach Park. This 2-mile stretch of white sand, usually dotted with tanning teenagers, has it all: from fishing and kite surfing to swings for the kids to volleyball courts. Beachgoers looking for quiet or privacy should head elsewhere. Stay alert in the water: the surf is rough and inconsistent. **Amenities:** food and drink; lifeguards; parking; showers; toilets. **Best for:** partiers; sunset; swimming; walking. ⊠ *30000 Pacific Coast Highway, Malibu* ☎ *310/305–9503* ⊕ *beaches.lacounty.gov* ⊠ *$10 parking.*

WORTH NOTING

Dan Blocker State Beach (*Corral Beach*). The narrow stretch of fine sand and rocks here make this little beach great for walking, light swimming, kayaking, and scuba diving. Clustered boulders create cozy spots for couples and picnickers, and because of the limited parking available along PCH, it's rarely crowded. Originally owned by the stars of the *Bonanza* TV series, the beach was donated to the state after Blocker (who played Hoss) died in 1972. Locals still know this as Corral Beach. **Amenities:** lifeguards; toilets. **Best for:** solitude; walking. ⊠ *26000 PCH, at Corral Canyon Rd., Malibu* ☎ *310/305–9503* ☞ *Lifeguard (yr-round, except only as needed in winter), restrooms.*

Las Tunas State Beach. This small beach known for its groins (metal gates constructed in 1929 to protect against erosion) has good swimming, diving, and fishing conditions, and a rocky coastline that wraps elegantly around the Pacific Coast Highway. **Amenities:** lifeguards; food and drink. **Best for:** swimming; solitude. ⊠ *19444 Pacific Coast Hwy., Malibu* ☎ *310/305–9503* ☞ *Parking on highway only, lifeguard (yr-round, except only as needed in winter).*

Nicholas Canyon County Beach. Sandier and less private than most of the rocky beaches surrounding it, this little beach is great for picnics. You can sit at a picnic table high up on a bluff overlooking the ocean, or cast out a fishing line. Surfers call it Zero Beach because the waves take the shape of a hollow tube when winter swells peel off the reef. **Amenities:** parking (fee); toilets; showers. **Best for:** surfing; solitude. ⊠ *33805 Pacific Coast Highway, Malibu* ☎ *310/305–9503* ⌖ *Parking, lifeguard (year-round), restrooms, showers, picnic tables, barbecues.*

Topanga State Beach. The beginning of miles of public beach, Topanga has good surfing at the western end (at the mouth of the canyon). Close to a busy section of the PCH and rather narrow, Topanga is hardly serene; hordes of teenagers zip over Topanga Canyon Boulevard from the Valley. Fishing and swings for children are available. **Amenities:** food and drink; lifeguards; parking (fee); toilets; showers. **Best for:** surfing. ⊠ *18700 block of Pacific Coast Highway, Malibu* ☎ *310/305–9503* ⌑ *Parking $10* ⌖ *Parking, lifeguard (year-round, except only as needed in winter), restrooms, food concessions.*

Westward Beach–Point Dume. Go tide-pooling, fishing, snorkeling, or bird-watching (prime time is late winter–early spring). Hike to the top of the sandstone cliffs at Point Dume to whale-watch—their migrations can be seen between December and April–and take in dramatic coastal views. Westward is a favorite surfing beach, but the steep surf isn't for novices. The Sunset restaurant is between Westward and Point Dume (at 6800 Westward Beach Road). **Amenities:** food and drink; lifeguards; parking (fee); toilets; showers. **Best for:** surfing; walking. ■**TIP→** Bring your own food, since the nearest concession is a long hike away. ⊠ *71030 Westward Beach Rd., Malibu* ☎ *310/305–9503* ⌑ *Parking $10* ⌖ *Parking, lifeguard (yr-round, except only as needed in winter), restrooms, showers.*

▌QUICK BITES

The Sunset Restaurant and Bar. This local secret is as close to the beach as you can get for some food without getting sand in your drink. Stop in for a cocktail at the friendly bar or a light meal of grilled fish tacos or one of their unique salads. It also serves breathtaking views of the surf, dolphins, surfers, and celebrity locals taking a break on the protected patio. ⊠ *Off Pacific Coast Hwy., just north of Zuma Beach, 6800 Westward Beach Rd., Malibu* ☎ *310/589–1007* ⊕ *www.thesunsetrestaurant.com.*

MANHATTAN BEACH

Chic boutiques, multimillion-dollar homes, and some of the best restaurants in Los Angeles dot the hilly downtown streets of this tony community. While the glamour and exclusivity are palpable, with attractive residents making deals over cocktails, this is still a beach town. Annual volleyball and surfing tournaments, crisp ocean breezes, and a very clean walking and biking path invite all visitors.

WORTH NOTING

Manhattan Beach. A wide, sandy strip with good swimming and rows of volleyball courts, Manhattan Beach is the preferred destination of muscled, tanned young professionals and dedicated bikini-watchers. There are also such amenities as a bike path, a playground, a bait shop, fishing equipment for rent, and a sizable fishing pier. Amenities: food and drink; lifeguards; parking (fee); toilets; showers. Best for: swimming; walking. ⊠ *Manhattan Beach Blvd. and N. Ocean Dr., Manhattan Beach* ☎ *310/372–2166* ⊠ *Metered parking; there are long-term and short-term lots* ☞ *Parking, lifeguard (yr-round), restrooms, food concessions, showers.*

HERMOSA BEACH

This energetic beach city boasts some of the priciest real estate in the country. But down by the sand, the vibe is decidedly casual, with plenty of pubs and ambling young couples. Volleyball courts line the wide beach, drawing many amateur and pro tournaments. The 300-meter pier invites strolling and features dramatic views of coastline winding southward.

WORTH NOTING

Hermosa Beach. South of Manhattan Beach, Hermosa Beach has all the amenities of its neighbor but it attracts more of a rowdy party crowd. Swimming takes a backseat to the volleyball games and parties on the pier and boardwalk, but the water here is consistently clean and inviting. Amenities: food and drink; lifeguards; parking (fee); toilets; showers. Best for: partiers; swimming. ⊠ *1201 The Strand, Hermosa Ave. and 33rd St., Hermosa Beach* ☎ *310/372–2166* ⊠ *Parking (metered) at 11th St. and Hermosa Ave., and 13th St. and Hermosa Ave.* ☞ *Parking, lifeguard (yr-round), restrooms, food concessions, showers, wheelchair access to pier.*

REDONDO BEACH

With its worn-in pier and cozy beach, Redondo is a refreshingly unglamorous counterpoint to neighboring beach cities. This was the first port in Los Angeles County in the early 1890s, before business shifted south to San Pedro Harbor, and the community still retains a working-class persona. The best way to soak up the scene these days is with a stroll along the sprawling pier, which features shops, casual restaurants, a live-fish market, and fantastic sunset views.

WORTH NOTING

Redondo Beach. The pier here marks the starting point of this wide, sandy, busy beach along a heavily developed shoreline community. Restaurants and shops flourish along the pier, excursion boats and privately owned crafts depart from launching ramps, and a reef formed by a sunken ship creates prime fishing and snorkeling conditions. If you're adventurous, you might try to kayak out to the buoys and hobnob with pelicans and sea lions. A series of free rock and jazz concerts takes place at the pier every summer. **Amenities:** food and drink; lifeguards; parking; showers; toilets; water sports. **Best for:** snorkeling; sunset; swimming; walking. ⊠ *Torrance Blvd. at Catalina Ave., Redondo Beach* ☎ *310/372–2166.*

Torrance Beach. This little-known gem of a beach, where the Strand walkway–bicycle path finally comes to an end, has no pier or other loud attractions, just a humble snack shop that's open in the summer. But it's a great place to escape the crowds of Redondo to the north and has a park with great vistas and volleyball. ⊠ *387 Paseo de la Playa, Torrance* ☎ *310/372–2166.*

PASADENA

GETTING ORIENTED

Pasadena and Environs

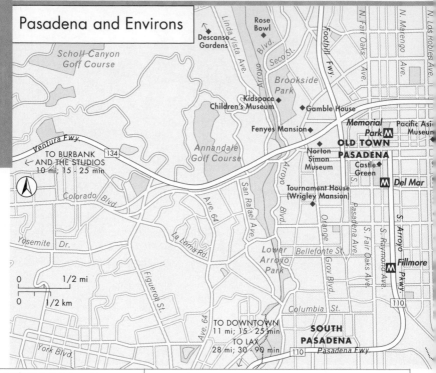

TO BURBANK
← AND THE STUDIOS
10 mi; 15 - 25 min

TO DOWNTOWN
11 mi; 15 - 25 min
TO LAX
28 mi; 30 - 90 min

DRIVING TIMES AND DISTANCES

Minimum times listed *below* represent little to no traffic; maximum times assume the worst.

Adjust accordingly taking rush hour and peak weekend travel time into account.

■ **From LAX:** 30–90 min/ 28 miles

■ **From Los Feliz/Silver Lake:** 20–30 min/13 miles

■ **From Beverly Hills:** 30–60 min/19 miles

■ **From Burbank:** 15–25 min/12 miles

GETTING HERE

Driving Strategy

To reach Pasadena from Downtown Los Angeles, drive north on the Pasadena Freeway (I-110).

From Hollywood and the San Fernando Valley, use the Ventura Freeway (Highway 134, east), which cuts through Glendale, skirting the foothills, before arriving in Pasadena.

Parking

There are several city lots located in Old Town Pasadena with low rates, all close to Colorado Boulevard, the main drag. On-street parking here is also widely available with few restrictions.

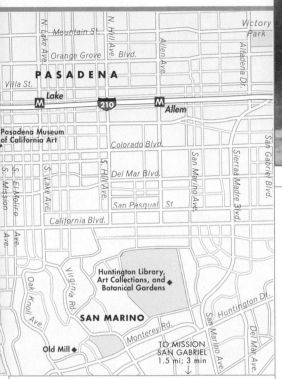

6

PLANNING YOUR TIME

With its lush lawns, intricate gardens, and elegant buildings, the Huntington Library should command most of your time. Just be sure to keep the summer heat in mind when you visit—the gardens are more pleasant during the cooler morning hours.

A stop at the beautiful Gamble House shouldn't take more than an hour, leaving plenty of time for an afternoon visit to the Norton Simon Museum, one of the area's best spots to enjoy world-class art. Unless you're planning on seeing a game or hitting the flea market, you will probably want to skip the Rose Bowl.

After visiting the Huntington, take in the prime architectural offerings dotting the city. Head to Old Pasadena in the evening, when the wide boulevards and leafy side streets come to life. Shops, restaurants, and craft beer pubs stay open late in this relatively safe neighborhood, and it's easy to find affordable parking in nearby garages.

TOP REASONS TO GO

Visit the Huntington Library. In addition to a collection of 18th-century British art, this library has 4 million manuscripts and 700,000 books, including the Gutenberg Bible.

Walk through the Huntington's Botanical Gardens. Set aside a couple of hours to enjoy the expansive lawns and stately trees surrounding the Huntington Library.

See American Craftsmanship at the Gamble House. The teak staircase and cabinetry are just a few of the highlights at this home, built in 1908.

Check Out the Norton Simon Museum. This small museum's fine collection features works by Renoir, Degas, Gauguin, and others.

Hang Out in Old Town Pasadena. Spend the afternoon walking around this 12-block historic town filled with cafés, restaurants, and shops.

Sightseeing
★★★★
Nightlife
★
Dining
★★
Lodging
★★
Shopping
★★

Although seemingly absorbed into the general Los Angeles sprawl, Pasadena is a separate and distinct city. It's most well known for the Tournament of Roses, or more commonly, the Rose Bowl, seen around the world every New Year's Day. But the city has sites worth seeing year-round—from gorgeous Craftsman homes to exceptional museums, particularly the Norton Simon and the Huntington Library, Art Collections, and Botanical Gardens. Note that the Huntington and the Old Mill reside in San Marino, a wealthy, 4-square-mile residential area just over the Pasadena line.

Updated
by Sarah
Amandalore

First-time visitors to L.A. only here for a short time might find it hard to get out to Pasadena. However, if you've had your fill of city life and are looking for a nearby escape that feels much farther away than it is, with open space and fresher air, it's the perfect trip.

The **Botanical Gardens** is a great place to start, with or without plans to see the **Huntington Library** and **Art Collections.** For a true small-town experience, spend the afternoon strolling around **Old Town Pasadena,** with shops and restaurants filling its 19-century brick buildings. Art and architecture lovers shouldn't miss the city's top site, the **Norton Simon Museum,** most noted for its excellent collection of Degas, as well as works by Rembrandt, Goya, and Picasso. The **Gamble House** is an immense three-story house and one of the country's shining examples of American Arts and Crafts bungalow architecture. The thing that might surprise you the most about visiting Pasadena is that even the drive here—on the freeway, though not during rush hour—is a pleasant one, with lovely scenery. The Pasadena Freeway follows the curves of the *arroyo* (creek bed), lined with old sycamores. It was the main road north during the early days of Los Angeles, when horses and buggies made their way through the countryside to the small town of Pasadena. In 1939 the road became the Arroyo Seco Parkway, the first freeway in Los Angeles, later renamed the Pasadena Freeway.

TOP ATTRACTIONS

Gamble House. Built by Charles and Henry Greene in 1908, this is a spectacular example of American Arts and Crafts bungalow architecture. The term *bungalow* can be misleading, since the Gamble House is a huge three-story home. To wealthy Easterners such as the Gambles (as in Procter & Gamble), this type of vacation home seemed informal compared with their mansions back home. What makes admirers swoon is the incredible craftsmanship, including a teak staircase and cabinetry, Greene and Greene–designed furniture, and an Emil Lange glass door. The dark exterior has broad eaves, with sleeping porches on the second floor. An hour-long, docent-led tour of the Gamble's interior will draw your eye to the exquisite details. If you want to see more Greene and Greene homes, buy a self-guided tour map of the neighborhood in the bookstore. ✉ *4 Westmoreland Pl., Pasadena* ☎ *626/793–3334* ⊕ *www. gamblehouse.org* 🎟 *$13.75* ⊙ *Thur.–Sun. noon–3; tickets go on sale Thur.–Sat. at 10, Sun. at 11:30. 1-hr tour every 20–30 min.*

Fodor'sChoice | **Huntington Library, Art Collections, and Botanical Gardens.** If you have time
★ | for just one stop in the Pasadena area, be sure to see this sprawling estate built for railroad tycoon Henry E. Huntington in the early 1900s. Henry and his wife, Arabella (who was also his aunt by marriage), voraciously collected rare books and manuscripts, botanical specimens, and 18th-century British art. The institution they established became one of the most extraordinary cultural complexes in the world. Among the highlights are John Constable's intimate *View on the Stour near Dedham* and the monumental *Sarah Siddons as the Tragic Muse,* by Joshua Reynolds.

The Virginia Steele Scott Gallery of American Art, a new addition in 2014, includes paintings by Mary Cassatt, Frederic Remington, and others from colonial times to the 20th century. The library contains more than 700,000 books and 4 million manuscripts, including one of the world's biggest history-of-science collections. The recently renovated Library Main Hall combines early-20th-century opulence with digital-age panache. The thoughtful permanent exhibit is organized around 12 focal points, like a Gutenberg Bible and Shakespeare's early editions, illuminating connections between events, images and texts from the 14th through mid-20th centuries.

Don't resist being lured outside into the stunning Botanical Gardens, which extend out from the main building. The 10-acre Desert Garden, for instance, has one of the world's largest groups of mature cacti and other succulents (visit on a cool morning or late afternoon). The Shakespeare Garden, meanwhile, blooms with plants mentioned in Shakespeare's works. The recently renovated Japanese Garden features an authentic ceremonial teahouse built in Kyoto in the 1960s. A waterfall flows from the teahouse to the ponds below. In the Rose Garden Tea Room, afternoon tea is served (reserve in advance).

The Rose Hills Foundation Conservatory for Botanical Science, a massive greenhouse-style center, has dozens of hands-on exhibits perfect for the whole family. And the Bing Children's Garden lets tiny tots explore the ancient elements of water, fire, air, and earth. A 1¼-hour

DID YOU KNOW?

The Huntington Botanical Gardens span 120 acres and are made up of more than a dozen themed gardens—including a rose garden, desert garden, and children's garden.

guided tour of the botanical gardens is led by docents at posted times, and a free brochure with map and highlights is available in the entrance pavilion. ✉ *1151 Oxford Rd., San Marino* ☎ *626/405–2100* ⊕ *www. huntington.org* ✉ *$20 weekdays, $23 weekends* ⊘ *Mon. and Wed.–Fri. noon–4:30, weekends 10:30–4:30.*

Fodor's Choice
★

Norton Simon Museum. Long familiar to TV viewers of the New Year's Day Tournament of Roses Parade, this low-profile brown building is more than just a background for the passing floats. It's one of the finest small museums anywhere, with an excellent collection that spans more than 2,000 years of Western and Asian art. It all began in the 1950s when Norton Simon (Hunt-Wesson Foods, McCalls Corporation, and Canada Dry) started collecting works by Degas, Renoir, Gauguin, and Cézanne. His collection grew to include old masters, impressionists, and modern works from Europe, as well as Indian and Southeast Asian art.

Today the Norton Simon Museum is richest in works by Rembrandt, Picasso, and, most of all, Degas—this is one of the only two U.S. institutions to hold the complete set of the artist's model bronzes (the other is New York's Metropolitan Museum of Art). Renaissance, baroque, and rococo masterpieces include Raphael's profoundly spiritual *Madonna with Child with Book* (1503), Rembrandt's *Portrait of a Bearded Man in a Wide-Brimmed Hat* (1633), and a magical Tiepolo ceiling, *The Triumph of Virtue and Nobility Over Ignorance* (1740–50). The museum's collections of impressionist (Van Gogh, Matisse, Cézanne, Monet, Renoir) and cubist (Braque, Gris) works are extensive. The popular 19th-Century Art Wing was renovated in 2013 to better showcase these paintings. Several Rodin sculptures are placed throughout the museum. Head down to the bottom floor to see rotating exhibits and phenomenal Southeast Asian and Indian sculptures and artifacts, where graceful pieces like a Ban Chiang blackware vessel date to well before 1000 BC. Don't miss a living artwork outdoors: the garden, conceived by noted Southern California landscape designer Nancy Goslee Power. The tranquil pond was inspired by Monet's gardens at Giverny. ✉ *411 W. Colorado Blvd., Pasadena* ☎ *626/449– 6840* ⊕ *www.nortonsimon.org* ✉ *$10, free 1st Fri. of month 6–9 pm* ⊘ *Wed., Thurs., and Sat.–Mon. noon–6, Fri. noon–9.*

Old Town Pasadena. Revitalized in the 1990s, this area blends restored 19th-century brick buildings with a contemporary overlay. A phalanx of chain stores has muscled in, but there are still some homegrown shops, plenty of tempting cafés and restaurants, and a vibrant craft beer scene. In the evening and on weekends, the streets are packed with people. The 22-block historic district is anchored along Colorado Boulevard between Pasadena Avenue and Arroyo Parkway. ✉ *Pasadena.*

QUICK BITES

Tutti Gelati. To cool off, follow the intoxicating aroma of freshly pressed waffle cones to Tutti Gelati, an Italian *gelateria* behind Crate & Barrel on Colorado Boulevard. Flavors include hazelnut and *stracciatella* (chocolate chip). Many ingredients come directly from Milan, and everything is made on the premises. ✉ *62 W. Union St., No. 1* ☎ *626/440–9800.*

DID YOU KNOW?

Raphael's Madonna and Child with Book is part of the wide-ranging collection of the Norton Simon Museum.

WORTH NOTING

Castle Green. One block south of Colorado Boulevard stands the one-time social center of Pasadena's elite. This Moorish building is the only remaining section of a turn-of-the-20th-century hotel complex. Today the often-filmed tower (see *The Sting, Edward Scissorhands, The Last Samurai, The Prestige*) is residential. The building is not open to the public on a daily basis, but it does organize a seasonal tour on the first Sunday of December. Call about occasional spring tours. ⊠ *99 S. Raymond Ave., Pasadena* ☎ *626/385–7774* ⊕ *www.castlegreen.com.*

Descanso Gardens. Getting its name from the Spanish word for "rest," this lovely oasis is a truly tranquil setting, shaded by massive oak trees. Known for being a smaller, mellower version of the nearby Huntington, Descanso Gardens features denser foliage, quaint dirt paths, and some hilly climbs that can make for good exercise. It's the perfect place to come in search of wonderful scents—between the lilacs, the acres of roses, and the forest of California redwoods, pines, and junipers, you can enjoy all sorts of fragrances. A forest of California live oak trees makes a dramatic backdrop for thousands of camellias, azaleas, and a breathtaking 5-acre International Rosarium holding 1,700 varieties of antique and modern roses. A small train ride draws families on weekends. There are also a child's train, a gift shop, and a café. ⊠ *1418 Descanso Dr., La Cañada/Flintridge* ☎ *818/949–4200* ⊕ *www.descansogardens.org* ⬚ *$8* ☉ *Daily 9–5.*

Fenyes Mansion. With its elegant dark-wood paneling and floors, curved staircases, and a theatrical stage in the parlor, it's easy to envision how this 1905 mansion along Pasadena's Millionaire's Row once served as gathering place for the city's elite (it also housed the Finnish Consulate until 1965). Most rooms on the ground and second floors are still fitted with original furniture; you can peek into these roped-off spaces, now home to mannequins dressed in period clothing, to get a sense of what life was like a century ago. You can visit the mansion (on your own or on a 90-minute tour), the adjacent Finnish Folk Art Museum, and the Historical Center Gallery, which has rotating exhibits dedicated to the art and culture of Pasadena. ⊠ *470 W. Walnut St., Pasadena* ☎ *626/577–1660* ⊕ *www.pasadenahistory.org* ⬚ *$7; tours $15* ☉ *Wed.–Sun. noon–5. Tours Fri.–Sun. 12:15.*

Heritage Square Museum. Looking like a prop street set up by a film studio, Heritage Square resembles a row of bright dollhouses in the modest Highland Park neighborhood. Five 19th-century residences, a train station, a church, a carriage barn, and a 1909 boxcar that was originally part of the Southern Pacific Railroad, all built between the Civil War and World War I, were moved to this small park from various locations in Southern California to save them from the wrecking ball. The newest addition, a re-creation of a World War I–era drugstore, has a vintage soda fountain and traditional products. Docents dressed in period costume lead visitors through the lavish homes, giving an informative picture of what life in Los Angeles was like a century ago. Don't miss the unique 1893 Octagon House, one of just a handful of its kind built in California. ⊠ *3800 Homer St., off Ave.*

43 exit, Highland Park ☎ *323/225–2700* ⊕ *www.heritagesquare.org* ✉ *$10; tour $10* ⊙ *Fri.–Sun. 11:30–4:30.*

The Old Mill (El Molino Viejo). Built in 1816 as a gristmill for the San Gabriel Mission, the mill is one of the last remaining examples in Southern California of Spanish Mission architecture. The thick adobe walls and textured ceiling rafters give the interior a sense of quiet strength. Be sure to step into the back room, now a gallery with rotating quarterly exhibits. Outside, a chipped section of the mill's exterior reveals the layers of brick, ground seashell paste, and oxblood used to hold the structure together. The surrounding gardens are reason enough to visit, with a flower-decked arbor and old sycamores and oaks. In summer the California Philharmonic ensemble performs in the garden. ⊠ *1120 Old Mill Rd., San Marino* ☎ *626/449–5458* ⊕ *www.old-mill.org* ✉ *Free* ⊙ *Tues.–Sun. 1–4.*

FAMILY **Kidspace Children's Museum.** Looking like a Looney Tunes cartoon, this activity-focused playground with oversize replicas of familiar objects offers lessons along with some fun. The whole family can gain tidbits of knowledge on earthquakes, animals, and insects. Explore gravity in the Physics Forest, featuring 13 interactive experiences. In the sunny atrium, kids assume the role of ants on their daring ascent. Outside they can run and climb along a running river or take on a tricycle race. It's a place practically built to wear out the little ones and give parents a much-needed break. ⊠ *480 N. Arroyo Blvd., Pasadena* ☎ *626/449–9144* ⊕ *www.kidspacemuseum.org* ✉ *$10* ⊙ *Sept.–May, Tues.–Fri. 9:30–5, weekends 10–5; June–Aug., weekdays 9:30–5, weekends 10–5.*

Los Angeles County Arboretum. Wander through a re-created tropical forest, a South Africa landscape, or the Australian outback at this arboretum. One highlight is the tropical greenhouse, with carnivorous-looking orchids and a pond full of brilliantly colored goldfish. The house and stables of the eccentric real-estate pioneer Lucky Baldwin are well preserved and worth a visit. Kids will love the many peacocks and waterfowl that roam the property. The Santa Anita Racetrack is across the street, but you'll seldom see it as you wander these 127 acres. To get here, head east on I-210 just past Pasadena, exit in Arcadia on Baldwin Avenue and go south, and you will soon see the entrance. ⊠ *301 N. Baldwin Ave., Arcadia* ☎ *626/821–3222* ⊕ *www.arboretum.org* ✉ *$9* ⊙ *Daily 9–5.*

Pacific Asia Museum. Devoted to the arts and culture of Asia and the Pacific Islands, this manageably sized museum displays changing exhibits drawn from its permanent collection of 17,000 artworks and artifacts. It's not the place for blockbuster shows—instead, you'll find modest displays of ceramics, calligraphy, textiles, traditional robes, and the like. The building itself is worth a look: it's inspired by Han Dynasty structures and surrounds a courtyard with a koi pond. Don't miss the newly refurbished Chinese Gallery, which houses a wide array of Chinese art. ⊠ *46 N. Los Robles Ave., Pasadena* ☎ *626/449–2742* ⊕ *www.pacificasiamuseum.org* ✉ *$10* ⊙ *Wed.–Sun. 10–6.*

6

DID YOU KNOW?

Pasadena's Tournament of Roses Parade, famed for its fanciful floats, has been an annual event since 1890.

Pasadena Museum of California Art. The first thing you see when you approach this museum is the graffiti-riddled parking structure. Was it vandalized by local taggers? Nope—it's the handiwork of artist George Kenny Scharf as part of this museum's dedication to all forms of Californian art, architecture, and design from 1850 to the present. The regularly changing exhibits are focused and thoughtfully presented; you might find anything from early California landscapes to contemporary works on car culture. The rooftop terrace affords views of the San Gabriel Mountains and the dome of the 1927 City Hall. ⊠ *490 E. Union St., Pasadena* ☎ *626/568–3665* ⊕ *www.pmcaonline. org* 🖃 *$7, free 1st Fri. of month* ☉ *Wed.–Sun. noon–5.*

Rose Bowl. With an enormous rose on its exterior, this 100,000-plus-seat stadium, host of many Super Bowls and home to the UCLA Bruins, is impossible to miss. Set at the bottom of a wide arroyo in Brookside Park, the facility is closed except during games and special events like the monthly Rose Bowl Flea Market. ⊠ *1001 Rose Bowl Dr., at Rosemont Ave., Pasadena* ☎ *626/577–3100* ⊕ *www. rosebowlstadium.com.*

Rose Bowl Flea Market. This massive flea market, held rain or shine inside the Rose Bowl, features antique and vintage finds along with new items from more than 2,500 vendors. Considered one of the best and most eclectic flea markets in the country, it draws hoards of fashion devotees and everyday bargain-seekers. Arrive early to beat the crowds, which tend to peak midday. Food and drink are readily available, and parking is free. ⊠ *1001 Rose Bowl Dr., at Rosemont Ave., Pasadena* ⊕ *www.rgcshows.com/rosebowl.aspx* 🖃 *$8* ☉ *2nd Sun. of each month 9–4:30.*

OFF THE BEATEN PATH

Mission San Gabriel Archangel. Established in 1771 as the fourth of 21 missions founded in California, this massive adobe complex was dedicated by Father Junípero Serra to St. Gabriel. Within the next 50 years, the San Gabriel Archangel became the wealthiest of all California missions. In 1833 the Mexican government confiscated the mission, allowing it to decline. The U.S. government returned the mission to the church in 1855, but by this time the Franciscans had departed. In 1908 the Claretian Missionaries took charge and poured much care into preserving the rich history. The cemetery here, the first in L.A. County, is said to contain approximately 6,000 Gabrieleno Indians. Tranquil grounds are lushly planted and filled with remnants of what life was like nearly two centuries ago. Public mass is held at

6

the mission Sunday morning at 7 and 9:30, but call ahead as times are subject to change. If you're lucky, you'll hear the six bells that ring out during special services—a truly arresting experience. You can take a self-guided tour of the grounds here by purchasing a map in the gift shop, or come for History Day the first Saturday of every month. Docent-led tours can be reserved in advance. ⊠ *428 S. Mission Dr., San Gabriel* ☎ *626/457–3048* ⊕ *www.sangabrielmission.org* ⊠ *$5* ⊙ *Mon.–Sat. 9–4:30, Sun. 10–4.*

Tournament House (Wrigley Mansion). Chewing-gum magnate William Wrigley purchased this white Italian Renaissance–style house in 1914. When his wife died in 1958, Wrigley donated the house to the city of Pasadena under the stipulation that it be used as the headquarters for the Tournament of Roses. The mansion features a green-tile roof and manicured rose garden with 1,500 varieties. The interior provides a glimpse of the over-the-top style of the area in the early 20th century. Tours of the house last about an hour; fans of the Rose Parade will see the various crowns and tiaras worn by former Rose Queens, plus trophies and memorabilia. ⊠ *391 S. Orange Grove Blvd., Pasadena* ☎ *626/449–4100* ⊕ *www.tournamentofroses.com* ⊠ *Free* ⊙ *Tours every Thurs. 2–4, Feb.–Aug.*

NIGHTLIFE

Updated by
Dianne de
Guzman

Lines down the block, strict dress codes, impossible traffic, endless parking tickets. . . . The list of complaints people have about Los Angeles nightlife is not short. The fact that they fan out across the city in search of the latest hot spot is a testament to the excitement that's available in Los Angeles.

The reward for being determined, however, can be a night that can simultaneously surprise and impress. That unscheduled set by an A-list comedian at the standup comedy club, being talked into singing karaoke at the diviest place you've ever seen, dancing at a bar with no dance floor because, well, the DJ is just too good at his job—going out isn't always what you expect, but it certainly is never boring.

The focus of nightlife once centered on the Sunset Strip, with its multitude of bars, rock clubs, and dance spots, but more neighborhoods are competing with each other and forcing the nightlife scene to evolve. Although the Strip can be a worthwhile trip, other areas of the city are catching people's attention. Downtown Los Angeles, for instance, is becoming a destination in its own right, drawing cocktail connoisseurs at Seven Grand and rooftop revelers at the Standard.

Other areas are fostering more of a neighborhood vibe. Silver Lake and Los Feliz have both cultivated a fun environment where you can be drinking in a tiki bar so small you wind up talking with the person at the next stool over (Tiki-Ti) or bringing in a 45 to play on an old-fashioned record player (El Prado).

The point is this: If you find yourself disappointed with a rude bouncer, or drinks that are too watery, or a cover charge that just isn't worth it, try again. Eventually you'll find that perfect place where each time is the best time. That, or at least you'll have a very good story to tell.

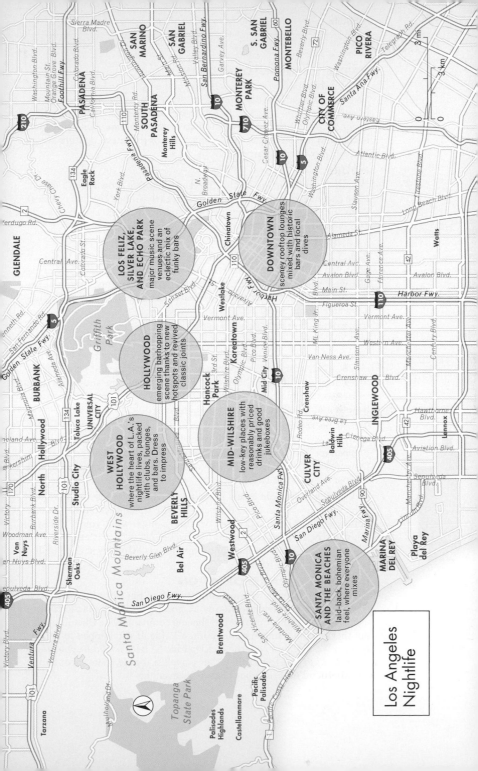

Los Angeles Nightlife

LOS FELIZ, SILVER LAKE, AND ECHO PARK major music scene venues and an eclectic mix of funky bars

DOWNTOWN scency rooftop lounges mixed with historic bars and local dives

HOLLYWOOD emerging barhopping scene thanks to new hotspots and revived classic joints

WEST HOLLYWOOD where the heart of L.A.'s nightlife lives, packed with clubs, lounges, and bars. Dress to impress

MID-WILSHIRE low-key places with reasonably priced drinks and good jukeboxes

SANTA MONICA AND THE BEACHES laid-back, bohemian feel, where everyone mixes

PLANNING

WHERE TO GET INFORMATION

Local publications *Los Angeles* magazine (⊕ *www.la.com*) and *LA Weekly* (⊕ *www.laweekly.com*) are great places to discover what's happening in Los Angeles. Lifestyle websites UrbanDaddy (⊕ *www.urbandaddy.com/home/la*) and Flavorpill (⊕ *www.flavorpill.com/losangeles*) do a good job of keeping track of the latest nightlife events and recently opened bars and clubs.

HOURS

Despite the high energy level of the L.A. nightlife crowd, don't expect to be partying until dawn—this is still an early-to-bed city. Bars close at 2 am, and it's safe to say that by this time, with the exception of a few after-hours venues, most clubs have closed for the night.

PARKING

Parking can be a pain if you're the type who insists on circling the block until you find a space. Most neighborhoods near party-heavy areas like West Hollywood require residential parking permits, so sometimes you're better off with a garage or valet parking. Either option costs anywhere from $5 to $20.

BEST NIGHTLIFE EXPERIENCES

Embrace another era. Los Angeles is rife with historic buildings, and the bars inside them are using this as a selling point, creating truly interesting locations that can transport you to another time and place. Places like Formosa Cafe and Musso & Frank's have long and interesting stories to tell, and upstarts like the Edison are aiming to re-create a bygone era, all of which adds up to an enjoyable drinking experience.

Drink in the scenery. The wonderful weather in Los Angeles makes for enjoyable nights outdoors, with plenty of spots offering rooftop pools or open-air patios where you can enjoy a cocktail. The Standard in Downtown, Yamashiro in Hollywood, or the Blue Lounge in Malibu are just a few places to start.

Rock (or laugh) the night away. Los Angeles is the town that most wannabe entertainers run to so they can "make it," and you'd be missing out if you didn't try a rock show or comedy night while you're in town. Big-name performers command high ticket prices, but it's easy to find less-expensive shows with up-and-coming acts. Monday at the Satellite you can hear bands for free.

LATE-NIGHT TRANSPORTATION

Taxis are a great way to hop from bar to bar, but can get costly when traveling between neighborhoods. A good alternative that locals are using for their nights out are ride sharing companies like Uber and Lyft, but they require a smartphone to hitch a ride. If you happen to be partying in West Hollywood, the PickUp Line (⊕ *www.weho.org/business/weho-pickup*) is a free trolley that travels a 4-mile route through the neighborhood on Friday and Saturday evenings.

WHAT A NIGHT OUT COSTS

A night out on the town doesn't come cheap, with hipper clubs charging $15 to $25 to get in the door. Tipping the doorman to bypass the line is still a thing, but expect to drop more than $20 into the bouncer's hand to get anywhere. Drink prices are also getting more expensive, with cocktails commanding anywhere from $12 to $18.

DOWNTOWN

Once pretty much ignored, Downtown is now on everyone's list of after-dark options. An amazing array of posh bars and downright divey places shows where nightlife is heading.

BARS AND LOUNGES

Bar 107. Those looking for a lively dive bar will probably appreciate the no-frills ambience here. The look of the bar is eclectic (Is that the grill of a 1961 Corvair van in the back bar?), but that just adds to its appeal. Happy-hour specials draw a crowd on weekdays. DJs spin tunes Tuesday to Saturday night. ⊠ *107 W. 4th St., Downtown* ☎ *213/625–7382.*

Broadway Bar. If you're looking for a swank-looking watering hole, Broadway Bar might be up your alley. In an up-and-coming section of Broadway (neighbors include the swank Ace Hotel), expect bartenders mixing creative cocktails and DJs spinning tunes nightly. The two-story space includes a smoking balcony overlooking the street. Leave the beachwear, baggy clothes, and baseball caps at home. ⊠ *830 S. Broadway, Downtown* ☎ *213/614–9909.*

Fodor's Choice
★

Downtown L.A. Standard. With a backdrop of city skyline, the rooftop bar of the Standard is a longtime favorite. Where else can you find drinks, dancing, a tempting swimming pool, and waterbeds (yes, waterbeds)? It's easy to spend the whole evening here—which is probably a good idea, considering the lengthy weekend lines. The west side of the roof is an enclosed *biergarten* where you can order food or play a game of table tennis. Expect to pay a $20 cover charge on Friday and Saturday after 7 pm. ⊠ *550 S. Flower St., at 6th St., Downtown* ☎ *213/892–8080* ⊕ *www.standardhotels.com.*

Edison. The glitz and glam of the Roaring Twenties is alive and well in the Edison, where the decor serves as tribute to the power plant that once occupied these premises. Black-and-white silent films are projected onto the walls, and tasty nibbles and artisanal cocktails are served (in a private room, if you prefer). There's live entertainment many nights, from jazz bands to burlesque shows. ⊠ *108 W. 2nd St., Downtown* ☎ *213/613–0000* ⊕ *www.edisondowntown.com.*

Golden Gopher. With craft cocktails, beers on tap, an outdoor smoking patio, and retro video games, this bar combines a long list of amenities with a swanky but laid-back vibe. With one of the oldest liquor licenses in Los Angeles (issued in 1905), the Golden Gopher is the only bar in Los Angeles with an on-site liquor store for to-go orders—just in case you want to buy another bottle before you head home. ⊠ *417 W. 8th St., Downtown* ☎ *213/614–8001.*

7

The Lash. In Downtown, where most bars aim for a speakeasy atmosphere, this bar is bold enough to break away from the pack and embrace a minimalist vibe. From the razzle-dazzle mural on the exterior to the black-and-white subway tiles in the hallways to the geometric back bar, the look is courtesy of artist Erik Hart, who helps gives this place its edge. Enter from the alley. ⊠ *117 Winston St., Downtown* ☎ *213/687–7723* ⊕ *www.thelashsocial.com.*

Redwood Bar & Grill. If you're looking for a place with potent drinks and fabulous food, this kitschy bar fits the bill perfectly. Known today as the "pirate bar" because of its nautical decor, the place dates back to the 1940s, when it was rumored to attract mobsters, politicians, and journalists due to its prime location next to City Hall, the Hall of Justice, and the *Los Angeles Times*. There's nightly music from local rock bands and a cover charge, although you can head to the back bar without paying if you just want drinks. ⊠ *316 W. 2nd St., Downtown* ☎ *213/680–2600* ⊕ *www.theredwoodbar.com.*

Seven Grand. The hunting lodge vibe makes it feel like you need to have a whiskey in hand—a good thing, since this Downtown establishment stocks more than 500 different kinds. The place attracts whiskey novices and connoisseurs, and the bartenders are more than willing to help you make a selection. Live jazz and blues bands play Sunday to Thursday, so even if you're not a big drinker there's still some appeal (although you're definitely missing out). The newly opened **Bar Jackalope**, a bar within a bar, has a "whisky tasting library" and holds just a dozen people. ⊠ *515 W. 7th St., 2nd fl., Downtown* ☎ *213/614–0737* ⊕ *www.sevengrandbars.com.*

CLUBS

La Cita. This dive bar may not look like much, but it more than makes up for it with an interesting mix of barflies, urban hipsters, and reasonable drink prices. Friday and Saturday night, DJs mix Top 40s hits and a tiny dance floor packs in the crowd. For those more interested in drinking and socializing, the Mexican-theme place has a back patio with a TV playing local sports. ⊠ *336 S. Hill St., Downtown* ☎ *213/687–7111* ⊕ *site.lacitabar.com.*

MUSIC

Blue Whale. This unassuming jazz club in Little Tokyo caters to a serious crowd, bringing progressive and modern jazz to the stage. Although the venue is focused on the music (yes, you may get shushed for talking—that's how small it is), there is a kitchen and bar for snacks and drinks. The club is on the third floor of Weller Court, and the cover runs around $10 to $20. ⊠ *123 Astronaut E. S. Onizuka St., Downtown* ☎ *213/620–0908* ⊕ *www.bluewhalemusic.com.*

The Smell. Reconnect with your punk roots at this live music and art space where you-either-know-'em-or-you-don't rock bands perform. There's no liquor license, but everyone comes to this tiny space for the underground musicians that play for a $5 cover charge. There's no ambience in this raw, no-frills space. Enter through the back alley. ⊠ *247 S. Main St., Downtown* ⊕ *www.thesmell.org.*

HOLLYWOOD

In terms of nightlife, this area gives you a lot of bang for your buck. In addition to Hollywood, you'll find that the nearby communities of Los Feliz, Echo Park, and Silver Lake offer plenty of after-dark options.

HOLLYWOOD

No longer merely a magnet for tourists, Hollywood has become an attractive place for locals to hang out. With the renewed interest in discovering Hollywood history, this area is once again a decent night-life destination.

BARS AND LOUNGES

Burgundy Room. Around since 1919, this rockin' place attracts a fiercely loyal local crowd, as well as the occasional wandering tourists. The bar is supposedly haunted (check out the Ouija boards toward the back), but that just adds to its charm. The drinks are strong and the jukebox plays classic 45s. The attached gallery is worth taking a quick spin through if it's open. ✉ 1621½ N. Cahuenga Blvd., Hollywood ☎ 323/465–7530.

Cat & Fiddle Pub. This English pub's most bragworthy point is the gorgeous courtyard and patio where most patrons go to hang out (and drink, of course). The crowd is a mix of locals, tourists, and expats who enjoy the Sunday jazz concerts and Tuesday trivia nights. The food is typical pub grub, with an L.A. spin (hello, gluten-free menu options). ✉ 6530 Sunset Blvd., Hollywood ☎ 323/468–3800 ⊕ www.thecatandfiddle.com.

Happy Ending. This place has a neighborhood college bar atmosphere for those who miss their days of beer pong (which they have here), karaoke (on Monday), and dancing to Top-40 hits on the weekend. It's not sophisticated, but that's the point. ✉ 7038 Sunset Blvd., Hollywood ☎ 323/469–7038 ⊕ www.thehappyendingbar.com.

Fodor'sChoice ★ **Musso & Frank Grill.** The prim and proper vibe of this old-school steak house won't appeal to those looking for a raucous night out, but its appeal lies more in its history and sturdy drinks. Established in 1919, its dark-wood decor, red tuxedo-clad waiters, and bartenders of great skill can easily shuttle you back to its Hollywood heyday when Marilyn Monroe, F. Scott Fitzgerald, and Greta Garbo used to hang around. ✉ 6667 Hollywood Blvd., Hollywood ☎ 323/467–7788.

Playhouse. Reminiscent of Las Vegas, this splashy spot continues to attract the crowds with its DJs spinning everything from house to hip-hop (and even hits from the '90s). Your best bets are the nights when hip-hop is the main event, as guest artists like Chris Brown and Too Short drop in from time to time. Dress fashionably and you should get in, although expect to drop anywhere from $20 to $30 for the cover charge. ✉ 6506 Hollywood Blvd., Hollywood ☎ 323/656–4800 ⊕ www.playhousenightclub.com.

The Room. This place maintains its reputation as a hip-hop club, serving cool cocktails in a chill environment. Cherry Poppin' Wednesday is a local favorite, with funk, soul, and old-school hip-hop played all night long. The bar likes to maintain a Rat Pack vibe (check out the photo of Frank Sinatra by the bar). ✉ 1626 N. Cahuenga Blvd., Hollywood ☎ 323/462–7196 ⊕ www.theroomhollywood.com.

7

Three Clubs. Whether its claim of being the area's first martini bar lounge is true or not, this bar does take its martinis (and other cocktails) seriously. The focus is fresh and local ingredients for all its cocktails. Around since the 1940s, the bar has a stage featuring live entertainment in the back. Watching the burlesque and comedy shows will incur a small cover charge, but if you just want to drink in the front room, it's free. Don't be surprised by all the well-coiffed young people hanging about. ⊠ *1123 Vine St., Hollywood* ☎ *323/462–6441* ⊕ *www.threeclubs.com.*

Tropicana Bar. This bar still manages to attract a crowd—enjoying perfectly mixed cocktails beside a shimmering pool while you're surrounded by beautiful people never gets old. There's never a cover charge, but the drinks can get pricey and the lines are long on busy nights (it is Hollywood, after all). If you can't wait, the hotel's swanky **Library Bar** serves drinks topped with ingredients from the farmers' markets. ⊠ *Hollywood Roosevelt Hotel, 7000 Hollywood Blvd., Hollywood* ☎ *323/466–7000* ⊕ *www.hollywoodroosevelt.com.*

Yamashiro Hollywood. Modeled after a mansion in Kyoto, this Japanese place has spectacular koi ponds and gardens, as well as sweeping views of the city from its hillside perch. There's a tasty (but pricey) food menu, delicious drinks, and the twinkly lights of Hollywood below. ■TIP➜ Valet parking is mandatory and runs $8. ⊠ *1999 N. Sycamore Ave., Hollywood* ☎ *323/466–5125* ⊕ *www.yamashirohollywood.com.*

CLUBS

Boardner's. This neighborhood bar has been around for decades, and its dim lighting and leather booths give it a well-worn feel. There aren't many tourists here—thanks to its location a half block off Hollywood Boulevard—and it draws a local crowd and the occasional celeb. The adjoining dance floor now has its own entrance and cover charge. The long-running Saturday Goth night still remains popular, even after 15 years in this space. ⊠ *1652 N. Cherokee Ave., Hollywood* ☎ *323/462–9621* ⊕ *www.boardners.com.*

Circus Disco. This club eschews the frou-frou style of its neighbors with a warehouse space that's less about the scene and more about the dancing. Hosting a diverse gay and straight crowd, there's a Tuesday Boyz Night Out and a trance-themed Saturday night party that often keeps going until 4 am. ⊠ *6655 Santa Monica Blvd., Hollywood* ☎ *323/462–1291.*

COMEDY

Groundlings Theatre. This improv and sketch comedy troupe has been entertaining audiences for 40 years, with famous alums often turning up in films and on television. (*Saturday Night Live* snagged Will Ferrell, Will Forte, and Kristin Wiig, to name a few.) Shows often sell out Wednesday to Sunday, and cover charges run from $10 to $20. ⊠ *7307 Melrose Ave., Hollywood* ☎ *323/934–4747* ⊕ *www.groundlings.com.*

iO West. This theater troupe offers nightly shows, "The Harold" being among its most popular. There's a bar in the waiting area—more common for comedy clubs than improv theaters—which is a bonus if you're staying for a few shows. ⊠ *6366 Hollywood Blvd., Hollywood* ☎ *323/962–7560* ⊕ *www.ioimprov.com/west.*

Upright Citizens Brigade. The L.A. offshoot of New York's famous troupe continues its tradition of sketch comedy and improv shows with weekly shows like "Facebook" (where the audience's online profiles are mined for material). Nearing its 10th year on the West Coast, UCB's shows attract celebrity guest stars from time to time, along with a rotating cast of regulars like *30 Rock*'s Jack McBrayer and *The League*'s Paul Scheer. ✉ *5919 Franklin Ave., Hollywood* ☎ *323/908–8702* ⊕ *www.ucbtheatre.com.*

MUSIC

Avalon. This multitasking art deco venue offers both live music and club nights because, well, why not? The killer sound system, cavernous space, and multiple bars make it a perfect venue for both. The club is best known for its DJs, who often spin well past the 2 am cutoff for drinks. The crowd can be a mixed bag, depending on the night, but those looking to dance usually aren't disappointed. Upstairs is **Bardot,** a loungier version of Avalon with its own musical offerings. ✉ *1735 N. Vine St., Hollywood* ☎ *323/462–8900* ⊕ *www. avalonhollywood.com.*

Baked Potato. This small club showcases contemporary jazz and blues every evening, along with regular Monday night jam sessions. The cover is usually $15, although it gets pricier, depending on the musical act. Baked potatoes, served in every shape and form, rule the menu. ✉ *3787 Cahuenga Blvd. W, North Hollywood* ☎ *818/980–1615* ⊕ *www. thebakedpotato.com.*

California Institute of Abnormal Arts. Better known as the CIA, this bar manages to make its circus theme seem kooky and fun (imagine Tim Burton directing *Pee-Wee's Big Adventure,* then add a twist of David Lynch). The list of events varies, from magic shows to burlesque performances to the occasional film screening. Expect a $5 to $10 cover, which isn't bad given the fact that there's so much to look at and ogle over. ✉ *11334 Burbank Ave., North Hollywood* ☎ *818/506–6353.*

Catalina Bar & Grill. This club is a favorite among jazz enthusiasts, featuring well-known and award-winning musicians in an intimate dinner-and-drinks setting. The wide range of jazz, cabaret, and blues played here means a widely varying cover (anywhere from $5 to $50, depending on the talent), but the musicians are always pleasing and worthy of the price. ✉ *6725 W. Sunset Blvd., Hollywood* ☎ *323/466–2210* ⊕ *www.catalinajazzclub.com.*

Dragonfly. Although this bar may come off as dark and gritty, it manages to attract patrons that you wouldn't necessarily suspect. Both "Point Break Live!" and "Terminator Too Judgment Play"—theatrical offerings based on iconic movies in which audience members are invited to play lead roles—draw crowds, as does Helter Skelter, the monthly Goth dance party. Every Thursday is drum-and-bass night, with a rotating mix of events the rest of the week. ✉ *6510 Santa Monica Blvd., Hollywood* ☎ *323/466–6111* ⊕ *www.thedragonfly.com.*

Fodor's Choice ★ **El Floridita.** Although the exterior might not look like much, El Floridita is a popular live salsa music spot on Monday, Friday, and Saturday, with dancers ranging from enthusiasts to those just trying to keep up. There's

7

DID YOU KNOW?

A cruise down Sunset Boulevard takes you to the heart
of Los Angeles nightlife.
Whether you're looking for
someplace seedy or swank,
you can find it here.

a $10 cover to listen to the band, although admission is free with dinner. Reservations are recommended to guarantee a table. ✉ *1253 N. Vine St., Hollywood* ☎ *323/871–8612* ⊕ *www.elfloridita.com.*

Genghis Cohen Cantina. Chinese food and live music is not a pairing you see often, but the success of this place will make you wonder why it's not done more often. A wide range of musicians plays here Monday to Saturday (many are singer-songwriter types), along with the occasional comedy show. ✉ *740 N. Fairfax Ave., Hollywood* ☎ *323/653–0640* ⊕ *www.genghiscohen.com.*

King King. Performances at this club range from salsa to hip-hop to rock, punctuated by truly unique shows that take place monthly. "The Floor Improv" and "Mental Head Circus" are among the more popular events, the former featuring bands performing on the ground level surrounded by dancing patrons, the latter a circus-theme show with aerialists descending from the ceiling. ✉ *6555 Hollywood Blvd., Hollywood* ☎ *323/960–9234* ⊕ *www.kingkinghollywood.com.*

Largo. The comfortable, welcoming vibe of this venue attracts big-name performers who treat this stage as their home base in Los Angeles. Standouts include musician and music producer Jon Brion regularly, who appears here with special drop-in guests (Fiona Apple and Andrew Bird, to name a few). Comedians Sarah Silverman and Patton Oswalt each hosts a monthly comedy show. Bring cash for drinks in the Little Room before the show. ✉ *366 N. La Cienega Blvd., Hollywood* ☎ *310/855–0350* ⊕ *www.largo-la.com.*

LOS FELIZ
BARS AND LOUNGES

Bigfoot Lodge. The cabin-in-the-woods decor and winky attitude toward all things forest-themed (hence the oversize Smokey the Bear statue) makes Bigfoot Lodge a fun destination. Despite (or because of?) the decor, there's a serious focus on the variety of libations, and the mix of DJs ensures that you'll have some good tunes in the background. ✉ *3172 Los Feliz Blvd., Los Feliz* ☎ *323/662–9227* ⊕ *www.bigfootlodge.com.*

Dresden Room. This bar's 1940s lounge decor makes it a favorite with folks in Los Angeles. The long-running house band, Marty and Elayne, has entertained patrons for more than three decades. (They've found a new generation of fans, thanks to the film *Swingers*.) There's never a cover, but expect a two-drink minimum if you want to stay for the entertainment. ✉ *1760 N. Vermont Ave., Los Feliz* ☎ *323/665–4294* ⊕ *www.thedresden.com.*

Good Luck Bar. Around for almost 20 years, this Asian-theme bar is a favorite with young locals looking to pair up. Many dates have started (or ended) here, and that might have something to do with the place's most popular drink, the Potent Potion. DJs spin on weekends (despite the lack of dance floor), and Tuesday is stand-up comedy night. ✉ *1514 Hillhurst Ave., Los Feliz* ☎ *323/666–3524* ⊕ *www.goodluckbarla.com.*

SILVER LAKE

Silver Lake's scene may not make much sense to outsiders, but its eclectic collection of bars and clubs is a perfect reflection of the hipster neighborhood.

BARS AND LOUNGES

4100. With swaths of fabric draped from the ceiling, this place's bohemian vibe makes it perfect for dates. Groups of locals also come through for the night, making the crowd a plentiful mix of, well, everyone. The bartenders know how to pour drinks that are both tasty and potent. There's plenty of seating at the tables and stools along the central bar, which gets crowded on the weekends. ⊠ *4100 Sunset Blvd., Silver Lake* ☎ *323/666–4460.*

Akbar. This bar's welcoming feel is one of the reasons many people consider it their neighborhood bar, even if they don't live in the neighborhood. The mostly gay crowd is friendly and inviting, and theme nights attract all sorts of folks, gay or straight. The comedy nights are favorites, as are weekends when DJs get everyone on the dance floor. ⊠ *4356 Sunset Blvd., Silver Lake* ☎ *323/665–6810* ⊕ *www. akbarsilverlake.com.*

Cha Cha Lounge. This place's decor—part tiki hut, part tacky party palace—shouldn't work, but it does. An import from Seattle, its cheap drinks, foosball tables, and jovial atmosphere make it a natural party scene. It draws a hipster crowd, which can be good or bad, depending on who you ask. ⊠ *2375 Glendale Blvd., Silver Lake* ☎ *323/660–7595* ⊕ *www.chachalounge.com.*

Smog Cutter. The exterior may seem sketchy and the interior not much better, but that doesn't detract from this dive bar's main attraction: nightly karaoke with a fun and rowdy (in a good way) crowd. You have to meet the two-drink minimum at this cash-only hole in the wall. ⊠ *864 N. Virgil Ave., Silver Lake* ☎ *323/660–4626.*

Thirsty Crow. This whiskey bar serves up seasonal cocktails in a fun, rustic-looking environment. Despite its diminutive size, the place manages to find space for live musicians, including for Saturday's open mike night. Events pop up on the calendar (toga party, anyone?), but that's what makes this place so endearing to locals. ⊠ *2939 W. Sunset Blvd., Silver Lake* ☎ *323/661–6007* ⊕ *www.thirstycrowbar.com.*

Tiki-Ti. The cozy feel of this Polynesian-theme bar is due in part to its small size—12 seats at the bar, plus a few tables along one side. Open since 1961, it serves a wide array of strong rum drinks that draw the crowds on the weekend. Don't be surprised to find a line outside. ⊠ *4427 Sunset Blvd., Silver Lake* ☎ *323/669–9381* ⊕ *www. tiki-ti.com.*

MUSIC

The Satellite. This venue hosts a variety of bands, mostly indie rockers. Monday nights are free and feature exciting up-and-coming bands. Cover charges on other days range from $8 to $15. ⊠ *1717 Silver Lake Blvd., Silver Lake* ☎ *323/661–4380* ⊕ *www.thesatellitela.com.*

Silverlake Lounge. This lounge offers a varying roster of indie, rock, and classical (yep) performers. It's not really the space to see bands you might have heard of, but if you're patient you might discover one that could hit the big time. The cover charge can reach $8. ⊠ *2906 Sunset Blvd., Silver Lake* ☎ *323/663–9636* ⊕ *www.thesilverlakelounge.com.*

ECHO PARK

Music factors into the nightlife scene at Echo Park, with quite a few places where you can see up-and-coming performers take to the stage. Even more traditional bars are bringing in local bands.

BARS AND LOUNGES

El Prado. This neighborhood bar certainly doesn't have a huge variety—there are only eight beer taps, for instance—but it isn't trying to be all things to all people. It stocks a constantly rotating selection that guarantees the most interesting wine and beer selection it can get its hands on. A record player serves as the main source of music—while the idea may seem twee, it's the heart of a popular Tuesday night record club, where patrons bring in their own vinyl. ⊠ *1805 W. Sunset Blvd., Echo Park* ⊕ *www.elpradobar.com.*

Short Stop. Other than its brightly lit "Cocktails" sign, this bar's exterior barely hints at the scene inside. It got its name thanks to its proximity to Dodger Stadium, and many patrons are coming or going to a game. On weekends the place caters to dance-hungry crowds who don't want to put up with any drama. ⊠ *1455 Sunset Blvd., Echo Park* ☎ *213/482–4942.*

MUSIC

The Echo. This favorite music spot in Echo Park features an eclectic array of up-and-coming bands. Soul or reggae dance nights and DJ mash-up sessions are thrown in to round out the calendar. The basement-level Echoplex has twice the space, so it can book bigger names. ⊠ *1154 Glendale Blvd.* ☎ *213/413–8200* ⊕ *www.attheecho.com.*

The Echoplex. The Echoplex books bigger national tours and events. ⊠ *1822 Sunset Blvd., Echo Park* ☎ *213/413–8200* ⊕ *www.attheecho.com.*

WEST HOLLYWOOD

Gay or straight, head to West Hollywood if you're looking for a party-loving crowd. This town has plenty of bars and clubs within walking distance, so if you don't like one, head to the next. Santa Monica Boulevard has everything from low-key sports bars to trendy clubs with raised dancing platforms. If you're clueless about what to wear, dress up. Everyone's looking.

BARS AND LOUNGES

The Abbey. Don't let the church theme scare you off: this club's fun atmosphere makes it a central gathering point for West Hollywood. Most folks partying in the area often wind up here at one point or another, whether for drinking or dancing (or even a champagne brunch the next morning). The patio is perfection both day and night, with music keeping everyone in an upbeat mood. ⊠ *692 N. Robertson Blvd., West Hollywood* ☎ *310/289–8410* ⊕ *www.abbeyfoodandbar.com.*

Bar Marmont. Depending on the night and what time you arrive, the mood here can switch from cozy and comfortable to unbearably packed, thanks to its reputation as being a favorite with celebs. Music from the house DJ usually kicks in around 10, and the crowd is generally well-dressed. The highly skilled bartenders can pour a stiff libation, and the food is worth trying: the burger and buttermilk fried chicken are favorites. ✉ *8171 Sunset Blvd., West Hollywood* ☎ *323/650–0575* ⊕ *www.chateaumarmont.com.*

Barney's Beanery. Open since 1920, Barney's Beanery is an iconic spot that drew legendary regulars Janis Joplin and Jim Morrison (among others) to its doorstep. There's an extensive menu, but all anyone talks about is the famous chili and the list of more than 250 beers. There are plenty of distractions, including three pool tables, a foosball table, and arcade games. ✉ *8447 Santa Monica Blvd., West Hollywood* ☎ *323/654–2287* ⊕ *www.barneysbeanery.com.*

The Dime. Despite its diminutive size, the Dime manages to pack in the drinking hordes on the weekend. There's a DJ, a daily happy hour, and an all-around good vibe. The music usually gets going by 10 pm and can span the decades. Come on Sunday night if you're looking for a chiller vibe. ✉ *442 N. Fairfax Ave., Fairfax District* ☎ *323/651–4421* ⊕ *www.thedimela.net.*

Formosa Café. Open since 1939, this restaurant and bar celebrates its Hollywood roots with more than 400 photos of Hollywood celebrities who ate and drank here. The restaurant maintains a neighborhood feel, with generations of loyal regulars who still remember the café in its earlier days. ✉ *7156 Santa Monica Blvd., West Hollywood* ☎ *323/850–9050.*

HMS Bounty. Hanging out in this ship-theme bar and restaurant is enough to make you forget the weekday traffic outside on Wilshire Boulevard. Locals make this their neighborhood bar of choice, and with good reason: the cheap drink prices are certainly enough of a draw, but the food is good enough to turn anyone into a regular. ✉ *3357 Wilshire Blvd., Mid-Wilshire* ☎ *213/385–7275* ⊕ *www.thehmsbounty.com.*

Jones. Italian food, serious cocktails, and hipster cred? You must be at Jones. Whiskey is usually the choice for the classic cocktails, although the bartenders are crafty enough to do up martinis properly (read: strong). The Beggar's Banquet is the place's version of happy hour, with specials on drinks and pizza. ✉ *7205 Santa Monica Blvd., West Hollywood* ☎ *323/850–1726.*

Molly Malone's. A stone's throw from the Los Angeles County Museum of Art, this Irish pub has been a cozy neighborhood spot since 1969. There's a dartboard, some tasty things to nibble, and a decent selection of beers. A small stage in the back hosts bands playing country, blues, and rock for a cover charge of $5 to $10. ✉ *575 S. Fairfax Ave., Fairfax District* ☎ *323/935–1577* ⊕ *www.mollymalonesla.com.*

Rainbow Bar & Grill. Its location next door to a long-running music venue, the Roxy, helped cement this bar and restaurant's status as a legendary watering hole for musicians (as well as their entourages and groupies). The Who, Guns 'n Roses, Poison, Kiss—and many others—have all passed through the doors. Expect a $5 to $10 cover, but you'll get the money back in drink tickets or a food discount. ✉ *9015 Sunset Blvd., West Hollywood* ☎ *310/278–4232* ⊕ *www.rainbowbarandgrill.com.*

Continued on page 149

L.A. STORY
THE CITY'S HISTORY THROUGH ITS BARS

Los Angeles is known as a place where dreams are realized, but it is also a place where pasts are forgotten. Despite what people say about L.A.'s lack of memory, however, there are quite a few noteworthy old-school bars that pay tribute to the city's vibrant past and its famous patrons.

Collectively, these eclectic watering holes have hosted everyone from ex-presidents to rock legends to famed authors and, of course, a continual stream of countless movie stars.

The bars are located in virtually every corner of the city—from Downtown to West Hollywood to Santa Monica.

In terms of character, they run the gamut from dive to dressy and serve everything from top-shelf whisky to bargain-basement beer.

While it's their differences that have kept people coming back through the decades, they all have something in common: Each has a story to tell.

EIGHT OF L.A.'S BEST

Mixing at Cole's

Chez Jay

Cole's

CHEZ JAY RESTAURANT (1959)
Noteworthy for: Located down the block from the Santa Monica Pier, this steak-and-seafood joint walks the line between celebrity hangout and dive bar.
Signature drink: Martini
Celeb clientele: Members of the Rat Pack, Leonard Nimoy, Sean Penn, Julia Roberts, Renée Zellweger, Owen Wilson, Drew Barrymore
Don't miss: The little booth in the back of the restaurant, known to insiders as Table 10, is a favorite celebrity hideout.
Filmed here: *Maverick*
Join the crowd: *1657 Ocean Ave., Santa Monica, 310/395–1741*

COLE'S (1908)
Noteworthy for: Found inside the Pacific Electric building, touted as Los Angeles's oldest public house, and once the epicenter of the Red Car railway network, this watering hole has its original glass lighting, penny-tile floors, and 40-foot mahogany bar.

Signature drink: The Red Car, a heady concoction with Rittenhouse rye, ginger liqueur, and lemon juice
Celeb clientele: Bill Murray, members of the cast of *Mad Men*
Don't miss: The Varnish at Cole's is an in-house speakeasy with 11 booths that can be accessed through a hidden door marked by a tiny framed picture of a cocktail glass.
Filmed here: *Forrest Gump, L.A. Confidential, Mad Men*
Join the crowd: *118 E. 6th St., Los Angeles, 213/622–4049*

FORMOSA CAFE (1929)
Noteworthy for: You can't miss West Hollywood's iconic bright red building with black-and-white-striped awnings. Once a trolley car, this Asian-inspired restaurant is an entertainment-industry favorite, with tons of autographed photos on its walls.
Signature drink: Mai tai, martini
Celeb clientele: Marilyn Monroe, Clark Gable, Elizabeth Taylor, Humphrey Bogart

Chez Jay

Harvelle's

Kibitz Room

A regular at Formosa's

Don't miss: Booths are named after the movie stars who sat in them during Hollywood's Golden Age.
Filmed here: *L.A. Confidential*
Join the crowd: *7156 Santa Monica Blvd., West Hollywood, 323/850–9050.*

FROLIC ROOM (1935)
Noteworthy for: This Hollywood favorite next door to the famed Pantages Theater has served actors and writers from Elizabeth Short to Charles Bukowski.
Signature drink: Cheap Budweiser ($2.75 during happy hour)
Celeb clientele: Kiefer Sutherland
Don't miss: A bowl of popcorn from the old-fashioned machine; the Hirschfeld mural depicting Marilyn Monroe, Charlie Chaplin, Louis Armstrong, Frank Sinatra, and others.
Filmed here: *L.A. Confidential, Southland*
Join the crowd: *6245 Hollywood Blvd., Los Angeles, 323/462–5890*

HARVELLE'S (1931)
Noteworthy for: Located one block off the Third Street Promenade, this dark and sexy jazz bar is said to be the oldest live-music venue on the Westside.
Signature drink: The Deadly Sins martini menu offers house-made mixes named after the seven sins, from Pride to Lust.
Don't miss: The Toledo Show is a pulse-quickening weekly burlesque-and-jazz performance on Sunday nights.
Join the crowd: *1432 4th St., Santa Monica, 310/395–1676.*

THE KIBITZ ROOM AT CANTER'S DELI (1961)
Noteworthy for: Adjacent to the famous Canter's Deli, which opened in 1948, this Fairfax District nightspot is definitely a dive bar, but that doesn't keep the A-listers away. Jakob Dylan and the Wallflowers got their start playing a weekly gig here.
Signature drink: Cheap beer
Celeb clientele: Dustin Hoffman, Tim Robbins, Kiefer Sutherland,

In golden days

Canter's

La Dolce Vita

Pastrami at Canter's

Julia Roberts, Javier Bardem, Penélope Cruz

Don't miss: The decor is pure retro 1960s, including vinyl booths and a fall-leaf motif on the ceiling.

Filmed here: *I Ought to Be in Pictures, Entourage, Curb Your Enthusiasm, Sunset Strip, Enemy of the State, What's Eating Gilbert Grape*

Join the crowd: *1 N. Fairfax Ave., Los Angeles, 323/651–2030.*

DOLCE VITA (1966)

Noteworthy for: Located in tony Beverly Hills, this staple for northern Italian has a classy clubhouse atmosphere, round leather booths, white tablecloths, and exposed-brick walls.

Signature drink: Martini

Celeb clientele: Members of the Rat Pack; several ex presidents, including Ronald Reagan. The place prides itself on being a safe haven from pesky paparazzi.

Don't miss: The burgundy-hued round leather booths.

Join the crowd: *9785 Santa Monica Blvd., Los Angeles, 310/278–1845*

MUSSO & FRANK GRILL (1919)

Noteworthy for: This swanky old-timer is called the oldest bar in Hollywood. While that title may spark jealousy among some of its Tinseltown counterparts, there is no doubt that this famed grill conjures Hollywood's halcyon days with its authentic '30s-era decor—and serves a mean martini.

Signature drink: The Mean Martini

Celeb clientele: Charlie Chaplin, Greta Garbo, Ernest Hemingway, F. Scott Fitzgerald, Marilyn Monroe

Don't miss: The red tuxedo–clad waiters are famous in their own right; some have been at the restaurant for more than 40 years.

Filmed here: *Ocean's Eleven, Charlie's Angels 2, Mad Men*

Join the crowd: *6667 Hollywood Blvd., Los Angeles, 323/467–7788*

Musso & Frank Grill

THE OLDEST RESTAURANT IN HOLLYWOOD
Since 1919

Skybar. This beautiful poolside bar is well worth a visit, but it can be a hassle to get into if you're not staying at the hotel, on the guest list, or know someone who can pull strings. The drinks are on the pricier side, but in this part of town that's to be expected. ⊠ *Hotel Mondrian, 8440 Sunset Blvd., West Hollywood* ☎ *323/650–8999* ⊕ *www. mondrianhotel.com.*

The Standard. Summer weekend pool parties are downright notorious at the Standard Hollywood. A cushy spot among the party places on Sunset Boulevard, the Pool Deck has DJs at the ready to welcome the masses. Wednesday offers live acoustic music—a definite contrast to the weekend music scene. ⊠ *The Standard Hollywood, 8300 Sunset Blvd., West Hollywood* ☎ *323/650–9090* ⊕ *www.standardhotels.com.*

Trunks. If the sceney vibe of the bars along Santa Monica Boulevard has you craving something calmer, head to this sports bar where the drinks are strong but cheap. Open for more than 25 years, it's welcoming and friendly. Although a DJ usually plays music after 10 pm, there's no dance floor to speak of—which can work in your favor if you're there to catch a game or play some pool. ⊠ *8809 Santa Monica Blvd., West Hollywood* ☎ *310/652–1015* ⊕ *www.trunksbar.com.*

Vignette. In a quieter section of West Hollywood, this small club is hopping on Tuesday night, when DJs play hip-hop and Top 40. Along with bottle service, patrons can request a tableside stripper pole, which could account for some of the club's popularity. The decor mixes Old Hollywood movie magic—think green velvet show curtains and rope pulleys along the wall—and a modern vibe, thanks to art hanging along one side of the club. ⊠ *8623 Melrose Ave., at Huntley Dr., West Hollywood* ☎ *310/289–8623* ⊕ *www.villalounge.com.*

COMEDY

Comedy Store. Three stages give seasoned (and unseasoned) comedians a place to perform and try out new material, with popular comics like Louis C. K. and Sarah Silverman dropping by just for fun. The front bar along Sunset Boulevard is a popular hangout after or between shows, oftentimes with that night's comedians mingling with fans. ⊠ *8433 Sunset Blvd., West Hollywood* ☎ *323/650–6268* ⊕ *www. thecomedystore.com.*

Improv. This standup comedy spot on Melrose Avenue has been making audiences laugh for years. Wednesday's ComedyJuice is popular with locals, while weekend shows draw out-of-towners to see more-well-known comedians. The cover charge is anywhere from $10 to $26. ⊠ *8162 Melrose Ave., West Hollywood* ☎ *323/651–2583* ⊕ *www. improv.com.*

Laugh Factory. Top standup comics appear at this Sunset Boulevard mainstay, often working in material in advance of national tours. Popular comics like Kevin Hart tend to drop by unannounced. Midnight Madness on the weekends is extremely popular, with comics performing more daring sets. ⊠ *8001 Sunset Blvd., West Hollywood* ☎ *323/656–1336* ⊕ *www.laughfactory.com.*

7

CLUBS

Greystone Manor Supperclub. From its chandeliers to its modern couches, this luxurious club attracts the young Hollywood crowd and music industry folks, with occasional appearances by rappers like the Game or Roscoe Dash. One of the more popular events is Sunday's hip-hop night, with DJs entertaining the (still) partying weekend crowds. ⊠ *643 N. La Cienega Blvd., West Hollywood* ☎ *310/652–2012* ⊕ *www. greystonemanorla.com.*

Rage. Those ready to mingle often drop by this club, and with good reason: the variety of events draws different crowds, depending on what scene you're into. There's lots of eye candy, and on weekends things certainly never get boring. ⊠ *8911 Santa Monica Blvd., West Hollywood* ☎ *310/652–7055* ⊕ *www.theragenightclub.com.*

MUSIC

El Rey Theater. This former movie house from the 1930s has been given a second life as a live music venue. All types of notable musicians play here—both the Pixies and Ringo Starr have recently appeared here while on tour. ⊠ *5515 Wilshire Blvd., Mid-Wilshire* ☎ *323/936–6400* ⊕ *www.theelrey.com.*

House of Blues. This club functions like a concert venue, hosting popular jazz, rock, and blues performers. Every Sunday there's a gospel brunch. ⊠ *8430 Sunset Blvd., West Hollywood* ☎ *323/848–5100* ⊕ *www. houseofblues.com.*

The Mint. This music venue has been around since 1937, with notable musicians like Stevie Wonder, Ray Charles, and Earth, Wind, and Fire gracing the stage over the years. Nowadays, the club hosts a mix of jazz, bluegrass, and rock bands and serves up your typical bar food along with its drinks. ⊠ *6010 W. Pico Blvd.* ☎ *323/954–9400* ⊕ *www. themintla.com.*

The Troubadour. The intimate vibe of the Troubadour helps make this club a favorite with music fans. This music venue has been open since 1957 and has a storied past. These days, the eclectic lineup is still attracting the crowds, with the focus mostly on rock, indie, and folk music. Those looking for drinks can imbibe at the adjacent bar. ⊠ *9081 Santa Monica Blvd., West Hollywood* ⊕ *www.troubadour.com.*

Viper Room. This club's been around for more than 20 years, and its rock and alternative shows still attract a crowd. The cover charge usually runs around $15 but can go up from there, depending on the act. ⊠ *8852 W. Sunset Blvd., West Hollywood* ☎ *310/358–1881* ⊕ *www.viperroom.com.*

Whisky A Go Go. The hardcore metal and rock scene is alive and well at the legendary Whisky A Go Go, which first made its name as the place where Led Zeppelin, Alice Cooper, Van Halen, and the Doors (who served as the house band for a short while) have all played. Celebrating its 50th anniversary on the Sunset Strip, the club still leans toward more underground acts. ⊠ *8901 Sunset Blvd., West Hollywood* ☎ *310/652–4202* ⊕ *www.whiskyagogo.com.*

SANTA MONICA AND THE BEACHES

In Santa Monica, the focus of nightlife shifts toward more live music, historic dives, and any space that has a view of the ocean.

SANTA MONICA

BARS AND LOUNGES

Basement Tavern. In the basement of the Victorian, this small bar has clusters of couches and ottomans pushed together to welcome groups. There's live music (anything from bluegrass to reggae to rock) or DJs each night, along with a creative cocktail menu. Go through the parking lot and down a flight of stairs. ⊠ *2640 Main St., Santa Monica* ☎ *310/396–2469* ⊕ *www.basementtavern.com.*

Chez Jay. Around since 1959, this dive bar continues to be a well-loved place in Santa Monica. Everyone from the young to the old (including families) frequents this historical landmark. It's a charming place, from the well-worn booths with their red checkered tablecloths to the ship's wheel near the door. ⊠ *1657 Ocean Ave., Santa Monica* ☎ *310/395–1741* ⊕ *www.chezjays.com.*

Circle Bar. Established in 1949, this place has always kept its oval-shape bar front and center—hence the name. Even with the dim lighting, the people-watching is usually fun, especially when DJs are playing the house, indie, or dance music and the crowd is packed in tight. ⊠ *2926 Main St., Santa Monica* ☎ *310/450–0508* ⊕ *www.circle-bar.com.*

The Galley. The boatlike exterior of this restaurant-bar certainly stands out, especially the wavy blue neon lights and porthole windows. Inside, the nautical theme continues with fishing nets and anchors adorning the walls and twinkling lights everywhere to brighten up the place. Most patrons tend to crowd the center bar, with the more dinner-oriented folks frequenting the booths. ⊠ *2442 Main St., Santa Monica* ☎ *310/452–1934.*

Monsoon Café. Whether you consider the decor of this Bali-theme place authentic or overdone, it does its job of transporting you away from the busy crowds outside on Santa Monica's Third Street Promenade. It's the second-floor dance space that attracts most people. ⊠ *1212 3rd St. Promenade, Santa Monica* ☎ *310/576–9996* ⊕ *www.globaldiningca.com.*

MUSIC

Harvelle's. The focus of this bar and music club is on jazz, blues, and soul. The club is small, with an even smaller checkerboard dance floor. There's usually a cover ($5 to $10, depending on the day), with a two-drink minimum. Some shows do get crowded, so reserve a table in advance. ⊠ *1432 4th St., Santa Monica* ☎ *310/395–1676* ⊕ *www.harvelles.com.*

McCabe's Guitar Shop. You can easily spend your time browsing at this famous guitar shop, but this place is also known for its weekend concerts. You may not recognize all the musicians that come through here, but the shows sell out quickly. Don't expect food or drinks (it's a music shop, after all). ⊠ *3101 Pico Blvd., Santa Monica* ☎ *310/828–4497* ⊕ *www.mccabes.com.*

7

Rusty's Surf Ranch. At the start of Santa Monica Pier, this surf-theme place features live music on weekends. The options range from rock to pop to country. ⊠ *256 Santa Monica Pier, Santa Monica* ☎ *310/393–7437* ⊕ *www.rustyssurfranch.com.*

Zanzibar. Spinning everything from salsa to reggae to classic hip-hop, this club has only one goal: to get you on the dance floor. The crowd is diverse and the go-go dancers definitely get everyone moving in this Moroccan-theme club. Old school hip-hop on Friday is popular, along with salsa (and salsa lessons) on Monday. ⊠ *1301 5th St., Santa Monica* ☎ *310/451–2221* ⊕ *www.zanzibarlive.com.*

VENICE
BARS AND LOUNGES
The Brig. This charming bar has its pluses (interesting drinks, talented DJs) and minuses (ugh, parking), but is generally worth a look if you're in the area. There's always a food truck around, and the bar's fine with you bringing in outside food. ⊠ *1515 Abbot Kinney Blvd., Venice* ☎ *310/399–7537* ⊕ *www.thebrig.com.*

Otheroom. With a focus on craft beers and fine wines, this bar has become a favorite local hangout. The space is welcoming, especially with its large front windows thrown open on particularly gorgeous days. The bar doesn't serve food, but allows patrons to bring their own—a wise decision, given the number of food trucks in the area. ⊠ *1201 Abbot Kinney Blvd., Venice* ☎ *310/396–6230* ⊕ *www.theotheroom.com.*

MALIBU
BARS AND LOUNGES
Duke's Barefoot Bar. With a clear view of the horizon from almost everywhere, a sunset drink at Duke's Barefoot Bar is how most beachgoers like to end their day. The entertainment is in keeping with the bar's Hawaiian theme, with Hawaiian dancers performing on Friday and a band on Saturday. If you're hungry, the food is worth checking out (don't expect beach-bum prices, though). ⊠ *21150 Pacific Coast Hwy., Malibu* ☎ *310/317–0777* ⊕ *www.dukesmalibu.com.*

Blue Lounge. This outdoor lounge attracts customers with its modern look and views of the ocean. DJs are constantly spinning lounge music in the background, and there's never a cover charge. ⊠ *20356 Pacific Coast Hwy.* ☎ *310/456–3010* ⊕ *www.moonshadowsmalibu.com.*

HERMOSA BEACH
BARS AND LOUNGES
Lighthouse Cafe. This place offers a wide range of live music, including jazz, reggae, and karaoke (either backed by a DJ or a live band, depending on when you go). There is a $5 cover on weekends, and a jazz brunch on Sunday. ⊠ *30 Pier Ave., Hermosa Beach* ☎ *310/376–9833* ⊕ *www.thelighthousecafe.net.*

PERFORMING
ARTS

Updated by
Dianne de
Guzman

To think of Los Angeles as simply a place where movies and television shows are made is to ignore a city that is teeming with culture beyond the cinema. With the arts, Los Angeles is both a place of innovation and history: venturing forward with new works in dance and theater—REDCAT Theater in Downtown Los Angeles is a prime example of a space working toward pushing the boundaries of art, media, and performance—but still holding a healthy respect for tradition with its restored theaters and classic plays.

This diverse city attracts a heavily artistic bunch and that's evident from the wide range of theaters, plays, and events available to the public. There's a play for any group or budget; East West Players at the David Henry Hwang Theatre focuses on Asian-American themed plays, for instance. If an opera at the Dorothy Chandler Pavilion seems out of your budget, the Actors' Gang in Culver City offers a free Shakespeare play (with a twist on the classic story) in Media Park in summer.

And, speaking of summer: the gorgeous weather offers an extended season of outdoor shows and that's where Los Angeles can truly shine. Whether it's enjoying a classic summer picnic listening to the Los Angeles Philharmonic at the Hollywood Bowl or watching a play outdoors with your family at the John Anson Ford Amphitheater, it's a glorious way to celebrate the warmth and beauty Southern California has to offer.

Last but not least, let's not forget our moneymaker: movies. Although we're known for our blockbusters—those blow-'em-up, shoot-'em-down $500 million action films—in town there's still a love for the classic film that turns up where you least expect it. Cinefamily at the Silent Film Theatre is one of the few places that still plays silent films, but they've also gone beyond that with its unabashed love for all things movies: campy films, indie films, even podcasts *about* film all happen here. American Cinémathèque operates out of the Aero Theatre in Santa Monica, as well as the Egyptian Theatre in Hollywood, with its old-school Egyptian-themed courtyard, and gets away with showing Hitchcock one night and a triple-feature of *Back to the Future* the next.

Los Angeles offers more than one might expect, and that's okay: it's one city that's always looking to prove the naysayers wrong.

PERFORMING ARTS PLANNER

WHERE TO GET INFORMATION

To find up-to-date listings of local events, ⊕ *www.la.com,* ⊕ *www. experiencela.com,* ⊕ *www.discoverlosangeles.com,* and *Los Angeles* magazine are all great sources to see what's happening or where the locals are going. Also, local site ⊕ *laist.com* offers readers a list of standout events for the week or weekend, in case you don't have time to do the research. The free alternative publication *LA Weekly* (⊕ *www. laweekly.com*) is issued every Thursday and is also a good resource that's available in newspaper boxes along the street.

WHERE TO GET TICKETS

Most venues can be contacted directly when looking for tickets—even if you've decided to try out a show last-minute—but the sources below are also worth looking at, in case there are discounted tickets available.

Razor Gator. High-demand tickets for sporting events, concerts, and theater are usually found on this site; sometimes at a discount, but generally not. ☏ *800/542–4466* ⊕ *www.razorgator.com.*

Ticketmaster. Although Ticketmaster doesn't sell tickets for all L.A. performances, it is the top seller for live events in Los Angeles. ☏ *800/745–3000* ⊕ *www.ticketmaster.com.*

BEST PERFORMING ARTS EXPERIENCES

Head Outdoors for a Summer Event. Whether you're headed to the Hollywood Bowl to see the L.A. Philharmonic play or attending the Friday Night Sing-Along in the outdoor garden of the Walt Disney Concert Hall at the Music Center *(see Hollywood Bowl),* spending time in the inviting weather while watching a show is the way to go.

Watch a Classic Movie. Even if you aren't the most serious of movie buffs, watching a classic film in Los Angeles has more intrigue than say, watching it on your TV back home, because you can muse about where nearby it was likely filmed or produced. Attending a screening at any number of the restored movie theaters will further heighten the moviegoing experience.

Visit a Smaller Theater. Although it's easy to be wowed by the events going on at any of the larger stages, such as those part of the Center Theatre Group, it's the smaller theaters that are getting braver and bolder with their original plays or reworked classics—oftentimes, at a cheaper price.

8

CONCERTS

These days, you're just as likely to meet a musician as you are an actor, and that's a plus if you're looking to attend a music show. Los Angeles is crawling with bands trying to break into the industry and you stand a decent chance of seeing the Next Big Thing.

There are many places to see live music in Los Angeles, and the variety of clubs and venues can satisfy just about any music cravings you might have. The venues below are the major players in concert halls, but if you're looking for something more off the beaten path, *LA Weekly* is great for finding out what's happening that night, in any given neighborhood.

MAJOR CONCERT HALLS

Fodor's Choice **Dorothy Chandler Pavilion.** Los Angeles opera and ballet fans make the
★ Dorothy Chandler Pavilion a must-go-to and with good reason: Performances here manage to remain fresh with a balance of both new and classic opera and ballet performances. L.A. Opera continues as the long-running resident company and touring ballet companies perform here also.

Another treat in itself: As the Dorothy Chandler Pavilion nears its 50th anniversary—the first performance was held on December 6, 1964—the music hall still looks as elegant as ever, from the requisite theater curtain, large-scale crystal chandeliers, and resident art collection. ■**TIP→** Ticket holders can attend free pre-opera talks, which happen one hour before the performance. Music Director James Conlon hosts the talks, although other scholars have hosted as well. Reservations aren't necessary, but early arrival is suggested due to the limited space. ⊠ *135 N. Grand Ave., Downtown* ☎ *213/972–7211* ⊕ *www.musiccenter.org.*

Greek Theatre. New as well as seasoned musical acts frequent the outdoor Greek Theatre and this venue does a good job of hosting a variety of concerts to please most music lovers. Taking advantage of the pleasant Los Angeles weather from May through November, acts like the Weeknd, the Flaming Lips, and Chicago have all graced the stage. The 5,800-seat amphitheater is in Griffith Park—this means that concert attendees may navigate through some preshow traffic driving to the venue, however, they will also venture past some beautiful Hollywood Hills homes and park foliage in the meantime. Pay lots are available for parking, but wear comfortable shoes and expect to do some walking, as some parking lots are a farther trek than others. ⊠ *2700 N. Vermont Ave., Los Feliz* ☎ *323/665–5857* ⊕ *www.greektheatrela.com.*

Fodor's Choice **Hollywood Bowl.** For those truly looking for a Los Angeles experience,
★ you can't get any better than a summer night at the Bowl. The Hollywood Bowl is Los Angeles's most iconic outdoor venue, with gorgeous views of nature serving as background to its concerts since it opened in 1920. The L.A. Philharmonic performs in summer here from June to September; both it and other events draw large crowds. Parking is limited, but the venue does the best it can by offering remote parking locations and shuttles to the venue. The L.A. Philharmonic allows patrons to bring their own food and drinks (including alcohol) to performances, if they prefer (most Los Angelenos do). Patrons are advised

The Los Angeles Master Chorale onstage at the Walt Disney Concert Hall

to bring a jacket despite whatever the temperatures are during the day, as the venue does get quite cold at night. ■ TIP→ Visitors can watch the L.A. Philharmonic practice for free on certain dates; call ahead for times. Past open practices have been held during weekdays, but times and dates vary. ⊠ *2301 Highland Ave., Hollywood* ☎ *323/850–2000* ⊕ *www.hollywoodbowl.com.*

Nokia Theatre L.A. Live. Hosting a variety of concerts and big-name awards shows—the Emmys, American Music Awards, and the BET Awards have all taken place here—this theater and the surrounding L.A. Live complex is a draw for those looking for a fun night out. The emphasis the building places on acoustics and versatile seating arrangements means that all seats are good seats, whether it's an intimate John Legend concert you're attending, or the People's Choice Awards (complete with screaming crowds). Outside, the L.A. Live complex hosts a number of restaurants and attractions (including the Grammy Museum) to keep patrons entertained before, after, or without a concert. ⊠ *777 Chick Hearn Court, Downtown* ☎ *213/763–6030* ⊕ *www.nokiatheatrelalive.com.*

Shrine Auditorium. Although the variety of shows at the Shrine Auditorium (and adjacent Expo Hall) lean toward the eclectic—anything from musical concerts to cheerleading competitions take place here—this historical venue is worth going to, should an event interest you. Opened in 1926, this venue has hosted just about every awards show that has been broadcast out of Los Angeles, including the Academy Awards, the Emmy Awards, and the Grammys, plus its Moorish Revival–style architecture is a thing to marvel over. ⊠ *665 W. Jefferson Blvd., Downtown* ☎ *213/748–5116* ⊕ *www.shrineauditorium.com.*

Staples Center. The epicenter for Los Angeles sports fans—the Lakers, Clippers, and Kings all play their local games here—this stadium also plays host to large-scale concerts. Headliner names of all different genres pass through here, from Beyoncé to the Rolling Stones to, yes, Taylor Swift. ✉ *1111 S. Figueroa St., Downtown* ☎ *213/742–7300* ⊕ *www.staplescenter.com.*

Wiltern LG Theater. Built in 1931, this historical landmark serves mainly as a space for music—such as rock, jazz, and pop—but a few other events wind up here as well, including comedy and dance. The main floor is generally standing room only for most shows, but there are some seating areas available, if desired. ✉ *3790 Wilshire Blvd., Mid-Wilshire* ☎ *213/388–1400.*

> **WORD OF MOUTH**
>
> "I took the Walt Disney Concert Hall's free guided tour on my last trip, but we didn't have time this time. I bought our concert tickets about a month before our trip. Our seats were in the "bench" section, which is behind the orchestra. I liked these seats because we got a good view of the orchestra plus we were able to watch the conductor."
>
> —yk

DANCE

The dance scene in Los Angeles isn't where most dancers would like it to be, but it's getting there. A number of dance companies are looking to reinvigorate the scene and make Los Angeles more of a destination for dance enthusiasts, meaning new companies and talent are setting up shop by the month.

BODYTRAFFIC. Named as one of the choices for Best of Culture for 2013 by the *Los Angeles Times,* this dance company works with both local and international dance stars to bring innovative, contemporary dance performances to Los Angeles. In 2014, the Broad Stage in Santa Monica named BODYTRAFFIC a resident dance company, so the dancers will now regularly be seen there. ✉ *708 Machado Dr., Venice* ☎ *646/221–7811* ⊕ *www.bodytraffic.com.*

Cal State L.A.'s Dance Department. This department puts on dance productions throughout the year, performed by students majoring in dance. The theater and music departments hold regular performances as well. The website has the latest on all events by these three departments and tickets are also sold online. ✉ *5151 State University Dr., East Los Angeles* ☎ *323/343–4118* ⊕ *www.calstatela.edu/academic/musictheatredance.*

Los Angeles Ballet. This company performs both classical and contemporary ballet, including new works, from December to June. Lacking a permanent theater space, this dance company rotates its performances among a number of venues in the Los Angeles area. ☎ *310/998–7782* ⊕ *www.losangelesballet.org.*

Center for the Art of Performance at UCLA. For dance, head to the Center for the Art of Performance at UCLA. The Los Angeles Ballet is one of the frequent guests in the performance space in Royce Hall. Some performances are also held at Glorya Kaufman Hall. ✉ *Royce Hall, 340 Royce Dr.* ☎ *310/825–4401* ⊕ *cap.ucla.edu.*

FILM

Watching movies here isn't merely an efficient way to kill time, but it's an *event*. Being in the midst of movie studios makes it extremely easy—and worthwhile—to attend screenings with a major director (or actor) participating in a postfilm discussion. A number of the theaters on this list are also attractions in themselves, with restorations paying close attention to the history of the building. Whether it's a first-run film or a revival, the show will likely be worth the trip out.

ART AND REVIVAL HOUSES

The American Cinemathèque at the Aero and Egyptian Theatres. Film enthusiasts will enjoy the roster of movies put on by the American Cinemathèque, with classic and independent films screening on a constantly rotating schedule at its two theaters: the Aero Theatre and the Egyptian Theatre. Expect everything from suspenseful Hitchcock to anime from Hayao Miyazaki, along with occasional question-and-answer sessions with directors and actors following film screenings. The Egyptian Theatre in Hollywood has the distinction of hosting the first-ever movie premiere, back when it opened in 1922, and its Egyptian-themed courtyard and columns have been lovingly restored to preserve its history. The Aero Theatre is in Santa Monica and first opened in 1940. ✉ *6712 Hollywood Blvd., Hollywood* ☎ *323/466–3456* ⊕ *www.americancinematheque.com.*

Aero Theatre. This Santa Monica–based American Cinemathèque theater first opened in 1940 and shows movies on a big screen. ✉ *1328 Montana Ave., Santa Monica* ☎ *323/466–3456* ⊕ *www.americancinematheque.com.*

Cinefamily at The Silent Movie Theatre. Although the name may imply that silent movies are all that show here, this theater has bloomed beyond that with its schedule of quirky indie films and events put together by the organization that runs it, Cinefamily. Regular events include podcast recordings by comedians Doug Benson and Greg Proops, along with the "Heavy Midnites" Friday night movie screenings of offbeat films (recent selections include *Blue Velvet* and *Ghost World*). Silent films do still show here, of course. They run on the first Wednesday of every month, although that's subject to change. ✉ *611 N. Fairfax Ave., Fairfax District* ☎ *323/655–2510* ⊕ *www.cinefamily.org.*

New Beverly Cinema. Indies and classic films are the draw here, along with a low admission price for daily double features. Open since 1978, the theater has yet to upgrade to digital projectors, meaning it is 35-mm-film heaven for those longing for the rich look of film. A bonus is the budget-friendly concession stand. ✉ *7165 Beverly Blvd., Hollywood* ☎ *323/938–4038* ⊕ *www.newbevcinema.com.*

Nuart. Foreign, indie, documentaries, classics, recent releases: there's not much the Nuart doesn't show here, but its eclectic mix of movies attract plenty of L.A. residents. Its film selections, paired with a love for guilty pleasure midnight showings—the title for longest-running performance of Rocky Horror Picture Show belongs to Nuart—constantly places the theater on lists of favorite movie theaters in Los

Angeles. Question-and-answer sessions with directors and actors also happen from time to time here. ✉ *11272 Santa Monica Blvd., West L.A.* ☎ *310/473–8530.*

MOVIE PALACES

ArcLight. Beyond the historically important Cinerama Dome on Sunset Boulevard—that impossible-to-miss golf ball-looking structure built in 1963 to show widescreen Cinerama films—ArcLight is the theater that attempts to problem-solve the issues associated with going to the movies. Assigned seating for movies, space for parking, a shopping area, a restaurant, and a bar—the 15-screen ArcLight has a lot going for it. The event calendar is worth paying attention to, as directors and actors stop in from time to time to chat with audiences; for example, Leonardo DiCaprio stopped in for a Q&A for his role in *The Wolf of Wall Street.* ■TIP→ **Evening shows on the weekend feature "21+" shows, where moviegoers can bring alcoholic beverages into the screening rooms.** Check the website for showtimes. ✉ *6360 Sunset Blvd., Hollywood* ☎ *323/464–4226* ⊕ *www.arclightcinemas.com.*

FAMILY **El Capitan Theatre.** The theater packs in as much preshow entertainment as it can before each movie, adding to the fun activities for children. The ever-changing roster of preshow entertainment includes such antics as onstage ice carving, for Disney's *Frozen,* for instance. El Capitan has an on-site organ player to entertain folks as they find their seats. The "VIP" tickets are pricier than general admission, but the added benefit is reserved seating with popcorn and a drink built into the price. ■TIP→ **The theater also offers a character breakfast before the first showing of certain films.** ✉ *6838 Hollywood Blvd., Hollywood* ☎ *323/467–7674* ⊕ *elcapitan.go.com.*

iPic Theaters. If you're one who loves going out for dinner and a movie, the luxurious iPic Theaters (formerly the Pasadena Gold Class Cinema) takes that concept and upgrades it: patrons can order from an extensive cocktail and food menu and have it brought to their seats during the movie. Current films are what play in the six intimate theaters (seating capacity doesn't go over 48 seats) and members get discounted tickets for movies, which tend to be pricey for nonmembers. The seats are fully reclining and come with a pillow and blanket, in case you want to play up the coziness factor. ✉ *42 Miller Alley, Pasadena* ☎ *626/639–2260* ⊕ *www.ipictheaters.com.*

Vista Theater. Beyond offering first-run films, this theater features a unique, restored Egyptian-style interior—the hieroglyphic details, busts, and red velvet curtains all add to the movie atmosphere. Other bragging points include larger-than-usual leg room—the theater removed nearly half its seats to gain 7 feet of space between rows—and celebrity hands and footprints in cement in the front forecourt (à la TCL Chinese Theatre in Hollywood). ✉ *4473 Sunset Dr., Los Feliz* ☎ *323/660–6639* ⊕ *www.vintagecinemas.com/vista.*

THEATER

The Los Angeles theater scene is still living under the shadow of Broadway, with many theaters choosing to host productions of shows from there, but that doesn't mean one should expect sloppy rehashes of already-seen plays. Indeed, some of the shows may look familiar, but there's still a lot of original work to be seen if you look.

Many of the companies are extremely hardworking and the theater community is constantly on the lookout to develop new talent through supportive programs and workshops. This means there's an eclectic mix of innovative work and well-worn classics; as a theatergoer, that certainly works in your favor.

LA Stage Tix. Working with theaters and arts organizations across Los Angeles, LA Stage Alliance's ticket service provides descriptions of currently running plays (at both large and smaller theaters), along with ways to purchase tickets. Tickets purchased through LA Stage Tix are often available at a discount, so it's worth checking out if you're browsing for a play to attend (or even if you have a certain one in mind). ☎ *213/614–0556* ⊕ *www.lastagetix.com.*

MAJOR THEATERS

Center Theatre Group. Comprising three theaters, Center Theatre Group is the natural go-to for fans of theater in Los Angeles (and, well, Broadway). Each theater has its own style of notable shows, whether they're premieres of plays or touring productions. ✉ *135 N. Grand Ave., Downtown* ☎ *213/972–7211* ⊕ *www.musiccenter.org.*

Mark Taper Forum. The focus at Mark Taper Forum, next door to the Ahmanson Theater in Downtown, is on dramas and comedies. Plenty of shows that premiere here go on to Broadway and off-Broadway theaters (a number of Pulitzer Prize–winning plays have also been developed here). ✉ *135 N. Grand Ave., Downtown* ☎ *213/628–2772* ⊕ *www.centertheatregroup.org.*

Ahmanson Theatre. The largest of L.A.'s Center Group's three theaters is Ahmanson Theatre in Downtown Los Angeles with a varying audience capacity of 1,600 to 2,000, and a number of larger-scale classic revivals, dramas, musicals, and comedies happen here. Recent musical *Leap of Faith* had its world premiere at Ahmanson Theatre and went on to earn a Tony Award nomination in 2012. ✉ *135 N. Grand Ave., Downtown* ☎ *213/628–2772* ⊕ *www. centertheatregroup.org.*

Kirk Douglas Theatre. This Culver City theater, which stages new, modern works, is the smallest venue of the group at 317 seats. It uses its small size to its advantage by hosting more intimate workshops and readings. ✉ *9820 W. Washington Blvd., Culver City* ☎ *213/628–2772* ⊕ *www.centertheatregroup.org.*

Geffen Playhouse. Consistently hosting world premieres (or West Coast premieres) of plays, the Geffen Playhouse is a constant source of critically acclaimed works. Recognizable actors are sometimes featured on the bill (Annette Bening, for example), and plays launched here have wound up on Broadway. With its two stages, there is always something

8

Big-budget musical comedies often find a home at the Ahmanson Theatre.

to watch here. ■ TIP➔ Free events are frequently offered to ticket hold-ers, including "Wine Down Sundays" featuring music and wine sampling before Sunday evening shows. Check the website for details and avail-ability. ✉ *10886 Le Conte Ave., Westwood* ☎ *310/208–5454* ⊕ *www. geffenplayhouse.com.*

John Anson Ford Theatres. It's quite possible that every personality type can find an event here that suits them: this space presents a wide variety of music, dance, theater, film, jazz, Latin, and family events from May to October. The outdoor amphitheater, which holds 1,200, teams up with L.A. County–based organizations to host these events for the summer; they focus on the local communities and artists. A smaller indoor theater, **Inside the Ford,** is used during the win-ter months; however at this writing it is closed for construction. ✉ *2580 Cahuenga Blvd. E., Hollywood* ☎ *323/461–3673* ⊕ *www. fordamphitheater.org.*

Pantages Theatre. If you're looking to see the grand-scale theatrics of a Broadway show in Los Angeles, such as *The Lion King* and *The Book of Mormon,* the 2,703-seat Pantages Theatre is one of the first places to check out. ✉ *6233 Hollywood Blvd., Hollywood* ☎ *800/982–2787* ⊕ *www.hollywoodpantages.com.*

Montalbán Theatre. Plays, musicals, and concerts all happen here, mostly focusing on Latin culture. This midsize theater collaborates with local arts groups and also hosts the occasional sports-themed event, thanks to a basketball court installed on the rooftop. ✉ *1615 N. Vine St., Hol-lywood* ☎ *323/871–2420* ⊕ *www.themontalban.com.*

Saban Theatre. This art deco–style theater was recently named a historic building in Beverly Hills and plays host to concerts and the occasional comedy show. ✉ *8440 Wilshire Blvd., Beverly Hills* ☎ *323/655–0111* ⊕ *www.sabantheatre.org.*

SMALLER THEATERS

The Actors' Gang. Socially conscious, unconventional, and politically themed shows are a focus of the plays here, and beyond the performances, the company focuses on education and outreach programs that form the backbone of its work within the community. Helmed by artistic director Tim Robbins (who was also one of its founders in 1981), the Actors' Gang has managed to go beyond the stage and form programs that benefit not only local students but also prisoners through Prison Project, which conducts acting workshops at California state prisons. Famous actors are also known to do acting stints in plays at the theater from time to time. ■ **TIP→ In summer, the Actors' Gang offers adaptations of Shakespeare for free in Media Park.** Call or check the website for the schedule. ✉ *9070 Venice Blvd., Culver City* ☎ *310/838–4264* ⊕ *www.theactorsgang.com.*

Atwater Village Theatre. Look to this new theater for fresh works by artists that occasionally win local theater awards. With two stages available for year-round performances, Atwater Village Theatre has aligned with three known area theater companies: Ensemble Studio Theatre/Los Angeles (an offshoot of the Ensemble Studio Theatre in New York), Circle X Theatre Co., and the recently added Echo Theater Company. ✉ *3269 Casitas Ave.* ☎ *323/644–1929* ⊕ *www. ensemblestudiotheatrela.org.*

FAMILY **Bob Baker Marionette Theater.** Enchanting marionette puppetry is a decidedly lo-fi way to spend a day with children, but perhaps this is the breath of fresh air parents are looking for. Children can sit on the floor as marionettes walk by, or some lucky young patrons get a head pat from a puppet. The ice-cream treat after the show is a staple of the 53-year-old theater, so plan in some extra time to stay and have a snack. There's a tiny counter with some marionettes available for purchase, in case the show has made you curious about the art. Reservations are required and tickets can be purchased online or over the phone. ✉ *1345 W. 1st St., at Glendale Blvd., Downtown* ☎ *213/250– 9995* ⊕ *www.bobbakermarionettes.com.*

David Henry Hwang Theatre at the Union Center for the Arts. For engaging plays that voice the Asian-American experience, this theater in the Union Center for the Arts is the place to go. The East West Players organization is nearing its 50th anniversary with plenty of theater experience under its belt. The group does some show revivals, but it focuses on original works featuring an Asian-American cast. East West Players also produces plays in conjunction with its Theatre for Youth Program, aiming to get kids of all ages involved with theater. ✉ *120 Judge John Aiso St., Little Tokyo* ☎ *213/625–7000* ⊕ *www. eastwestplayers.org.*

8

Edgemar Center for the Arts. Serving as both a working acting school and theater, Edgemar hosts a variety of events, from original productions by students to plays by outside theater companies (with most material being family-friendly). Beyond its plays, the center also hosts a number of other notable events, including "Cinema at the Edge," its annual independent film festival. The acting school offers classes for adults, children, and teens. ✉ *2437 Main St., Santa Monica* ☎ *310/392–0815* ⊕ *www.edgemarcenter.org.*

Fremont Centre Theatre. The focus of this theater centers on original material and world premieres of plays with professional actors year-round. This small venue is known for its inviting atmosphere, with "talkbacks" arranged after certain shows, encouraging audience members to engage in Q&As with its actors. Ray Bradbury regularly produced shows here for five years before his death in 2012, including a stage adaptation of *Fahrenheit 451.* ✉ *1000 Fremont Ave., South Pasadena* ☎ *626/441–5977* ⊕ *www.fremontcentretheatre.com.*

Hudson Theatres. Typifying plays at the Hudson Theatres is a tall order and with good reason: this triple-threat theater/café/art gallery hosts a variety of local and traveling companies and shows run the gamut of genres. Nestled among a number of small-scale theaters on Theatre Row in Hollywood, this unique space houses three stages as well as Comedy Central, which regularly stages standup comedy shows. ✉ *6539 Santa Monica Blvd., Hollywood* ☎ *323/856–4249* ⊕ *www.hudsontheatre.com.*

Odyssey Theatre. Known for its strong acting, the Odyssey Theatre presents largely traditional dramas (plays you may not know but should) in an intimate space, typically with astute direction and taut, powerful acting. It also produces contemporary, experimental plays (or thoughtful explorations of the classics) throughout the season and plays host to visiting companies and limited run plays. In 2014 the Odyssey celebrates its 45th anniversary as a theater group. ✉ *2055 S. Sepulveda Blvd., West L.A.* ☎ *310/477–2055* ⊕ *www.odysseytheatre.com.*

Pacific Resident Theatre. Focusing on lesser-known plays by recognizable playwrights and new works, this theater has earned local theater awards and a respectable following. ✉ *703 Venice Blvd., Venice* ☎ *310/822–8392* ⊕ *www.pacificresidenttheatre.com.*

The Pasadena Playhouse. Solidly done plays and musicals, occasionally featuring known TV and movie actors are what this theater is mostly known for. Although not all of the plays are first-run works, the theater is committed to original plays through its theater program, HOTHOUSE at The Playhouse, which helps develop new plays. The playhouse also holds the honor of official state theater of California. Tours of the venue are available by arrangement. ✉ *39 S. El Molino Ave., Pasadena* ☎ *626/356–7529* ⊕ *www.pasadenaplayhouse.org.*

The REDCAT (Roy and Edna Disney Cal Arts Theater). Inside the Walt Disney Concert Hall, this theater serves as a space for innovative performance and visual art. Shows can be anything from dance to theater, music, film, and lectures, and the gallery features changing art installations. Tickets are also reasonably priced at $25 and under for most events. ✉ *631 W. 2nd St., Downtown* ☎ *213/237–2800* ⊕ *www.redcat.org.*

FAMILY **Santa Monica Playhouse.** Housing three theaters, this venue brings a number of original plays, touring companies, poetry readings, spoken word events, and revival shows to the stage. A number of plays are done with families in mind as part of the Family Theatre Musical Matinee Series, featuring reworked classic plays. A number of educational programs and workshops are available for people of all ages. ✉ *1211 4th St., Santa Monica* ☎ *310/394–9779* ⊕ *www.santamonicaplayhouse.com.*

Theatre of NOTE. Preferring to stick with experimental plays by cutting-edge (albeit, lesser-known) authors, this theater focuses on producing unique works and encouraging new artists through its Young Writers Program and NOTEworthy, a staged reading series focused on developing new work. ✉ *1517 N. Cahuenga Blvd., north of Sunset Blvd., Hollywood* ☎ *323/856–8611* ⊕ *www.theatreofnote.com.*

FAMILY **Theatre West.** Performing classic plays and new works year-round, this theater co-op has been in operation since 1962 and has won awards for its work over the years. **Storybook Theatre** performs interactive plays for a younger age set (three- to nine-year-olds). ✉ *3333 Cahuenga Blvd. W, Hollywood* ☎ *323/851–7977 Theatre West, 818/761–2203 Storybook Theatre* ⊕ *www.theatrewest.org.*

FAMILY **Will Geer Theatricum Botanicum.** This open-air theater puts on classic, as well as new and relevant, plays from June to October. The gardens have sitting areas for picnics before the show; the company also hosts dinner (and a show) on certain nights. ■**TIP→** Sunday is a great day for families with special shows performed with children in mind. ✉ *1419 N. Topanga Canyon Blvd., Topanga* ☎ *310/455–3723* ⊕ *www.theatricum.com.*

THEATER ENSEMBLES

Cornerstone Theater Company. Performances by this theater company not only hit on socially conscious themes, but get attendees into the heart of Los Angeles: works are performed not in regular theaters but in untraditional venues that center on community. One of their more recent plays, *Love on San Pedro* was performed at Los Angeles Mission on Skid Row, for instance. ✉ *708 Traction Ave., Downtown* ☎ *213/613–1700* ⊕ *www.cornerstonetheater.org.*

InterACT Theatre Company. Beyond its renowned acting and original plays, this theater ensemble also puts on educational programs and readings, despite not having a permanent space. ☎ *818/765–8732* ⊕ *www.interactla.org.*

Fodor'sChoice **Walt Disney Concert Hall.** One of the architectural wonders of Los Angeles, the 2,265-seat Walt Disney Concert Hall is a sculptural monument ★ of gleaming, curved steel designed by master architect Frank Gehry. It's part of a complex that includes a public park, gardens, and shops, as well as two outdoor amphitheaters. This is the home of Los Angeles Master Chorale as well as Los Angeles Philharmonic, under the baton of Music Director Gustavo Dudamel, an international celebrity in his own right. Audio tours and guided tours are available. The complimentary walking tours, which start at noon, take an hour and begin in the lobby. ✉ *111 S. Grand Ave., Downtown* ☎ *323/850–2000* ⊕ *www.laphil.org.*

8

Billy Wilder Theater. Serving as the movie theater for both the Hammer Museum (where it is located) and the UCLA Film & Television Archive, this shared space presents a number of acclaimed film and television screenings, including movies from the early days of cinema, foreign films, and those recently restored by the archive. The Hammer Museum (⊕ *http://hammer.ucla.edu/programs/programs*) produces its own events for the theater, including readings, lectures, and conversations with artists (recent appearances include film director David Lynch, as well as author Jonathan Lethem). ∎TIP➔ **Programs put on by the Hammer Museum are free; however, screenings by the UCLA Film & Television Archive have charged admission with a ticket.** It's best to check in advance to determine whether a paid ticket is necessary. ✉ *10899 Wilshire Blvd.* ☎ *310/206–8013 UCLA Film & Television Archive, 310/443–7074 Hammer Museum* ⊕ *www. cinema.ucla.edu*

SHOPPING

Updated
by Sarah
Amandalore

Los Angeles is known as the City of Angels, and it really is heaven for shopping. The scene is incredibly varied: up-and-coming local designers, the highest of high-end boutiques, and plenty of flea markets combine to cement the city's relaxed yet stylish reputation. Thanks to the notorious L.A. sprawl, far-flung neighborhoods offer different duds for different tastes. Residents generally split the city in two—by Eastside (the Hollywood side) and Westside (the beach side)—but many enclaves between are peppered with shops you won't want to miss.

The sun-and-sand beach culture and Hollywood stars provide big influences on the shopping scene. Stylists are always on the lookout for the newest trends and looks for the pretty young things they dress, and emerging designers take inspiration from what's being worn on the street.

Paparazzi are right there to capture the looks of the stylish starlets the second they're worn, whether they're parading on a red carpet or seen emerging from a hot spot. Together the style makers set the cutting-edge pace—what you see here on the racks will be big back home but maybe not for another six months.

"Sunny and 70" is the weather forecast for a good part of the year, and the climate means that most shopping centers are open-air, to allow you to park your car and walk from shop to shop. This foot traffic also means that good eateries open near good shops, and you can always find somewhere delicious to dine and covertly star-watch.

Those new to Los Angeles usually start at Rodeo Drive in Beverly Hills, not far from Hollywood. This tourist hot spot is a destination for window-shopping along the cluster of blocks and can provide a few hours of entertainment—or, if you're looking for a designer logo bag or red-carpet wear, get ready to do some serious spending.

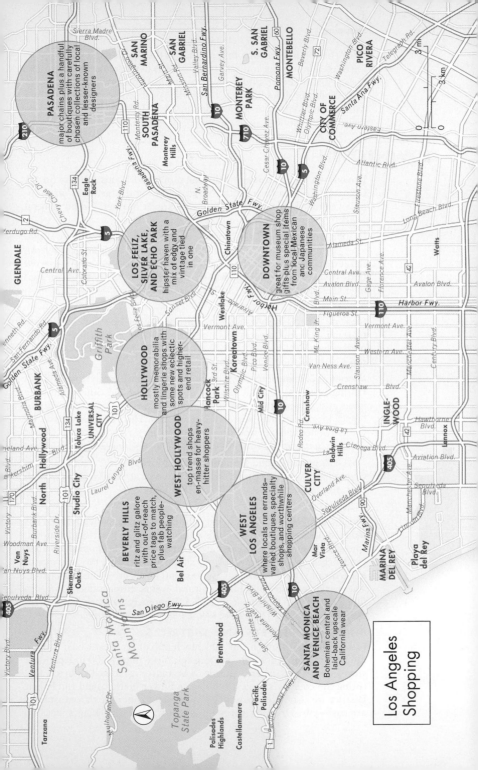

PASADENA
major chains plus a handful of boutiques with carefully chosen collections of local and lesser-known designers

LOS FELIZ, SILVER LAKE, AND ECHO PARK
hipster haven with a mix of edgy and vintage tied in one

DOWNTOWN
great for museum shop gifts plus special items from local Mexican and Japanese communities

HOLLYWOOD
mostly memorabilia and lingerie shops with some new eclectic spots and higher-end retail

WEST HOLLYWOOD
top trend shops en-masse for heavy-hitter shoppers

BEVERLY HILLS
ritz and glitz galore with out-of-reach price tags to match, plus fab people-watching

WEST LOS ANGELES
where locals run errands—varied boutiques, specialty shops, and worthwhile shopping centers

SANTA MONICA AND VENICE BEACH
Bohemian central and laid-back upscale California wear

Los Angeles Shopping

Then you can hop in your car and absorb the city's artsier side, exploring eclectic boutiques and scouring for deals in the numerous neighborhoods: finding down-and-dirty bargains in Downtown, hitting funky West Hollywood, kicking back with the laid-back beach vibe of Santa Monica and Venice, or going edgy in Silver Lake, Echo Park, or Los Feliz. Let the games begin.

DOWNTOWN

Downtown L.A. is dotted with ethnic neighborhoods (Olvera Street, Chinatown, Koreatown, Little Tokyo) and several large, open-air shopping venues (the Fashion District, the Flower Market, Grand Central Market, the Toy District, and the Jewelry District).

It offers an urban bargain hunter's dream shopping experience if you know precisely what you're looking for (like diamonds and gems from the Jewelry District) or if you're willing to be tempted by unexpected finds (piñatas from Olvera Street, slippers from Chinatown, or lacquered chopsticks from Little Tokyo).

HOME FURNISHINGS

Skeletons in the Closet. At this gift shop run by the Los Angeles County Coroner, you can snag everything from toe-tag key chains to body-outline beach towels. ⊠ *1104 N. Mission Rd., at Morengo St., Downtown* ☎ *323/343–0760.*

Museum of Contemporary Art Store. Find Ed Ruscha beach towels, Keith Haring watches, Comme des Garçons wallets, and other high-style items at the Museum of Contemporary Art Store. There are plenty of books, magazines, and posters from exhibits. There are branches at the Geffen Contemporary and the Pacific Design Center. ⊠ *250 S. Grand Ave., Downtown* ☎ *213/621–1710* ⊕ *www.moca.org.*

MOCA at the Pacific Design Center. MOCA at the Pacific Design Center has a selection of art catalogs and rare art books. ⊠ *8687 Melrose Ave., West Hollywood* ☎ *310/289–5223.*

MARKETS

Grand Central Market. For almost 100 years, this open-air market has tempted Angelenos with all kinds of produce, fresh meats and seafood, spices, and fresh tortillas. These days, while overstuffed *pupusas,* Cuban sandwiches, and kebabs still satisfy shoppers on the go, the oft-expanding array of vendors make it easy to spend hours browsing and tasting. The market occasionally hosts cultural events, from coffee tastings to film screenings to live music. ⊠ *317 S. Broadway, between 3rd and 4th Sts., Downtown* ☎ *213/624–2378* ⊕ *www.grandcentralmarket.com.*

SHOPPING STREETS AND DISTRICTS

Fashion District. Although this 100-block hub of the West Coast fashion industry is mainly a wholesale market, more than 1,000 independent stores sell to the general public. The massive Flower District, featuring the country's largest wholesale flower market, and the Fabric District are also here. Bargaining is expected, but note that most sales are cash-only. Dressing rooms are scarce, as are parking spaces on

TOP SHOPPING EXPERIENCES

3rd Street and The Grove. Stores on 3rd Street range from independent designer boutiques to chic houseware havens. And just blocks away, The Grove, an open-air shopping area, has brand name stores, restaurants, the adjoining Farmers Market, and celebrity sighting.

Main Street, Santa Monica. Three blocks away from the ocean, this is the choice for easy Sunday shopping after the Farmers Market or when you'd like to also visit the Santa Monica Pier. An added draw is the variety of street performers who are actually quite good.

Melrose Avenue, Melrose Place, and Nearby Robertson. This is clothing for It-girls and It-guys and the paparazzi who chase them. Come for unique purchases that say "I'm on the list" even before the bouncer opens the red rope to let you in.

Rodeo Drive. There are a surprising variety of shops that are reasonably priced on the surrounding streets—but Rodeo Drive is not to be missed for the quintessential Beverly Hills experience.

Sunset Boulevard in Silver Lake. If you have a penchant for perfectly worn jeans and a countercultural vibe, this laid-back locale will suit your tastes. With its fashionably rough edges and dirty-chic clientele, Silver Lake is the edgy counterpart to more upscale Los Feliz.

weekends. ⊠ *Roughly between I-10 and 7th St., San Pedro and Main Sts., Downtown* ⊕ *www.fashiondistrict.org.*

Santee Alley. Situated in the Fashion District, Santee Alley is known for back-alley deals on knock-offs of designer sunglasses, jewelry, handbags, shoes, and clothing. Be prepared to haggle, and don't lose sight of your wallet. Weekend crowds can be overwhelming, but there's plenty of street food to keep your energy up. ⊠ *Santee St. and Maple Ave. from Olympic Blvd. to 11th St., Downtown* ⊕ *www.thesanteealley.com.*

Jewelry District. Filled with bargain hunters, these crowded sidewalks resemble a slice of Manhattan. Expect to save big on everything from wedding bands to sparkling belt buckles. The more upscale stores are along Hill Street between 6th and 7th streets. There's a parking garage next door on Broadway. ⊠ *Between Olive St. and Broadway from 5th to 8th St., Downtown.*

Fodor's Choice ★ **Olvera Street.** Historic buildings line this redbrick walkway overhung with grape vines. At dozens of clapboard stalls you can browse south-of-the-border goods—leather sandals, woven blankets, devotional candles, and the like—as well as cheap toys and souvenirs. With the musicians and cafés providing the soundtrack, the area is constantly lively. ⊠ *Between Cesar Chavez Ave. and Arcadia St., Downtown* ⊕ *www.olvera-street.com.*

Toy District. This 14-block area of wholesale toy dealers is for adventurous shoppers in search of knock-off versions of popular toys. Find stuffed animals you can buy for loose change or electronic games for bigger bills. Most vendors are in the wholesale business, but plenty will also sell to anyone with cash. ⊠ *Bordered by 3rd and 5th Sts., and Los Angeles and San Pedro Sts., Downtown.*

HOLLYWOOD AND THE STUDIOS

Local shops may be a mixed bag, but at least you can read the stars below your feet as you browse along Hollywood Boulevard. In the past, lingerie and movie memorabilia stores have predominated here, but now there are numerous options in the retail-hotel-dining-entertainment complex Hollywood & Highland welcome addition to the scene.

Hollywood impersonators (Michael Jackson, Marilyn Monroe, Johnny Depp's Jack Sparrow) join break-dancers and other street entertainers in keeping tourists entertained on Hollywood Boulevard's sidewalks near the Dolby Theatre, home to the Oscars.

Along La Brea Avenue, there is plenty of trendy, quirky, and hip merchandise, from records to furniture and clothing.

HOLLYWOOD

BOOKS AND MUSIC

Fodor's Choice ★ Amoeba Records. Touted as the "World's Largest Independent Record Store," Amoeba is a playground for music lovers, with a knowledgeable staff and a focus on local artists. Catch in-store appearances by artists and bands that play sold-out shows at venues down the road. Find a rich stock of new and used CDs and DVDs, LPs, and 45s, an impressive cache of collectibles, and walls filled with concert posters. ⊠ *6400 W. Sunset Blvd., at Cahuenga Blvd., Hollywood* ☎ *323/245–6400* ⊕ *www.amoeba.com.*

Larry Edmunds Bookshop. After more than 70 years on the boulevard, this cinema and theater bookstore maintains old-school courtesy and charm. Books on movies and about the craft of moviemaking are the main draw, but you can also find thousands of posters from shows and movies from *Ain't Misbehavin'* to *Zelig.* ⊠ *6644 Hollywood Blvd., Hollywood* ☎ *323/463–3273* ⊕ *www.larryedmunds.com.*

Meltdown. The largest comic-book store on the West Coast is a monument to the artistry, wit, and downright weirdness of titles ranging from *Ghost World* to *Booty Babe.* Graphic novels, toys, posters, and a gallery with comic-related art and photography supplement the scores of comic books, making for a sophisticated blend of offerings. The NerdMelt Showroom in the back of the store hosts a variety of smart, quirky events, including some of the best comedy performances in the city. ⊠ *7522 Sunset Blvd., Los Angeles, CA* ☎ *323/851–7223* ⊕ *www.meltcomics.com.*

Samuel French, Theatre & Film Bookshop. If you're interested in theater or film, this longtime local favorite has an astounding collection of books on subjects ranging from how to write your first screenplay to where to find an agent. There's also a huge selection of plays. ⊠ *7623 Sunset Blvd., Hollywood* ☎ *866/598–8449* ⊕ *www.samuelfrench.com/bookstore.*

CLOTHING

Jet Rag. Be prepared to dig for treasure. Racks and stacks are filled with everything from bell-bottom jeans to polyester tops to weathered leather jackets. Known for its reasonable prices, Jet Rag takes things one step further on Sunday with an all-day parking-lot sale where everything goes for $1. ⊠ *825 N. La Brea Ave., Hollywood* ☎ *323/939–0528.*

Lost & Found. The owner of this place describes it as "Alice in Wonderland meets Jimi Hendrix." It's actually six storefronts offering clothing for men, women, and children; brass jewelry from France; African silk batiks; and other goodies handpicked from around the world. ✉ *6320 Yucca St., Hollywood* ☎ *323/856–5872.*

MALLS AND SHOPPING CENTERS

Bowl Store. Music buffs can appreciate the cheeky fun of eating corn flakes from a "Hollywood Bowl" bowl available at this shop next to the outdoor music venue. ✉ *2301 N. Highland Ave., Hollywood* ☎ *213/972–3440* ⊕ *www.laphilstore.com* ⊙ *Closed Oct.–June.*

Hollywood & Highland. Full of designer shops (BCBGMaxAzria, Louis Vuitton) and chain stores (Victoria's Secret, Fossil, and Sephora), this entertainment complex is a huge tourist magnet. The design pays tribute to the city's film legacy, with a grand staircase leading up to a pair of three-story-tall stucco elephants, a nod to the 1916 movie *Intolerance.* Pause at the entrance arch, called Babylon Court, which frames a picture-perfect view of the Hollywood Sign. On the second level, next to the Dolby Theatre, is a visitor information center with maps, brochures, and a multilingual staff. The streets nearby provide the setting for Sunday's Hollywood Farmers Market, where you're likely to spot a celebrity or two picking up fresh produce or stopping to eat breakfast from the food vendors. ✉ *Hollywood Blvd. and Highland Ave., Hollywood* ☎ *323/817–0220* ⊕ *www.hollywoodandhighland.com.*

Space 15 Twenty. A unique retail space in the heart of Hollywood, Space 15 Twenty is anchored by an Urban Outfitters that's flanked by galleries and boutiques, a skateboard shop, and an art and architecture bookstore. They're all connected by an outdoor courtyard near the Sunday Hollywood Farmers Market. ✉ *1520 N. Cahuenga, at Cahuenga Blvd., Hollywood* ☎ *323/465–1893* ⊕ *www.space15twenty.com.*

STUDIO CITY

Although Studio City offers plenty of strip mall styles, this enclave not far from Hollywood gets a dose of sophistication from Tejunga Village, a leafy stretch between Tejunga Avenue and Moorpark Street filled with cafés and restaurants.

CLOTHING

Dari. Bohemian chic kicked up a notch is what you'll get at this boutique, which offers separates in warm, rich colors, balanced by a selection of structured dresses and blazers from the likes of Equipment and Iro. ✉ *12184 Ventura Blvd., Studio City* ☎ *818/762–3274* ⊕ *www. shopdari.com.*

Faire Frou Frou. This is a lingerie shop first and foremost, but the pretty shop also stocks lace-trimmed chemises, silk camisoles, and bustiers. Find lacy and racy underthings along with more practical, but still sexy, options from La Perla and Fleur de England. ✉ *13017-A Ventura Blvd., near Coldwater Canyon Ave.* ☎ *818/783–4970* ⊕ *www. fairefroufrou.com.*

BURBANK

It's not a major shopping destination, but Burbank has some offbeat shops that are well worth exploring.

CLOTHING

It's a Wrap. Looking for castoffs from *Hannah Montana, All My Children, Star Trek,* or dozens of other productions? The wardrobe departments of movie and TV studios and production companies ship clothes here daily. A "letter of authenticity" accompanies each bargain (that's 35%–95% off retail). Another store is open near Beverly Hills, on South Robertson Boulevard. ✉ *3315 W. Magnolia Blvd., at California St., Burbank* ☏ *818/567–7366* ⊕ *www.itsawraphollywood.com.*

Playclothes Vintage Fashions. This off-the-beaten-path shop offers tons of vintage clothing from all eras and an especially impressive selection of accessories found in cases and on display throughout the store. ✉ *3100 W. Magnolia Blvd., Burbank* ☏ *818/557–8447* ⊕ *www. vintageplayclothes.com.*

LOS FELIZ

Stroll past the mansions on Los Feliz Boulevard before hitting the vintage shops and sophisticated boutiques with old-school tendencies—think refurbished brick and classic decor.

BOOKS

Skylight Books. A neighborhood bookstore through and through, Skylight has excellent sections devoted to kids, fiction, and film, plus lots of magazines and journals and a space devoted to urban culture. The owners play host to book discussion groups and present panels and author readings with hip literati. ✉ *1818 N. Vermont Ave., Los Feliz* ☏ *323/660–1175.*

CLOTHING

La La Ling. This shop offers more than your run-of-the-mill kiddies clothes—it stocks a particularly hip take on tot-size versions of adult staples (Splendid T-shirts, Joe's jeans). There are also stylish baby slings and diaper bags for parents. ✉ *1810 N. Vermont Ave., Los Feliz* ☏ *323/664–4400* ⊕ *www.lalaling.com.*

Panty Raid. It's all about fun and functional undergarments here, including low-rise thongs from Cosabella and Hanky Panky. The staff is likely to guess a bra size on sight, too. ✉ *1953 Hillhurst Ave., Los Feliz* ☏ *323/668–1888* ⊕ *www.pantyraidshop.com.*

SquaresVille. Vintage and recent clothing, including loads of fun shoes and accessories, share rack space at this shop with a rockin' vibe. Buy, sell, trade—it's all good here. ✉ *1800 N. Vermont Ave., Los Feliz* ☏ *323/669–8464* ⊕ *squaresvillevintage.tumblr.com.*

GIFTS AND SOUVENIRS

Soap Plant Wacko/La Luz de Jesus Gallery. This pop-culture supermarket offers a wide range of items, including rows of books on art and design. But it's the novelty stock that makes the biggest impression, with animal masks, X-ray specs, and hula dancer lamps. The in-store gallery in the back focuses on underground art. ⊠ *4633 Hollywood Blvd., Los Feliz* ☎ *323/663–0122* ⊕ *www.soapplant.com.*

Y-Que Trading Post. Here you can find T-shirts emblazoned with celebrity mug shots, or opt for a design of your own. There are also Sea Monkeys, Magic Gardens, and other kitschy items. On weekends, crowds of revelers often shop here until midnight. ⊠ *1770 N. Vermont Ave., Los Feliz* ☎ *323/668–0117* ⊕ *www.yque.com.*

SILVER LAKE

The action here is concentrated along Sunset Boulevard, where the young and hip come to sip artisanal coffee and peruse the one-of-a-kind wares.

BOOKS

Secret Headquarters. This could be the coolest comic-book store on the planet, with a selection to satisfy both the geekiest of collectors and those more interested in artistic and literary finds. Rich wood floors and a leather chair near the front window mark the sophisticated setting, which features wall displays neatly organized with new comics and filing cabinets marked DC and Marvel filled with old classics like *Superman* and newer favorites like *Buffy* and *Saga.* ⊠ *3817 W. Sunset Blvd., Silver Lake* ☎ *323/666–2228* ⊕ *www.thesecretheadquarters.com.*

CLOTHING

Clare Vivier. Clare Vivier's chic handbags are classic French glamour by way of laid-back California, and her eponymous Silver Lake boutique follows the same aesthetic. Inside, find her full line of messenger bags, fold-over clutches, and iPad cases, all of them made locally in Los Angeles. ⊠ *3339 Sunset Blvd., Silver Lake* ☎ *323/665–2476* ⊕ *www.clarevivier.com.*

Lake. Styles here are for the sophisticated Eastsider: a little edgy and always comfortably chic. Find Isabel Marant shoes, Clare Vivier handbags, and John Derian decoupage trinkets. The airy shop, flooded with natural light, has lovely gifts like sweet-smelling French soaps. ⊠ *1618 1/2 Silverlake Blvd., Silver Lake* ☎ *323/664–6522* ⊕ *www.lakeboutique.com.*

COSMETICS

Le Pink & Co. This small and friendly beauty shop is decorated with vintage perfume bottles. In stock are cult beauty brands such as Dr. Hauschka, Rosebud Salve, and Caswell Massey, as well as such hard-to-find brands as Eminence Organics. ⊠ *3820 W. Sunset Blvd., Silver Lake* ☎ *323/661–7465* ⊕ *www.lovelepink.com.*

FOOD AND WINE

Silver Lake Wine. Boutique wineries from around the world provide this shop with the vintages that fill the floor-to-ceiling racks. Looking unassuming in jeans and T-shirts, the knowledgeable staff can steer you to the right wine or spirits for any occasion. You can wet your whistle at tastings on Sunday, Monday, and Thursday. Summer social events are held at nearby Barnsdall Art Park. ⊠ *2395 Glendale Blvd., Silver Lake* ☎ *323/662–9024* ⊕ *www.silverlakewine.com.*

9

HOUSEWARES

Yolk. Stocked with a little bit of everything you'll want to get or give, this shop has a spot-on selection of fresh designer goods. Look for Le Feu de L'eau candles, AMT bags, and Design House Stockholm barware, as well as a back room with children's organic cotton clothing and bedding and nontoxic wood toys. You'll also find handcrafted jewelry by local designers and works by local artists. ⊠ *1626 Silver Lake Blvd., Silver Lake* ☎ *323/660–4315* ⊕ *www.shopyolk.com.*

ECHO PARK

Scruffier than neighboring Silver Lake, this increasingly cool area has a scrappy, do-it-yourself appeal. Secondhand stores squeeze in alongside vegan restaurants, hip dive bars, and friendly boutiques stocked with clothes by local designers.

CLOTHING

Flounce Vintage. Flowy scarves, rhinestone baubles, beaded cardigans, and a great stock of solid and print dresses, including chiffon flapper dresses from the 1920s and swingy 1940s styles, await in this girlishly sweet store. ⊠ *1555 Echo Park Ave., Echo Park* ☎ *213/481–1975* ⊕ *www.flouncevintage.com.*

BEVERLY HILLS AND THE WESTSIDE

BEVERLY HILLS

BEAUTY

MAC. This beauty emporium is what's called a "professional" store, with lines of products not available at the chain's regular outlets. This is also a place to arrange makeup lessons or all-out makeovers, or even to prepare for red carpet or other special events. The artists here are fashion show and award-season veterans. ⊠ *133 N. Robertson Blvd., West Hollywood* ☎ *310/271–9137* ⊕ *www.maccosmetics.com.*

BOOKS

Taschen. Philippe Starck designed the space to evoke a cool 1920s Parisian salon—a perfect showcase for the coffee-table books about architecture, travel, culture, and (often racy) photography. A suspended glass-cube gallery space in back hosts rotating art, photo exhibits, and limited edition books. ⊠ *354 N. Beverly Dr., Beverly Hills* ☎ *310/274–4300* ⊕ *www.taschen.com.*

CLOTHING

Anto Distinctive Shirt Maker. This atelier has been in the custom shirt-making business since the 1950s and has had an impressive list of clients, from Frank Sinatra to Arnold Schwarzenegger. ⊠ *258 N. Beverly Dr., Beverly Hills* ☎ *310/278–4500* ⊕ *www.antoshirt.com.*

BCBG Max Azria. This designer offers affordable designs that attract young celebs: romantic dresses, teeny tops, and fun accessories. ⊠ *443 N. Rodeo Dr., Beverly Hills* ☎ *310/275–3024* ⊕ *www.bcbg.com.*

The Farmers Market in West Hollywood, an L.A. institution

Burberry. Here's proof that everything old can be new again—British designer Christopher Bailey put this distinctive plaid on everything from tot-size kilts to sexy swimwear. Classic trench coats and English lace also get sexy, modern updates. There's another location in the Beverly Center mall. ⊠ *9560 Wilshire Blvd., Beverly Hills* ☎ *310/550–4500* ⊕ *us.burberry.com.*

Carroll & Co. Dapper is the name of the game at this long-standing traditional men's clothing store, which has dressed such icons as Cary Grant and Clark Gable. You can still find quality goods, excellent service, and styles that endure. ⊠ *425 N. Canon Dr., Beverly Hills* ☎ *310/273–9060* ⊕ *www.carrollandco.com.*

Céline. French designer Phoebe Philo creates fearlessly eclectic ensembles, pairing bright colors and bold patterns in a way that feels fun and fresh. ⊠ *319 N. Rodeo Dr., Beverly Hills, Beverly Hills* ☎ *310/888–0120* ⊕ *www.celine.com.*

Chanel. Ladylike classics—tailored tweed suits and softly scented perfumes—from this gleaming white corner flagship are sure to be staples for years to come. ⊠ *400 N. Rodeo Dr., Beverly Hills* ☎ *310/278–5500* ⊕ *www.chanel.com.*

Christian Dior. Fans of the French label can browse the latest fashions, accessories, fragrances, and beauty products in a sparkling glass-fronted space. ⊠ *309 N. Rodeo Dr., Beverly Hills* ☎ *310/859–4700* ⊕ *www.dior.com.*

Curve. This shop helped set the tone for Robertston Boulevard. Layers of chiffon, lace, silk, and leather create a tough yet feminine aesthetic. Curve's own line rubs elbows with fresh designers like Rochas and Pierre Balmain. ✉ *154 N. Robertson Blvd., between Beverly Hills and West Hollywood, West Hollywood* ☎ *310/360–8008* ⊕ *www.shopcurve.com.*

Dolce & Gabbana. Ornately designed and vividly colored attire and accessories by the renowned Italian design team is on full display at these adjoining men's and women's boutiques. ✉ *312 N. Rodeo Dr., Beverly Hills* ☎ *310/888–8701* ⊕ *www.dolcegabbana.com.*

Emporio Armani. Sleek suits, separates, and accessories are the draw at this spot that offers a more casual take on the traditional Armani cachet. ✉ *9533 Brighton Way, Beverly Hills* ☎ *310/271–7790* ⊕ *www.armani. com/us/emporioarmani.*

Fendi. Karl Lagerfield's latest designs have more-subtle branding, but the signature Double F logo can still be found on some of the fashions and accessories at this West Coast outpost. ✉ *355 N. Rodeo Dr., Beverly Hills* ☎ *310/276–8888* ⊕ *www.fendi.com.*

Giorgio Armani. Heavy-hitter Armani is known for great tailoring and fine fabrics in clothing for both men and women. ✉ *436 N. Rodeo Dr., Beverly Hills* ☎ *310/271–5555* ⊕ *www.armani.com.*

Gucci. This designer goes for a completely modernist aesthetic. Look for lean, sexy, and mainly black clothing upstairs and the signature bags downstairs. ✉ *347 N. Rodeo Dr., Beverly Hills* ☎ *310/278–3451* ⊕ *www.gucci.com.*

Juicy Couture. Wearing drawstring pants and matching hoodies in bright colors only became acceptable on Rodeo Drive after Juicy hit the fashion scene. Cute and casual dresses round out the offerings. ✉ *456 N. Rodeo Dr., Beverly Hills* ☎ *310/550–0736* ⊕ *www.juicycouture.com.*

Lily et Cie. Rita Watnick's red-carpet shop is more a museum of Hollywood's golden-era garments than a run-of-the-mill vintage boutique. You might find a price tag marked $100,000 on a vintage Chanel cocktail dress or a Givenchy evening gown. ✉ *9044 Burton Way, Beverly Hills* ☎ *310/724–5757* ⊕ *www.lilyetcie.com.*

Prada. The Rem Koolhaas–designed Italian showcase is so cool it doesn't even have a sign out front, but its 20-foot-wide staircases and funhouse curves offer an inviting way to see the classy clothes, shoes, and bags. ✉ *343 N. Rodeo Dr., Beverly Hills* ☎ *310/278–8661.*

Roberto Cavalli. With wild prints and sexy designs, this decadent Italian style is perfect for the men and women of the club scene. ✉ *362 N. Rodeo Dr., Beverly Hills* ☎ *310/276–6006* ⊕ *www.robertocavalli.com.*

Ted Baker. Preppy menswear with quirky touches, including polo shirts with plaid collars, is what you'll find here. The selection of women's clothing includes lots of pastels and classic tailoring. ✉ *131 N. Robertson Blvd., West Hollywood, Beverly Hills* ☎ *310/550–7855* ⊕ *www.tedbaker.com.*

Theodore. One of the few indie clothing stores in the area, Theodore is a haven for the young and perhaps rebellious to find James Perse T-shirts, jeans of all labels, and hoodies aplenty. Upstairs, browse the avant-garde designer duds from names like Ann Demeulemeester and

Jean Paul Gaultier. Next door, Theodore Man has faux-scruffy leather jackets and other items for the guys. ⊠ *336 N. Camden Dr., Beverly Hills* ☎ *310/276–0663* ⊕ *www.theodorebh.com.*

Tory Burch. Preppy, stylish, and colorful clothes appropriate for a road trip to Palm Springs or a flight to Palm Beach fill this flagship boutique. ⊠ *366 N. Rodeo Dr., Beverly Hills* ☎ *310/274–2394* ⊕ *www. toryburch.com.*

Traffic. Men with a taste for luxe without stuffiness come here for Paul Smith, Jil Sander, or Comme des Garcons. Traffic has everything from J Brand Jeans to Alexander McQueen. ⊠ *Beverly Center, 8500 Beverly Blvd., 6th fl., West Hollywood* ☎ *310/659–4313* ⊕ *www.shoptrafficla.com.*

Versace. With its temple dome ceiling and recherché design, this is just the place for a dramatic red-carpet gown, along with bold bags, sunglasses, and accessories. It also stocks primo menswear. ⊠ *248 N. Rodeo Dr., Beverly Hills* ☎ *310/205–3921* ⊕ *us.versace.com.*

Yves Saint Laurent. Adorned with a simple YSL, this spacious boutique carries an extensive collection of ready-to-wear fashions, shoes, and handbags from the French label. ⊠ *469 N. Rodeo Dr., Beverly Hills* ☎ *310/271–4110.*

DEPARTMENT STORES

Barneys New York. This is truly an impressive one-stop shop for high fashion. The Co-op section introduces indie designers before they make it big. Shop for beauty products, shoes, and accessories on the first floor, then wind your way up the staircase for couture. Keep your eyes peeled for fabulous and/or famous folks eating deli-style lunches at Barney Greengrass on the top floor. ⊠ *9570 Wilshire Blvd., Beverly Hills* ☎ *310/276–4400* ⊕ *www.barneys.com.*

Henri Bendel. This beloved New York boutique has found its way to Los Angeles replete with high-end handbags, jewelry, and accessories. ⊠ *Beverly Center, 8500 Beverly Blvd., West Hollywood* ☎ *310/358–9378* ⊕ *www.henribendel.com.*

Neiman Marcus. This is luxury shopping at its finest. The couture salon frequently trots out designer trunk shows, and most locals go right for the shoe department. ⊠ *9700 Wilshire Blvd., Beverly Hills* ☎ *310/550–5900* ⊕ *www.neimanmarcus.com.*

FOOD AND WINE

American Tea Room. Some like it hot; some like it iced. Silver tins lining the walls contain 300 varieties of tea, with each color-coded by the tea's region of origin. Baskets, boxes, and teapots make unique souvenirs. ⊠ *401 N. Canon Dr., at Brighton Way, Beverly Hills* ☎ *310/271–7922* ⊕ *www.americantearoom.com.*

HOUSEWARES

Gearys of Beverly Hills. Since 1930, this has been the ultimate destination for those seeking the most exquisite fine china, crystal, silver, and jewelry, mostly from classic sources like Wedgwood, Baccarat, and Royal Crown Derby. There's another location on Rodeo Drive. ⊠ *351 N. Beverly Dr., Beverly Hills* ☎ *310/273–4741* ⊕ *www.gearys.com.*

9

DID YOU KNOW?

Rodeo Drive is the main drag of the chic shopping district bordered by Santa Monica Boulevard, Wilshire Boulevard, and Beverly Drive.

Moss at SLS Beverly Hills. For home design that's a notch above luxurious, Moss can't be beat. Next to the lauded restaurant Baazar, Moss's offerings are both whimsical and surreal. A square pedestal of Moliere? An artisan model boat? Be surprised at how much you just may think that you need them. ⊠ *SLS Hotel at Beverly Hills, 465 S. La Cienega, near Beverly Hills* ☎ *310/246–5565.*

JEWELRY AND ACCESSORIES

Bulgari. Bold, contemporary Italian jewelry, watches, and other luxurious necessities are the order of the day at Bulgari. ⊠ *401 N. Rodeo Dr., Beverly Hills* ☎ *310/858–9216* ⊕ *us.bulgari.com.*

Cartier. Cartier has a bridal collection to sigh for in its chandeliered and respectfully hushed showroom, along with more playful colored stones and an Asian-inspired line. ⊠ *370 N. Rodeo Dr., Beverly Hills* ☎ *310/275–4272* ⊕ *www.cartier.com.*

Harry Winston. Perhaps the most locally famous jeweler is Harry Winston, *the* source for Oscar-night jewelry. The three-level space, with a bronze sculptural facade, velvet-panel walls, private salons, and a rooftop patio, is as glamorous as the gems. ⊠ *310 N. Rodeo Dr., Beverly Hills* ☎ *310/271–8554* ⊕ *www.harrywinston.com.*

Louis Vuitton. Holding court on a prominent corner, Louis Vuitton carries it's recognizable monogram on all manner of accessories and leather goods. ⊠ *295 N. Rodeo Dr., Beverly Hills* ☎ *310/859–0457* ⊕ *www. louisvuitton.com.*

Tiffany & Co. There's a bauble for everyone at Tiffany's, with three floors for its classic and contemporary jewelry and watches, crystal, and china. There are also some somewhat-more-accessible sterling silver pieces. ⊠ *210 N. Rodeo Dr., Beverly Hills* ☎ *310/273–8880* ⊕ *www.tiffany.com.*

Van Cleef & Arpels. In business for more than a century, Van Cleef & Arpels still designs elegant and distinctive pieces. ⊠ *300 N. Rodeo Dr., Beverly Hills* ☎ *310/276–1161* ⊕ *www.vancleef-arpels.com.*

MALLS AND SHOPPING CENTERS

Beverly Center. This is one of the more traditional malls you can find in L.A., with eight levels of stores, including Macy's, Bloomingdale's, and the newer addition: luxury retailer Henri Bendel. Fashion is the biggest draw and there's a little something for everyone, from D&G to H&M, and many shops in the midrange, including Banana Republic, Club Monaco, and Coach. Look for inexpensive accessories at Aldo or edgy dresses at new addition Maje; there's even a destination for the race-car obsessed at the Ferrari Store. Inside there are casual dining choices at the top-floor food court, and several popular chain restaurants are outside on the ground floor. ⊠ *8500 Beverly Blvd., West Hollywood* ☎ *310/854–0071* ⊕ *www.beverlycenter.com.*

SHOES

Bottega Veneta. With rich colors and chic designs, these buttery leather goods are never overly trendy. ⊠ *457 N. Rodeo Dr., Beverly Hills* ☎ *310/858–6533* ⊕ *www.bottegaveneta.com.*

9

Jimmy Choo. Find splurge-worthy heels and equally glamorous handbags from the line made famous on *Sex and the City.* ⊠ *240 N. Rodeo Dr., Beverly Hills* ☎ *310/860–9045* ⊕ *www.jimmychoo.com.*

SHOPPING NEIGHBORHOODS

Rodeo Drive. New York City has 5th Avenue, but L.A. has famed Rodeo Drive (pronounced Ro-DAY-o). The triangle, between Santa Monica and Wilshire boulevards and Beverly Drive, is one of the city's biggest tourist attractions and is lined with shops featuring the biggest names in fashion. You can see well-coiffed, well-heeled ladies toting multiple packages to their Mercedes and paparazzi staking out street corners. Steep price tags on designer labels make it a "just looking" experience for many residents and tourists alike. ⊠ *Beverly Hills* ⊕ *www. rodeodrive-bh.com.*

WEST HOLLYWOOD

West Hollywood is prime shopping real estate. And as they say with real estate, it's all about location, location, location. Depending on the street address, West Hollywood has upscale art, design, and antiques stores, clothing boutiques for the ladies-who-lunch set, megamusic stores, and specialty book vendors.

Melrose Avenue, for instance, is part bohemian-punk shopping district (from North Highland to Sweetzer) and part upscale art and design mecca (upper Melrose Avenue and Melrose Place). Discerning locals and celebs haunt the posh boutiques around Sunset Plaza (Sunset Boulevard at Sunset Plaza Drive), on Robertson Boulevard (between Beverly Boulevard and 3rd Street), and along upper Melrose Avenue.

The huge, blue Pacific Design Center, on Melrose at San Vicente Boulevard, is the focal point for this neighborhood's art- and interior design–related stores, including many on nearby Beverly Boulevard. The Beverly–La Brea neighborhood also claims a number of trendy clothing stores. Perched between Beverly Hills and West Hollywood, 3rd Street (between La Cienega Boulevard and Fairfax Avenue) is a magnet for small, friendly designer boutiques.

Melrose Place, not to be confused with the cheaper and trendier Melrose Avenue, is an in-the-know haven to savvy Los Angeles fashionistas and a charming anecdote to the city's addiction to strip-malls and mega-shopping centers. This three-block-long strip, east of La Cienega and a block north of Melrose Avenue lacks the pretentiousness of Rodeo. Reminiscent of the best of West Village shopping in New York, here haute couture meets pedestrian-friendly, tree-lined walkways.

Finally, the Fairfax District, along Fairfax Avenue below Melrose Avenue, encompasses the flamboyant, historic Farmers Market, at Fairfax Avenue and 3rd Street; the adjacent shopping extravaganza, The Grove; and some excellent galleries around Museum Row at Fairfax Avenue and Wilshire Boulevard.

ANTIQUES

Blackman Cruz. Browse among David Cruz and Adam Blackman's off-beat pieces (like 1940s New York subway signs) as well as fine European and Asian furniture from the 18th- to the mid-20th century. ⊠ *836 N. Highland Ave., near West Hollywood* ☎ *310/657–9228* ⊕ *www. blackmancruz.com.*

BOOKS AND MUSIC

Fodor'sChoice
★

Book Soup. One of the best independent bookstores in the country, Book Soup has been serving Angelinos since 1975. Given its Hollywood pedigree, it's especially deep in books about film, music, art, and photography. Fringe benefits include an international newsstand, a bargain-book section, and author readings several times weekly. ⊠ *8818 Sunset Blvd., West Hollywood* ☎ *310/659–3110* ⊕ *www. booksoup.com.*

Traveler's Bookcase. A massive collection of travel titles fills this shop, including guidebooks from Hong Kong, Barcelona, Delhi, and Singapore. Coffee table books, marvelous maps, and gifts for travelers (notebooks, pens, luggage tags, compact clocks) are also on offer. ⊠ *8375 W. 3rd St., West Hollywood* ☎ *323/655–0575* ⊕ *www. travelersbookcase.com.*

CLOTHING

AllSaints Spitalfields. The British store invaded Robertson Boulevard, bringing with it a rock-and-roll edge mixed with a dash of Downton Abbey. Look for leather biker jackets, tough shoes, edgy prints, and long sweaters and cardigans, which, worn correctly, let them know you're with the band. ⊠ *100 N. Robertson Blvd., Beverly Hills* ☎ *310–432-8484* ⊕ *www.us.allsaints.com.*

American Apparel. Simple yet sexy, these made-in-L.A. casual separates are the perfect California uniform. ⊠ *315 Robertson Blvd., Beverly Hills* ☎ *310/385–9183* ⊕ *www.americanapparel.net.*

9

Fodor'sChoice
★

American Rag Cie. Half the store features new clothing from established and emerging labels, and the other side is stocked with well-preserved vintage clothing organized by color and style. You'll also find plenty of shoes and accessories. ⊠ *150 S. La Brea Ave., Beverly–La Brea* ☎ *323/935–3154* ⊕ *www.amrag.com.*

Bleu. Ever dream of getting a fresh look without lifting a finger? The friendly, style-savvy staff will size you up in minutes and deliver just the right edgy basics for day or flirty party frocks for night (with the jewelry, shoes, and undies to match) to your dressing room. ⊠ *454 S. La Brea Ave., Beverly–La Brea* ☎ *323/939–2228* ⊕ *www.bleuclothing.com.*

Carolina Herrera. Sleek evening gowns and smart dresses share space at this always-chic Venezuelan-American designer's boutique. There's a second store on Rodeo Drive. ⊠ *8441 Melrose Pl., near West Hollywood* ☎ *323/782–9090* ⊕ *www.carolinaherrera.com.*

Chloé. This French luxury import is devoted to youthful, casual separates. ⊠ *8448 Melrose Pl., near West Hollywood* ☎ *323/602–0000* ⊕ *www.chloe.com.*

DID YOU KNOW?

The three-tiered staircase off Via Rodeo was built to resemble the Spanish Steps at the heart of Rome's most famous high-end shopping district.

Decades. A-listers scour these racks for dresses for awards season. Owner Cameron Silver's stellar selection includes dresses by Pucci and Ossie Clark and bags by Hermès. On the street level, Decades Two resells contemporary designer and couture clothing and accessories. ⊠ *8214 Melrose Ave., near West Hollywood* ☎ *323/655–0223* ⊕ *www. shopdecadesinc.com.*

Diane von Furstenberg. This famous designer's classic wrap dresses and casual clothing in distinctive geometric prints can be found here. ⊠ *8407 Melrose Ave., near West Hollywood* ☎ *323/951–1947* ⊕ *www.dvf.com.*

Fodor's Choice
★
Fred Segal. The ivy-covered building and security guards in the parking lot might tip you off that this is *the* place to be. Go during the lunch hour to stargaze at the super-trendy café. This longtime L.A. fashion landmark is subdivided into small boutiques that range from couture clothing to skateboard fashions. The entertainment industry's fashion fiends are addicted to these exclusive fashions, many from cult L.A. designers just making their marks. ⊠ *8118 Melrose Ave., near West Hollywood* ☎ *323/651–4129* ⊕ *www.fredsegal.com.*

H. Lorenzo. Funky, high-end designer clothes (Ann Demeulemeester, Junya Watanabe, and Comme des Garcons, to name a few) attract a young Hollywood crowd that doesn't blink at paying $250 for jeans. Next door, H. Men provides hot styles for the guys. ⊠ *8660 Sunset Blvd., West Hollywood* ☎ *310/659–1432* ⊕ *shop.hlorenzo.com.*

Intermix. NY-based Intermix is giving already established boutiques a run for their money. Racks feature looks that are both femme and fierce, with urban designs from Rag & Bone and brightly colored options from Vince, Robert Rodriguez, and more. The dress selection is especially notable. ⊠ *110 N. Robertson Blvd., West Hollywood* ☎ *310/860–0113* ⊕ *www.intermixonline.com.*

James Perse. These soft cotton T-shirts (and sweaters and fleece pullovers) are quintessentially L.A. Find them here in an immaculate, gallerylike space with sleek furnishings. ⊠ *8914 Melrose Ave., near West Hollywood* ☎ *310/276–7277* ⊕ *www.jamesperse.com.*

Kate Somerville. This is where the stars go to get their skin red-carpet ready. The historic space is done up in hues of light blue and white that instantly transport you to spa heaven. Her well-known products are on sale here as well. ⊠ *8428 Melrose Pl., near West Hollywood* ☎ *323/655–7546* ⊕ *www.katesomerville.com.*

Kitson. Stars that want to be seen (and seen shopping) come here to choose from piles of neon Geneva watches, sequined Converse sneakers, bejeweled backpacks, and unusual pampering products like Wine Wipes for teeth. It's pure girly glitz. Across the street, Kitson Kids provides mini-me versions of trends. Nearby Kitson Men has jeans, hoodies, sneakers, and accessories like sleep masks printed with the word "pimp." ⊠ *115 S. Robertson Blvd., Beverly Hills* ☎ *310/859–2652* ⊕ *www.shopkitson.com.*

Lotta. True bohemian glamour prevails here, with halters and tunics from hippie-chic designers. Piles of accessories complete the look. Look for magazine spreads of celebs wearing the same styles you see on the racks. ⊠ *8372 W. 3rd St., near West Hollywood* ☎ *323/852–0520* ⊕ *www.lottanyc.com.*

9

Madison/Diavolina. This veteran of the fashion scene showcases what is hot right this minute, including shoes, accessories, and clothing. From Rag & Bone jeans to Missoni dresses, what's in common here is that they're all stylish. ✉ *8745 W. 3rd St., near West Hollywood* ☎ *310/275–1930* ⊕ *www.madisonlosangeles.com.*

Marc Jacobs. Bold prints and boyish cuts sweetened with girly details make this American designer a favorite among Hollywood starlets. His fresh, forward-thinking look occupies four boutiques in West Hollywood. ✉ *8400 Melrose Pl., near West Hollywood* ☎ *310/653–5100* ⊕ *www.marcjacobs.com* ✉ *men's, 8409 Melrose Pl.* ☎ *323/866–8255* ✉ *Marc by Marc, 8410 Melrose Ave.* ☎ *323/653–0100.*

Fodor'sChoice   **Maxfield.** This modern concrete structure holds one of L.A.'s too-cool-
★   for-school sources for high fashion, with sleek-as-can-be offerings from Chanel, Saint Laurent, Balmain, and Rick Owen. It's for serious shoppers (or gawkers) only. ✉ *8825 Melrose Ave., at Robertson Blvd., West Hollywood* ☎ *310/274–8800* ⊕ *www.maxfieldla.com.*

MILK. Milk bottles and old trunks and suitcases line the shelves at this spacious shop, which has become a destination for new trends and emerging designers. T-shirts and jeans are carefully arranged on the tables and racks feature well-edited picks, from silky dresses to lacy tops to luxe sweaters. Part of the back is devoted to menswear. ✉ *8209 W. 3rd St., near West Hollywood* ☎ *323/951–0330.*

Monique Lhuillier. Neutral tones provide a brilliant backdrop to seductive red-carpet dresses and princess-worthy gowns at this elegant boutique. ✉ *8485 Melrose Pl., near West Hollywood* ☎ *323/655–1088* ⊕ *www. moniquelhuillier.com.*

Moods of Norway. This Norwegian brand has a quirky and playful sensibility, with blazers and shirts in bright plaids and geometric patterns, along with a nice variety of sporty and classically tailored outerwear. ✉ *113 S. Robertson Blvd., Beverly Hills* ☎ *310/271–7172* ⊕ *www. moodsofnorway.com.*

Oscar de la Renta. All things feminine, from beaded ball gowns to satin cocktail dresses, make this boutique an epicenter for women preparing to attend glamorous events. ✉ *8446 Melrose Pl., near West Hollywood* ☎ *323/653–0200* ⊕ *www.oscardelarenta.com.*

Paul Smith. You can't miss the shocking fuchsia "shoebox" that houses Paul Smith's fantastical collection of clothing, boots, hats, luggage, and objets d'art. Photos and art line the walls above shelves of books on pop culture, art, and Hollywood. The clothing vibrates in signature colors like hot pink and mustard yellow, and you can find Smith's signature stripes on everything from socks to notebooks. ✉ *8221 Melrose Ave., near West Hollywood* ☎ *323/951 4800* ⊕ *www.paulsmith.co.uk.*

Resurrection. This shop offers a spot-on selection of high-quality vintage wear from the likes of Halston and Pucci, as well as vintage Levi's denim and Gucci accessories—all neatly arranged by color and style. ✉ *8006 Melrose Ave., near West Hollywood, West Hollywood* ☎ *323/651–5516* ⊕ *www.resurrectionvintage.com.*

Ron Herman. The vibe here is relaxed but plugged in, with an eclectic mix of local and European designs. ⊠ *8100 Melrose Ave., West Hollywood* ☎ *323/651–4129* ⊕ *www.ronherman.com.*

Satine. This small shop has a retro feel to it, matched by the selection of clothing by indie designers you won't find elsewhere. You'll also find well-known ones like Alexander Wang and Isabel Marant. A vintage-loving style permeates the air, with a playful touch of little-girl-grown-up. ⊠ *8134 W. 3rd St., near West Hollywood* ☎ *323/655–2142* ⊕ *www.satineboutique.com.*

Stacey Todd. The newly opened boutique, all wood, white and natural light, touts a denim bar stocked with brands like Rag & Bone and DSquared. Classic, menswear-inspired clothing by luxe labels, including Helmut Lang and Band of Outsiders, pair with bohemian-tough accessoires, like Isabel Marant boots. A selection of lifestyle products features candles, coffee table books, and bath and body products. A second store is in Studio City. ⊠ *454 N. Robertson Blvd., West Hollywood* ☎ *310/659–8633* ⊕ *www.staceytoddboutique.com.*

Stella McCartney. This ivy-covered boutique houses the British designer's cruelty-free ready-to-wear fashions. ⊠ *8823 Beverly Blvd., West Hollywood* ☎ *310/273–7051* ⊕ *www.stellamccartney.com.*

South Willard. Guys who aren't shy about wearing high-style designs from mostly European and Japanese lines head to this shop. ⊠ *8038 W. 3rd St., near West Hollywood* ☎ *323/653–6153* ⊕ *www. southwillard.com.*

Ten Over Six. If you love accessories, this is the place for you. This boutique stocks pieces by highly acclaimed designers such as Vena Cava, 3.1 Phillip Lim, and Pamela Love. ⊠ *8425 Melrose Ave., near West Hollywood* ☎ *323/330–9355* ⊕ *shop.tenover6.com.*

Theory. Sleek and sophisticated separates and suits are what you'll find in this open, airy space. ⊠ *8428 Melrose Ave. Blvd., West Hollywood* ☎ *323/782–0163* ⊕ *www.theory.com.*

Trina Turk. Interior designer Kelly Wearstler put her stamp on this beautiful space, with mod furnishings providing the perfect setting for Turk's bohemian-chic line. The place has a resort feel, with mannequins wearing big sunglasses and print scarves. ⊠ *8008 W. 3rd St., near West Hollywood* ☎ *323/651–1382* ⊕ *www.trinaturk.com.*

The Way We Wore. Overlook the over-the-top vintage store furnishings to find one of the city's best selections of well-cared-for and one-of-a-kind items, with a focus on sequins and beads. Upstairs, couture from Halston, Dior, and Chanel can cost up to $20,000. ⊠ *334 S. La Brea, Beverly–La Brea* ☎ *323/937–0878* ⊕ *www.thewaywewore.com.*

HOUSEWARES

Armani Casa. Enter Armaniland, where the clean and classic lines of black, white, and mocha furniture and home accessories cast their spell. ⊠ *157 N. Robertson Blvd., at Beverly Blvd., West Hollywood* ☎ *310/248–2440* ⊕ *www.armanicasa.com.*

9

Jonathan Adler. For fans of the New York–based kitsch-tastic designer, this recently expanded West Coast flagship store is the place to be. Mid-century and country-club styles get retooled in whimsical pottery, fun pillows, and graphic textiles. ⊠ *8125 Melrose Ave., near West Hollywood* ☎ *323/658–8390* ⊕ *www.jonathanadler.com.*

Heath Ceramics. This loftlike outpost of the beloved Sausalito-based ceramics company stocks everything from Coupe dishes, a line created by founder Edith Heath herself in the 1940s, to glass tumblers hand-blown in West Virginia. Also look for table linens, bud vases, and specialty foods like artisanal jams from Pasadena. ⊠ *7525 Beverly Blvd., Fairfax* ☎ *323/965–0800* ⊕ *www.heathceramics.com.*

OK. An über–gift shop, OK stocks the classy (such as Scandinavian stemware and vintage phones) and specializes in architecture and design books. There's a second Silver Lake location. ⊠ *8303 W. 3rd St., near West Hollywood, West Hollywood* ☎ *323/653–3501* ⊕ *okthestore.com.*

Santa Maria Novella. Soaps, candles, perfumes, and other gift-friendly items from Italy are on offer at this friendly boutique. ⊠ *8411 Melrose Pl., West Hollywood* ☎ *323/651–3754* ⊕ *www.santamarianovellausa.com.*

Soolip. If the desk accoutrements, custom stationery, and handmade paper from nearly 50 countries aren't enough, this *paperie* also does a brisk business in bespoke gift wrapping (think: linen paper tied with metallic twine and glass berries). Located inside the Pacific Design Center, the shop also sells European soaps and other gifts. ⊠ *Pacific Design Center, 8687 Melrose Ave., near West Hollywood* ☎ *310/360–0545* ⊕ *www.soolip.com.*

JEWELRY AND ACCESSORIES

Alpha. This spacious shop answers the questions on every guy's mind: What to wear to work or on a date? What to use for serving takeout? What to put on the coffee table? Super-cool and stylish accessories abound. ⊠ *8625 Melrose Ave., West Hollywood* ☎ *310/855–0775* ⊕ *www.alpha-man.com.*

MALLS AND SHOPPING CENTERS

Fodor's Choice
★

Farmers Market. The granddaddy of L.A. markets dates back to 1935, and the amazing array of clapboard stalls (selling everything from candy to hot sauce, just-picked fruit to fresh lamb), wacky regulars, and a United Nations of food choices must be experienced to be appreciated. Employees from the nearby CBS studios mingle with hungover clubbers and elderly locals at dozens of eateries, movie theaters, and shops under one huge roof. The green trolley shuttles visitors between the Farmers Market and the nearby Grove. ⊠ *6333 W. 3rd St., at Fairfax Ave., Fairfax District* ☎ *323/933–9211 Farmers Market* ⊕ *www.farmersmarketla.com/.*

The Grove. This wildly popular outdoor mall is fabulous for people-watching. Although many of the stores may sound familiar (Abercrombie & Fitch, American Girl Place, Nordstrom), the winding tile walkways, the central fountain with "dancing" water choreographed to music, and the "snow" that falls during the holiday season, put this place over the top. ⊠ *189 The Grove Dr., West Hollywood* ☎ *323/900–8080* ⊕ *www.thegrovela.com.*

MARKETS

Melrose Trading Post. Hollywood denizens love this hip market, where you're likely to find recycled rock T-shirts or some vinyl to complete your collection. Live music and fresh munchies entertain vintage hunters and collectors. The market is held 9 to 5 on Sunday in Fairfax High School's parking lot. Parking is free, but admission is $3. ✉ *Fairfax Blvd. and Melrose Ave.* ☎ *323/655–7679* ⊕ *www.melrosetradingpost.org.*

SHOES

Boot Star. This huge selection of boots spells heaven for urban cowboys and cowgirls. You can find materials ranging from calfskin to alligator, and most boots are handmade in Mexico and Texas. Custom sizing is available. ✉ *8493 Sunset Blvd., West Hollywood* ☎ *323/650–0475* ⊕ *www.bootstaronline.com.*

Christian Louboutin. These French shoes—famous for their red soles—are always eye-catching. Some designs have insanely high heels; others are done in neon colors or crazy patterns. ✉ *650 N. Robertson Blvd., West Hollywood* ☎ *310/247–9300* ⊕ *www.christianlouboutin.com.*

WESTWOOD

This is L.A.'s errand central, where entertainment executives and Industry types do their serious shopping. In general, it's more affordable than Beverly Hills.

A nascent art scene is blossoming in Culver City, along the intersection of La Cienega and Washington boulevards and the Santa Monica Freeway, and down side streets like Comey Avenue. To the west, Westwood is dominated by its largest resident, UCLA.

BOOKS AND STATIONERY

Children's Book World. One of the city's largest bookstores is as loved by parents as it is by kids. The Saturday-morning storytelling series is a huge hit, and the knowledgeable staffers have an insatiable love for children's literature. It's just southwest of Century City. ✉ *10580½ W. Pico Blvd., West L.A.* ☎ *310/559–2665* ⊕ *www.childrensbookworld.com.*

CLOTHING

Attire Los Angeles. In addition to amazing deals on past-season separates by designers like Prabal Gurung and Phillip Lim, this store stocks artworks, accessories and clothes by local designers and L.A. brands, like Velvet and 12th Street By Cynthia Vincent. ✉ *5879 Washington Blvd., Culver City* ☎ *310/287–2333* ⊕ *www.attirelosangeles.com.*

FOOD AND WINE

Surfas. You're likely to rub elbows with area chefs in their work whites at this spacious and well-organized restaurant supply store. Find aisles of spices and jarred delicacies along with all the pots, pans, and appliances you'll need to be your own Top Chef. The adjoining café serves salads, sandwiches, and baked goods. ✉ *8777 Washington Blvd., at National Blvd., Culver City* ☎ *310/559–4770* ⊕ *www.surfasonline.com.*

9

Wally's. It may be known as the wine store to the stars, but regular folks also delve into the vast selection of liquors and liqueurs, fine chocolates, and imported cheeses, as well as the impressive assortment of cigars. Saturday-afternoon wine tastings make a visit all the sweeter. ⊠ *2107 Westwood Blvd., West L.A.* ☎ *310/475–0606* ⊕ *www.wallywine.com.*

The Wine House. This warehouse carries everything from $10 table wines to $500 first-growth Bordeaux—and the right cigars to go with them. The scope of the selection can be daunting, but the friendly staffers help you find the perfect bottle. Don't miss the wine bar upstairs. ⊠ *2311 Cotner Ave., between Pico and Olympic Blvds., West L.A.* ☎ *310/479–3731* ⊕ *www.winehouse.com.*

PARKING TIPS

Parking in Santa Monica is next to impossible on Wednesday, when some streets are blocked off for the farmers' market, but there are several parking structures with free parking for an hour or two.

There are several well-marked, free (for two hours) parking lots around the core shopping area around Beverly Hills.

HOUSEWARES

Room & Board. Think of this furniture store as Crate & Barrel's more fashion-forward (but equally expensive) sibling, offering chic items with midcentury-modern appeal. ⊠ *8707 Washington Blvd., between Venice and Washington Blvds., Culver City* ☎ *310/736–9100* ⊕ *www.roomandboard.com.*

MALLS AND SHOPPING CENTERS

H.D. Buttercup. The lovingly restored Helms Bakery, an art deco gem, is more like a showroom than a traditional store. Manufacturers offer antiques, artworks, furniture, fashions, books, bedding, and more. A second-floor loft features discontinued items at prices that rival outlet stores. ⊠ *3225 Helms Ave., between Venice and Washington Blvds., Culver City* ☎ *310/558–8900* ⊕ *www.hdbuttercup.com.*

Westfield Century City. Known locally as the Century City Mall, this open-air shopping center is set among office buildings on what used to be the backlot of Twentieth Century Fox studios. You'll find a mix of luxury retailers (Louis Vuitton, Tourneau), department stores (Macy's, Bloomingdale's), clothing stores (Gap, Zara), and trendy shops (Madewell). ⊠ *10250 Santa Monica Blvd., Century City* ☎ *310/277–3898.*

TOYS

Allied Model Trains. Kids (and kids at heart) light up when visiting this huge shop that celebrates trains old and new. Look for model trains by Lionel and American Flyer. ⊠ *4371 S. Sepulveda Blvd., Culver City* ☎ *310/313–9353.*

SANTA MONICA AND THE BEACHES

The breezy beachside communities of Santa Monica and Venice are ideal for leisurely shopping. Scads of tourists (and some locals) gravitate to the Third Street Promenade, a popular pedestrians-only strolling–shopping area that is within walking range of the beach and historic Santa Monica Pier. The newly refurbished Santa Monica Place, at the south end of the promenade, draws the young and hip.

A number of modern furnishings stores are nearby on 4th and 5th streets. Main Street between Pico Boulevard and Rose Avenue offers upscale chain stores, cafés, and some original shops, while Montana Avenue is a great source for distinctive clothing boutiques and child-friendly shopping, especially between 7th and 17th streets.

In Venice, Abbot Kinney Boulevard is abuzz with midcentury furniture stores, art galleries and boutiques, and cafés.

SANTA MONICA

BEAUTY

Palmetto. The shelves at this longtime favorite are literally crammed with bath, body, and beauty treats from both little-known and sought-after lines. There's a strong focus on products made with natural ingredients. ⊠ *1034 Montana Ave., Santa Monica* ☎ *310/395–6687.*

Strange Invisible Perfumes. A custom-made fragrance by perfumer Alexandra Balahoutis might run you thousands of dollars, but you can pick up ready-made scents, such as citrusy Fair Verona and sultry Black Rosette, for much less. Her exquisitely designed shop is both modern and romantic. ⊠ *1138 Abbot Kinney Blvd., Venice* ☎ *310/314–1505* ⊕ *www.siperfumes.com.*

BOOKS AND MUSIC

Arcana. A treasure trove for art lovers, this store boasts a serious collection of new, rare, and out-of-print books on architecture, design, and fashion—with an especially impressive selection on photography. ⊠ *8675 W. Washington Blvd., Santa Monica* ☎ *310/458–1499* ⊕ *www. arcanabooks.com.*

Hennessey + Ingalls Bookstore. A stop here would make a perfect end to a day at the Getty. This is L.A.'s largest collection of books on graphic design, architecture, and photography. ⊠ *214 Wilshire Blvd., between 2nd and 3rd Sts., Santa Monica* ☎ *310/458–9074* ⊕ *www. hennesseyingalls.com.*

CLOTHING

Fodor's Choice
★

Fred Segal. The West Hollywood branch might draw more celebrities, but this location is larger and decidedly more laid-back. Across-the-street shops feature miniboutiques stocking everything from the latest denim styles to designer handbags. The selection of beauty products is particularly impressive. ⊠ *420 and 500 Broadway, Santa Monica* ☎ *310/458–8100.*

9

Heist. Owner Nilou Ghodsi sends thank-you notes to customers and employs a sales staff that is friendly and helpful but not at all overbearing. The focus at this airy boutique is on elegantly edgy separates from American designers like Nili Lotan and Gary Graham, as well as hard-to-find French and Italian designers. ⊠ *1100 Abbot Kinney Blvd., Venice* ☎ *310/450–6531* ⊕ *shopheist.com/.*

The Levi's Store. This busy location features endless stacks of jeans, perfectly organized by size for easy browsing. Vests, jackets, shirts, and boots break up the sea of denim. ⊠ *1409 3rd St. Promenade, Santa Monica* ☎ *310/393–4899* ⊕ *www.levisstore.com.*

Planet Blue. The quintessential Malibu style is found here, with baskets on the floor filled with flip-flops and an abundance of jeans, tops, dresses, and accessories. There's another location on Montana Avenue. ⊠ *2940 Main St., Santa Monica* ☎ *310/396–1767* ⊕ *www. shopplanetblue.com.*

Principessa. This warm and homey boutique stocks oh-so-cool clothes from Eugenia Kim, Biya, Rachel Pally, and more. An ample selection of jewelry, some from local designers, completes the look. ⊠ *1323 Abbot Kinney Blvd., Venice* ☎ *310/450–6696* ⊕ *www. principessavenice.com.*

Wasteland. This vintage emporium, a block from the Third Street Promenade, sells gently used items for both women and men. You'll find everything from wide-lapelled polyester shirts to last year's Coach bag. Other locations are on Melrose Avenue and Ventura Boulevard. ⊠ *1330 4th St., between Arizona and Santa Monica Blvd., Santa Monica* ☎ *310/395–2620* ⊕ *www.shopwasteland.com.*

ZJ Boarding House. One of the area's best surf, skate, and snow shops offers the essentials. You'll find everything from wax to wet suits. ⊠ *2619 Main St., Santa Monica* ☎ *310/392–5646* ⊕ *www. zjboardinghouse.com.*

MARKETS

Brentwood Country Mart. The dozen or so stores at this faux country market include Calypso (for beachy, bohemian clothing), Turpan (for luxury home goods), James Perse (for laid-back cotton knits), Sugar Paper (for exquisite paper goods), and Broken English (for fine jewelry). Grab a chicken basket at Reddi Chik and chow down on the open-air patio. ⊠ *225 26th St., at San Vicente Blvd., Santa Monica* ⊕ *www. brentwoodcountrymart.com.*

Third Street Promenade. Street performers of every stripe set the scene along this pedestrians-only shopping stretch dotted with ivy-covered fountains. Stores are mainly the chain variety, including Quiksilver and Rip Curl outposts for cool surf attire. Movie theaters, pubs, and restaurants ensure that virtually every need is covered. ⊠ *3rd St., between Broadway and Wilshire Blvd., Santa Monica.*

TOYS

Acorn. Remember when toys didn't require computer programming? Ellen West's old-fashioned shop sparks children's imaginations with dress-up clothes, picture books, and hand-painted wooden toys. No

Kites and spinners on display at Venice Beach

batteries or plastic allowed. ✉ *1220 5th St., near Wilshire Blvd., Santa Monica* ☎ *310/451–5845* ⊕ *theacornstore.hostasaurus.com.*

Jenny Bec's. Need ideas for designing the nursery, or a last-minute costume for your favorite pirate or fairy? Head to this toy store, which is jam-packed with puzzles, books, and crafts. A nice bonus is the colorful gift-wrapping and shipping service. ✉ *11710 San Vicente Blvd., Brentwood* ☎ *310/395–9505* ⊕ *www.jennybecs.com.*

VENICE

HOME FURNISHINGS AND GIFTS
Colcha. This gem-filled Abbot Kinney spot showcases statement-making furniture, fanciful lighting fixtures, and colorfully patterned throw pillows. ✉ *1416 Abbot Kinney Blvd., Venice* ☎ *310/392–3600* ⊕ *www.colchahome.com.*

MALIBU

MALLS AND SHOPPING CENTERS
Malibu Lumberyard. This shopping complex is a window into beachfront California living. Emblematic Malibu lifestyle stores include James Perse, Maxfield, and one of the chicest J. Crew stores you've ever seen. ✉ *3939 Cross Creek Rd., Malibu* ⊕ *www.themalibulumberyard.com.*

PASADENA

In Pasadena, the stretch of Colorado Boulevard between Pasadena Avenue and Arroyo Parkway, known as Old Town, is a popular pedestrian shopping destination, with retailers such as Crate & Barrel and H&M, and Tiffany's, which sits a block away from Forever 21. A few blocks east on Colorado, the open-air "urban village" known as Paseo Colorado mixes residential, retail, dining, and entertainment spaces along Colorado Boulevard between Los Robles and Marengo avenues. Enter on Colorado or Marengo for free parking.

BOOKS

Fodor'sChoice **Vroman's Bookstore.** Southern California's oldest and largest independent
★   bookseller is justly famous for its great service. A newsstand, café, and stationery store add to the appeal. Some 400 author events annually, plus a fab kids' zone complete with play area, make this a truly outstanding spot. ⊠ *695 E. Colorado Blvd., Pasadena* ☎ *626/449–5320* ⊕ *www.vromansbookstore.com.*

CLOTHING

Elisa B. This small but well-edited collection of up-and-coming L.A. designers (Love, Zooey) and established favorites (Michael Stars, Tracey Reese) draw women of all ages to this friendly Old Town boutique. ⊠ *12 Douglas Alley, Pasadena* ☎ *626/792–4746* ⊕ *www.elisab.com.*

MARKETS

Pasadena City College Flea Market. For bargain hunting, head to the Pasadena City College Flea Market on the first Sunday of each month. With 500 vendors (70 of them selling records), this is a great source for collectibles, furniture, and clothing at prices that won't break the bank. ⊠ *1570 E. Colorado Blvd., at Hill Ave., Pasadena* ☎ *626/585–7906.*

Rose Bowl Flea Market. Huge and hyped, the Rose Bowl Flea Market takes place on the second Sunday of every month, rain or shine. This extremely popular market attracts more than 2,500 vendors looking for top dollar for their antiques, crafts, and new furniture. It's an especially good source for pop culture odds and ends—a *Partridge Family* lunchbox was recently spotted going for $100. ⊠ *1001 Rose Bowl Dr., Pasadena* ☎ *323/560–7469* ⊕ *www.rgcshows.com.*

WHERE TO EAT

10

Updated by
Cindy Arora

Los Angeles may be known for its beach living and celebrity-infused backdrop, but it was once a farm town. The hillsides were covered in citrus orchards and dairy farms, and agriculture was a major industry. These days, although L.A. is urbanized, the city's culinary landscape has re-embraced a local, sustainable, and seasonal philosophy at many levels — from fine dining to street snacks.

With a growing interest in farm-to-fork, the city's farmers' market scene has exploded, becoming popular at big-name restaurants and small eateries alike. In Hollywood and Santa Monica you can often find high-profile chefs scouring farm stands for fresh produce.

Yet the status of the celebrity chef continues to carry weight around this town. People follow the culinary zeitgeist with the same fervor as celebrity gossip. You can queue up with the hungry hordes at **Mozza** or try and snag a reservation to the ever-popular **Trois Mec** that's much like getting a golden ticket these days. Elsewhere, the seasonally driven bakery and insanely popular **Huckleberry** in Santa Monica has been given a Brentwood counterpart with the rustically sweet Milo & Olive created by the same owners. In Culver City, a run-down International House of Pancakes has been turned into a ski chalet-inspired **A-Frame Tavern**. And in Downtown Los Angeles, the stylish Ace Hotel has opened LA Chapter and created a haven for local designers and artists to bring their laptops and get inspired by food and design.

Ethnic eats continue to be a backbone to the L.A. dining scene. People head to the San Gabriel Valley for dim sum, ramen, and unassuming taco lounges, Koreatown for epic Korean cooking and late night coffeehouses and West L.A. and "the Valley" for phenomenal sushi. Latin food is well represented in the city, making it tough to choose between Guatemalan eateries, Peruvian restaurants, nouveau Mexican bistros, and Tijuana-style taco trucks. With so many dining options, sometimes the best strategy is simply to drive and explore. Just don't mind the traffic.

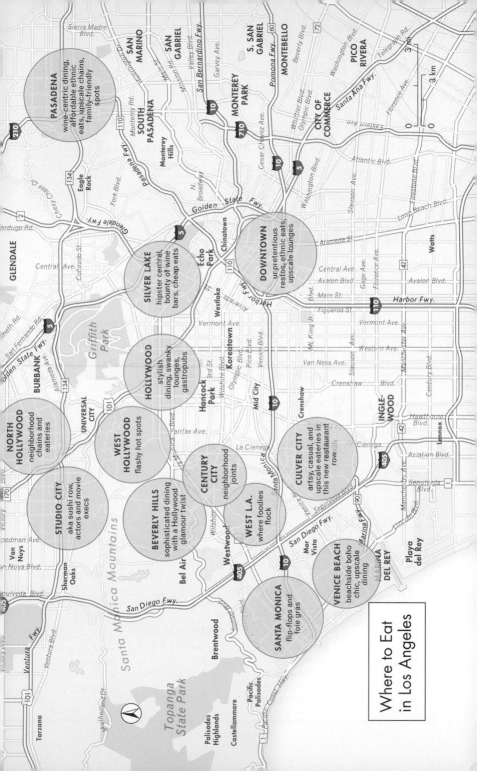

Where to Eat
in Los Angeles

PASADENA wine-centric dining, affordable ethnic eats, upscale chains, family-friendly spots

SILVER LAKE hipster central, bounty of wine bars, cheap eats

DOWNTOWN unpretentious restos, ethnic eats, upscale lounges

HOLLYWOOD stylish dining, swanky lounges, gastropubs

NORTH HOLLYWOOD neighborhood chains and eateries

WEST HOLLYWOOD flashy hot spots

STUDIO CITY aka sushi row, actors and movie execs

BEVERLY HILLS sophisticated dining with a Hollywood glamour twist

CENTURY CITY neighborhood joints

WEST L.A. where foodies flock

CULVER CITY artsy, casual, and upscale eateries in this new restaurant row

SANTA MONICA flip-flops and foie gras

VENICE BEACH beachside boho chic, upscale dining

BEST BETS FOR LOS ANGELES DINING

With thousands of restaurants to choose from, how will you decide where to eat? Fodor's writers and editors have selected their favorite restaurants by price, cuisine, and experience in the Best Bets lists *below*. You can also search by neighborhood—just peruse the following pages to find specific details about a restaurant in the full reviews later in the chapter.

INDIAN

Badmaash, $$, p. 203

ITALIAN

Angelini Osteria, $$$$, p. 221

Fodor's Choice★

Angelini Osteria $$$$, p. 221
A.O.C. $$$$,1 p. 222
The Apple Pan $, p. 227
Badmaash, $$, p. 203
Bottega Louie $$, p. 203
Bouchon Bistro $$$, p. 218
Cube Café and Marketplace $$, p. 210
Little Dom's $$$, p. 214
Mélisse, $$$$, p. 233
Philippe the Original $, p. 206
Pizzeria Mozza $$, p. 211
Providence $$$$, p. 211
Spago Beverly Hills, $$$$, p. 221
Urasawa $$$$, p. 221
Yuca's Hut $, p. 215

By Price

$

The Apple Pan, p. 227
Artisan Cheese Gallery, p. 215
Little Flower Candy Company, p. 236
Pink's Hot Dogs, p. 211
Philippe the Original, p. 206
Porto's Bakery, p. 213
Yuca's Hut, p. 215
Zankou Chicken, p. 212

$$

Bottega Louie, p. 203
Cube Café and Marketplace, p. 210
Father's Office, p. 232
Gjelina, p. 234
Pizzeria Mozza, p. 211

$$$

Animal, p. 207
Bouchon Bistro, p. 218
Little Dom's, p. 214
Oliverio, p. 219

$$$$

Angelini Osteria, p. 221
A.O.C., p. 222
Gordon Ramsay at The London, p. 223
Providence, p. 211
Spago Beverly Hills, p. 221
Urasawa, p. 221
Water Grill, p. 206

By Cuisine

AMERICAN

The Apple Pan, $, p. 227
Philippe the Original, $, p. 206

FRENCH

Comme Ça, $$$$, p. 222
Mélisse, $$$$, p. 233
Patina, $$$$, p. 206

Cube Café and Marketplace, $$, p. 210
Pecorino, $$$, p. 225
Pizzeria Mozza, $$, p. 211
Valentino, $$$$, p. 234

JAPANESE

Asanebo, $$$$, p. 215
Matsuhisa, $$$$, p. 219
Mori Sushi, $$$, p. 227
Urasawa, $$$$, p. 221
Wa Sushi & Bistro, $$$$, p. 224

MEDITERRANEAN

A.O.C., $$$$, p. 222

MEXICAN

Lotería! Grill Hollywood, $$, p. 211
Monte Alban, $$, p. 227
Yuca's Hut, $, p. 215

NEW AMERICAN

Craft Los Angeles,
$$$$, p. 225
Lucques, $$$, p. 223
Spago Beverly Hills,
$$$$, p. 221

SEAFOOD

Providence, $$$$,
p. 211
Water Grill, $$$$,
p. 206

SPANISH

Bar Pintxo, $$, p. 228
The Bazaar by José
Andrés, $$$$, p. 217

STEAK

CUT, $$$$, p. 218
Nick & Stef's Steak-
house, $$$$, p. 206

VIETNAMESE

Crustacean, $$$$,
p. 218
Gingergrass, $$,
p. 216

By Experience

BAR SCENE

Father's Office, $$,
p. 232
Nobu Malibu, $$$$,
p. 235

BRUNCH

The Belvedere, $$$$,
p. 217
Bottega Louie, $$,
p. 203
Girasol, $$$, p. 215
Oliverio, $$$, p. 219

CELEB-SPOTTING

Bouchon Bistro, $$$,
p. 218
Craft Los Angeles,
$$$$, p. 225
CUT, $$$$, p. 218
The Grill on the Alley,
$$$, p. 219
Hinoki and the Bird,
$$$, p. 226
Matsuhisa, $$$$,
p. 219
Nobu Malibu, $$$$,
p. 235
Spago Beverly Hills,
$$$$, p. 221

CHILD-FRIENDLY

Border Grill, $$$,
p. 229
Fred 62, $, p. 214
Little Flower Candy
Company, $, p. 236
Lotería! Grill Holly-
wood, $$, p. 211
Philippe the Original,
$, p. 206
Porto's Bakery, $,
p. 213
Warren's Blackboard,
$$, p. 213

GOOD FOR GROUPS

25 Degrees, $$,
p. 207
A.O.C., $$$$, p. 222
Bottega Louie, $$,
p. 203
Craft Los Angeles,
$$$$, p. 225
Girasol, $$$, p. 215
Little Dom's, $$$,
p. 214
Gordon Ramsay at
The London, $$$$,
p. 223

GREAT VIEW

Gladstone's Malibu,
$$$$, p. 232

HISTORIC

Cicada, $$$$, p. 204
Engine Co. No. 28, $$,
p. 204
Philippe the Original,
$, p. 206
Pink's Hot Dogs, $,
p. 211
Santa Monica
Seafood, $$, p. 233

LATE-NIGHT DINING

25 Degrees, $$,
p. 207
Animal, $$$, p. 207
Canter's, $, p. 222
Fred 62, $, p. 214
Kate Mantilini, $$,
p. 219

MOST ROMANTIC

Allumette, $$, p. 216
A.O.C., $$$$, p. 222
Bouchon Bistro, $$$,
P. 218
Cicada, $$$$, p. 204
Gjelina, $$, p. 234
Mélisse, $$$$, p. 233
Patina, $$$$, p. 206

10

SOUTH-OF-THE-BORDER FLAVOR

From Cal-Mex burritos to Mexico City–style tacos, Southern California is a top stateside destination for experiencing Mexico's myriad culinary styles.

Many Americans are surprised to learn that the Mexican menu goes far beyond Tex-Mex (or Cal-Mex) favorites like burritos, chimichangas, enchiladas, fajitas, and nachos—many of which were created or popularized stateside. Indeed, Mexico has rich, regional food styles, like the complex mole sauces of Puebla and Oaxaca and the fresh ceviches of Veracruz, as well as the trademark snack of Mexico City: tacos.

In Southern California, tacos are an obsession, with numerous blogs and websites dedicated to the quest for the perfect taco. They're everywhere—in ramshackle taco stands, roving taco trucks, and strip-mall *taquerias*. Whether you're looking for a cheap snack or a lunch on the go, SoCal's taco selection can't be beat. But be forewarned: there may not be an English menu. Here we've noted unfamiliar taco terms, along with other potentially new-to-you items from the Mexican menu.

THIRST QUENCHERS

Spanish for "fresh water," *agua fresca* is a nonalcoholic Mexican drink made from fruit, rice, or seeds that are blended with sugar and water. Fruit flavors like lemon, lime, and watermelon are common. Other varieties include *agua de Jamaica*, flavored with red hibiscus petals; *agua de horchata*, a cinnamon-scented rice milk; and *agua de tamarindo*, a bittersweet variety flavored with tamarind. If you're looking for something with a little more kick, try a *michelada*, a beer enhanced with lime juice, chili sauce, and other ingredients. It's served in a salt-rimmed glass with ice.

DECODING THE MENU

Ceviche—Citrus-marinated seafood appetizer from the Gulf shores of Veracruz. Often eaten with tortilla chips.

Chili relleno—Roasted poblano pepper that is stuffed with ingredients like ground meat or cheese, then dipped in egg batter, fried, and served in tomato sauce.

Clayuda—A Oaxacan dish similar to pizza. Large corn tortillas are baked until hard, then topped with ingredients like refried beans, cheese, and salsa.

Fish taco—A specialty in Southern California, the fish taco is a soft corn tortilla stuffed with grilled or fried white fish (mahimahi or wahoo), pico de gallo, and shredded cabbage.

Gordita—"Little fat one" in Spanish, this dish is like a taco, but the cornmeal shell is thicker, similar to pita bread.

Mole—A complex, sweet sauce with Aztec roots made from more than 20 ingredients, including chilis, cinnamon, cumin, anise, black pepper, sesame seeds, and Mexican chocolate. There are many types of mole using various chilis and ingredient combinations, but the most common is *mole poblano* from the Puebla region.

Quesadilla—A snack made from a fresh tortilla that is folded over and stuffed with simple fillings like cheese, then toasted on a griddle. Elevated versions of the quesadilla may be stuffed with

sautéed *flor de calabaza* (squash blossoms) or *huitlacoche* (corn mushrooms).

Salsa—A class of cooked or raw sauces made from chilis, tomatoes, and other ingredients. Popular salsas include *pico de gallo*, a fresh sauce made from chopped tomatoes, onions, chilis, cilantro, and lime; *salsa verde*, made with tomatillos instead of tomatoes; and *salsa roja*, a cooked sauce made with chilis, tomatoes, onion, garlic, and cilantro.

Sopes—A small, fried corn cake topped with ingredients like refried beans, shredded chicken, and salsa.

Taco—Tacos are made from soft, palm-size corn tortillas filled with meat, chopped onion, cilantro, and salsa. Common taco fillings include *al pastor* (spiced pork), *barbacoa* (braised beef), *carnitas* (roasted pork), *cecina* (chili-coated pork), *carne asada* (roasted, chopped beef), *chorizo* (spicy sausage), *lengua* (beef tongue), *sesos* (cow brain), and *tasajo* (spiced, grilled beef).

Tamales—Sweet or savory corn cakes that are steamed, and may be filled with cheese, roasted chilis, shredded meat, or other fillings.

Torta—A Mexican sandwich served on a crusty sandwich roll. Fillings include meat, refried beans, and cheese.

10

(top left) Ceviche; (top right) Fish taco;
(bottom left) Tamales

PLANNING

CHILDREN

Although it's unusual to see children in the dining rooms of L.A.'s most elite restaurants, dining with youngsters here does not have to mean culinary exile.

SMOKING

Smokers should keep in mind that California law forbids smoking in all enclosed areas, including bars.

RESERVATIONS

You'll be happy to hear it's getting easier to snag a desired reservation, but it's still a good idea to plan ahead. Some renowned restaurants are booked weeks or even months in advance. If that's the case, you can get lucky at the last minute if you're flexible—and friendly. Most restaurants keep a few tables open for walk-ins and VIPs. Show up for dinner early (6 pm) or late (after 9 pm) and politely inquire about any last-minute vacancies or cancellations.

Occasionally, an eatery may ask you to call the day before your scheduled meal to reconfirm: don't forget or you could lose out. While making your reservation, also inquire about parking. You'll find most places, except small mom-and-pop establishments, provide valet parking at dinner for reasonable rates (often around $5, plus tip).

DINING HOURS

Despite its veneer of decadence, L.A. is not a particularly late-night city for eating. (The reenergized Hollywood dining scene is emerging as a notable exception.) The peak dinner times are from 7 to 9, and most restaurants won't take reservations after 10 pm. Unless otherwise noted, the restaurants listed in this guide are open daily for lunch and dinner. Generally speaking, restaurants are closed either Sunday or Monday; a few are shuttered both days. Most places—even the upscale spots—are open for lunch on weekdays, since many of Hollywood megadeals are conceived at that time.

WHAT TO WEAR

Dining out in Los Angeles tends to be a casual affair, and even at some of the most expensive restaurants you're likely to see customers in jeans (although this is not necessarily considered in good taste). It's extremely rare for L.A. restaurants to actually require a jacket and tie, but all of the city's more formal establishments appreciate a gentleman who dons a jacket—let your good judgment be your guide.

TIPPING AND TAXES

In most restaurants, tip the waiter 16%–20%. (To figure out a 20% tip quickly, just move the decimal point one place to the left on your total and double that amount.) Note that checks for parties of six or more sometimes include the tip already. Tip at least $1 per drink at the bar, and $1 for each coat checked. Never tip the maître d' unless you're out to impress your guests or expect to pay another visit soon. Also, be prepared for a sales tax of 9.75% to appear on your bill.

PRICES

If you're watching your budget, be sure to ask the price of daily specials recited by the waiter. The charge for specials at some restaurants is noticeably out of line with the other prices on the menu. Beware of the $10 bottle of water; ask for tap water instead. And always review your bill.

If you eat early or late, you may be able to take advantage of a prix-fixe deal not offered at peak hours. Most upscale restaurants are offering great lunch deals with special menus at cut-rate prices designed to give customers a true taste of the place.

Credit cards are accepted unless otherwise noted in the review. While many restaurants do accept credit cards, some smaller places accept only cash. If you plan to use a credit card it's a good idea to double-check its acceptability when making reservations or before sitting down to eat.

Prices in the restaurant reviews are the average cost of a main course at dinner or, if dinner is not served, at lunch.

RESTAURANT REVIEWS

Listed alphabetically within neighborhoods; use the coordinate (✥ 1:B2) at the end of each listing to locate a site on the corresponding map.

DOWNTOWN

The Eastside is home to L.A.'s boho community, a mixture of aspiring artists, musicians, scribes, and young families who grow their own vegetables and motor around on vintage Vespas. The neighborhood has been changing the last few years as Downtown's culinary renaissance has rippled through the area, making it a popular dining destination where people come in search of the edgy and creative menus that celebrate the artistic spirit of these communities. Here you'll find plenty of cozy wine bars, quaint bistros, historical landmarks, ethnic eats, and upscale restaurants that lack pretension.

$$ INDIAN Fodor's Choice ★ 🍴 **Badmaash.** This popular Indian eatery has quickly become beloved for its boundary-stretching menu, irreverent posters of Ghandi and other cultural icons, and Bollywood movies projected onto the soaring white walls. Challenging the formality of Indian cusine, curry has never been quite this cool before. Try the popular and indulgent chicken tikka *poutine* (a nod to Montreal's gravy covered fries), the short-rib samosas, or the chili cheese naan (which has been referred to as the Indian version of an enchilada.) [$] *Average main: $18* ✉ *108 W. 2nd St. No. 104, Downtown* ☎ *213/221–7466* 🌐 *www.badmaashla.com* ✍ *Reservations essential* 🕒 *No lunch weekends* ✥ *1:C2.*

$$ ITALIAN Fodor's Choice ★ 🍴 **Bottega Louie.** In a former Brooks Brother's suit store, this lively Italian restaurant and gourmet market quickly became Downtown's culinary darling. Vast open spaces, stark white walls, and windows that stretch from floor to ceiling give it a grand and majestic appeal. An army of stylish servers weaves in and out of the dining room carrying bowls of pasta and trays of thin-crust pizzas. Pick and choose from a bevy of salads, pastas, pizzas, and entrées that range from shrimp scampi to

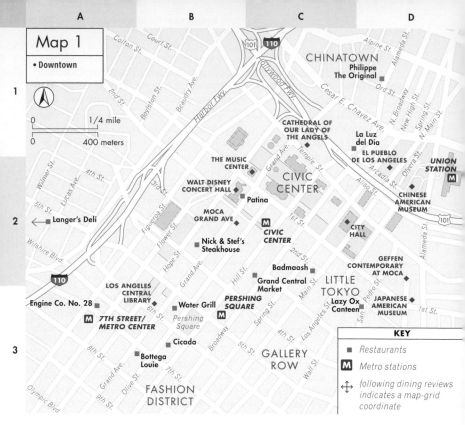

a hearty New York strip steak. Or simply order from the small plates menu: asparagus with fried egg, burrata, and roasted vine tomatoes, tomato bruschetta, and fried calamari. Don't let the crowd waiting for a table deter you, order a glass of Prosecco from the bar and nibble on a brightly colored macaroon. $ *Average main: $18* ⊠ *700 S. Grand Ave., Downtown* ☎ *213/802–1470* ⊕ *www.bottegalouie.com* ⌲ *Reservations not accepted* ⊕ *1:A3.*

$$$$ ✕ **Cicada.** One of the most romantic and architecturally dramatic din-
ITALIAN   ing venues in L.A., Cicada occupies the ground floor of the 1928 art deco Oviatt Building. Carved maple columns soar two stories to a gold leaf ceiling, and a mezzanine-level bar overlooks the spacious dining room. The menu leans on Italy, but with global influences, featuring dishes like tuna carpaccio with lemon-ginger sauce, and lamb chops with rosemary-mirin sauce. Fans rave about the restaurant's Lalique glass accents, live music, and widely spaced tables. Others complain about its banquet hall feel and so-so food. $ *Average main: $36* ⊠ *617 S. Olive St., Downtown* ☎ *213/488–9488* ⊕ *www.cicadarestaurant. com* ⌲ *Reservations essential* ⊙ *Closed Mon. No lunch* ⊕ *1:B3.*

$$ ✕ **Engine Co. No. 28.** A lovingly restored 1912 fire station where every-
AMERICAN   thing—even the original brass sliding pole—has been preserved, Engine
FAMILY   Co. No. 28 now rushes out solid, old-fashioned comfort food. The long bar is a popular hangout for Downtown workers delaying their

rush-hour commute. The kitchen does a fine job with chili, crab cakes, macaroni and cheese, and thick slabs of meat loaf. Specials showcase recipes inspired by firehouse cooking across the country. [$] *Average main: $18* ✉ *644 S. Figueroa St., Downtown* ☎ *213/624–6996* 🌐 *www.engineco.com* ⏲ *No lunch weekends* ✥ *1:A3.*

$ INTERNATIONAL
🍴 **Grand Central Market.** The Grand Central Market has long been a hub for ethnic eats that drew on crowds from the Downtown business district. A historical part of Los Angeles since 1917, the market, much like the rest of the area itself has gone through a culinary renaissance and these days you can find the area's hottest food curators and purveyors setting up shop. For breakfast make a stop at the popular **Egg Slut,** a former food truck that has opened its first brick and mortar, try the Slut which is coddled egg served in a glass jar with two pieces of toast. For lunch, meander over to **Valerie Bakery and Coffeeshop** and try their smoked salmon *bánh mì* with salmon, daikon pickle, seared jalapeno, Persian cucumber, red pepper, mint, cilantro, and ginger mayonnaise and don't skip their delectable sweets. [$] *Average main: $12* ✉ *317 S. Broadway, Downtown* ☎ *213/624-2378* 🌐 *www.grandcentralmarket.com/* ✍ *Reservations not accepted* ⏲ *Closed for dinner* ✥ *1:C2.*

$ MEXICAN FAMILY
La Luz del Dia. The most authentic Mexican food can be found at La Luz del Dia. Discover traditional Michoachan favorites such as chilis rellenos and *nopales* (pickled cactus), as well as handmade tortillas patted out in a practiced rhythm by the women behind the counter. [$] *Average main: $6* ✉ *W-1 Olvera St., Downtown* ☎ *213/628–7495* ✥ *1:C1.*

$ DELI
🍴 **Langer's Deli.** With fluorescent lighting and Formica tables, Langer's has the look of a no-frills Jewish deli back in New York. The draw here is the hand-cut pastrami, which is relatively lean, peppery, and robust in flavor—those who swear it's the best in town have a strong case. Some regulars opt for the legendary No. 19 (pastrami with Swiss and coleslaw piled high on twice-baked rye), but purists prefer it straight up with Russian dressing. The neighborhood is rough around the edges, but the nearby Metro station brings plenty of adventurous foodies who come in search of this James Beard Award–winning spot. [$] *Average main: $10* ✉ *704 S. Alvarado St., Downtown* ☎ *213/483–8050* 🌐 *www.langersdeli.com* ✍ *Reservations not accepted* ⏲ *Closed Sun. No dinner* ✥ *1:A2.*

10

$$$ INTERNATIONAL
🍴 **Lazy Ox Canteen.** In the artsy Little Tokyo section of Downtown Los Angeles, Lazy Ox Canteen is a neighborhood favorite often filled with Downtown dwellers who tuck themselves into a communal table for the night. The dimly lit restaurant brings together flavorful food, great wine, and moderate prices, along with an outdoor patio for enjoying L.A.'s great weather. The kitchen is led by Chef Josef Centeno, whose diverse culinary background has resulted in a hodgepodge of seasonal eats that range from caramelized onion soup to porcini rosemary ragu. Try the toad in the hole (crispy pork, brie, and poached egg on a brioche), the seared albacore ratatouille, or the burger with white cheddar and whole grain mustard. They have a lively weekend brunch, and desserts that don't disappoint. [$] *Average main: $20* ✉ *241 S. San Pedro, Downtown* ☎ *213/626–5299* 🌐 *www.lazyoxcanteen.com* ✥ *1:D3.*

$$$$
STEAKHOUSE

✕**Nick & Stef's Steakhouse.** Run by restaurateurs Joachim and Christine Splichal and named after their twin boys, this contemporary beef palace has been so successful they've replicated the concept in other cities. Despite a sleek, modern aesthetic, elements of the traditional steak house—comfortable booths, crisp white linen, and wood accents—remain. The premium steaks come from a glassed-in aging room; build up your order by choosing from a diverse array of sauces, starches, and vegetables that give honored steak-house traditions a little sex appeal. The wine list, deep in California reds, is predictably strong. $ *Average main: $35* ✉ *330 S. Hope St., Downtown* ☎ *213/680–0330* ⊕ *www.patinagroup.com* ⚖ *Reservations essential* ⊙ *No lunch weekends* ✛ *1:B2.*

> **DINING BY DESIGN**
>
> Architecture buffs needn't go hungry in L.A. The **Restaurant at the Getty Center** (✉ *1200 Getty Center Dr., Brentwood* ☎ *310/440–6810* ⊕ *www.getty. edu*) places sophisticated fare in the midst of Richard Meier's travertine–clad museum, and acclaimed **Patina** sits inside Frank Gehry's stainless steel–plated Walt Disney Concert Hall. **Cicada,** in the Oviatt Building (an art deco masterpiece), serves modern Italian cuisine.

$$$$
FRENCH

✕**Patina.** Opened by chef Joachim Splichal, Patina has Downtown's most striking address: inside the Frank Gehry–designed Walt Disney Concert Hall. The contemporary space, surrounded by a rippled "curtain" of rich walnut, is an elegant, dramatic stage for the acclaimed restaurant's contemporary French cuisine. Seasonally changing specialties include copious amounts of foie gras, butter-poached lobster, and medallions of venison served with lady apples. Finish with a hard-to-match cheese tray (orchestrated by a genuine *maître fromager*) and the elegant fromage blanc soufflé served with house-made bourbon ice cream. $ *Average main: $46* ✉ *Walt Disney Concert Hall, 141 S. Grand Ave., Downtown* ☎ *213/972–3331* ⊕ *www.patinagroup.com* ⚖ *Reservations essential* ⊙ *Closed Mon.* ✛ *1:B2.*

$
AMERICAN
FAMILY
Fodor's Choice
★

✕**Philippe the Original.** Dating from 1908, L.A.'s oldest restaurant claims that the French dip sandwich originated here. You can get one made with beef, pork, ham, lamb, or turkey on a freshly baked roll; the house hot mustard is as famous as the sandwiches. Its reputation is earned by maintaining traditions, from sawdust on the floor to long communal tables where customers debate the Dodgers or local politics. The home cooking—orders are taken at the counter where some of the motherly servers have managed their long lines for decades—includes huge breakfasts, chili, pickled eggs, and a generous pie selection. The best bargain: a cup of java for 49¢. $ *Average main: $7* ✉ *1001 N. Alameda St., Downtown* ☎ *213/628–3781* ⊕ *www.philippes.com* ⚖ *Reservations not accepted* ▭ *No credit cards* ✛ *1:D1.*

$$$$
SEAFOOD

✕**Water Grill.** There's a bustling, enticing rhythm here as platters of glistening shellfish get whisked from the oyster bar to the bright dining room. The menu is seasonally driven; all the seafood greats are represented. Start with steamed mussels, the Fijian albacore tuna Niçoise salad, or a New England–style lobster roll. For entrées, consider the line-caught Baja mahimahi sautéed with a pomegranate glaze, the Atlantic cod fish-and-chips, and the bigeye tuna rubbed with maitake mushrooms. Excellent desserts and a fine wine list round out this top-notch (albeit pricey) Downtown dining experience. [$] *Average main: $36 ⊠ 544 S. Grand Ave., Downtown* ☎ *213/891–0900* ⊕ *www. watergrill.com* ⚐ *Reservations essential* ⊘ *No lunch weekends* ✛ *1:B3.*

HOLLYWOOD AND THE STUDIOS

HOLLYWOOD

Hollywood has two faces. Although a hub for tourists who come here to take photos along the Hollywood Walk of Fame, it is still in touch with its irreverent rock-and-roll roots. The result is a complex dining scene made up of cheap fast food, upscale eateries, and provocative hot spots helmed by celebrity chefs.

$$
AMERICAN
✕ **25 Degrees.** Named after the difference in temperature between a medium-rare and well-done burger, this upscale burger joint sits in one of Hollywood's hippest hotels. The action at 25 Degrees revolves around a counter constructed of rich oak instead of Formica, and Cabernet is favored over cola. Order the No. 1 (caramelized onions, Gorgonzola and Crescenza cheeses, bacon, arugula, and Thousand Island dressing) or create your own masterpiece from a selection of premium meats, artisanal cheeses, and house-made condiments. A long list of half bottles makes wine pairings easy for solo diners. It's open 24 hours—and does offer other choices, including a good fried egg sandwich, if you're unsure about burgers for breakfast. [$] *Average main: $15 ⊠ Hollywood Roosevelt Hotel, 7000 Hollywood Blvd., Hollywood* ☎ *323/785–7244* ⊕ *www.25degreesrestaurant.com* ⚐ *Reservations not accepted* ✛ *2:E2.*

$$
AMERICAN
✕ **Ammo.** This hip canteen proves that designers and photographers (regulars here) have good taste in food as well as fashion. The ever-evolving menu at this neighborhood favorite changes with the seasons: lunch might be French lentil salad, a perfectly cooked burger, or a pro-sciutto, mozzarella, and arugula sandwich. Start dinner with one of the kitchen's market-fresh salads, then follow up with a baby artichoke pizza or a grilled hanger steak. The crisp, minimal setting is cool but not chilly. [$] *Average main: $18 ⊠ 1155 N. Highland Ave., Hollywood* ☎ *323/871–2666* ⊕ *www.ammocafe.com* ✛ *2:E2.*

$$$
AMERICAN
✕ **Animal.** When foodies in Los Angeles need a culinary thrill, they come to this restaurant in the Fairfax District, which is light on the flash but heavy on serious food. The James Beard Award–winning restaurant is owned by Jon Shook and Vinny Dotolo, two young chefs who shot to fame with a stint on *Iron Chef* and later with their own show called *Two Dudes Catering.* With a closing time of midnight, the small restaurant is one of the few late-night spots in L.A. The menu consists of small plates and entrées that make it easy to explore many items, like barbecue pork belly sandwiches, *poutine* with oxtail gravy, foie gras *loco moco* (a hamburger topped with foie gras, quail egg, and Spam), and grilled quail served with plum *char-siu.* For dessert, the house specialty is a multilayer bacon-chocolate crunch bar. [$] *Average main: $25 ⊠ 435 N. Fairfax Ave., Hollywood* ☎ *323/782–9225* ⊕ *www.animalrestaurant. com* ⚐ *Reservations essential* ⊘ *No lunch* ✛ *2:D3.*

10

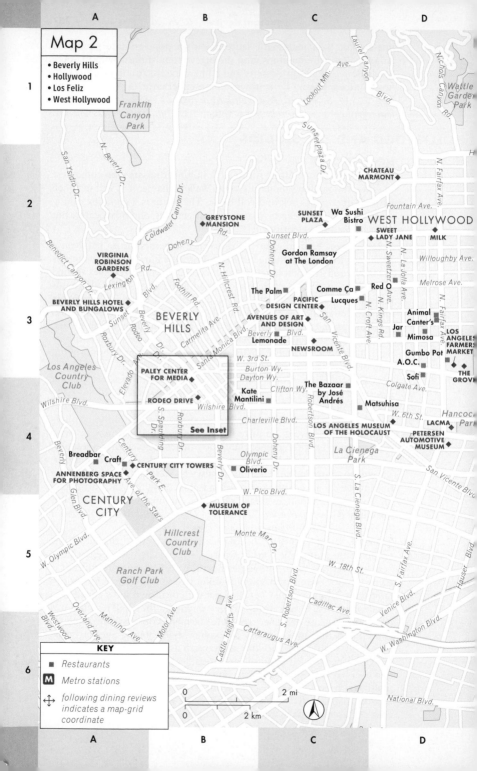

$$$$ LATIN AMERICAN 🍴 **Beso.** Celebrity chef Todd English takes on Hollywood, collaborating with television star Eva Longoria at this stylish Latin-theme restaurant. Glittering chandeliers dangle over a dramatic scene: young hipsters sipping mojitos at a marble bar and couples sliding into cozy booths with a view of the prominent exhibition kitchen. Begin with one of the inventive appetizers, such as the artichoke guacamole or the addictive crispy ribs with apple slaw. For the main course, move on to a steak with chimichurri sauce or jumbo sea scallops with pomegranate sauce. Churros with chocolate and fried-banana splits make for the sweetest finale. Beso (the name means "kiss" in Spanish) is pure Hollywood, but because it doesn't take itself too seriously, it adds plenty of fun to the legendary neighborhood. [$] *Average main: $35* ✉ *6350 Hollywood Blvd., Hollywood* ☎ *323/467–7991* 🌐 *www.besohollywood.com* ✍ *Reservations essential* 🕒 *Closed Sun. No lunch* ✥ *2:F2.*

$$$ MEDITERRANEAN 🍴 **Cleo.** Tucked away in the Redbury Hotel, this hip restaurant buzzes with energy in both its ambience and its fresh approach to Mediterranean cuisine. Start with a trio of dips including hummus with tahini, thick yogurt with feta, and a *muhammara* (walnut garlic spread) that comes with fresh-from-the-oven flatbread. Chicken and lamb kebabs are an ideal segue into the main courses, as are the perfectly roasted lamb shank or the moussakah made with eggplant, beef ragù, and feta and sprinkled with pine nuts. Get your veggie allowance with the Brussels sprouts made with capers, parsley, and almonds, or mushrooms with hazelnuts and dates. The thoughtful cocktail menu, decent wine list, and enthusiastic staff make Cleo a great place to spend the evening—Hollywood style. [$] *Average main: $30* ✉ *Redbury Hotel, 1717 Vine St., Hollywood* ☎ *323/962–1711* 🌐 *www.cleorestaurant.com* 🕒 *No lunch* ✥ *2:F2.*

$$ ITALIAN Fodor'sChoice ★ 🍴 **Cube Café & Marketplace.** Cheese, charcuterie, and pasta lovers take heed: this seasonally inspired Italian restaurant will ruin you for all the others. With more than 30 varieties of cheese, an enviable salami selection, picture-perfect pastries and a passionate staff, this former pasta company turned café and gourmet market is one of L.A.'s more affordable culinary gems. Take a seat at the bar, order the cheesemonger's choice, and pair it with a glass of Italian wine. For dinner, start with the antipasti of braised octopus, then move on to the English pea tortellini or cavatelli with house-made sausage served with sprouting baby broccoli. [$] *Average main: $22* ✉ *615 N. La Brea Blvd., Hollywood* ☎ *323/939–1148* 🌐 *www.eatatcube.com* 🕒 *Closed Sun. and Mon.* ✥ *2:D3.*

$$ MODERN MEXICAN 🍴 **El Cholo.** The first of what's now a small chain, this landmark south of Hollywood has been packing them in since the 1920s. A hand-painted adobe ceiling and an outdoor patio with a fountain create a partylike atmosphere, which the bar's legendary margaritas can only enhance. The fare includes all kinds of Cal–Mex standards, including tacos, chicken enchiladas, *carnitas* (shredded fried pork), and—from July to October—their famous green-corn tamales. [$] *Average main: $15* ✉ *1121 S. Western Ave., Hollywood* ☎ *323/734–2773* 🌐 *www.elcholo.com* ✥ *2:G5.*

$$ MEXICAN 🍴 **Guelaguetza.** Catering to a largely Spanish-speaking clientele, this in-the-know spot has a festive mood and exotic scents filling the small, cheerful space. Surely one of L.A.'s best Mexican eateries, it serves the complex but not overpoweringly spicy cooking of Oaxaca, one of Mexico's most renowned culinary capitals. The standouts are the moles, whose intense flavors come from intricate combinations of nuts, seeds, spices, chilis, and bitter chocolate. But be sure to check out barbecued goat tacos or pizzalike *clayudas* topped with white cheese and *tasajo* (dried beef) or *cecina* (chili-marinated pork) and chorizo. [$] *Average main: $14* ✉ *3014 W. Olympic Blvd, Mid-Wilshire* ☎ *213/427–0608* 🌐 *www.ilovemole.com* ✥ *2:G4.*

$$ MEXICAN FAMILY 🍴 **Lotería! Grill Hollywood.** After drawing an almost cultlike following from a stand in the Farmers Market, Lotería! takes on Hollywood with a sleek sit-down restaurant with essentially the same time-tested menu. Start with banana squash and corn soup or *chicharron de queso* (a crunchy, paper-thin sheet of addictive griddle-toasted cheese) with guacamole while sipping on the tequila you've selected from a long list. Then tuck into tacos or burritos stuffed with mushrooms and cheese, meatballs in tomato-chipotle sauce, or *cochinita pibil* (Yucatán-style pork). To tame the heat, nothing soothes the palate like its homemade Mexican ice cream. [$] *Average main: $16* ✉ *6627 Hollywood Blvd., Hollywood* ☎ *323/465–2500* 🌐 *www.loteriagrill.com* ✥ *2:F1.*

$ AMERICAN FAMILY 🍴 **Pink's Hot Dogs.** Orson Welles ate 18 of these hot dogs in one sitting, and you, too, will be tempted to order more than one. The chili dogs are the main draw, but the menu has expanded to include a Martha Stewart Dog (a 10-inch frank topped with mustard, relish, onions, tomatoes, sauerkraut, bacon, and sour cream). Since 1939, Angelenos and tourists alike have been lining up to plunk down some modest change for one of the greatest guilty pleasures in L.A. Pink's is open until 3 am on weekends. [$] *Average main: $4* ✉ *709 N. La Brea Ave., Hollywood* ☎ *323/931–4223* 🌐 *www.pinkshollywood.com* ✍ *Reservations not accepted* 💳 *No credit cards* ✥ *2:E2.*

$$ ITALIAN Fodor's Choice ★ 🍴 **Pizzeria Mozza.** This casual venue gives newfound eminence to the humble "pizza joint." With traditional Mediterranean items like white anchovies, squash blossoms, and Gorgonzola, Mozza's pies—thin-crusted delights with golden, blistered edges—are much more Campania than California, and virtually every one is a winner. Antipasti include simple salads, roasted bone marrow, and platters of *salumi*. All sing with vibrant flavors thanks to superb market-fresh ingredients, and daily specials may include favorites like lasagna. Like the menu, the Italian-only wine list is both interesting and affordable. Walk-ins are welcome at the bar. [$] *Average main: $20* ✉ *641 N. Highland Ave., Hollywood* ☎ *323/297–0101* 🌐 *www.pizzeriamozza.com* ✍ *Reservations essential* ✥ *2:E3.*

$$$$ SEAFOOD Fodor's Choice ★ 🍴 **Providence.** Chef-owner Michael Cimarusti has elevated Providence to the ranks of America's finest seafood restaurants. The elegant dining room, outfitted with subtle nautical accents, is smoothly overseen by co-owner Donato Poto. Obsessed with quality and freshness, the meticulous chef maintains a network of specialty purveyors, some of

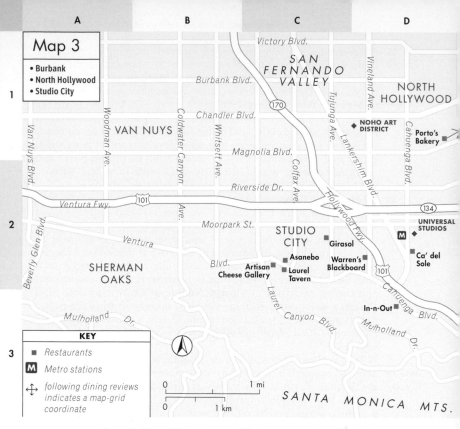

Map 3

- Burbank
- North Hollywood
- Studio City

A   **B**   **C**   **D**

Victory Blvd.

SAN FERNANDO VALLEY

Burbank Blvd.

NORTH HOLLYWOOD

Woodman Ave.

Van Nuys Blvd.

VAN NUYS

Coldwater Canyon

Whitsett Ave.

Chandler Blvd.

Magnolia Blvd.

Colfax Ave.

Tujunga Ave.

Lankershim Blvd.

Vineland Ave.

Cahuenga Blvd.

NOHO ART DISTRICT

Porto's Bakery

Riverside Dr.

Ventura Fwy.

Ave.

Moorpark St.

Ventura

SHERMAN OAKS

Beverly Glen Blvd.

Blvd.

STUDIO CITY

Girasol

Asanebo

Artisan Cheese Gallery

Warren's Blackboard

Laurel Tavern

Hollywood Fwy.

UNIVERSAL STUDIOS

Ca' del Sole

Cahuenga Blvd.

In-n-Out

Mulholland Dr.

Laurel Canyon Blvd.

Mulholland Dr.

KEY

- ■ Restaurants
- Ⓜ Metro stations
- ⬌ following dining reviews indicates a map-grid coordinate

0   1 mi
0   1 km

SANTA MONICA MTS.

whom tip him off to their catch before it even hits the dock. This exquisite seafood then gets the Cimarusti treatment of French technique, traditional American themes, and Asian accents, often presented in elaborate tasting menus. Pastry chef David Rodriguez's exquisite desserts are not to be missed. For a splurge, consider the six-course dessert tasting menu. $ *Average main: $43* ✉ *5955 Melrose Ave., Hollywood* ☎ *323/460–4170* ⊕ *www.providencela.com* ☞ *Reservations essential* ⊙ *No lunch Mon.–Thurs. and weekends* ⬌ *2:F3.*

$ ✕ **Roscoe's House of Chicken 'n Waffles.** Don't be put off by the name of
SOUTHERN   this casual eatery, which honors a late-night combo popularized in
FAMILY   Harlem jazz clubs. Roscoe's is *the* place for real down-home Southern cooking. Just ask the patrons, who drive from all over L.A. for Roscoe's bargain-price fried chicken, wonderful waffles (which, by the way, turn out to be a great partner for fried chicken), buttery chicken livers, and toothsome grits. Although Roscoe's has the intimate feel of a smoky jazz club, those musicians hanging out here are just taking five. $ *Average main: $10* ✉ *1514 N. Gower St., Hollywood* ☎ *323/466–7453* ⊕ *www.roscoeschickenandwaffles.com* ☞ *Reservations not accepted* ⬌ *2:F2.*

$ ✕ **Zankou Chicken.** This aromatic, Armenian-style rotisserie chicken
MIDDLE EASTERN   with perfectly crisp, golden skin is one of L.A.'s truly great budget
FAMILY   meals. It's served with pita bread, veggies, hummus, and unforgettable

garlic sauce. If this doesn't do it for you, try the kebabs, falafel, or sensational *shawarma* (spit-roasted lamb or chicken) plates. Ⓢ *Average main: $9* ⊠ *5065 W. Sunset Blvd., Hollywood* ☎ *323/665–7845* ⚏ *Reservations not accepted* ✛ *2:H2.*

NORTH HOLLYWOOD

North Hollywood has a burgeoning dining scene that has made this a great place for a night out. Tapas restaurants, stylish bars, and an up-and-coming hotel restaurant can be discovered in the NoHo Arts District.

$$ ✕ **Ca' del Sole.** With antique wood hutches, copper moldings, and a
ITALIAN fireplace, this establishment draws a diverse clientele in search of grilled octopus drizzled with a spicy limoncello vinaigrette, soulful spaghetti carbonara, pumpkin-filled *mezzelune* (half moon–shaped ravioli), and classic osso buco. The wine list is moderately priced and, weather permitting, you can sit on the walled patio that, despite its proximity to L.A. traffic, feels wonderfully escapist. Ⓢ *Average main: $18* ⊠ *4100 Cahuenga Blvd., North Hollywood* ☎ *818/985–4669* ⊕ *www.cadelsole.com* ☽ *No lunch Sat.* ✛ *3:D2.*

$$ ✕ **Warren's Blackboard.** For years, the diner at the Beverly Garland
DINER Hotel was sadly overlooked. No longer. Led by Executive Chef Warren Schwartz, the menu at Warren's Blackboard is simple, seasonal, and approachable. A comfortable dining area that's great for families is on one side of the room, and a bar area with television screens playing classic movies can be found on the other. Start with a buratta and pear salad and a spectacularly savory mushroom and bacon popover. Dinner entrées include grilled salmon with yams, Treviso radicchio and tangerines, or seared scallops with carrot risotto, grapefruit, and tarragon. Ⓢ *Average main: $20* ⊠ *Beverly Garland Hotel, 4222 Vineland Ave., North Hollywood* ☎ *818/255–7290* ✛ *3:D2.*

BURBANK

Home to movie and television studios, there's a quiet sophistication to this part of town. Great restaurants are tucked away in strip malls and side streets. Don't be surprised if you spot celebrities while grabbing lunch.

$ ✕ **Porto's Bakery.** Waiting in line at Porto's is as much a part of the expe-
CUBAN rience as is indulging in a roasted pork sandwich and chocolate-dipped
FAMILY croissant. Locals love this neighborhood bakery and café that has been an L.A. staple for more than 50 years. Just minutes away from Griffith Park, it's a great spot to take a stroll and peruse the consignment shops run by former movie fashion stylists. The café bustles with an ambitious lunch crowd, but counter service is quick and efficient. Go for one of its tasty sandwiches like the *pan con lechon* (roasted pork), or try the filling plate of *ropa vieja* (shredded beef). Skipping dessert here would just be wrong. Your sweet tooth will thank you later. Ⓢ *Average main: $10* ⊠ *3614 W. Magnolia Blvd., Burbank* ☎ *818/846–9100* ⊕ *www.portosbakery.com* ✛ *3:D1.*

10

LOS FELIZ

This affluent hillside community has a laid-back dining scene. Wine bars, burger joints, and a pint-size taco stand are among the options for a family night out.

$ ✗ **Cha Cha Cha.** Left-of-center Cha Cha Cha attracts an eclectic crowd. It's
CARIBBEAN   hip without being pretentious or overly trendy. A giant map on the wall suggests the restaurant's Caribbean influences. You can sit in the small dining room or on the enclosed tropical patio where Carmen Miranda would feel at home. Standard options include empanadas, Jamaican jerk chicken or pork, curried shrimp, fried plantain chips, and paella. Sangría is the drink of choice. $ *Average main: $10* ✉ *656 N. Virgil Ave., Los Feliz* ☎ *323/664–7723* ⊕ *www.theoriginalchachacha.com* ✛ *2:H3.*

$ ✗ **Fred 62.** This tongue-in-cheek take on the American diner was created
ECLECTIC   by funky L.A. chef-restaurateur Fred Eric. The usual burgers and shakes
FAMILY   are joined by such eclectic dishes as the Fried Chicken Salad (made with jicama, pico de gallo, and a habanero-cilantro dressing), the Poorest Boy sandwich (crispy fried chicken, onions, and rémoulade on a French roll) and the Coffee Shop Grilled Cheese, served on a brioche. Breakfasts range from tofu scrambles to "Hunka Hunka Burnin' Love"—pancakes made with peanut butter, chocolate chips, and banana. Like the neighborhood itself, nobody is out of place here, with everybody from button-down business executives to tattooed musicians showing up at some point. $ *Average main: $10* ✉ *1850 N. Vermont Ave., Los Feliz* ☎ *323/667– 0062* ⊕ *www.fred62.com* ⌂ *Reservations not accepted* ✛ *2:H1.*

$$$ ✗ **Little Dom's.** With a vintage bar and dapper barkeep who mixes up sea-
ITALIAN   sonally inspired retro cocktails, an attached Italian deli where you can pick
Fodor'sChoice   up a pork cheek sub, and a $15 Monday night supper, it's not surprising
★   why Little Dom's is a neighborhood gem. Cozy and inviting, with big leather booths you can sink into for the night, Little Dom's has a menu that blends classic Italian fare with a modern sensibility, with dishes like the baked ricotta and wild boar soppressatta, rigatoni with homemade sausage, whitefish picatta, and New York strip steak with a fennel béarnaise. This is a terrific spot for weekend brunch; order a bottle of the well-priced house wine and take a seat in the sidewalk patio for an L.A. experience. $ *Average main: $24* ✉ *2128 Hillhurst Ave., Los Feliz* ☎ *323/661–0055* ⊕ *www.littledoms.com* ⌂ *Reservations essential* ✛ *2:H1.*

$ ✗ **Umami Burger.** There's sweet, salty, bitter, and sour, and now, there's
AMERICAN   Umami. This burger joint, named after the pleasant savory taste discovered by the Japanese, has found a loving following by locals who come here for gourmet burgers that awaken all the senses. A simple dining room with lively music creates a casual environment that's home to locals, gourmets, and families who come in search of a savory burger with unique fixings. Go for the Umami burger made with a juicy patty and served medium rare with a parmesan crisp and the signature ketchup that's both sweet and savory. Or try the SoCal burger that's made with oven-dried tomato spread, butter lettuce, and house-made American cheese. Add a side of sweet potato fries or ask for the off-the-menu cheesy tater tots that come with jalapeño ranch dressing. $ *Average main: $13* ✉ *4655 Hollywood Blvd., Los Feliz* ☎ *323/669–3922* ⊕ *www.umamiburger.com* ✛ *2:H2.*

$ 🍴 **Yuca's Hut.** Blink and you can miss this place, whose reputation far exceeds its size (it may be the tiniest place to have ever won a James Beard Award). It's known for *carne asada*, (marinated beef), *cochinita pibil* (Yucatán-style roasted pork) tacos, burritos, and banana leaf-wrapped tamales. This is a fast-food restaurant in the finest tradition—independent, family-owned, and sticking to what it does best. The liquor store next door sells lots of Coronas to Yuca's customers soaking up the sun on the makeshift parking-lot patio. There's no chance of satisfying a late-night craving, though; it closes at 6 pm. [$] *Average main: $10* ✉ *2056 N. Hillhurst Ave., Los Feliz* ☎ *323/662–1214* 🌐 *www.yucasla.com* ✍ *Reservations not accepted* 💳 *No credit cards* ⏲ *Closed Sun. No dinner* ✥ *2:H1.*

MEXICAN
FAMILY
Fodor's Choice ★

STUDIO CITY

The dining scene here continues to grow as restaurateurs realize how many locals are looking for stylish and swanky places to eat. Japanese, Mexican, and Italian eateries can all be found in this dynamic city.

$ 🍴 **Artisan Cheese Gallery.** Taste your way through triple creams, goat's milk, blues, and other aromatic cheeses from all over the globe at this charming locale that offers cheese and charcuterie plates, super sandwiches, and oversize salads. Taste-testing is encouraged, so don't be shy to ask. Grab a table on the small outdoor patio and enjoy the scenery. [$] *Average main: $10* ✉ *12023 Ventura Blvd., Studio City* ☎ *818/505–0207* 🌐 *www.artisancheesegallery.com* ✍ *Reservations not accepted* ✥ *3:C2.*

DELI
FAMILY

$$$$ 🍴 **Asanebo.** Don't let its nondescript minimal location deter you: Asanebo is one of L.A.'s finest Japanese restaurants—and still relatively undiscovered. Once strictly a sashimi bar, this inviting establishment introduced top-quality sushi to satisfy increasing local demand and also offers a wealth of innovative dishes. From a simple morsel of pristine fish dusted with sea salt to intricately cooked items, Asanebo continues to impress. The affable chefs will introduce you to memorable specialties such as a caviar-topped lobster cocktail and succulent seared *toro* (tuna belly) drizzled with a light garlic cream. [$] *Average main: $35* ✉ *11941 Ventura Blvd., Studio City* ☎ *818/760–3348* ✍ *Reservations essential* ⏲ *Closed Mon. No lunch weekends* ✥ *3:C2.*

JAPANESE

$$$ 🍴 **Girasol.** A white-wood sunflower with swirling vines and petals covers the wall at Girasol creating a woodsy and cozy mood to complement the seasonally driven menu. Found along a busy street made up of apartments, condos, and strip malls, Girasol is a Valley favorite thanks to its chef CJ Jacobson (of Top Chef fame) who celebrates California's sunny days and year-round Farmers Market. Start with the rustic beets and berries that is served atop whipped Soledad goat cheese, leafy herbs and hazelnuts or the Frog Hollow pears with burrata, crispy lentils and basil. For dinner, the whole fried red snapper with kumquats and sorrel is a crowd pleaser or the braised leg of lamb with crispy Brussels sprouts, charred juniper, parsnip purée and huckleberry. Leave room for the wild acorn panna cotta with whipped crème fraîche and a wild sage shortbread; it won't disappoint your inner wood nymph. [$] *Average main: $28* ✉ *11334 Moorpark St., Studio City* ☎ *818/824–2323* 🌐 *www.girasolrestaurant.com* ✍ *Reservations essential* ⏲ *No lunch Mon.–Sat.* ✥ *3:C2.*

ECLECTIC

$ BURGER 🍴 **In-N-Out.** Quintessentially California, In-N-Out is beloved by the masses, which is easy to see with the lines of cars wrapped around the driveway. Whether it's the double-double you love, with or without grilled onions, or the grilled cheese (on their secret menu), the best thing about In-N-Out is the complete West Coast experience you can have with a burger, order of fries, and a chocolate shake. This branch is close to Universal Studios. [$] *Average main: $8* ✉ *3640 Cahuenga Blvd., Studio City* ☎ *1-800/786–1000* 🌐 *www.in-n-out.com* ✣ *3:D3.*

WORD OF MOUTH

"The word 'casual' always throws me here—just about EVERY restaurant in California is casual."
—rjw_lgb_ca

$ AMERICAN 🍴 **Laurel Tavern.** This classic American pub—in a handsome package of exposed brick, leather walls, and two huge picture windows—serves gourmet bar food and craft beers. The menu is classic burgers, beers, and fries, but with an upscale twist. Top choices include chorizo sliders, pork belly skewers, and lollipop chicken wings. There are 10 beers on draft that were handpicked by the restaurant's "beer chick." [$] *Average main: $10* ✉ *11938 Ventura Blvd., Studio City* ☎ *818/506–0777* 🌐 *www.laureltavern.net* ✣ *3:C2.*

SILVER LAKE

With plenty of hipster appeal, the eateries of Silver Lake draw an eclectic crowd that likes its neighborhood hangouts.

$$ ECLECTIC 🍴 **Allumette.** This critically acclaimed restaurant is led by young chef Miles Thompson, who has worked in the kitchens of L.A.'s best and brightest. Thompson has created an innovative menu that the staff calls "avant-garde comfort food," and the result has been met with success. The small-plate menu is not meant to be shared, but savored individually. Start with the house-made potato chips served with smoked white fish and sea urchin cream or the Dungeness crab custard known as "Mermaid Cereal" because of the layers of texture in each bite. The gnocchetti with wood pigeon ragu and the branzino with shellfish tapioca are house favorites. Try the Jerusalem artichoke panna cotta made with dulce de leche for a sweet and savory dessert. [$] *Average main: $20* ✉ *1320 Echo Park Blvd., Echo Park* ☎ *213/935–8787* 🌐 *allumettela.com* ✍ *Reservations essential* ⏲ *No lunch. Closed Sun. and Mon.* ✣ *2:H2.*

$$ VIETNAMESE FAMILY 🍴 **Gingergrass.** Traditional Vietnamese favorites emerge from this café's open kitchen, sometimes with a California twist. With a minimalist decor marked by tropical wood banquettes, Silver Lake's bohemian past and über-trendy present converge at Gingergrass. Consider classic crispy-skinned imperial rolls (filled with chicken, veggies, or crab and shrimp, served with lettuce and mint for wrapping), variations on *pho* (Vietnam's ubiquitous noodle soup), and Cal-light versions of *bánh mì* (baguette sandwiches that fuse French and Southeast Asian traditions), along with a refreshing basil-lime elixir. [$] *Average main: $17* ✉ *2396 Glendale Blvd., Silver Lake* ☎ *323/644–1600* 🌐 *www.gingergrass.com* ✍ *Reservations not accepted* ✣ *2:H2.*

$$ CAFÉ 🍴 **LAMILL Coffee Boutique.** With a sleek, neoclassical design, and menu designed by Providence chef Michael Cimarusti and his acclaimed pastry chef Adrian Vasquez, this is no ordinary neighborhood coffeehouse. For coffee connoisseurs, LAMILL features the finest beans from around the world, brewed in a French press or through a siphon apparatus that looks like it was salvaged from the laboratory of a mad scientist. For foodies, house-cured Tasmanian sea trout with wasabi crème fraîche are followed by exquisitely presented desserts like chocolate lollipops and an exotic Asian twist on s'mores. [$] *Average main: $22* ✉ *1636 Silver Lake Blvd., Silver Lake* ☎ *323/663–4441* 🌐 *www.lamillcoffee.com* ✥ *2:H2.*

BEVERLY HILLS AND THE WESTSIDE

Never short on sophistication, Beverly Hills, West Hollywood, and the Westside are known for their high-profile eateries that often have paparazzi camped outside.

BEVERLY HILLS

Dining in the 90210 is always an elegant experience, especially when you're leaving your car with the valet at one of the hot new restaurant along Wilshire Boulevard. But meals here don't need to break the bank, as there are also eateries that are cool, casual, and relatively affordable.

$$ DELI 🍴 **Barney Greengrass.** Unlike your corner lox-and-bagel joint, this *haute* deli on the fifth floor of Barneys department store has an appropriately runway-ready aesthetic: limestone floors, mahogany furniture, and a wall of windows. On the outdoor terrace, at tables shaded by large umbrellas, you can savor flawless smoked salmon, sturgeon, and whitefish flown in fresh from New York. The deli closes at 6 pm. [$] *Average main: $20* ✉ *Barneys, 9570 Wilshire Blvd., Beverly Hills* ☎ *310/777–5877* ✥ *2:H6.*

$$$$ SPANISH 🍴 **The Bazaar by José Andrés.** Celebrity Spanish chef José Andrés conquers L.A. with a multifaceted concept that includes two dining rooms (one classic, one modern), a cocktail bar stocked with liquid nitrogen, and a flashy patisserie. Half the menu is dedicated to traditional Spanish tapas: *bacalao* (salt cod) fritters with honey aioli, creamy chicken *croquetas*, and plates of chorizo or prized *jamón Ibérico*. The other half involves some wild inventions of molecular gastronomy, including "liquid" olives (created through a technique called spherification), and an ethereal version of the traditional tortilla Española in which an egg is cooked slowly at 63 degrees, just short of coagulation. A splendid list of Spanish wines is offered. For dessert, the patisserie offers playful items like beet meringue with pistachios and chocolate lollipops. [$] *Average main: $36* ✉ *SLS Hotel at Beverly Hills, 465 S. La Cienega Blvd., Beverly Hills* ☎ *310/246–5555* 🌐 *www.thebazaar.com* ✍ *Reservations essential* ⏲ *No lunch* ✥ *2:C4.*

$$$$ AMERICAN 🍴 **The Belvedere.** In the entertainment industry's A-list hotel, the Belvedere practically guarantees that you'll be rubbing elbows with power brokers. The refined cooking here elevates the opulent restaurant far above the usual hotel dining room. You may want to start with the signature house-smoked salmon with scallion pancakes, chive crème fraîche, and caviar, then indulge in osso bucco, Kansas City strip steak, or grilled Alaskan halibut with pomegranate gastrique. At lunch, deal makers convene over salads and such "glamburgers" as sautéed salmon with fennel-kumquat jam and dill mayonnaise. The execs who favor this place are prone to special ordering—and the staff graciously obliges. [$] *Average main: $36* ✉ *The Peninsula Beverly Hills, 9882 S. Santa Monica Blvd., Beverly Hills* ☎ *310/975–2306* 🌐 *www.peninsula.com* ⊕ *2:F6.*

$$$ FRENCH Fodor's Choice ★

🍴 **Bouchon Bistro.** Famed chef Thomas Keller has set up his unforgettable bistro right in the center of swanky Beverly Hills. Grand and majestic, there is nothing about Bouchon that doesn't make you feel pampered. With little details that separate it from the pack, look for filtered Norwegian water served at every table, twig-shape baguettes made fresh in the kitchen, and an expansive wine list celebrating California and French wines. It's a foodie scene that welcomes L.A.'s high-profile chefs, celebrities, and locals. Start with its classic onion soup that arrives with a bubbling lid of cheese, or the salmon rillettes, which are big enough to share. For dinner, there's a traditional steak and *frites*, roasted chicken, steamed Maine mussels, and a delicious grilled *croque madame*. For a sweet bite, order an espresso and the profiteroles or the bite-size brownies served with homemade vanilla ice cream. Special menus come with a tour of the multimillion-dollar kitchen. [$] *Average main: $27* ✉ *235 N. Canon Dr., Beverly Hills* ☎ *310/271–9910* 🌐 *www.bouchonbistro.com* ✍ *Reservations essential* ⊕ *2:H6.*

$$$$ VIETNAMESE

🍴 **Crustacean.** This head-turning venue is a surreal reproduction of colonial Vietnam. Exotic fish swim in a floor-to-ceiling aquarium and through a glass-topped "river" sunk into the marble floor, which meanders toward the bar. The French-influenced Southeast Asian menu includes lemongrass–scented bouillabaisse and filet mignon with a ponzu glaze. Colossal tiger prawns and whole Dungeness crab simmered in sake, Chardonnay, and Cognac parade out of the "secret kitchen" where only the owner's family members are allowed, thereby protecting treasured recipes. [$] *Average main: $36* ✉ *9646 Santa Monica Blvd., Beverly Hills* ☎ *310/205–8990* 🌐 *houseofan.com/wp* ✍ *Reservations essential* ⏲ *No lunch weekends* ⊕ *2:G5.*

$$$$ STEAKHOUSE

🍴 **CUT.** In a true collision of artistic titans, celebrity chef Wolfgang Puck presents his take on steak-house cuisine in a space designed by Getty Center architect Richard Meier. The restaurant's contemporary lines and cold surfaces recall few of the comforts of this beloved culinary tradition. And, like Meier's design, Puck's fare doesn't dwell much on the past; a thoroughly modern Crab Louis salad is the closest thing to nostalgia on the menu. Playful dishes like bone-marrow flan take center stage before diners dive into perfectly dry-age and seared hunks of Nebraskan sirloin—a few bites prove that the Austrian-born super-chef understands our beefy American love affair. [$] *Average main: $36* ✉ *Regent Beverly Wilshire, 9500 Wilshire Blvd., Beverly Hills* ☎ *310/276–8500* 🌐 *www.wolfgangpuck.com* ✍ *Reservations essential* ⏲ *Closed Sun. No lunch* ⊕ *2:H6.*

$$ ✗ **Da Pasquale.** In a neighborhood dominated by the likes of Gucci and
ITALIAN Prada, an affordable meal is harder to spot than a pair of sensible shoes.
And that's one reason to visit Da Pasquale. An even better reason is the
wonderful thin-crust pizza topped with ingredients like fresh tomato,
garlic, and basil or three cheeses with prosciutto. The kitchen also excels
at familiar pastas and roasted chicken. Despite talent-agency regulars,
the homey Old Napoli interior and friendly staff makes everybody feel
welcome. $ *Average main: $20* ✉ *9749 S. Santa Monica Blvd., Beverly
Hills* ☎ *310/859–3884* ⊕ *www.dapasqualecaffe.com* ⊙ *Closed Sun. and
Mon. No lunch Sat.* ✛ *2:G6.*

$$$ ✗ **The Grill on the Alley.** Beverly Hills restaurants can take you many
AMERICAN places, from Provence to Polynesia, but in this case it's just up the
Golden State Freeway to a traditional San Francisco–style grill with
dark-wood paneling and brass trim. This clubby chophouse, where
movie industry execs power-lunch, creates tasty, simple American fare
including steaks, chicken potpies, jumbo crab cakes, chowders, and an
enormous Cobb salad. If you've really made it in Hollywood, you've
got your usual booth at the Grill. $ *Average main: $30* ✉ *9560 Dayton
Way, Beverly Hills* ☎ *310/276–0615* ⊕ *www.thegrill.com* ⌒ *Reservations essential* ⊙ *No lunch Sun.* ✛ *2:H6.*

$$ ✗ **Kate Mantilini.** Casual but cool, this is a good place to remember for
AMERICAN brunch or a late-night snack (it's open until midnight on weekends).
The lengthy menu lines up all-American staples like New England clam
chowder, macaroni and cheese, meat loaf, and chili made with white
beans and chicken. Despite its truck stop–style comfort food, the cav-
ernous ultramodern space exudes a hip urban vibe and the prices are
not surprising for Beverly Hills. $ *Average main: $22* ✉ *9101 Wilshire
Blvd., Beverly Hills* ☎ *310/278–3699* ✛ *2:C4.*

$$$$ ✗ **Matsuhisa.** Freshness and innovation are the hallmarks of this flagship
JAPANESE restaurant of Nobu Matsuhisa's empire. The prolific chef-restaurateur's
surprisingly modest-looking place draws celebrities and serious sushi
buffs alike. Reflecting his past stint in Peru, Matsuhisa incorporates
intriguing Latin ingredients into traditional Japanese cuisine. Here you
can encounter such dishes as the Chilean sea bass with foie gras, scal-
lop sashimi with black garlic sauce and kiwi, or kampachi served with
agua de chili. Daring diners should ask for the *omakase,* a seven-course
chef-selected menu for an amazing culinary experience (with a tab to
match). $ *Average main: $35* ✉ *129 N. La Cienega Blvd., Beverly Hills*
☎ *310/659–9639* ⊕ *www.nobumatsuhisa.com* ⌒ *Reservations essential*
⊙ *No lunch weekends* ✛ *2:C4.*

$$$ ✗ **Oliverio.** This restaurant feels straight out of the *Valley of the Dolls*
ITALIAN movie. Midcentury modern design gives vintage appeal that blends
in with the restaurant's updated Italian cuisine and Californian sensibility. Fresh food concepts are created by chef Mirko Paderno, who
favors seasonal ingredients. Enjoy a starter of *fritto misto* or a cau-
liflower soufflé; for dinner try the classic chicken *diavolo,* beef short
ribs, or a risotto Milanese. Private poolside cabanas are a favorite
for celebratory occasions. $ *Average main: $25* ✉ *Avalon Hotel,
9400 W. Olympic Ave., Beverly Hills* ☎ *310/277–5221* ⊕ *www.
avalonbeverlyhills.com* ✛ *2:B4.*

10

Local Chains Worth Stopping For

It's said that the drive-in burger joint was invented in L.A., probably to meet the demands of an ever-mobile car culture. Burger aficionados line up at all hours outside **In-N-Out Burger** (⊕ www.in-n-out. com, multiple locations), still a family-owned operation whose terrific made-to-order burgers are revered by Angelenos. Visitors may recognize the chain as the infamous spot where Paris Hilton got nabbed for drunk driving, but locals are more concerned with getting their burger fix off the "secret" menu, with variations like "Animal Style" (mustard-grilled patty with grilled onions and extra spread), a "4 x 4" (four burger patties and four cheese slices, for big eaters) or the bun-less "Protein Style" that comes wrapped in a bib of lettuce. The company's website lists explanations for other popular secret menu items.

Tommy's sells a delightfully sloppy chili burger; the original location (⊠ 2575 Beverly Blvd., Los Angeles ☎ 213/389–9060) is a no-frills culinary landmark. For rotisserie chicken that will make you forget the Colonel forever, head to **Zankou Chicken** (⊠ 5065 Sunset Blvd., Hollywood ☎ 323/665–7845 ⊕ www.zankouchicken.com), a small chain noted for its golden crispy-skinned birds, potent garlic sauce, and Armenian specialties. Homesick New Yorkers will appreciate **Jerry's Famous Deli** (⊠ 10925 Weyburn Ave., Westwood ☎ 310/208–3354 ⊕ www.jerrysfamousdeli.com), where the massive menu includes all the classic deli favorites. With a lively bar scene, good barbecued ribs, and contemporary takes on old favorites, the more upscale **Houston's** (⊠ 202 Wilshire Blvd., Santa Monica ☎ 310/576–7558 ⊕ www.hillstone. com) is a popular local hangout. And **Señor Fish** (⊠ 422 E. 1st St., Downtown ☎ 213/625–0566 ⊕ www. senorfish.net) is known for its healthy Mexican seafood specialties, such as scallop burritos and ceviche tostadas.

$$$$
MODERN
AMERICAN
Fodor's Choice
★

✕**Spago Beverly Hills.** The famed flagship restaurant of Wolfgang Puck is justifiably a modern L.A. classic. Spago centers on a buzzing outdoor courtyard shaded by 100-year-old olive trees. From an elegantly appointed table inside, you can glimpse the exhibition kitchen and, on rare occasions, the affable owner greeting his famous friends (these days, compliments to the chef are directed to Lee Hefter). The people-watching here is worth the price of admission, but the clientele is surprisingly inclusive, from the biggest Hollywood stars to Midwestern tourists to foodies more preoccupied with vintages of Burgundy than with faces from the cover of *People*. Foie gras has disappeared, but the daily-changing menu might offer a pizza with wild mushrooms, baby asparagus, and sun-dried tomatoes, Cantonese-style duck, and some traditional Austrian specialties. Dessert is magical, with everything from an ethereal apricot soufflé to Austrian *kaiserschmarrn* (crème fraîche pancakes with fruit). $ *Average main: $35* ✉ *176 N. Cañon Dr., Beverly Hills* ☎ *310/385–0880* ⊕ *www. wolfgangpuck.com* ⚱ *Reservations essential* ☽ *No lunch Sun.* ✛ *2:H6.*

$$$$
JAPANESE
Fodor's Choice
★

✕**Urasawa.** This understated sushi bar has precious few seats, resulting in incredibly personalized service. At a minimum of $375 per person for a strictly *omakase* (chef's choice) meal, Urasawa remains the priciest restaurant in town, but the endless parade of masterfully crafted, exquisitely presented dishes renders few regrets. The maple sushi bar, sanded daily to a satinlike finish, is where most of the action takes place. You might be served velvety bluefin toro paired with beluga caviar, slivers of foie gras to self-cook *shabu shabu* style, or egg custard layered with *uni* (sea urchin), glittering with gold leaf. This is also the place to come during *fugu* season, when the legendary, potentially deadly blowfish is artfully served to adventurous diners. $ *Average main: $375* ✉ *218 N. Rodeo Dr., Beverly Hills* ☎ *310/247–8939* ⚱ *Reservations essential* ☽ *Closed Sun. and Mon. No lunch* ✛ *2:H6.*

BEL AIR

A mostly residential area, Bel Air also has some well-regarded eateries.

$$$$
AMERICAN

✕**Vibrato.** Co-owned by trumpeter Herb Albert, Vibrato takes a high-road approach to a jazz club: this is a stylish, acoustically perfect venue where every table has a view of the stage. The kitchen is as notable as the music; it turns out contemporary American fare such as pan-roasted sea bass with a fennel-leek ragu, macaroni and cheese with bacon-parmesan crust, and USDA Prime steaks. Art on the walls was painted by the Grammy-winning owner himself. $ *Average main: $36* ✉ *2930 Beverly Glen Circle, Bel Air* ☎ *310/474–9499* ⊕ *www.vibratogrilljazz. com* ⚱ *Reservations essential* ☽ *Closed Mon. No lunch* ✛ *4:D1.*

WEST HOLLYWOOD

Lively, stylish, and surrounded by the best restaurants and nightlife in Los Angeles, WeHo (as locals call it) is a magnet for celebrity sightings. There are great bakeries, well-regarded burger joints, and upscale bars serving couture cocktails.

$$$$
ITALIAN
Fodor's Choice
★

✕**Angelini Osteria.** You might not guess it from the modest, rather congested dining room, but this is one of L.A.'s most celebrated Italian restaurants. The key is chef-owner Gino Angelini's thoughtful use of superb ingredients, evident in dishes such as a chopped salad with

10

white beans, cucumbers, pistachios, and avocado, and cavatelli with mussels, clams, shrimp, peas, and saffron. Whole branzino, liberally crusted in sea salt, and boldly flavored rustic specials like tender veal kidneys or rich oxtail stew, consistently impress. An intelligent selection of mostly Italian wines complements the menu. [$] *Average main: $32* ✉ *7313 Beverly Blvd., West Hollywood* ☎ *323/297–0070* 🌐 *www.angeliniosteria.com* ✍ *Reservations essential* 🕒 *Closed Mon. No lunch weekends* ✢ *2:E3.*

$$$$ MEDITERRANEAN Fodor's Choice ★ 🍴 **A.O.C.** This restaurant and wine bar revolutionized L.A.'s dining scene, pioneering the small-plate format that has now swept the city. The space is dominated by a long, candle-laden bar serving more than 50 wines by the glass. There's also a charcuterie bar, an L.A. rarity. The tapas-like menu is perfectly calibrated for the wine list; you could pick duck confit, lamb roulade with mint pistou, an indulgent slice of ricotta tartine, or just plunge into one of the city's best cheese selections. Named for the acronym for Appellation d'Origine Contrôlée, the regulatory system that ensures the quality of local wines and cheeses in France, A.O.C. upholds the standard of excellence. [$] *Average main: $35* ✉ *8700 W. 3rd St., West Hollywood* ☎ *323/653–6359* 🌐 *www.aocwinebar.com* ✍ *Reservations essential* 🕒 *No lunch weekdays* ✢ *2:D3.*

$$ AMERICAN 🍴 **BLD.** Chef Neal Fraser concentrates on simple, approachable fare at this casual yet sophisticated eatery that's open from morning to night. With its versatile menu, you can start the day with a vegan Benedict (with house-smoked tofu bacon, wilted arugula, and dairy-free hollandaise) or ricotta and blueberry pancakes. Snack on an excellent selection of cheeses and charcuterie, enjoy an all-American burger for lunch, or tuck into a perfectly seared steak at dinner. The prices are reasonable, too, which helps explain the line out the door. [$] *Average main: $22* ✉ *7450 Beverly Blvd., West Hollywood* ☎ *323/930–9744* 🌐 *www.bldrestaurant.com* ✢ *2:E3.*

$ DELI FAMILY 🍴 **Canter's.** This granddaddy of L.A. delicatessens (it opened in 1928) cures its own corned beef and pastrami and has an in-house bakery. It's not the best deli in town, or the friendliest, but it's a true L.A. classic and open around the clock. Next door is the Kibitz Room, where there's live music every night. [$] *Average main: $10* ✉ *419 N. Fairfax Ave., Fairfax District* ☎ *323/651–2030* 🌐 *www.cantersdeli.com* ✍ *Reservations not accepted* ✢ *2:D3.*

$$$$ FRENCH 🍴 **Comme Ça.** This brasserie from Sona chef David Myers, with polished service and a menu with something for everyone, is styled for those craving a decidedly French joie de vivre. Simple tables covered in butcher paper offset elegant antique mirrors, and a long chalkboard doubles as a wall. Comme Ça can't help but encourage a love affair with food and wine. Savor specialties like tarte flambée, steak frites, and the perfectly roasted chicken for two. Drain a carafe of Côtes du Rhône with French cheeses before concluding with profiteroles or a chocolate-whiskey soufflé while you longingly imagine yourself in Montparnasse. [$] *Average main: $35* ✉ *8479 Melrose Ave., West Hollywood* ☎ *323/782–1104* 🌐 *www.commecarestaurant.com* ✍ *Reservations essential* 🕒 *No lunch* ✢ *2:C3.*

$$$$ FRENCH 🍴 **Gordon Ramsay at the London.** The foul-mouthed celebrity chef from *Hell's Kitchen* demonstrates why he nevertheless ranks among the world's finest chefs at this fine-dining restaurant in a West Hollywood boutique hotel. Two pastel-color dining rooms with city views flank a formidable white marble bar, creating a space that feels stylish yet surprisingly unpretentious. A menu of small plates accommodates both light suppers and indulgent feasts. Highlights include Ramsay's signature beef Wellington for two, filet mignon and braised short ribs, and a Maine lobster with coconut froth and mushroom ravioli. To maximize the experience, consider one of the flexible tasting menus ($120 on average), artfully crafted by Ramsay's local culinary team and orchestrated by a polished, gracious staff. [$] *Average main: $38* ✉ *The London, 1020 N. San Vicente Blvd., West Hollywood* ☎ *310/358–7788* 🌐 *www.thelondonwesthollywood.com/gordon-ramsay* ✍ *Reservations essential* ✥ *2:C2.*

$ CAJUN 🍴 **Gumbo Pot.** While it's not exactly "down by the bayou," this order-at-the-counter outdoor café does serve a mean gumbo rich in shrimp, chicken, and andouille sausage. It's also the place for New Orleans–style po'boy and *muffaletta* sandwiches, jambalaya, and beignets (the Big Easy's take on doughnuts). [$] *Average main: $10* ✉ *Farmers Market, 6333 W. 3rd St., West Hollywood* ☎ *323/933–0358* 🌐 *www.thegumbopotla.com* ✍ *Reservations not accepted* ✥ *2:D3.*

$$$ AMERICAN 🍴 **Jar.** At this modern chophouse, refined style meets classic, comfort-food favorites. Chef Suzanne Tracht cooks up a hit parade of all-American dishes, executed with a refined touch. After crab-accented deviled eggs, dressed-up fried clams, or endive Caesar salad, consider a rack of lamb, roasted salmon, or a massive slab of tender pot roast that's a few steps above Mom's recipe. Appropriately, steaks also are stellar, and well-priced to boot. Homey desserts like rich chocolate pudding or banana cream pie summon a sweet ending. [$] *Average main: $30* ✉ *8225 Beverly Blvd., West Hollywood* ☎ *323/655–6566* 🌐 *www.thejar.com* ⏲ *No lunch Mon.–Sat.* ✥ *2:D3.*

$ MODERN AMERICAN 🍴 **Lemonade.** Take a seat on the patio of this charming eatery and indulge in unique salads, perfectly braised meats, tasty pot roast sandwiches, and—of course—fresh-squeezed lemonade. The seasonally driven menu pulls from the aisles of the Farmers Market and includes a litany of comfort foods that you can mix-and-match. Grab a tray and order chicken over aromatic basmati rice, a mixed green salad with a slice of ahi tuna draped atop, and a tall glass of cucumber-mint lemonade. Finish off your meal with a slice of banana mascarpone cake. Get here early, as the place closes at 7:30. [$] *Average main: $10* ✉ *9001 Beverly Blvd., West Hollywood* ☎ *310/247–2500* 🌐 *www.lemonadela.com* ✥ *2:C3.*

$$$ MODERN AMERICAN 🍴 **Lucques.** Formerly silent-film star Harold Lloyd's carriage house, this brick building has morphed into a chic restaurant that has elevated chef Suzanne Goin to national prominence. In her veggie-intense contemporary American cooking, she uses finesse to balance tradition and invention. Consider starting with the chickpea soup with pasta, kale, and pecorino cheese, then moving on to the fish with black rice and curried cauliflower. Finish with the orange blossom panna cotta with candied tangerines, dates, and pistachio brittle. [$] *Average main: $30* ✉ *8474 Melrose Ave., West Hollywood* ☎ *323/655–6277* 🌐 *www.lucques.com* ✍ *Reservations essential* ⏲ *No lunch Sun. and Mon.* ✥ *2:C3.*

$$$$ STEAKHOUSE 🍴 **The Palm.** All the New York elements are present at this West Coast replay of the famous Manhattan steak house—mahogany booths, tin ceilings, a boisterous atmosphere, and no-nonsense waiters rushing you through your cheesecake (flown in from the Bronx, of course). This is where you'll find the biggest and best lobster; good steaks, prime rib, and chops; and great onion rings. [$] *Average main: $35* ✉ *9001 Santa Monica Blvd., West Hollywood* ☎ *310/550–8811* 🌐 *www.thepalm.com* ✍ *Reservations essential* ⏲ *No lunch weekends* ✥ *2:C3.*

$$$ MEXICAN 🍴 **Red O.** With a luxurious setting, fun tequila lounge, loveseat swings by the main bar, and a menu that blends classic Mexican dishes with innovative ingredients, Red O has won over the hearts and palates of everyone in town. Scoring a seat at Red O—an honest-to-goodness celebrity magnet—makes you privy to some of the best people-watching in town. Pull up a white wicker chair and start your evening with a margarita made with serrano pepper-infused syrup, and ask for the yellowtail ceviche with homemade tortilla chips. Small-plate offerings allow for sampling: try the soft tacos made with braised short rib, or the slow-cooked Sonoma duck taquitos. The goat-cheese tamales are a tasty rendition of a Mexican classic, and the shrimp empanaditas seal the deal. [$] *Average main: $26* ✉ *8155 Melrose Ave., West Hollywood* ☎ *323/655–5009* 🌐 *www.redorestaurant.com* ⏲ *No lunch* ✥ *2:D3.*

$$ GREEK 🍴 **Sofi.** Hidden from bustling, increasingly hip 3rd Street, this friendly little taverna offers all the Greek classics: dolmades, spanakopita, souvlaki, and *taramasalata* (a creamy, salty dip made from fish roe). The smart, casual dining room is more than comfortable, but consider sitting outside on the lovely bougainvillea-shaded garden patio. All that's missing is a view of the Aegean Sea. [$] *Average main: $20* ✉ *8030¾ W. 3rd St., West Hollywood* ☎ *323/651–0346* 🌐 *www.sofisrestaurant.com* ✥ *2:D3.*

$$$$ JAPANESE 🍴 **Wa Sushi & Bistro.** Founded by three alums of trendsetting Matsuhisa, Wa offers a more personalized experience with high-quality ingredients and intriguing Japanese cooking. Particularly enticing are dishes enhanced with French-inspired sauces. For instance, the Chilean sea bass is layered with foie gras and bathed in a port reduction, while the Santa Barbara prawns are dosed with a perfect *beurre blanc* prepared on a rickety range behind the sushi bar. Wa's hillside location allows for seductive city views from a small handful of tables dressed up with linen and candles. [$] *Average main: $35* ✉ *1106 N. La Cienega Blvd., West Hollywood* ☎ *310/854–7285* ✍ *Reservations essential* ⏲ *Closed Mon. No lunch* ✥ *2:C2.*

BRENTWOOD

Fashionable eateries are easy to find in Brentwood. Many of this upscale neighborhood's restaurants end up on annual "best of" lists put together by local publications.

$$$$ JAPANESE 🍴 **Katsuya.** This sushi places caters to a beautiful, trend-conscious clientele. Katsuya ups the ante with a seductive, ultramodern look created by celebrated designer Philippe Starck featuring glowing murals of a geisha's face. Glossy lips kiss the room's clientele from one wall, while kohl-rimmed eyes peer out from behind the sushi bar. Highly regarded sushi chef Katsuya Uechi turns out spicy tuna atop crispy rice, whimsical wonton cones filled with scoops of silky crab and tuna tartare, and

larger plates like miso-marinated black cod. Don't neglect the plates from the *robata* bar, where skewers of veggies, seafood, and meats are grilled over hot coals. [$] *Average main: $35* ✉ *11777 San Vicente Blvd., Brentwood* ☎ *310/207–8744* 🌐 *www.sbe.com/katsuya* ✍ *Reservations essential* ⏲ *No lunch weekends* ✣ *4:C2.*

$$$ ITALIAN 🍴 **Pecorino.** San Vicente Boulevard is lined with trendy trattorias, but Pecorino presents a delightful compromise between old-world charm and modern sensibilities. Wrought-iron chandeliers hang from a beamed ceiling above a room dressed up with white-linen tablecloths and red velvet curtains. The pleasures of the namesake sheep's milk cheese are explored in simply sauced pastas and the Abruzzese-style lamb casserole. A huge baked onion filled with eggplant, raisins, and pine nuts is a terrific vegetarian beginning; a plate of pecorino cheeses from every corner of Italy is a perfect finish. [$] *Average main: $27* ✉ *11604 San Vicente Blvd., Brentwood* ☎ *310/571–3800* 🌐 *www.pecorinorestaurant.com* ✍ *Reservations essential* ⏲ *No lunch Sun.* ✣ *4:C2.*

CENTURY CITY

This is the town where deals are made, ideas are discussed, and some of the best meals can be discovered.

$$ ECLECTIC 🍴 **Breadbar.** The art of bread hasn't always been celebrated in carb-watching L.A., but at Breadbar it's all grains and glory. Breadbar is known for its tasty homemade artisanal breads—redwood rye, golden fig loaf, and a traditional rustic white, for starters. These loaves star (or co-star) in an appetizing array of sandwiches, salads, and entrées. Start with a cheese plate or an order of steamed mussels in a white-wine broth that's perfect for dipping crusty bread. Order a grilled cheese, the signature corned beef sandwich, or a chopped frisée salad made with hazelnuts and feta cheese. Pair these with a crisp glass of wine or a jasmine iced tea for a lazy lunch. Stop in for dinner and try the roasted chicken breast in a mushroom sauce or tandoori chicken brochettes. A lively coffee bar makes this a great place to charge up before heading out for some L.A. shopping. [$] *Average main: $19* ✉ *10250 Santa Monica Blvd., Century City* ☎ *310/277–3770* 🌐 *www.breadbar.net* ✣ *2:A4.*

$$ BAKERY 🍴 **Clementine.** In fast-paced Century City, this quaint restaurant pays homage to comfort food classics. Look for chicken pot pie, macaroni and cheese, and roast beef sandwiches. There's a slew of hearty salads, including one that's dolled up with roasted chicken, apples, and grapes. A great breakfast or lunch detour as you make your way up to the beaches, this place has a bakery case that's filled to the brim with slices of banana cake with cream-cheese frosting, chocolate-cherry cookies, and freshly made cinnamon rolls (Saturday only) studded with plump raisins. [$] *Average main: $15* ✉ *1751 Ensley Ave., Century City* ☎ *310/552–1080* 🌐 *www.clementineonline.com* ✍ *Reservations not accepted* ⏲ *Closed Sun.* ✣ *4:D2.*

$$$$ MODERN AMERICAN 🍴 **Craft Los Angeles.** New York chef Tom Colicchio (a judge on TV's *Top Chef*) expands his burgeoning empire with this sleek Southern California outpost. Thanks to Century City's growing legions of agents and lawyers, Craft has emerged as a major film industry hangout. In its open, airy dining room, deals are brokered over lunches featuring seasonal, artisanal ingredients. In the evening, Craft is ideal for groups

sharing plates from the signature à la carte menu that often includes Peruvian octopus with roasted pineapple, braised beef short ribs, and veal sweetbreads with plums. Boutique produce goes into a plethora of side dishes, and desserts may include butterscotch pudding with dates and hazelnuts or beignets with blackberry honey and chocolate. The endless menu can be frustrating, and some dishes miss the mark—but just as many sparkle. [$] *Average main: $35* ✉ *10100 Constellation Blvd., Century City* ☎ *310/279–4180* 🌐 *www.craftrestaurant.com* ✍ *Reservations essential* 🕓 *No lunch weekends* ✣ *2:A4.*

$$$ ECLECTIC 🍴 **Hinoki and the Bird.** A brilliant combination of East and West is unveiled at Hinoki and the Bird, the latest restaurant by Michelin star–studded chef David Meyers. In a condo tower on Avenue of the Stars, Hinoki could easily be dismissed as another celebrity hot spot with all the flash and none of the substance, but the small-plates menu tells a different story. Pick and choose between fun appetizers and inspirational entrées, including the delicate red snapper accented with grapefruit and lime, the crispy marinated chicken with lemon aioli, and the lobster roll with green curry and Thai basil. The signature black cod arrives at your table with paper-thin layers of *hinoki* (cypress) still smoldering—it's a feast for all your senses. [$] *Average main: $30* ✉ *10 Century Dr., Century City* ☎ *310/552–1200* 🌐 *hinokiandthebird.com* ✍ *Reservations essential* 🕓 *No lunch weekends* ✣ *4:E2.*

CULVER CITY

Sandwiched between some of L.A.'s coolest neighborhoods, Culver City has spent the past few years forming its own identity. It's the place for adventurous eaters, as you can find cuisines spanning the globe.

$ SOUTHERN FAMILY 🍴 **Honey's Kettle Fried Chicken.** This family-operated business has updated the old-fashioned practice of kettle cooking—frying its chicken with intense heat in stainless steel drums, allowing the juices to be sealed beneath a crackly, generously battered skin. This is soulful Southern goodness, and for folks who appreciate this kind of food—it's a bit greasy, but you can say that about any respectable fried chicken—Honey's is well worth a visit. In addition to the golden bird, the menu also offers a satisfying fried catfish, hot cakes, and some of the fluffiest biscuits in town. Hang out on the patio with a glass of homemade lemonade and observe the hipsters filing into the high-end eateries that surround unpretentious Honey's. [$] *Average main: $9* ✉ *9537 Culver Blvd., Culver City* ☎ *310/202–5453* 🌐 *www.honeyskettle.com* ✍ *Reservations not accepted* ✣ *4:E3.*

$$ AMERICAN FAMILY 🍴 **Tender Greens.** In Culver City's burgeoning restaurant district, Tender Greens turns out the kind of fast food your mom, accountant, and nutritionist would unanimously approve of—emphasizing health and value without compromising quality. After you stand in line for a bit, locally grown greens are tossed in front of you in a big metallic bowl, plated with perfectly grilled meats or fish. Enjoy a grilled chicken salad or a chipotle-barbecue-chicken salad with a creamy lime dressing while sitting on the sidewalk patio with a glass of homemade lemonade. [$] *Average main: $15* ✉ *9523 Culver Blvd., Culver City* ☎ *310/842–8300* 🌐 *www.tendergreensfood.com* ✍ *Reservations not accepted* ✣ *4:E3.*

$$$ MODERN BRITISH

🍴 **Waterloo & City.** In a renovated greasy spoon on the outskirts of Culver City, Waterloo & City is a British gastropub that has fine-dining lineage from its owners and kitchen staff. But the mood here is definitely easygoing. A communal table anchors the lounge area, vintage mirrors adorn the walls, and suede banquettes make for cozy seating. Start your night with a pint or a cocktail and order from the beloved one-of-a-kind charcuterie menu, which has given this eatery some meat-curing street cred. Order the rabbit and pistachio terrine, duck and walnut paté, and pig trotters. Balance out the rich meats with an arugula salad tossed with roasted almonds, tangerines, and Parmesan cheese. The fettuccini with spicy Thai lobster, mussels, and lime is a fresh approach to pasta, while the lamb "bangers" and carrot "mash" is a great spin to an English classic. The sticky toffee pudding with salted caramel is an absolute must. [$] *Average main: $23* ✉ *12517 W. Washington Blvd., Culver City* ☎ *310/391–4222* 🌐 *www.waterlooandcity.com* 🕒 *No lunch* ✥ *3:D4.*

WEST LOS ANGELES

The Westside has a cutting-edge dining scene that's slightly more family-friendly, with more moderate and casual spots.

$ AMERICAN Fodor's Choice ★

🍴 **The Apple Pan.** A favorite since 1947, this unassuming joint with a horseshoe-shape counter—no tables here—turns out one heck of a good burger. Try the cheeseburger with Tillamook cheddar, or perhaps the hickory burger topped with barbecue sauce. You can also find great fries and, of course, an apple pie indulgent enough to christen the restaurant (although many regulars argue that the banana cream deserves the honor). Be prepared to wait, but the veteran countermen turn the stools at a quick pace. In the meantime, grab a cup of Sanka and enjoy a little LA vintage. [$] *Average main: $7* ✉ *10801 W. Pico Blvd., West L.A.* ☎ *310/475–3585* ✍ *Reservations not accepted* 💳 *No credit cards* 🕒 *Closed Mon.* ✥ *4:D2.*

$$ MEXICAN FAMILY

🍴 **Monte Alban.** This family-owned café serves the subtle cooking of one of Mexico's most respected culinary regions, warm and wonderful Oaxaca. The flavors here are intense without being fiery. Try this version of *chilis rellenos* (bright green chili peppers stuffed with chicken, raisins, and nuts). Don't miss any of the complex moles ladled over chicken, pork, salmon, or extra-tender stewed goat. For dessert, there's fried sweet plantains topped with crème fraîche that's *delicioso.* [$] *Average main: $15* ✉ *11927 Santa Monica Blvd., West L.A.* ☎ *310/444–7736* 🌐 *montealbanrestaurante.com/location.html* ✥ *4:C2.*

$$$ JAPANESE

🍴 **Mori Sushi.** Only a small fish logo identifies the facade of this restaurant, but many consider it the best sushi bar in L.A. The austere white-washed space stands in contrast to the artful presentations of pristine morsels of seafood, all served on ceramic plates made by Morihiro Onodera himself. Allow him to compose an entire meal for you—this can be an expensive proposition—and he'll send out eye-popping presentations of sushi or sashimi accented with touches of rare sea salts, yuzu, and freshly ground wasabi, as well as intricately conceived salads, house-made tofu, and soups. [$] *Average main: $25* ✉ *11500 Pico Blvd., West L.A.* ☎ *310/479–3939* 🌐 *morisushi.net* 🕒 *Closed Sun. No lunch Sat.* ✥ *4:D3.*

$$
SOUTHERN
FAMILY
✕ **Mr. Cecil's California Ribs.** A rib-loving movie-studio exec opened this eatery in a tiny, circular hatbox of a building. The meaty, tender St. Louis–style ribs are particularly outstanding, with a spirited but not overpowering sauce. Aficionados of pecan pie should also beat a path here. A bonus: It's the only rib joint in town where you can order a bottle of Château Lafite Rothschild. $ Average main: $18 ✉ 12244 W. Pico Blvd., West L.A. ☎ 310/442–1550 ⊕ www.mrcecilscaribs. com ✛ 4:C3.

$
CUBAN
FAMILY
✕ **Versailles.** Despite its no-frills dining room in which noise echoes off Formica surfaces, people line up outside the door for Versailles's respectable, bargain-price Cuban food. Most are crazy about the citrusy *mojo*-marinated chicken seasoned with loads of garlic. Others prefer flank steak, paella, or *ropa vieja* (shredded beef). $ Average main: $13 ✉ 10319 Venice Blvd., West L.A. ☎ 310/558–3168 ⊕ www. versaillescuban.com ⚠ Reservations not accepted ✛ 4:E3.

$$
AMERICAN
FAMILY
✕ **Westside Tavern.** The rare mall restaurant to make a culinary splash, this modern gastropub is known for its casual, lively, and engaging atmosphere and well-executed food. The comfy bar is your first stop; grab a peach-and-basil gimlet before heading to your table. Start with the ceviche of the day or a platter of tempura green beans. If you're craving a sandwich, order the lamb French dip, a BLT with a soft fried egg, or an open-faced portobella melt. Entrées include Niman Ranch flat-iron steak and fried halibut-and-chips. For a sweet finish, try the cinnamon sugar donuts that arrive with raspberry and chocolate dipping sauces. $ Average main: $19 ✉ Olympic Collection, 10850 Pico Blvd., West L.A. ☎ 310/470–1539 ⊕ www.westsidetavernla.com ✛ 4:D2.

SANTA MONICA AND THE BEACHES

In these neighborhoods, choose from a diverse collection of eateries—from taco stands to upscale seafood houses—that cater to the healthy and active lifestyle of locals. But beware of overpriced eateries betting that an ocean view will help you forget about substandard value and quality. Fortunately, they're easy to avoid by sticking to our list here. As for budget eats, there are plenty of cafés, burger shacks, and casual chains that won't raise an eyebrow when you walk in with your sandy flip-flops.

SANTA MONICA

This idyllic seaside town is a hotbed of culinary activity, with a dynamic farmers' market that attracts chefs from all over Los Angeles. Local restaurants celebrate seasonal dining.

$$
SPANISH
✕ **Bar Pintxo.** Inspired by his trips to Spain, chef Joe Miller (of Joe's restaurant in Venice) opened this lively, warmly appointed tapas bar. In the Basque region, tapas are called pintxos, and this narrow slice of the Iberian Peninsula carries the spirit of the genuine article, despite having a view of the Pacific Ocean instead of the Bay of Biscay. It's occupied by SoCal surfer dudes and struggling screenwriters taking advantage of the good values. Sip a glass of sangría while snacking on *croquetas de pollo y jamón* (chicken and ham croquettes),

morcilla (blood sausage), or paprika-laden chorizo with fried quail eggs. A bowl of Andalusian gazpacho is perfect on a hot California evening. $ *Average main: $21* ⊠ *109 Santa Monica Blvd., Santa Monica* ☎ *310/458–2012* ⊕ *www.barpintxo.com* ⚲ *Reservations not accepted* ☾ *No lunch* ✛ *4:F6.*

$$$$ ✕ **BOA Steakhouse.** This is not your father's steak house—the fun-loving
STEAKHOUSE crowd is surrounded by sleek surfaces and bathed in a warm glow from modern lighting fixtures. You can still start with a prawn cocktail or a traditional Caesar salad prepared tableside before slicing your Laguiole knife into a dry-aged prime New York strip or rib eye. Genuine Japanese Wagyu and certified organic beef are also available. Although the steaks are delicious without any frills, you can opt for an embellishment such as a blue cheese rub or Cabernet reduction sauce. $ *Average main: $45* ⊠ *101 Santa Monica Blvd., Santa Monica* ☎ *310/899–4466* ⊕ *www.innovativedining.com/restaurants/boa* ⚲ *Reservations essential* ✛ *4:F6.*

$$$ ✕ **Border Grill.** At this busy restaurant, massive murals are a perfect
MEXICAN complement to modern interpretations of such ancient Mayan dishes
FAMILY as *cochinita pibil* (achiote-marinated pork). Other favorites include a wild-mushroom quesadilla, green-corn tamales, plantain empanadas, and daily ceviche specials. Celebrity chef-owners Mary Sue Milliken and Susan Feniger display a passion for Mexican cuisine here, but they do mellow the dishes to suit a broad audience. $ *Average main: $23* ⊠ *1445 4th St., Santa Monica* ☎ *310/451–1655* ⊕ *www.bordergrill.com* ✛ *4:F6.*

$$$$ ✕ **Chinois on Main.** A once-revolutionary outpost in Wolfgang Puck's rep-
ASIAN ertoire, this is still one of L.A.'s most crowded—and noisy—restaurants. The jazzy interior is just as loud as the clientele. Although the menu has expanded, the restaurant's happy marriage of Asian and French cuisines shows best in such signature dishes as Chinois chicken salad, Shanghai lobster with a spicy ginger-curry sauce, and Cantonese duck with fresh plum sauce. $ *Average main: $35* ⊠ *2709 Main St., Santa Monica* ☎ *310/392–9025* ⊕ *www.wolfgangpuck.com* ⚲ *Reservations essential* ✛ *4:G6.*

$ ✕ **The Counter.** Angelenos love their old-fashioned burger joints, but
BURGER have also embraced this upscale, contemporary eatery. Check off your
FAMILY preferences on an order sheet—choose between beef, turkey, or veggie patties, then add cheeses, toppings, and one of 18 different sauces (anything from spicy sour cream to sweet BBQ sauce). You can even select your bun, although carb counters go for the "burger-in-a-bowl." Even with the slick surroundings and wild combinations, this emerging chain is a nostalgic reminder of L.A.'s ongoing love affair with the burger. $ *Average main: $10* ⊠ *2901 Ocean Park Blvd., Santa Monica* ☎ *310/399–8383* ⊕ *www.thecounterburger.com* ⚲ *Reservations not accepted* ✛ *4:H5.*

$$$ ✕ **Farmshop.** Southern California native Jeffrey Cerciello brought a
AMERICAN little Napa Valley to this classic spot that pays attention to the details but also keeps things refreshingly simple. Order the buttermilk biscuits served with quince preserves, French toast with pear marmalade and raisins, and baked eggs with wild greens, fennel cream, and flavorful

10

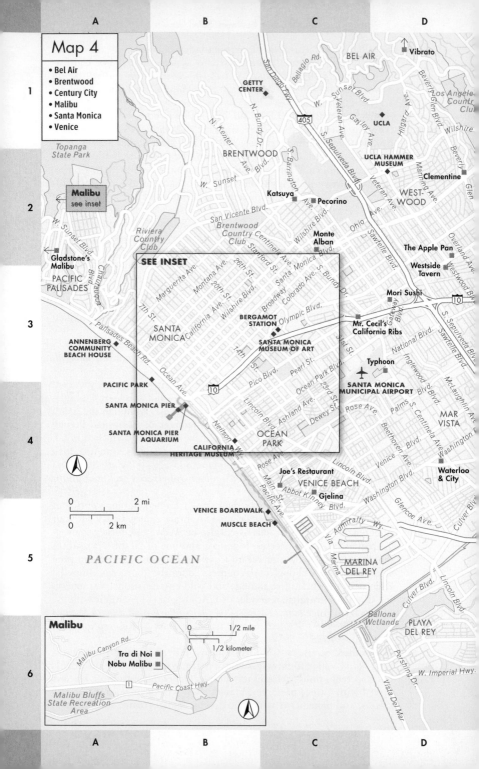

Map 4

- Bel Air
- Brentwood
- Century City
- Malibu
- Santa Monica
- Venice

A **B** **C** **D**

1

2

3

4

5

6

Vibrato

BEL AIR

Bellagio Rd.

San Diego Fwy.

GETTY CENTER

W. Sunset Blvd.

405

Sunset Blvd.

Veteran Ave.

Gayley Ave.

Hilgard Ave.

Beverly Glen Blvd.

Los Angeles Country Club

Wilshire

UCLA

N. Kenter Ave.

N. Bundy Dr.

BRENTWOOD

S. Barrington Ave.

S. Sepulveda Blvd.

Veteran Ave.

UCLA HAMMER MUSEUM

Marmac Ave.

Beverly Glen

Clementine

WEST-WOOD

Topanga State Park

W. Sunset

San Vicente Blvd.

Brentwood Country Club

Centinela Ave.

Stanford St.

Wilshire Blvd.

Katsuya

Pecorino

Ohio

Sawtelle Blvd.

Overland Ave.

Westwood Blvd.

Malibu see inset

Riviera Country Club

Chautauqua Blvd.

Wilshire Blvd.

Santa Monica Blvd.

S. Bundy Dr.

Monte Alban

The Apple Pan

Westside Tavern

10

Gladstone's Malibu

W. Sunset Blvd.

PACIFIC PALISADES

SEE INSET

Marguerita Ave.

Montana Ave.

26th St.

20th St.

California Ave.

Wilshire Blvd.

Broadway

Colorado Ave.

Olympic Blvd.

Mori Sushi

National Blvd.

Sawtelle Blvd.

S. Sepulveda Blvd.

7th St.

SANTA MONICA

BERGAMOT STATION

SANTA MONICA MUSEUM OF ART

3rd St.

Mr. Cecil's California Ribs

ANNENBERG COMMUNITY BEACH HOUSE

Palisades Beach Rd.

Ocean Ave.

14th

Pico Blvd.

Pearl St.

Typhoon

SANTA MONICA MUNICIPAL AIRPORT

Inglewood Blvd.

McLaughlin Ave.

MAR VISTA

PACIFIC PARK

SANTA MONICA PIER

Neilson Wy.

Ocean Park Blvd.

23rd St.

Ashland Ave.

Dewey St.

Rose Ave.

Palms Blvd.

S. Centinela Ave.

Beethoven Ave.

Washington Blvd.

SANTA MONICA PIER AQUARIUM

CALIFORNIA HERITAGE MUSEUM

Lincoln Blvd.

Main St.

OCEAN PARK

Rose Ave.

Lincoln Blvd.

Venice Blvd.

Waterloo & City

Joe's Restaurant

VENICE BEACH

Gjelina

Pacific St.

Abbot Kinney Blvd.

Washington Blvd.

Glencoe Ave.

Culver Blvd.

VENICE BOARDWALK

MUSCLE BEACH

Admiralty Wy.

Via Marina

MARINA DEL REY

Culver Blvd.

Lincoln Blvd.

PACIFIC OCEAN

0   2 mi

0   2 km

Ballona Wetlands

PLAYA DEL REY

Pershing Dr.

Vista Del Mar

Malibu

Malibu Canyon Rd.

Tra di Noi

Nobu Malibu

1

Pacific Coast Hwy.

Malibu Bluffs State Recreation Area

0   1/2 mile

0   1/2 kilometer

W. Imperial Hwy.

A **B** **C** **D**

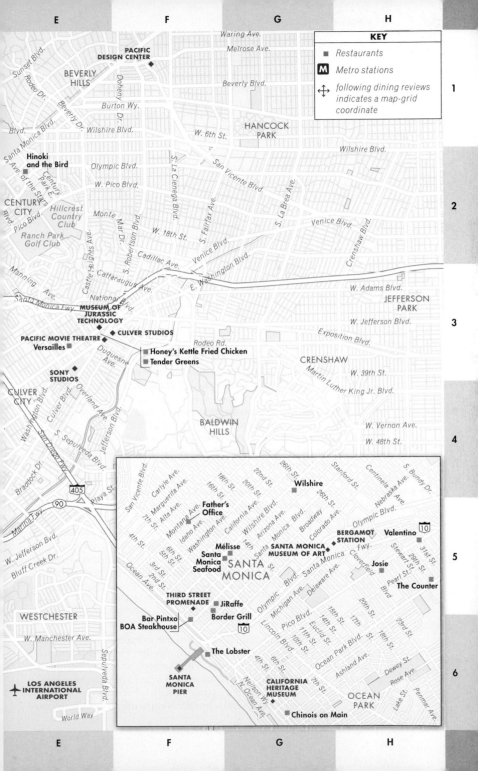

sourdough toast. Lunch is an assortment of farm-fresh salads, savory soups, and sandwiches. Try the warm Dungeness crab salad made with butter lettuce, sunchokes, and curly mustard greens, or the smoked salmon tartine dressed with caper berries and pickled vegetables on rye bread. Meander over to the gourmet market and take a culinary tour of the senses. [$] *Average main: $28* ✉ *Brentwood Country Mart, 225 26th St., Santa Monica* ☎ *310/566–2400* 🌐 *www.farmshopla.com* ✥ *3:B2.*

$$ AMERICAN 🍴 **Father's Office.** With a facade distinguished by a vintage neon sign, this pub is famous for handcrafted beers and what has been called L.A.'s best burger. Topped with Gruyère and Maytag blue cheeses, caramelized onions, and applewood-smoked bacon compote, the "Office Burger" is a guilty pleasure worth waiting in line for (which is usually required). Get a side order of the addictive sweet potato fries served in a miniature shopping cart with aioli—don't even think of asking for ketchup, because FO enforces a strict no-substitutions policy. Other options include steak frites and Spanish-style tapas. Note: Because Father's Office is a bar, it's strictly 21 and older. [$] *Average main: $15* ✉ *1018 Montana Ave., Santa Monica* ☎ *310/393–2337* 🌐 *www.fathersoffice.com* ✍ *Reservations not accepted* ⏲ *No lunch weekdays* ✥ *4:F5.*

$$$$ SEAFOOD FAMILY 🍴 **Gladstone's Malibu.** This is one of the most popular restaurants along the Southern California coast. The food is notable mostly for its over-size portions: giant bowls of crab chowder, lobsters up to six pounds, spectacular seafood towers, and the famous mile-high chocolate cake that could easily feed a regiment. But the real reason to visit Gladstone's is the glorious vista of sea, sky, and beach. Sip on one of the iconic mojitos and watch the sun dip into the ocean at sunset. There's a sister restaurant at Universal Studios, though the lack of beachfront makes it far less attractive. [$] *Average main: $35* ✉ *17300 Pacific Coast Hwy., at Sunset Blvd., Pacific Palisades* ☎ *310/454–3474* 🌐 *www.gladstones.com* ✥ *4:A2.*

$$$ MODERN AMERICAN 🍴 **JiRaffe.** This two-story California bistro with ceiling-high windows and polished dark-wood accents is as handsome as the menu is tasteful. Chef-owner Raphael Lunetta, also an accomplished surfer, turns out such seasonal appetizers as a delicately roasted tomato tart or a beet salad with caramelized walnuts and dried cherries. Main dishes include a truly memorable coriander-crusted yellowfin tuna with baby bok choy, and an oven-dried ravioli with lemon basil and garlic croutons. Enjoy the playful chocolate chip ice cream sandwich or Meyer lemon soufflé for a sweet ending. [$] *Average main: $30* ✉ *502 Santa Monica Blvd., Santa Monica* ☎ *310/917–6671* 🌐 *www.jirafferestaurant.com* ✍ *Reservations essential* ⏲ *No lunch. Closed Sun.* ✥ *4:F5.*

$$$ AMERICAN 🍴 **Josie.** Done in understated hues and featuring warm wood floors and generously spaced tables, this cosmopolitan establishment feels as if it belongs in San Francisco. The kitchen, however, blends that sophistication with inspirations from the Great Outdoors, resulting in "campfire trout" cooked in a cast-iron skillet, bacon-wrapped quail, and a Gruyere-stuffed buffalo burger with truffle fries. [$] *Average*

main: $30 ✉ *2424 Pico Blvd., Santa Monica* ☎ *310/581–9888* 🌐 *www.josierestaurant.com* ✍ *Reservations essential* ⏲ *No lunch* ⊕ *4:H5.*

$$$ SEAFOOD 🍴 **The Lobster.** Anchoring the beach end of the festive Santa Monica Pier, the Lobster usually teems with locals and tourists alike, who come here for the jubilant scene, the great view, and the seafood of chef Allyson Thurber. Start with lobster cocktail with tarragon-lemon aioli, lobster clam chowder, or lobster salad with sweet corn pancakes. For entrées, the theme continues with both Maine and Pacific spiny varieties, but dishes like king salmon in herb sauce are equally satisfying. Request a table on the terrace, both for the views and an escape from the high-decibel interior. [$] *Average main: $30* ✉ *1602 Ocean Ave., Santa Monica* ☎ *310/458–9294* 🌐 *www.thelobster.com* ✍ *Reservations essential* ⊕ *4:F6.*

$$$$ FRENCH Fodor's Choice ★ 🍴 **Mélisse.** In a city where informality reigns, this is one of L.A.'s more dressy, but not stuffy, establishments. The dining room is contemporary yet elegant, with well-spaced tables topped with flowers and fine china. Chef-owner Josiah Citrin enhances his modern French cooking with seasonal California produce. Consider white corn ravioli in brown butter–truffle froth, lobster bolognese, and elegant tableside presentations of Dover sole and stuffed rotisserie chicken. The cheese cart is packed with domestic and European selections. The tasting menus offered here including a creative vegetarian option. [$] *Average main: $115* ✉ *1104 Wilshire Blvd., Santa Monica* ☎ *310/395–0881* 🌐 *www.melisse.com* ✍ *Reservations essential* ⏲ *Closed Sun. and Mon. No lunch* ⊕ *4:F5.*

$$ SEAFOOD FAMILY 🍴 **Santa Monica Seafood.** The Cigliano family began its modest seafood business on Santa Monica Pier in the early 1930s. The restaurant remains a Southern California favorite in its swankier digs along Wilshire Boulevard. It expanded the retail market and made room for a café where you can enjoy oysters and champagne while wearing jeans and flip-flops. The simple menu includes Italian flavors in such dishes as the rainbow trout drizzled with olive oil and spices. There are also sandwiches, soups, and a children's menu. Take time to stroll around the market, read up on the history, and enjoy free tastings of the specials. [$] *Average main: $22* ✉ *1000 Wilshire Blvd., Santa Monica* ☎ *310/393–5244* 🌐 *www.santamonicaseafood.com* ⊕ *4:F5.*

$$ ASIAN 🍴 **Typhoon.** Owner Brian Vidor, who traveled the world as a rock musician and naturalist, brings home some of his favorite gastronomic experiences to this restaurant. Tear your attention away from the planes landing at nearby Santa Monica Airport and the chefs at work in the impressive exhibition kitchen so you can embark on a culinary grand tour of Asia. You'll find samosas from India, curries from Thailand, and salads from Korea. For even more adventure—or bragging rights—you can order stir-fried crickets, Manchurian mountain ants, or Singapore-style scorpions, all beautifully seasoned. [$] *Average main: $19* ✉ *3221 Donald Douglas Loop S., Santa Monica* ☎ *310/390–6565* 🌐 *www.typhoon.biz* ✍ *Reservations essential* ⏲ *No lunch Sat.* ⊕ *4:D3.*

$$$$ ITALIAN 🍴 **Valentino.** Valentino has a truly awe-inspiring wine list—with nearly 2,800 labels consuming 130 pages, backed by a cellar overflowing with more than 80,000 bottles, this restaurant is nothing short of heaven for serious oenophiles. In the 1970s, suave owner Piero Selvaggio introduced L.A. to his exquisite modern Italian cuisine, and he continues to impress with dishes like a timballo of wild mushrooms with rich Parmigiano-Reggiano–saffron *fonduta*, a fresh risotto with market vegetables, a memorable osso buco, and sautéed branzino with lemon emulsion. There's also a more casual wine bar with nibbles like carpaccio. [$] *Average main: $44* ✉ *3115 Pico Blvd., Santa Monica* ☎ *310/829–4313* 🌐 *www.valentinosantamonica.com* ✍ *Reservations essential* ⏲ *Closed Sun. and Mon. No lunch Sat. and Mon.–Thurs.* ✣ *4:H5.*

$$$ MODERN AMERICAN 🍴 **Wilshire.** The woodsy patio at Wilshire is one of the most coveted spaces on the L.A. dining circuit—its candlelight, firelight, and gurgling fountain reel in a hip crowd beneath a cloud of canvas. A passion for organic, market-fresh ingredients is reflected in dishes like lobster bisque with lemongrass cream and duck breast with dried cherry chutney. The eclectic wine list is first-rate, and there's a lively bar scene here, too. [$] *Average main: $29* ✉ *2454 Wilshire Blvd., Santa Monica* ☎ *310/586–1707* 🌐 *www.wilshirerestaurant.com* ✍ *Reservations essential* ⏲ *Closed Sun. No lunch weekends* ✣ *4:H4.*

VENICE

A bit rough around the edges, this urban beach town is home to many of L.A.'s artists, skaters, and surfers. The dining scene continues to grow, but remains true to its cool and casual roots.

$$ AMERICAN 🍴 **Gjelina.** This handsome restaurant comes alive the minute you walk through the rustic wooden door and into a softly lit dining room with long communal tables. The menu is smart and seasonal, with small plates, cheese and charcuterie, pastas, and pizza. Begin with a mushroom, goat cheese, and truffle oil pizza, heirloom spinach salad, mussels with chorizo, or grilled squid with lentils and salsa verde. For the main course, there's the duck leg confit or the hanger steak with watercress salsa verde. Typically crowded and noisy, the outdoor patio is the spot. [$] *Average main: $18* ✉ *1429 Abbot Kinney Blvd., Venice* ☎ *310/450–1429* 🌐 *www.gjelina.com* ✍ *Reservations essential* ✣ *4:C5.*

$$$ AMERICAN 🍴 **Joe's Restaurant.** In a century-old beach house, Joe Miller has created the definitive neighborhood restaurant with a citywide reputation. His imaginative French-influenced California cooking focuses on fresh ingredients. Start with tuna tartare or porcini ravioli in a mushroom-Parmesan broth, and continue with Berkshire pork *crépinette* (a type of sausage) or potato-crusted red snapper in port wine sauce. For dessert, try the chocolate crunch cake with hazelnuts and house-made coffee ice cream. Lunch is a terrific value—all entrées are $18 or less and come with soup or salad. [$] *Average main: $30* ✉ *1023 Abbott Kinney Blvd., Venice* ☎ *310/399–5811* 🌐 *www.joesrestaurant.com* ⏲ *Closed Mon.* ✣ *4:C4.*

MALIBU

The beauty of the coastline makes every meal here taste like the best you've ever had. Here you'll find quaint family spots and extravagant hot spots.

$$$$ ✕ **Nobu Malibu.** At famous chef-restaurateur Nobu Matsuhisa's coastal
JAPANESE outpost, the casually chic clientele sails in for morsels of the world's finest fish. In addition to stellar sushi, Nobu serves many of the same ingenious specialties offered at Matsuhisa in Beverly Hills or Nobu in West Hollywood. You can find exotic species of fish artfully accented with equally exotic South American peppers, tender Kobe beef, and a broth perfumed with matsutake mushrooms. Order the bento box chocolate soufflé and enjoy the ocean view from every seat in the house. $ *Average main: $35* ⊠ *22706 Pacific Coast Hwy., Malibu* ☎ *310/317–9140* ⊕ *www.noburestaurants.com* ⚓ *Reservations essential* ☽ *No lunch* ✛ *4:B6.*

$$$ ✕ **Tra di Noi.** The name means "among us," and Malibu natives try to
ITALIAN keep this simple *ristorante* just that—a local secret. A Tuscan villa-inspired hideaway, the homey Tra di Noi draws everyone from movie stars to well-heeled residents. Nothing too fancy or *nuovo* on the menu, just generous salads, hearty lasagna and other freshly made pastas, short ribs braised in Chianti wine, and a whole two-pound branzino served with herb sauce. An Italian buffet is laid out for Sunday brunch. $ *Average main: $28* ⊠ *3835 Cross Creek Rd., Malibu* ☎ *310/456–0169* ⊕ *www.tradinoimalibu.com* ✛ *4:B6.*

PASADENA

With the revitalization of Old Town Pasadena, more people are discovering the beauty of Rose City. They mingle at bistros, upscale eateries, and taco trucks, but are also discovering the newer innovative dining spots that are giving Pasadena a hipper feel.

$$ ✕ **All India Cafe.** At this authentic Indian eatery, the ingredients are fresh
INDIAN and the flavors are bold without being overpowering. Start with the *bhel puri,* a savory puffed rice-and-potato dish. In addition to meat curries and tikkas, there are many vegetarian selections and some hard-to-find items such as the burrito-like frankies, a favorite Bombay street food. The prices are as palatable as the meals: a full lunch still costs less than $10. $ *Average main: $14* ⊠ *39 S. Fair Oaks Ave., Pasadena* ☎ *626/440–0309* ⊕ *www.allindiacafe.com* ✛ *5:B1.*

$$$ ✕ **Bistro 45.** One of Pasadena's most stylish and sophisticated din-
FRENCH ing spots, Bistro 45 blends traditional French themes with modern concepts to create fanciful California hybrids that delight locals and visitors alike. Seared ahi tuna with a black-and-white-sesame crust, and duck with a tamari-ginger sauce incorporate Pacific Rim accents. The art deco bungalow has been tailored into a sleek environment. Oenophiles, take note: in addition to offering one of the best wine lists in town, owner Robert Simon regularly hosts lavish wine dinners. $ *Average main: $29* ⊠ *45 S. Mentor Ave., Pasadena* ☎ *626/795–2478* ⊕ *www.bistro45.com* ⚓ *Reservations essential* ☽ *Closed Mon. No lunch weekends* ✛ *5:C1.*

10

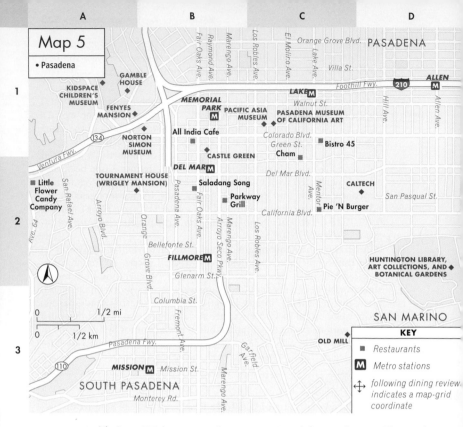

$ ✕ **Cham.** With a name that means "meal for workers," Cham takes

KOREAN   traditional Korean food and turns it into seasonally driven tapas, stews, and *ssam* (leafy vegetable wraps you make yourself). Don't miss the chicken or beef *bibimbap* that arrives with crunchy rice, or the purple sweet potato pie that adds a splash of color and taste. A boutique wine list, craft beers, and Korean cocktails match the lively flavors of the food. Relaxed and inviting, Cham has simple wood furnishing and oversize tables that make for comfy dining. $ *Average main: $11* ✉ *851 Cordova St., Pasadena* ☎ *626/792–2474* ⊕ *www. chamkoreanbistro.com* ⊗ *Closed Sun.* ⟷ *5:C2.*

$ ✕ **Little Flower Candy Co.** This quaint café charms the hearts and taste-

CAFÉ   buds of locals with its seasonally driven menu of sandwiches, salads,

FAMILY   soups, and incredible baked goods. The café is owned by Christine Moore, who made a name for herself in the candy world with sea-salt caramels and pillowy marshmallows. The café is nestled against sloping hills for an away-from-it-all feel (even though Downtown is just a few miles away). It's a terrific place to grab a coffee, a fresh berry pastry, or a light meal before heading out for an afternoon of shopping. $ *Average main: $10* ✉ *1424 W. Colorado Blvd., Pasadena* ☎ *626/304–4800* ⊕ *www.littleflowercandyco.com* ⊗ *Closed Sun.* ⟷ *5:A2.*

$$$$ ✕ **Parkway Grill.** This influential restaurant (once referred to as the
INTERNATIONAL Spago of Pasadena) sports all-American fixtures like exposed brick
walls, a carved wooden bar, and a prominent fireplace. The food
wanders farther afield, incorporating influences from Italy to Japan.
In one sitting you might have black bean soup or a tiger-shrimp corn
dog with Thai aïoli, then filet mignon with a wild mushroom ragout
or whole fried catfish with a yuzu–ponzu sauce. Don't pass up s'mores
for dessert. $ *Average main: $35* ⊠ *510 S. Arroyo Pkwy., Pasadena*
☎ *626/795–1001* ⊕ *www.theparkwaygrill.com* ⌕ *Reservations essential* ⊙ *No lunch weekends* ✛ *5:B2.*

$ ✕ **Pie 'N Burger.** A legendary hangout, this place serves up burgers that
AMERICAN locals justifiably worship, plus potpies, traditional fountain drinks,
FAMILY and tasty pies (especially peach, pecan, and peanut butter). There
are only a few tables, but you'll be treated right at a long counter filled with astrophysicists from the nearby California Institute of
Technology. $ *Average main: $10* ⊠ *913 E. California Blvd., Pasadena* ☎ *626/795–1123* ⊕ *www.pienburger.com* ⌕ *Reservations not
accepted* ▭ No credit cards ✛ *5:C2.*

$ ✕ **Saladang Song.** Surrounded by pierced-steel panels covered with fanci-
THAI ful designs, this eatery has a tucked-away feel. The Thai menu goes well
beyond the usual satays and pad thai. For lunch or dinner, consider the
spicy fish cakes or salmon with curry sauce. For a rarer treat, come for
a Thai breakfast, with *kao-tom-gui* (rice soup with various meats or
seafood) and *joak* (Thai-style rice porridge), with sweet potato, taro,
and pumpkin. $ *Average main: $10* ⊠ *383 S. Fair Oaks Ave., Pasadena*
☎ *626/793–5200* ✛ *5:B2.*

10

WHERE TO STAY

Updated by
Michele Bigley

When it comes to finding a place to stay, travelers have never been more spoiled for choice in today's Los Angeles. From luxurious digs in Beverly Hills and along the coast, to budget boutiques in Hollywood, hotels are stepping up service, upgrading amenities, and throwing in perks like free Wi-Fi, in-room espresso makers, and spa-quality bath products.

The ambitious revitalization of the city's Downtown has upped the game for hoteliers in one of L.A.'s most walkable neighborhoods. Around the L.A. Live complex, there's a 54- floor-tower that holds both a Ritz-Carlton and JW Marriott, together offering a set of grand hotel restaurants and services close to the convention center. Other new Downtown hotels, the Line and Ace Hotels have been erected near California Plaza and in Koreatown to cater to the hipsters who flock to this area to drink and eat on weekends.

Over in Hollywood, it seems every hotel has been getting some work done: most notably Loews Hollywood, Farmer's Daughter, and the historic Hollywood Roosevelt Hotel, which all had massive renovations.

This edition brings a dozen new listings, including some under-the-radar L.A. favorites like Culver Hotel, Sirtaj Beverly Hills, Moment Hotel, W Westwood, and Garden Cottage Bed and Breakfast—all of which offer a reasonably priced L.A. experience. On the design side the Palihouse empire has constructed three new properties in town to help anchor West Hollywood, Hollywood, and Santa Monica in cool.

Those emblematic luxury resorts popular with celebrities are not to be overlooked either, and this edition does not scrimp on ways to get your bling on. Seems almost every major upscale hotel has a new look, with Peninsula Beverly Hills, Le Meridien Delfina Santa Monica, Sunset Marquis, and Fairmont Miramar Hotel & Bungalows leading the pack. For beachfront escapes, Terranea and Shutters still remain at the top of Angelenos' lists as a choice getaway for staycations.

WHERE SHOULD I STAY?

	Neighborhood Vibe	Pros	Cons
Downtown	High-rises, office towers, commercial districts, and cultural institutions, with a growing residential scene.	Affordable hotels within walking distance of art museums, concert halls, and the new L.A. Live complex.	Homeless encampments, with some sketchy areas at night.
Hollywood	Historic theaters and the Walk of Fame, but much of the area is overly touristy.	Heart of the city's nightlife and see-and-be-seen spots, from lively nightclubs to popular eateries.	Steep parking fees, quirky celebrity-obsessed crowd, overpriced everything.
Studio City, Universal City, and North Hollywood	Residential and suburban feel, with some commercial (strip-mall) spots.	Safe, family-friendly, affordable accommodations, plentiful dining options.	Requires a car to get anywhere, even to a nearby coffee shop.
Beverly Hills	Upscale—one of the city's most sought-after addresses, with classy and elegant hotels.	Great shopping, celeb spotting, numerous restaurants all near quiet residential areas.	Big bucks to stay, dine, park, and shop here; limited diversity.
Century City and Culver City	Businesses mixed with residential buildings; centrally located.	Easy access to all points on the Westside; pedestrian-friendly strip in Culver City.	Some strictly office areas, no beach or ocean views.
Bel Air, Brentwood, West Hollywood, Westwood	Coveted neighborhood for elite; boutique hotels abound in West Hollywood.	Close proximity to Getty Center; ambitious restaurants and fun nightspots in West Hollywood.	Stuffy attitudes in Bel Air; spendy stays in West Hollywood.
LAX vicinity	Concentration of office towers and commercial buildings.	Convenient location near airport; incredibly affordable.	Little activity, dull nearby strip malls with restaurants and shopping.
Santa Monica and Malibu	Laid-back beach towns with waterfront hotels, cottages, and inns.	Ocean breezes, super-safe, family-friendly; walkable pockets with restaurants, cafés, and boutiques.	Some bars, but limited nightlife; steep prices for an ocean view.
Venice, Marina Del Rey, Manhattan, Hermosa, Long Beach	Edgy, artsy in Venice; residential in Manhattan Beach; sailing and biking in Marina del Rey.	Diverse neighborhoods but close to the ocean without Malibu's spendiness. Long Beach airport is a great travel alternative.	Mostly residential in some pockets; traffic along Highway 1 means long driving times.
Pasadena	Residential with walkable strip of shops and cafés.	Charming small town feel, family-friendly, historic.	Removed from Westside and beaches; lengthy driving time into the city.

PLANNING

RESERVATIONS

Hotel reservations are an absolute necessity when planning your trip to Los Angeles—although rooms are easier to come by these days. Competition for clients also means properties undergo frequent improvements, so when booking ask about any renovations, lest you get a room within earshot of construction. In this ever-changing city travelers can find themselves temporarily, and most inconveniently, without commonplace amenities such as room service or spa access if their hotel is upgrading.

SERVICES

Most hotels have air-conditioning and flat-screen cable TV. Those in the moderate and expensive price ranges often have voice mail, coffeemakers, bathrobes, and hair dryers as well. Most also have high-speed Internet access in guest rooms, with a 24-hour use fee (though at a number of hotels it's free). Wi-Fi is common even at budget properties. Southern California's emphasis on being in shape means most hotels have fitness facilities; if the one on-site is not to your liking, ask for a reference to a nearby sports club or gym.

STAYING WITH KIDS

From Disneyland to the beach cities, laid-back Los Angeles definitely has a reputation as a family-friendly destination. Resorts and hotels along the coast, in particular, attract plenty of beachgoing family vacationers looking for sun and sandcastles. Some properties provide such diversions as in-room movies, toys, and video games; others have suites with kitchenettes and foldout sofa beds. Hotels often provide cribs, rollaway beds, and references to babysitting services, but make arrangements when booking the room, not when you arrive. *Properties that are especially kid-friendly are marked FAMILY throughout the chapter.*

PARKING

Exploring Los Angeles, a sprawling city of wide boulevards and five-lane freeways, pretty much requires a car. Though you might stroll Rodeo Drive on foot or amble along the Hollywood Walk of Fame, to get from one part of town to another, you'll need wheels. Thankfully, there's street parking in most areas (read signs carefully as some neighborhoods are by permit only) and many public parking lots offer the first hour or two free. Though a few hotels have free parking, most charge for the privilege, and some resorts only have valet parking, with fees as high as $40 per night.

PRICES

Tax rates for the area will add 10% to 15.5% to your bill depending on where in Los Angeles County you stay; some hoteliers tack on energy, service, or occupancy surcharges—ask about customary charges when you book your room.

When looking for a hotel, don't write off the pricier establishments immediately. Price categories here are determined by "rack rates"—the list price of a hotel room—which is often higher than those you'll find online or by calling the hotel directly. Specials abound, particularly in Downtown on the weekends. Many hotels have packages that include breakfast, theater tickets, spa services, or exotic rental cars. Pricing is competitive, so always check with the hotel for current special offers.

Finally, when making reservations, don't forget to check the hotel's website for exclusive Internet specials.

Prices in the hotel reviews are the lowest cost of a standard double room in high season.

HOTEL REVIEWS

For expanded hotel reviews, visit Fodors.com.

Use the coordinate (✛ 1:B2) at the end of each listing to locate a site on the corresponding map.

DOWNTOWN

An ongoing revitalization in Downtown, anchored around the L.A. Live complex, along with a thriving, hipster vibe in Koreatown and Echo Park make these areas a great place to see Los Angeles in transition: Think affordable accommodations rubbing elbows with business hotels, streets lined with coffeehouses, and edgy boutiques that can be explored on foot. Note that some parts of Downtown should not be explored on foot after dark.

Take advantage of the proximity to the Griffith Park Observatory in summer or the burgeoning nightlife in Downtown.

$
HOTEL
Ace Hotel. L.A.'s newest hipster haven wears multiple hats as a hotel, theater, neighborhood diner/coffee shop, and series of lounges, where you can bar-hop by elevator. **Pros:** lively public areas; great rates; free Wi-Fi. **Cons:** expensive parking rates compared to nightly rates ($36); service needs to get the kinks worked out; compact and somewhat awkwardly designed rooms. **$** *Rooms from: $199* ✉ *929 S. Broadway, Downtown* ☎ *213/623–3233* ⊕ *www.acehotel.com/losangeles* ⟿ *182 rooms, 1 suite* ⦿ *No meals* ✛ *1:B3.*

$
HOTEL
Figueroa Hotel. On the outside, it feels like Spanish Colonial; on the inside, this 12-story hotel, built in 1926, is a mix of Mexican, Mediterranean, and Moroccan styles, with earth tones, hand-glazed walls, and wrought-iron beds. **Pros:** a short walk to Nokia Theatre, L.A. Live, and the convention center; great poolside bar; well-priced, including lowest parking charge in town ($12). **Cons:** somewhat funky and dark room decor; small bathrooms; gentrifying neighborhood. **$** *Rooms from: $148* ✉ *939 S. Figueroa St., Downtown* ☎ *213/627–8971, 800/421–9092* ⊕ *www.figueroahotel.com* ⟿ *285 rooms, 6 suites* ⦿ *No meals* ✛ *1:A3.*

$$
HOTEL
Hilton Checkers Los Angeles. Opened as the Mayflower Hotel in 1927, Checkers retains much of its original character, such as its charming period details, but it also has contemporary luxuries like pillow-top mattresses, coffeemakers, 24-hour room service, and plasma TVs. **Pros:** historic charm; business-friendly; rooftop pool and spa. **Cons:** no on-street parking and valet is almost $40; some rooms are compact; urban setting. **$** *Rooms from: $259* ✉ *535 S. Grand Ave., Downtown* ☎ *213/624–0000, 800/445–8667* ⊕ *www.hiltoncheckers.com* ⟿ *188 rooms, 5 suites* ⦿ *No meals* ✛ *1:B3.*

BEST BETS FOR LOS ANGELES LODGING

Fodor's offers a selective listing of lodging experiences at every price range. Here, we've compiled our top recommendations by price and experience. The best properties are designated with the Fodor's Choice logo.

Fodor'sChoice★

Beach House Hotel at Hermosa, $$$, p. 267

Channel Road Inn, $, p. 260

The Crescent Beverly Hills, $, p. 252

Farmer's Daughter Hotel, $, p. 257

Hollywood Roosevelt Hotel, $$$ p. 247

Hotel Bel-Air, $$$$, p. 256

The Langham Huntington, Pasadena, $$, p. 268

Magic Castle Hotel, $, p. 247

Montage Beverly Hills, $$$$, p. 253

Palihotel, $, p. 248

Peninsula Beverly Hills, $$$$, p. 253

The Redbury, $$$$, p. 248

The Ritz-Carlton Marina del Rey, $$$$, p. 266

Shore Hotel, $$$, p. 265

Shutters on the Beach, $$$$, p. 265

Sunset Marquis Hotel & Villas, $$$, p. 258

Terranea, $$$$, p. 267

By Price

$

Channel Road Inn, p. 260

The Crescent Beverly Hills, p. 252

Hotel Amarano Burbank, p. 250

Farmer's Daughter Hotel, p. 257

Figueroa Hotel, p. 243

Los Feliz Lodge, p. 251

Magic Castle Hotel, p. 247

Palihotel, p. 248

Sea Shore Motel, p. 264

$$

Hilton Checkers Hotel, p. 243

Hotel Erwin, p. 266

The Langham Huntington, Pasadena, p. 268

Palihouse West Hollywood, p. 258

$$$

Beach House Hotel Hermosa Beach, p. 267

Hollywood Roosevelt Hotel, p. 247

Shore Hotel, p. 265

Sunset Marquis Hotel & Villas, p. 258

$$$$

Beverly Wilshire, a Four Seasons Hotel, p. 252

Four Seasons Hotel, Los Angeles at Beverly Hills, p. 252

Montage Beverly Hills, p. 253

Peninsula Beverly Hills, p. 253

The Redbury, p. 248

Shutters on the Beach, p. 265

Terranea, p. 267

By Experience

BEST DESIGN

Avalon, $$, p. 251

Figueroa Hotel, $, p. 243

Mondrian Los Angeles, $$, p. 258

Mosaic Hotel, $$$, p. 253

Oceana, $$$, p. 264

Palihouse Santa Monica, $$, p. 264

The Standard, Downtown L.A., $$, p. 246

Viceroy Santa Monica, $$$$, p. 265

BEST SPAS

Beverly Wilshire, a Four Seasons Hotel, $$$$, p. 252

Four Seasons Hotel, Los Angeles at Beverly Hills, $$$$, p. 252

Hotel Bel-Air, $$$$, p. 256

Montage Beverly Hills, $$$$, p. 253

Shutters on the Beach, $$$$, p. 265

Westin Bonaventure Hotel & Suites, $, p. 246

GREEN FOCUS

The Ambrose, $$, p. 260

Hotel Palomar Los Angeles–Westwood, $$, p. 259

Hotel Shangri-La, $$$$, p. 264

Los Feliz Lodge, $, p. 251

Venice Beach Eco-Cottages, $$, p. 266

MOST KID-FRIENDLY

Loews Santa Monica Beach Hotel, $$$$, p. 264

Magic Castle Hotel, $, p. 247

Montage Beverly Hills, $$$$, p. 253

Sheraton Universal, $$, p. 265

Shutters on the Beach, $$$$, p. 265

Terranea, $$$$, p. 267

11

$
B&B/INN

⊡ **Inn at 657.** Proprietor Patsy Carter runs a homey, welcoming bed-and-breakfast near the University of Southern California that is decked out in period antiques with Far East accents. **Pros:** vintage home and quiet garden; homemade treats; accessible innkeeper. **Cons:** low-tech stay; no elevator. $ *Rooms from: $160 ⊠ 657 W. 23rd St., Downtown ☎ 213/741–2200 ⊕ www.patsysinn657.com ↩ 4 rooms, 2 suites ⦿ Breakfast ✢ 1:A3.*

$$$
HOTEL

⊡ **JW Marriott Los Angeles at L.A. Live.** Set in a shimmering blue-glass tower, the 878-room convention center–adjacent hotel anchors the L.A. Live entertainment complex that's home to the Nokia Theatre and more than a dozen bars, nightclubs, and eateries. **Pros:** Higher floors have jetliner views; movie theaters, restaurants, and a pro sports arena are just out the door. **Cons:** Imposing and crowded lobby; expensive dining choices and valet. $ *Rooms from: $339 ⊠ 900 W. Olympic Blvd., Downtown ☎ 213/765–8600 ⊕ www.lalivemarriott.com ↩ 826 rooms, 52 suites ⦿ No meals ✢ 1:A3.*

$$
HOTEL

⊡ **The Line.** L.A.'s newest boutique hotel pays homage to its Koreatown address with a dynamic new dining concept by superstar Roy Choi, artsy interiors, and a hidden karaoke speakeasy, aptly named Speek. **Pros:** free bikes to explore the area; cheery staff; celebratory atmosphere. **Cons:** design might feel cold and too ambitious for some; expensive parking ($32). $ *Rooms from: $240 ⊠ 3515 Wilshire Blvd., Hollywood ☎ 213/381–7411 ⊕ www.thelinehotel.com ↩ 362 rooms, 26 suites ⦿ No meals ✢ 1:A2.*

$
HOTEL

⊡ **Millennium Biltmore Hotel.** One of Downtown L.A.'s true treasures, the gilded 1923 Beaux-Arts masterpiece exudes ambience and history (which does mean that some of the rooms are small by today's standards). **Pros:** historic character; famed filming location; club-level rooms have many hospitable extras. **Cons:** pricey valet parking; standard rooms are truly compact. $ *Rooms from: $189 ⊠ 506 S. Grand Ave., Downtown ☎ 213/624–1011, 866/866–8086 ⊕ www.millenniumhotels.com ↩ 635 rooms, 48 suites ⦿ No meals ✢ 1:B3.*

$
HOTEL

⊡ **O Hotel.** A former residential hotel, the O has been completely cleaned up and redone in a minimalist, Zen-modern style complete with an on-site restaurant and the Oasis City Spa's array of massage and body treatments. **Pros:** boutique, European city–style hotel; ambitious restaurant cuisine. **Cons:** boxy, almost monastic cell-like rooms and few views; gentrifying neighborhood means numerous homeless people, and deserted streetscapes come nightfall. $ *Rooms from: $159 ⊠ 819 S. Flower St., Downtown ☎ 213/623–9904 ⊕ www.ohotelgroup.com ↩ 67 rooms ⦿ Breakfast ✢ 1:A3.*

$$$$
HOTEL
FAMILY

⊡ **Omni Los Angeles Hotel at California Plaza.** Fresh off a multimillion-dollar renovation, the 17-story Omni is in Downtown's cultural and business heart, just steps from the Museum of Contemporary Art and the Los Angeles Philharmonic's home, Walt Disney Concert Hall. **Pros:** western-facing rooms have stunning views including Disney Hall; a short walk to most Downtown culture and courthouses. **Cons:** confusing lobby layout (entrances on different floors); Olive Street super-traffic-y and not pedestrian-friendly. $ *Rooms from: $419 ⊠ 251 S. Olive St., Downtown ☎ 213/617–3300, 800/843–6664 ⊕ www.omnihotels.com ↩ 439 rooms, 14 suites ⦿ No meals ✢ 1:B2.*

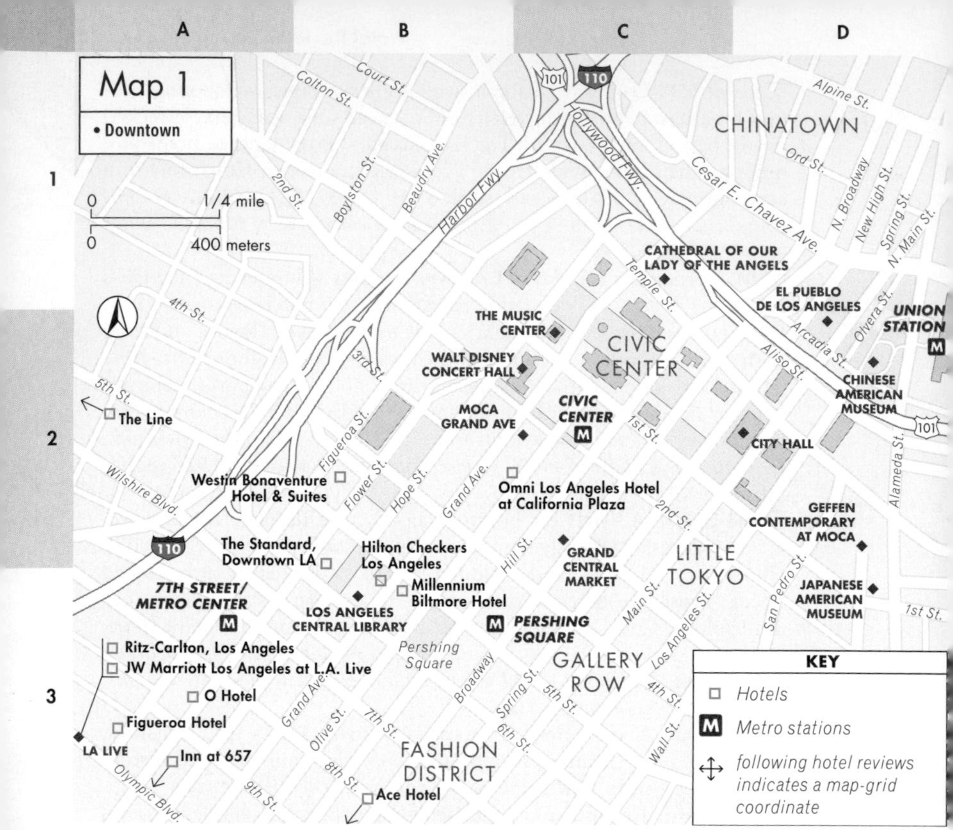
A
B
C
D
1
2
3
Map 1
• Downtown
0
1/4 mile
0
400 meters
Court St.
Colton St.
2nd St.
Boylston St.
Beaudry Ave.
Harbor Fwy.
Hollywood Fwy.
101
110
Alpine St.
CHINATOWN
Ord St.
Cesar E. Chavez Ave.
N. Broadway
New High St.
Spring St.
N. Main St.
CATHEDRAL OF OUR LADY OF THE ANGELS
Temple St.
EL PUEBLO DE LOS ANGELES
UNION STATION
Olvera St.
Arcadia St.
4th St.
THE MUSIC CENTER
CIVIC CENTER
3rd St.
WALT DISNEY CONCERT HALL
Aliso St.
CHINESE AMERICAN MUSEUM
5th St.
The Line
MOCA GRAND AVE
CIVIC CENTER
1st St.
CITY HALL
Figueroa St.
Alameda St.
Wilshire Blvd.
Westin Bonaventure Hotel & Suites
Flower St.
Hope St.
Grand Ave.
Omni Los Angeles Hotel at California Plaza
2nd St.
GEFFEN CONTEMPORARY AT MOCA
The Standard, Downtown LA
Hilton Checkers Los Angeles
Hill St.
GRAND CENTRAL MARKET
LITTLE TOKYO
San Pedro St.
7TH STREET/ METRO CENTER
Millennium Biltmore Hotel
Main St.
JAPANESE AMERICAN MUSEUM
1st St.
LOS ANGELES CENTRAL LIBRARY
PERSHING SQUARE
Los Angeles St.
Ritz-Carlton, Los Angeles
Pershing Square
GALLERY ROW
JW Marriott Los Angeles at L.A. Live
Broadway
Spring St.
5th St.
4th St.
O Hotel
Grand Ave.
Figueroa Hotel
Olive St.
7th St.
6th St.
Wall St.
LA LIVE
Inn at 657
FASHION DISTRICT
Olympic Blvd.
8th St.
9th St.
Ace Hotel
KEY
Hotels
Metro stations
following hotel reviews indicates a map-grid coordinate

$$$ HOTEL 🏨 **The Ritz-Carlton, Los Angeles.** This citified Ritz-Carlton on the 23rd and 24th floors of a 54-story tower within Downtown's L.A. Live entertainment complex features skyline views through expansive windows, blond woods, and smartened-up amenities such as flat-screen TVs (including one hidden in the bathroom mirror). **Pros:** designer spa with a *Jetsons*-esque relaxation room; well soundproofed; impressive views from the restaurant. **Cons:** somewhat confusing layout; expensive valet parking; pricey room service. [$] *Rooms from: $369* ✉ *900 West Olympic Blvd., Downtown* ☎ *213/742–6855* 🌐 *www.ritzcarlton.com* 🛏 *109 rooms, 14 suites* 🍴 *No meals* ✥ *1:A3.*

$$ HOTEL 🏨 **The Standard, Downtown L.A.** Though this hotel was built in 1955 as the company headquarters for Standard Oil, you might not know it, because the building was completely revamped in 2002 under the sharp eye of owner André Balazs, giving it a sleeky, cutting-edge feel. **Pros:** on-site Rudy's barbershop for grooming; 24/7 coffee shop for dining; rooftop pool and lounge for fun. **Cons:** disruptive party scene weekends and holidays; street noise; pricey valet parking. [$] *Rooms from: $250* ✉ *550 S. Flower St., Downtown* ☎ *213/892–8080* 🌐 *www.standardhotels.com* 🛏 *171 rooms, 36 suites* 🍴 *No meals* ✥ *1:B2.*

$ HOTEL 🏨 **Westin Bonaventure Hotel & Suites.** To keep up with the energizing of Downtown this historic, five-tower, 35-story property—L.A.'s largest hotel—recently underwent a $32 million renovation of its rooms and lobby. **Pros:** numerous restaurants including Korean barbecue; an Asian-theme spa with shiatsu or chair massage; revolving rooftop lounge is a classic experience. **Cons:** massive hotel might feel too corporate; mazelike lobby and public areas. $ *Rooms from: $189* ⊠ *404 S. Figueroa St., Downtown* ☎ *213/624–1000, 866/716–8132* ⊕ *www. westin.com* ↔ *1,354 rooms, 135 suites* ⦿ *No meals* ✛ *1:B2.*

HOLLYWOOD AND THE STUDIOS

For easy access to the Walk of Fame and trendy nightlife, Hollywood delights partygoers and those wanting to be in the heart of the action. Movie buffs may take days exploring the vicinity, but most travelers usually spend some time walking along Hollywood Boulevard, which is a congested strip of historic theaters, bars, restaurants, and kitschy (and sometimes tacky) shops. Many hotels in the area, however, offer great views of the Hollywood sign, and Universal Studios theme park is one or two Metro stops away. This area can be rough at night. Nearby in Los Feliz, you'll find a historic walkable neighborhood packed with boutiques and cafés.

The San Fernando Valley houses many of the major studios, making this a fine place to call home if you are here on work, or want more affordable accommodations. You'll need to drive to most places, as the Valley is a patchwork of strip malls packed with ethnic eateries.

HOLLYWOOD

$$$
HOTEL
Fodor's Choice
★

⛭ **Hollywood Roosevelt Hotel.** Think hip bachelor pad when considering the Roosevelt, which is known for its party-centric vibe in the heart of Hollywood and was once the home of the first Academy Awards. **Pros:** in the heart of Hollywood's action and a block from the Metro; lively social scene; great burgers at hotel's restaurant, 25 Degrees. **Cons:** reports of noise and staff attitude; stiff parking charges. $ *Rooms from: $399* ⊠ *7000 Hollywood Blvd., Hollywood* ☎ *323/466–7000, 800/950–7667* ⊕ *www.hollywoodroosevelt.com* ↔ *305 rooms, 48 suites* ⦿ *No meals* ✛ *2:E2.*

$$
HOTEL
FAMILY

⛭ **Loews Hollywood.** Part of the massive Hollywood & Highland shopping and entertainment complex, this 20-story Loew's Hotel is at the center of Hollywood's action but still manages to offer a quiet night's sleep with fantastic views of the Hollywood Sign. **Pros:** large rooms with new contemporary-styled furniture; free Wi-Fi; Red Line Metro station adjacent; attached to a mall with plentiful dining options. **Cons:** corporate feeling; very touristy; pricey parking fees. $ *Rooms from: $289* ⊠ *1755 N. Highland Ave., Hollywood* ☎ *323/856–1200, 800/769–4774* ⊕ *www.loewshotels.com/en/Hollywood-Hotel* ↔ *604 rooms, 33 suites* ⦿ *No meals* ✛ *2:E1.*

$
HOTEL
FAMILY
Fodor's Choice
★

⛭ **Magic Castle Hotel.** Close to the action (and traffic) of Hollywood, this former apartment building faces busy Franklin Avenue and is a quick walk to the nearby Red Line stop at Hollywood & Highland. **Pros:** remarkably friendly and able staff; free Wi-Fi; good value. **Cons:** traffic-heavy locale; no elevator; small bathrooms. $ *Rooms from: $184* ⊠ *7025 Franklin Ave., Hollywood* ☎ *323/851–0800, 800/741–4915* ⊕ *www. magiccastlehotel.com* ↔ *7 rooms, 36 suites* ⦿ *Breakfast* ✛ *2:E1.*

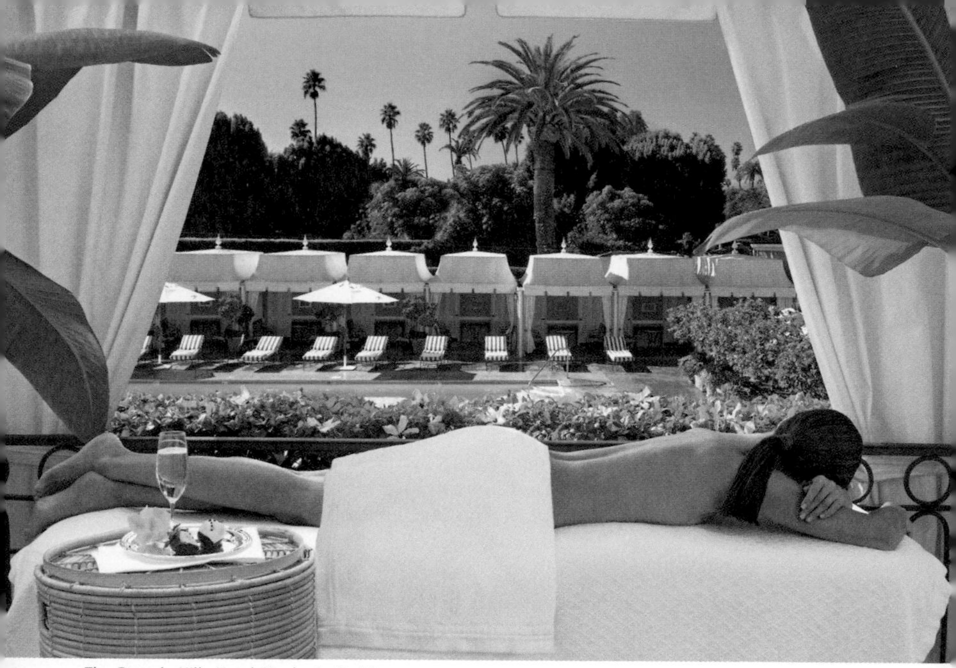

The Beverly Hills Hotel Spa by La Prairie

$$ HOTEL [🏨] **Moment Hotel.** Across from Guitar Center on bustling Sunset Boulevard, Hollywood's newest property caters to young party-people, who breeze in and out at all hours. **Pros:** central location; on-site food service; free Wi-Fi. **Cons:** street noise; not the safest neighborhood for walking at night. [$] *Rooms from: $239* ✉ *7370 Sunset Blvd., Hollywood* ☎ *323/822–5030* 🌐 *themomenthotel.com* 🛏 *38 rooms, 1 suite* 🍴 *No meals* ✣ *2:E2.*

$ HOTEL Fodor's Choice ★ [🏨] **Palihotel.** Catering to young and hip budget travelers, who crave style over space, this design-centric boutique property on lively Melrose Avenue is in the heart of Hollywood's best shopping and dining and contains Hollywood's dining hot-spot, Hart and the Hunter. **Pros:** funky aesthetic; fun communal massage room; fantastic location in a walkable neighborhood. **Cons:** small rooms; congested lobby; decor might not appeal to everyone. [$] *Rooms from: $179* ✉ *7950 Melrose Ave., Hollywood* ☎ *323/272–4588* 🌐 *www.pali-hotel.com* 🛏 *32 rooms* 🍴 *No meals* ✣ *2:D3.*

$$$$ HOTEL Fodor's Choice ★ [🏨] **The Redbury.** In the heart of Hollywood's nightlife, near the intersection of Hollywood and Vine, the Redbury's dark hues and suites (the smallest is 750 square feet) are designed to appeal to the inner Bohemian in most travelers. **Pros:** kitchenette, washer-dryer and spacious rooms are ideal for those staying a while; excellent dining. **Cons:** no pool or on-site gym; noisy on lower floors; a real Hollywood scene (which can be a pro, depending on your point of view). [$] *Rooms from: $500* ✉ *1717 Vine St., Hollywood* ☎ *323/962–1717, 977/962–1717* 🌐 *www.theredbury.com* 🛏 *57 suites* 🍴 *No meals* ✣ *2:F1.*

CLOSE UP

Spa Specialists

11

In a city where image is everything, spas are urban sanctuaries, but they're also places of pampering and rejuvenating for those willing to pay the price. A one-hour massage can set you back as much as $160. Along with massages, spas emphasize anti-aging treatments since everyone's after the fountain of youth here.

When booking a massage, specify your preference for a male or female therapist. Give yourself time to arrive early and relax via steam, sauna, or Jacuzzi depending on the spa's selection. Tip at least 15% to 20%.

Bliss. Want that red-carpet glow? In superslick, all-white treatment rooms, Bliss provides superhydrating triple-oxygen-treatment facials that plump and reinvigorate even the most blah skin. ⊠ *6250 Hollywood Blvd., Hollywood* ☎ *877/862–5477.*

Chuan Spa at the Langham Huntington. Chinese medicine–influenced therapies at the Huntington Spa help restore balance and harmony to the body via meditative breathing rituals and acupressure. ⊠ *1401 S. Oak Knoll Ave., Pasadena* ☎ *626/585–6414.*

Hotel Bel-Air Spa by La Prairie. This upscale spa in one of the city's poshest addresses delivers anti-aging treatments in relaxing treatment rooms. Some favorites include the caviar and the gold facials. ⊠ *701 Stone Canyon, Bel Air* ☎ *310/909–1681* ⊕ *www.dorchestercollection.com/en/los-angeles/hotel-bel-air/spa-hotel/la-prairie-spa* ⊙ *8 am–9 pm.*

One. Treatments at Santa Monica's One aim to relax the body and mind. Body treatments here, such as the Red Flower Hammam, turn skin silky soft using all-natural tonics from Red Flower. ⊠ *Shutters on the Beach, 1 Pico Blvd., Santa Monica* ☎ *310/587–1712.*

Peninsula Spa at the Peninsula Beverly Hills. Rarefied treatments at this exclusive rooftop retreat include massages with oils laced with pulverized precious stones. ⊠ *9882 S. Santa Monica Blvd., Beverly Hills* ☎ *310/551–2888.*

Spa at the Beverly Wilshire. Rub elbows with celebs (or play out your *Pretty Woman* fantasies) at the Spa at the Beverly Wilshire, with a mani-pedi and then an afternoon at the pool. Features include a fabulous rain shower (cascades vary from a cool mist to a brisk Atlantic storm); a supersize, mosaic-tile steam room; superstar facial treatments like hydra-facial and the Natura Bisse Diamond Collection; and oh-so-decadent massages. ⊠ *9500 Wilshire Blvd., Beverly Hills* ☎ *310/385–7023.*

Spa at the Four Seasons, Beverly Hills. Choose your own soundtrack in the deluxe treatment rooms at this spa that concentrates on traditional body treatments in small, seasonally scented private quarters. Try the fabulous Manipura experience body treatment that begins with a Himalayan salt scrub and ends with a body massage with argan oil. ⊠ *300 S. Doheny Dr., Beverly Hills* ☎ *310/273–2222, 310/786–2229.*

Spa Montage. The Moroccan décor, ornate steam room, glass-walled sauna, co-ed mineral pool, and indoor Jacuzzi at this hidden casbah of pampering will keep you relaxed for hours. ⊠ *225 N. Canon Dr., Beverly Hills* ☎ *310/860–7840.*

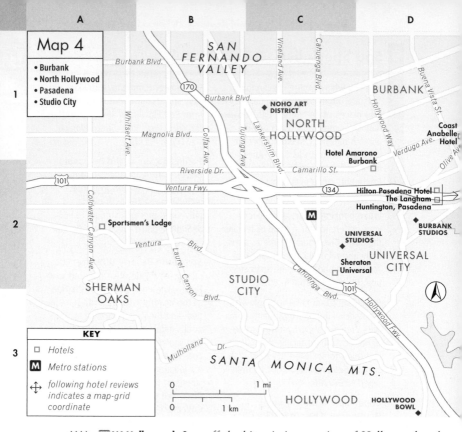

Map 4

- Burbank
- North Hollywood
- Pasadena
- Studio City

SAN FERNANDO VALLEY

Burbank Blvd.

Burbank Blvd.

NORTH HOLLYWOOD

NOHO ART DISTRICT

BURBANK

Coast Anabelle Hotel

Hotel Amarano Burbank

Magnolia Blvd.

Riverside Dr.

Camarillo St.

Ventura Fwy.

Hilton Pasadena Hotel

The Langham Huntington, Pasadena

Sportsmen's Lodge

BURBANK STUDIOS

UNIVERSAL STUDIOS

UNIVERSAL CITY

Ventura

Blvd.

Sheraton Universal

SHERMAN OAKS

STUDIO CITY

SANTA MONICA MTS.

Mulholland Dr.

HOLLYWOOD

HOLLYWOOD BOWL

KEY

☐ Hotels

Ⓜ Metro stations

⊕ following hotel reviews indicates a map-grid coordinate

0   1 mi

0   1 km

$$$$
HOTEL
🖥 **W Hollywood.** Just off the historic intersection of Hollywood and Vine and above a busy Metro station, the W Hollywood is ultramodern and outfitted for the wired traveler, though party people will enjoy the central location and rooftop pool deck. **Pros:** Metro stop outside the front door; you'll be equipped for an in-room party—from ice to cocktail glasses. **Cons:** small pool; pricey dining and valet parking; soundproofing issues. $ *Rooms from: $749* ✉ *6250 Hollywood Blvd., Hollywood* ☎ *323/798–1300, 888/625–4955* ⊕ *www.whotels.com/hollywood* ⤵ *265 rooms, 40 suites* ⦿ *No meals* ⊕ *2:F2.*

BURBANK

$
HOTEL
🖥 **Coast Anabelle Hotel.** The location of this small nonsmoking hotel—on Burbank's main drag—is handy, especially for those on studio business because it's a straight-shot mile from NBC and 3 miles from Warner Bros. **Pros:** near studios; free Burbank airport shuttle; use of pool at sister property next door. **Cons:** noise from traffic heard from first-floor rooms. $ *Rooms from: $199* ✉ *2011 W. Olive Ave., Burbank* ☎ *818/845–7800, 800/782–4373* ⊕ *www.coastanabelle.com/coast* ⤵ *45 rooms, 9 suites* ⦿ *No meals* ⊕ *4:D1.*

$
HOTEL
🖥 **Hotel Amarano Burbank.** Close to Burbank's TV and movie studios, the smartly designed Amarano feels like a Beverly Hills boutique hotel, complete with 24-hour room service, a homey on-site

restaurant and lounge, and newly spruced-up rooms. **Pros:** boutique style; location in the Valley; pleasant breakfast room. **Cons:** street noise. [$] *Rooms from: $199* ✉ *322 N. Pass Ave., Burbank* ☎ *818/842–8887, 888/956–1900* 🌐 *www.hotelamarano.com* 🛏 *98 rooms, 34 suites* 🍴 *No meals* ✥ *4:D2.*

LOS FELIZ

$ RENTAL

🏨 **Los Feliz Lodge.** Checking into this bungalow-style lodge is like crashing at an eco-minded and artsy friend's place: you let yourself into an apartment with fully stocked kitchen, washer and dryer, and a communal patio. **Pros:** homey feel; within walking distance to restaurants. **Cons:** no on-site restaurant or pool. [$] *Rooms from: $155* ✉ *1507 N. Hoover St., Los Feliz* ☎ *323/660–4150* 🌐 *www.losfelizlodge.com* 🛏 *4 rooms* 🍴 *No meals* ✥ *2:H2.*

UNIVERSAL CITY

$$ HOTEL FAMILY

🏨 **Sheraton Universal.** Because of its large meeting spaces and veteran staff, this Sheraton buzzes year-round with business types who also come for the high-tech extras like automated check-in, convenient in-room coffeemaker with to-go cup, and numerous business services. **Pros:** woodsy location straddling Hollywood Hills; Metro access; free shuttle to Universal Studios and CityWalk. **Cons:** average in-house restaurant; touristy. [$] *Rooms from: $299* ✉ *333 Universal Hollywood Dr., Universal City* ☎ *818/980–1212, 888/627–7184* 🌐 *www.sheratonuniversal.com* 🛏 *451 rooms, 31 suites* 🍴 *No meals* ✥ *4:C2.*

STUDIO CITY

$ HOTEL FAMILY

🏨 **Sportsmen's Lodge.** The sprawling five-story hotel, an L.A. landmark in the San Fernando Valley, is under new ownership and management and thus has a new contemporary look. **Pros:** close to Ventura Boulevard's plentiful restaurants; free shuttle and discounted tickets to Universal Hollywood; garden-view rooms are quietest. **Cons:** pricey daily self-parking fee; a bit of a drive to get to the city. [$] *Rooms from: $159* ✉ *12825 Ventura Blvd., Studio City* ☎ *818/769–4700, 800/821–8511* 🌐 *www.sportsmenslodge.com* 🛏 *177 rooms, 13 suites* 🍴 *No meals* ✥ *4:A2.*

BEVERLY HILLS AND THE WESTSIDE

A dream zip code for many, posh Beverly Hills, funky West Hollywood and the Westside are fantastic central addresses for accessing the beaches, the Getty Center, and midcity. The prime zip code means hotels here, including stylish newcomers like Palihouse West Hollywood, come with a hefty price tag. The silver lining is walkable areas, so you'll spend less time in a car, and the access to the glittering coast.

BEVERLY HILLS

$$ HOTEL

🏨 **Avalon.** Interior decorator Kelly Wearstler put her Midas touch on this midcentury Beverly Hills hotel, mixing original classic pieces by George Nelson and Charles Eames with her chic custom designs. **Pros:** Beverly Hills location; stylish. **Cons:** poolside social scene can be noisy. [$] *Rooms from: $250* ✉ *9400 W. Olympic Blvd., Beverly Hills* ☎ *310/277–5221, 800/670–6183* 🌐 *www.avalonbeverlyhills.com* 🛏 *76 rooms, 10 suites* 🍴 *No meals* ✥ *2:B4.*

$$$$ HOTEL FAMILY 🏨 **Beverly Hills Hotel.** Remarkably still at the top of her game, the "Pink Palace" continues to attract Hollywood's elite after 100 years. **Pros:** pool; spa; legendary, retro 20-seat Fountain Coffee room is a fun spot for dining with the stars. **Cons:** pricey fare at the Polo Lounge. [$] *Rooms from: $645* ✉ *9641 Sunset Blvd., Beverly Hills* ☎ *310/276–2251, 800/283–8885* 🌐 *www.beverlyhillshotel.com* 🛏 *145 rooms, 38 suites, 23 bungalows* 🍴 *No meals* ✢ *2:A3.*

$$ HOTEL 🏨 **Beverly Hills Plaza Hotel.** With a precious courtyard surrounding the pool, the well-maintained, all-suites Beverly Hills Plaza has a look that would be right at home in the south of France. **Pros:** European ambience; amiable staff; near golf. **Cons:** lowest-priced suites are accessible via stairs only; no services or restaurants close-by, so car is a must. [$] *Rooms from: $225* ✉ *10300 Wilshire Blvd., Beverly Hills* ☎ *310/275–5575, 800/800–1234* 🌐 *www.beverlyhillsplazahotel.com* 🛏 *116 suites* 🍴 *No meals* ✢ *2:A4.*

$$$ HOTEL FAMILY 🏨 **Beverly Hilton.** Home of the Golden Globe Awards, the Beverly Hilton is as polished as its glitzy address, offering spectacular views of Beverly Hills and sizeable balconies in many rooms. **Pros:** walking distance to Beverly Hills; complimentary car service for short jaunts; one of L.A.'s largest hotel pools. **Cons:** corporate feel; some rooms feel tired. [$] *Rooms from: $345* ✉ *9876 Wilshire Blvd., Beverly Hills* ☎ *310/274–7777, 877/414–8018* 🌐 *www.beverlyhilton.com* 🛏 *468 rooms, 101 suites* 🍴 *No meals* ✢ *2:A4.*

$$$$ HOTEL 🏨 **Beverly Wilshire, a Four Seasons Hotel.** Built in 1928, the Italian Renaissance–style Wilshire wing of this fabled hotel is replete with elegant details: crystal chandeliers, oak paneling, walnut doors, crown moldings, and marble. **Pros:** chic location; top-notch service; refined vibe. **Cons:** small lobby; valet parking backs up at peak times; expensive dining options. [$] *Rooms from: $775* ✉ *9500 Wilshire Blvd., Beverly Hills* ☎ *310/275–5200, 800/427–4354* 🌐 *www.fourseasons.com/beverlywilshire* 🛏 *258 rooms, 137 suites* 🍴 *No meals* ✢ *2:B4.*

$ HOTEL Fodor's Choice ★ 🏨 **The Crescent Beverly Hills.** Built in 1926 as a dorm for silent film actors, the Crescent is now a sleek boutique hotel with a great location—within the Beverly Hills shopping triangle—and with an even better price. **Pros:** the on-site restaurant CBH's tasty cuisine and convivial happy hour; the restaurant is fashionista central; upscale service at Beverly Hills' lowest price. **Cons:** dorm-size rooms; gym an additional fee and only accessed outside hotel via Sports ClubLA; no elevator. [$] *Rooms from: $198* ✉ *403 N. Crescent Dr., Beverly Hills* ☎ *310/247–0505* 🌐 *www.crescentbh.com* 🛏 *35 rooms* 🍴 *No meals* ✢ *2:B3.*

$$$$ HOTEL 🏨 **Four Seasons Hotel, Los Angeles at Beverly Hills.** High hedges and patio gardens make this hotel a secluded retreat that even the hum of traffic can't permeate, which is part of the reason it's a favorite of Hollywood's elite, so don't be surprised by a well-known face poolside or in the Windows bar—come awards season, expect to spot an Oscar winner or two. **Pros:** expert concierge; deferential service; celebrity magnet. **Cons:** Hollywood scene in bar and restaurant means rarefied prices. [$] *Rooms from: $445* ✉ *300 S. Doheny Dr., Beverly Hills* ☎ *310/273–2222, 800/332–3442* 🌐 *www.fourseasons.com/losangeles* 🛏 *185 rooms, 100 suites* 🍴 *No meals* ✢ *2:C3.*

$$ ▦ **Maison 140.** Colonial chic reigns in this three-story, 1930s grand Bev-
HOTEL erly Hills boutique hotel, where the look mixes French and Far East with
gleaming antiques, textured wallpaper, and colorfully painted rooms. **Pros:**
ultimate boutique stay; eye-catching design; short walk to all Beverly Hills
shopping. **Cons:** few amenities; room service from another hotel. $ *Rooms
from: $200* ✉ *140 S. Lasky Dr., Beverly Hills* ☎ *310/281–4000, 800/670–
6182* ⊕ *www.maison140.com* ⤳ *43 rooms* ❏ *No meals* ✣ *2:B4.*

$$$$ ▦ **Montage Beverly Hills.** The nine-story, Mediterranean-style palazzo
HOTEL is dedicated to welcoming those who relish luxury, providing classic
Fodor'sChoice style and exemplary service. **Pros:** a feast for the senses; architectural
★ details include crown moldings and muted colors; the highly trained
staff is most obliging. **Cons:** all this finery adds up to a hefty tab.
$ *Rooms from: $595* ✉ *225 N. Canon Dr., Beverly Hills* ☎ *310/860–
7800, 888/860–0788* ⊕ *www.montagebeverlyhills.com* ⤳ *146 rooms,
55 suites* ❏ *No meals* ✣ *2:B4.*

$$$ ▦ **Mosaic Hotel.** Stylish, comfortable, and decked out with the latest
HOTEL electronics, the Mosaic is on a quiet side street that's central to Beverly
Hills's business district. **Pros:** intimate and cozy; friendly service; free
Wi-Fi and local shuttle service. **Cons:** small and shaded pool; tiny lobby.
$ *Rooms from: $300* ✉ *125 S. Spalding Dr., Beverly Hills* ☎ *310/278–
0303, 800/463–4466* ⊕ *www.mosaichotel.com* ⤳ *44 rooms, 5 suites*
❏ *No meals* ✣ *2:B4.*

$$$$ ▦ **Peninsula Beverly Hills.** This French Rivera–style palace is a favorite
HOTEL of Hollywood boldface names, but all kinds of visitors consistently
Fodor'sChoice describe their stay as near perfect—though expensive. **Pros:** central,
★ walkable Beverly Hills location; stunning flowers; one of the best con-
cierges in the city. **Cons:** serious bucks required to stay here; room
decor might feel too ornate for some. $ *Rooms from: $695* ✉ *9882
S. Santa Monica Blvd., Beverly Hills* ☎ *310/551–2888, 800/462–7899*
⊕ *www.beverlyhills.peninsula.com* ⤳ *142 rooms, 37 suites, 16 villas*
❏ *No meals* ✣ *2:B4.*

$$$$ ▦ **L'Ermitage Beverly Hills.** Every indulgence and practicality is consid-
HOTEL ered here, from the smooth, crisp designer sheets, soaking tubs, and
oversize bath towels to the caviar and Champagne service in the lobby-
adjacent lounge. **Pros:** squeaky clean throughout; spacious work desk;
understated elegance. **Cons:** small spa and pool. $ *Rooms from: $459*
✉ *9291 Burton Way, Beverly Hills* ☎ *310/278–3344, 800/768–9009*
⊕ *www.viceroyhotelsandresorts.com/en/beverlyhills* ⤳ *103 rooms, 16
suites* ❏ *No meals* ✣ *2:C3.*

$$ ▦ **Sirtaj.** Hidden on a residential street, a block from Rodeo Drive, the new
HOTEL Sirtaj Hotel with an East-Indian design caters to travelers wanting to be
in Beverly Hills' Golden Triangle without the steep price tag. **Pros:** great
value for the neighborhood; free Wi-Fi; in-room espresso machines. **Cons:**
no pool or on-site gym; only nearby parking is valet ($28). $ *Rooms from:
$239* ✉ *120 South Reeves Dr., Beverly Hills* ☎ *310/248–2402* ⊕ *www.
sirtajhotel.com* ⤳ *28 rooms, 4 suites* ❏ *No meals* ✣ *2:C4.*

$$$$ ▦ **SLS Hotel at Beverly Hills.** Imagine dropping into Alice in Wonderland's
HOTEL rabbit hole: this is the sleek, textured, and tchotke-filled lobby of the
SLS from design maestro Philippe Starck. **Pros:** a vibrant destination
with lofty ambitions; excellent design and cuisine; great for celebrity

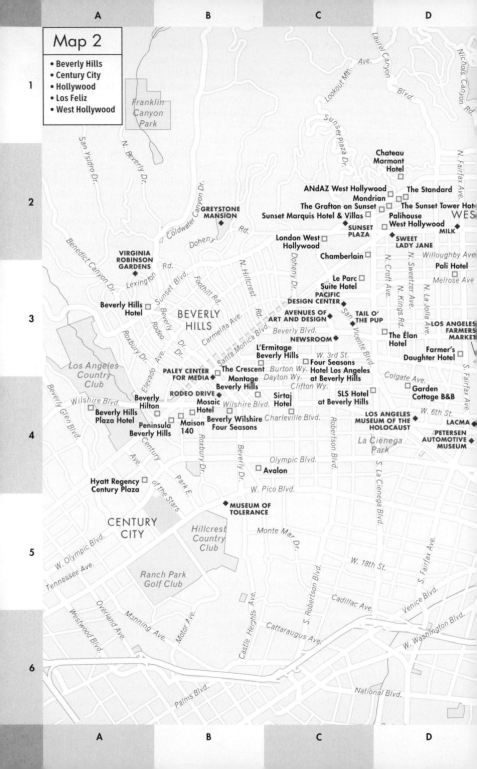

spotting. **Cons:** standard rooms are compact, with no tubs, but you pay for the scene; pricey hotel dining and parking; design might feel cold to some. $ *Rooms from: $489* ✉ *465 S. La Cienega Blvd., Beverly Hills* ☎ *310/247–0400* ⊕ *www.slshotels.com* ⤳ *236 rooms, 61 suites* ⓘ *No meals* ✛ *2:C4.*

BEL AIR

$$$$
HOTEL
Fodor'sChoice
★

🏨 **Hotel Bel-Air.** This Spanish Mission-style icon has been a discreet hillside retreat for celebrities and society types since 1946; and now courtesy of star designers Alexandra Champalimaud and David Rockwell, the rooms and suites, many of which feature fireplaces and private patios, are decidedly more modern. **Pros:** full of history (and stories); lovely pool; spacious rooms. **Cons:** attracts society crowd; hefty price tag; a car is essential. $ *Rooms from: $675* ✉ *701 Stone Canyon Rd., Bel Air* ☎ *310/472–1211, 800/648–4097* ⊕ *www.hotelbelair.com* ⤳ *52 rooms, 39 suites* ⓘ *No meals* ✛ *3:C1.*

$$
HOTEL
FAMILY

🏨 **Luxe Hotel Sunset Boulevard.** On seven landscaped acres near the Getty Center, the Luxe feels like a secluded country club—but it's also next to the I-405 for easy freeway access. **Pros:** country-club feel; oversize rooms; central for Westside business meetings. **Cons:** some freeway noise; off an extremely busy intersection; a car almost essential. $ *Rooms from: $239* ✉ *11461 Sunset Blvd., Bel Air* ☎ *310/476–6571, 800/468–3541* ⊕ *www.luxehotels.com* ⤳ *110 rooms, 51 suites* ⓘ *No meals* ✛ *3:C1.*

WEST HOLLYWOOD

$
HOTEL

🏨 **ANdAZ West Hollywood.** On the north side of the Sunset Strip, the ANdAZ is a youthful update of the former Hyatt West Hollywood, catering to hipsters, techies, and rock stars. **Pros:** sleek new interiors with the latest gadgets like free Wi-Fi throughout and sizable flat-screen TVs; ambitious hotel dining and bar concepts; excellent gym overlooks Sunset Boulevard's nonstop action. **Cons:** traffic congestion impedes access; Sunset Strip is wildly popular weekends and holidays; expensive parking. $ *Rooms from: $189* ✉ *8401 Sunset Blvd., West Hollywood* ☎ *323/656–1234, 800/233–1234* ⊕ *www.andaz.com* ⤳ *219 rooms, 19 suites* ⓘ *No meals* ✛ *2:C2.*

$$
HOTEL

🏨 **Chamberlain.** On a leafy residential side street, the Chamberlain is steps from Santa Monica Boulevard and close to the Sunset Strip, bringing in young business types, the fashion–design crowd, and 24-hour party people looking to roam West Hollywood and the Strip. **Pros:** excellent guests-only dining room and bar; pleasing design; close to Strip without the hassle. **Cons:** compact bathrooms. $ *Rooms from: $249* ✉ *1000 Westmount Dr., West Hollywood* ☎ *310/657–7400, 800/201–9652* ⊕ *www. chamberlainwesthollywood.com* ⤳ *114 suites* ⓘ *No meals* ✛ *2:C2.*

$$$$
HOTEL

🏨 **Chateau Marmont Hotel.** Celebs like Johnny Depp appreciate this swanky hotel for its secluded cottages, bungalows, and understated suites and penthouses. **Pros:** walking distance to all of Sunset Strip's action; great food and vibe at Bar Marmont; guaranteed celeb spotting. **Cons:** plenty of attitude from staff; ancient elevators. $ *Rooms from: $550* ✉ *8221 Sunset Blvd., West Hollywood* ☎ *323/656–1010, 800/242–8328* ⊕ *www.chateaumarmont.com* ⤳ *11 rooms, 63 suites* ⓘ *No meals* ✛ *2:D2.*

WORD OF MOUTH

"The Standard Hotel in West Hollywood usually has fair rates. The location is nice, but it can be loud on weekends."

—Browns

$$ HOTEL **The Élan Hotel.** Small and modest, and a favorite of international travelers, this hotel has an enviable location within walking distance of some of the city's best restaurants and the Beverly Center. **Pros:** friendly staff; free Wi-Fi; central location with many great restaurants nearby. **Cons:** super-compact rooms; no pool. [$] *Rooms from: $229* ✉ *8435 Beverly Blvd., West Hollywood* ☎ *323/658–6663, 866/203–2212* 🌐 *www.elanhotel.com* 🛏 *46 rooms, 3 suites* 🍴 *Breakfast 2:D3.*

$ HOTEL Fodor's Choice ★ **Farmer's Daughter Hotel.** A favorite of *The Price Is Right* and *American Idol* hopefuls (both TV shows tape at the CBS studios nearby) as well as local hipsters, this motel has a tongue-in-cheek country style with farm tools as art, a hopping Sunday brunch, and a little pool accented by giant rubber duckies and bean bags. **Pros:** great central city location; across from the cheap eats of the Farmers Market and The Grove's shopping and entertainment mix. **Cons:** shaded pool; no bathtubs. [$] *Rooms from: $189* ✉ *115 S. Fairfax Ave., Farmers Market* ☎ *323/937–3930, 800/334–1658* 🌐 *www.farmersdaughterhotel.com* 🛏 *63 rooms, 2 suites* 🍴 *No meals* ✥ *2:D3.*

$ B&B/INN **The Garden Cottage Bed and Breakfast.** In one of Los Angeles's most walkable and picturesque neighborhoods, this Spanish/Mediterranean-style duplex surrounded by fountains and foliage inspires travelers to make themselves at home, an easily accomplished mission with the help of the effusive hosts, Ahuva and Bob. **Pros:** fun neighborhood for all ages; free parking; hosts are a wealth of information. **Cons:** cottage has no bathtub; the cozy environment doesn't allow for anonymity; no credit cards accepted. [$] *Rooms from: $175* ✉ *8318 W. 4th St.* ☎ *323/653–5616* 🌐 *www.gardencottagela.com* 🛏 *2 rooms, 2 suites* 💳 *No credit cards* 🍴 *Breakfast* ✥ *2:D4.*

$$$ HOTEL **The Grafton on Sunset.** It's easy to tap into the Sunset Strip energy here, especially at the hotel's new Oliver's Prime steakhouse and rock 'n' roll–styled lounge, the Cutting Room. **Pros:** playful amenities; snazzy suites; heart of Strip's action. **Cons:** higher-priced weekend stays; Strip traffic; small standard rooms. [$] *Rooms from: $399* ✉ *8462 W. Sunset Blvd., West Hollywood* ☎ *323/654–4600, 800/821–3660* 🌐 *www.graftononsunset.com* 🛏 *105 rooms, 3 suites* 🍴 *No meals* ✥ *2:C2.*

$$$ HOTEL **Le Parc Suite Hotel.** On a tree-lined residential street close to CBS Television City and the Pacific Design Center, this congenial low-rise hotel aims to make guests feel coddled, with extremely personalized service and a strong commitment to privacy. **Pros:** great views from rooftop pool deck; lighted tennis court. **Cons:** small lobby. [$] *Rooms from: $309* ✉ *733 W. Knoll Dr., West Hollywood* ☎ *310/855–8888, 800/578–4837* 🌐 *www.leparcsuites.com* 🛏 *154 suites* 🍴 *No meals* ✥ *2:C3.*

$$$ HOTEL **The London West Hollywood.** Just off the Sunset Strip, cosmopolitan and chic in design, the London WeHo is a remake of 1984-built Bel Age, bringing those signature large suites and rooftop pool with citywide views to mix with the spiffed up luxury textures like Ultrasuede-covered

hallway walls, framed mirrors throughout, and glam gold lamé leather couches. **Pros:** perfectly designed interiors; hillside and city views from generous-size suites, all with balconies and steps from the strip. **Cons:** too refined for kids to be comfortable; lower floors have mundane views. [$] *Rooms from: $399* ✉ *1020 N. San Vicente Blvd., West Hollywood* ☎ *310/854–1111, 866/282–4560* 🌐 *www.thelondonwesthollywood.com* 🛏 *226 suites* 🍴 *No meals* ⊕ *2:C2.*

$$ HOTEL **Mondrian Los Angeles.** A city club attitude pervades at the spendy Mondrian Los Angeles, where everything from the artsy headboards to the mirrors are for sale. **Pros:** pool, spa, and nighttime social scene mean never having to leave the property. **Cons:** pricey valet parking only; late-night party scene; inflated prices. [$] *Rooms from: $279* ✉ *8440 Sunset Blvd., West Hollywood* ☎ *323/650–8999, 800/606–6090* 🌐 *www.mondrianhotel.com* 🛏 *54 rooms, 183 suites* 🍴 *No meals* ⊕ *2:D2.*

$$ RENTAL **Palihouse West Hollywood.** Inside an unassuming apartmentlike complex just off West Hollywood's main drag, you'll find DJs spinning tunes for fashionistas on the ground floor and a gorgeous collection of assorted suites with fully equipped kitchens upstairs. **Pros:** free Wi-Fi; eclectic design; fun scene at lobby bar. **Cons:** lobby can be loud in the evenings; no pool. [$] *Rooms from: $299* ✉ *8465 Holloway Dr., West Hollywood, West Hollywood* ☎ *323/656 4100* 🌐 *www.palihousewesthollywood.com* 🛏 *37 suites* 🍴 *No meals* ⊕ *2:D2.*

$$ HOTEL **The Standard.** Hotelier André Balazs created this playful Sunset Strip hotel with '70s kitsch out of a former retirement home. **Pros:** on-site, decent 24-hour coffee shop; poolside scene; live DJs. **Cons:** extended party place for twentysomethings; staff big on attitude rather than service. [$] *Rooms from: $250* ✉ *8300 Sunset Blvd., West Hollywood* ☎ *323/650–9090* 🌐 *www.standardhotel.com* 🛏 *137 rooms, 2 suites* 🍴 *No meals* ⊕ *2:D2.*

$$$ HOTEL Fodor's Choice ★ **Sunset Marquis Hotel & Villas.** If you're in town to cut your new hit single, you'll appreciate this near-the-Strip spot with two on-site recording studios; or if you're in the market to rock out with celebs, you, too, will appreciate this hidden retreat in the heart of West Hollywood. **Pros:** superior service; discreet setting just off the Strip; clublike atmosphere; free passes to Equinox nearby. **Cons:** rooms can feel dark; small balconies. [$] *Rooms from: $315* ✉ *1200 N. Alta Loma Rd., West Hollywood* ☎ *310/657–1333, 800/858–9758* 🌐 *www.sunsetmarquis.com* 🛏 *102 suites, 52 villas* 🍴 *No meals* ⊕ *2:C2.*

$$$$ HOTEL **Sunset Tower Hotel.** A clubby style infuses the 1929 art deco landmark once known as the Argyle, bringing out as many locals as tourists to this iconic Sunset Strip boutique hotel. **Pros:** incredible city views; Tower Bar a favorite of Hollywood's elite; exclusive spa favored by locals. **Cons:** wedged into the Strip, so the driveway is a challenge; small standard rooms. [$] *Rooms from: $445* ✉ *8358 Sunset Blvd., West Hollywood* ☎ *323/654–7100, 800/225–2637* 🌐 *www.sunsettowerhotel.com* 🛏 *20 rooms, 44 suites* 🍴 *No meals* ⊕ *2:D2.*

11

BRENTWOOD

$$
B&B/INN

Brentwood Inn. On busy Sunset Boulevard, a short drive from Brentwood's commercial strip and UCLA, Brentwood Inn is an under-the-radar bed-and-breakfast delivering solid service and simple, yet classy, interiors. **Pros:** value hotel in a pricey zip code; amicable service; great off-season rates. **Cons:** tight bathrooms; on a busy street; need a car to get around. $ *Rooms from: $209* ✉ *12200 Sunset Blvd., Brentwood* ☎ *800/840–3808, 310/476–9981* ⊕ *thebrentwood.com* ⬎ *21 rooms, 2 suites* ❍| *Breakfast* ✢ *3:B2.*

$
HOTEL

Hotel Angeleno. A thoroughly up-to-date remake of the landmark 1970s mod, cylindrical tower hotel, this building conveniently sits at the crossroads of Sunset Boulevard and I-405. **Pros:** complimentary shuttle to nearby Getty Center; free Wi-Fi; intriguing design throughout. **Cons:** compact rooms; small, shaded pool; old elevators; somewhat isolated location. $ *Rooms from: $199* ✉ *170 N. Church Lane, Brentwood* ☎ *310/476–6411, 866/264–3536* ⊕ *www.hotelangeleno.com* ⬎ *205 rooms, 3 suites* ❍| *No meals* ✢ *3:C1.*

CENTURY CITY AND CULVER CITY

$$
HOTEL

Culver Hotel. This 1924 triangular brick hotel smack in the center of town contains a slice of Culver City's history—and not just because it housed the munchkins during the *Wizard of Oz*. **Pros:** in a lively walkable neighborhood, a short walk to the Metro; historic design; close to studios and restaurants. **Cons:** small standard rooms; antique decor might not appeal to everyone. $ *Rooms from: $250* ✉ *9400 Culver Blvd., Culver City* ☎ *310/558–9400* ⊕ *www.culverhotel.com* ⬎ *40 rooms, 6 suites* ❍| *No meals* ✢ *3:E3.*

$$$
HOTEL

Hyatt Regency Century Plaza. For more than 40 years, the Century Plaza has been one of L.A.'s most frequented business hotels, with newly refreshed rooms featuring large bathrooms, balconies, and stunning city views. **Pros:** on-site power gym, Equinox Fitness Club and Spa, open to guests for an extra fee; stunning views to west; lower weekend rates. **Cons:** large, corporate hotel; isolated location in Century City. $ *Rooms from: $349* ✉ *2025 Ave. of the Stars, Century City* ☎ *310/228–1234, 800/233–1234* ⊕ *www.centuryplaza.hyatt.com* ⬎ *687 rooms, 39 suites* ❍| *No meals* ✢ *2:A4.*

WESTWOOD

$$
HOTEL

Hotel Palomar Los Angeles–Westwood. A convivial lobby and smartly designed rooms set this Kimpton-managed hotel apart from other chain hotels; and because of its proximity to UCLA, the Palomar also attracts those visiting the sprawling university for business and students' friends and families. **Pros:** visually appealing room design; in-room luxe touches like Frette linens and Aveda toiletries; friendly staff. **Cons:** isolated on a busy thoroughfare. $ *Rooms from: $250* ✉ *10740 Wilshire Blvd., Westwood* ☎ *310/475–8711, 800/472–8556* ⊕ *www.hotelpalomar-lawestwood.com* ⬎ *238 rooms, 26 suites* ❍| *No meals* ✢ *3:D2.*

$$$
HOTEL

W Westwood. Hip grown-ups retreat to this quiet and artful oasis steps from UCLA, where they find a cabana-lined pool and sleek lounge, two on-site restaurants with regional cuisine, and a spa that serves brownies postmassage. **Pros:** great location in the heart of Westwood; lovely pool area; live DJs on weekend. **Cons:** not as lively as other W properties; rooms in need of some updating; expensive valet parking. [$] *Rooms from: $399* ✉ *930 Hilgard Ave., Westwood* ☎ *310/208–8765* 🌐 *www.wlosangeles.com* 🛏 *258 suites* ✣ *3:D1.*

SANTA MONICA AND THE BEACHES

L.A.'s laid-back beach towns are the ideal place for enjoying the trifecta of coastal living: sun, sand, and surf. From moneyed Malibu to the original surf city, Huntington Beach, each city retains a character and feel of its own, but collectively, these beach towns are family-friendly, scenic, and dotted with waterfront hotels (try the Fairmont Miramar's Bungalow bar or Viceroy in Santa Monica for nighttime drinks at least, if you're not staying in the area). The farther south you venture, however, the more likely you are to encounter traffic while driving to the city's main attractions.

SANTA MONICA

$$ HOTEL 🏨 **The Ambrose.** An air of tranquillity pervades the four-story Ambrose, which blends right into its mostly residential Santa Monica neighborhood. **Pros:** L.A.'s most eco-conscious hotel with nontoxic housekeeping products and recycling bins in each room; newly added food service is a plus for weary travelers; free Wi-Fi and parking. **Cons:** quiet, residential area of Santa Monica. [$] *Rooms from: $249* ✉ *1255 20th St., Santa Monica* ☎ *310/315–1555, 877/262–7673* 🌐 *www.ambrosehotel.com* 🛏 *77 rooms* 🍴 *Breakfast* ✣ *3:G1.*

$$ HOTEL 🏨 **Bayside Hotel.** Tucked snugly into a narrow corner lot, the supremely casual Bayside's greatest asset is its prime spot directly across from the beach, within walkable blocks from the Third Street Promenade and Santa Monica Pier. **Pros:** cheaper weeknight stays; beach access and views. **Cons:** homeless encampments nearby; basic bedding; thin walls. [$] *Rooms from: $249* ✉ *2001 Ocean Ave., Santa Monica* ☎ *310/396–6000, 800/525–4447* 🌐 *www.baysidehotel.com* 🛏 *45 rooms* 🍴 *No meals* ✣ *3:G2.*

$ B&B/INN Fodor's Choice ★ 🏨 **Channel Road Inn.** A quaint surprise in Southern California, the Channel Road Inn is every bit the country retreat B&B lovers adore, with four-poster beds with fluffy duvets and a cozy living room with fireplace. **Pros:** quiet residential neighborhood close to beach; free Wi-Fi and evening wine and hors d'oeuvres. **Cons:** no pool. [$] *Rooms from: $175* ✉ *219 W. Channel Rd., Santa Monica* ☎ *310/459–1920* 🌐 *www.channelroadinn.com* 🛏 *13 rooms, 2 suites* 🍴 *Breakfast* ✣ *3:A3.*

$$$$ HOTEL 🏨 **Fairmont Miramar Hotel & Bungalows Santa Monica.** A mammoth Moreton Bay fig tree dwarfs the main entrance of the 4-acre Santa Monica retreat that plays host to families, businesspeople, couples, and friends wanting a wellness retreat a short walk to the sand. **Pros:** walking distance to beach and Third Street Promenade shopping and dining. **Cons:** all this luxury comes at a big price. [$] *Rooms from: $499* ✉ *101 Wilshire Blvd., Santa Monica* ☎ *310/576–7777, 866/540–4470* 🌐 *www.fairmont.com/santamonica* 🛏 *251 rooms, 51 suites, 32 bungalows* 🍴 *No meals* ✣ *3:F2.*

$$ HOTEL 🏨 **The Georgian Hotel.** Driving by, you can't miss the Georgian: the art deco exterior is aqua, with ornate bronze grillwork and a charming oceanfront veranda. **Pros:** many ocean-view rooms; front terrace is a

Lodging Alternatives

CLOSE UP

11

For your trip to Los Angeles, you may want a beachfront location and more space than a typical hotel can provide. Some travelers consider apartment and beach house rentals, but we tend to recommend hotel suites and B&Bs instead. Why? Unfortunately, rental scams are prevalent. In some cases, potential guests have arrived to find that the apartment they rented does not exist, or that they are paying for an illegal sublet. Unfortunately, travelers have also lost their deposit money, or their prepaid rent in the past. Note: Never wire money to an individual's account.

There are few reputable providers of short-term rentals, *noted below.* But many Fodorites have turned to suite hotels, lodges, and B&Bs with apartment-like accommodations to guard themselves from possible scams.

Vacation rentals from reputed websites like **HomeAway** (⊕ *www. homeaway.com*) and its affiliate websites like **VRBO** (⊕ *www.vrbo. com*) come with the Carefree Rental Guarantee (for a fee), which protects travelers in sticky situations, whether the home has been foreclosed on, or the owner has double-booked guests,

misrepresented a property, or withheld a security deposit.

From Malibu in the north to Long Beach farther south, most of the city's beach towns have waterfront hotels and inns with spacious suites and rooms. Some favorites include the pricey **Malibu Beach Inn** and **Shutters on the Beach** in Santa Monica, while the New England cottage–styled, all-suites **Beach House Hotel at Hermosa** and **Hotel Erwin** are comparative bargains with great ocean breezes.

Also consider cottages and B&Bs like the beloved **Inn at 657,** near the University of Southern California in L.A.'s Downtown or the **Los Feliz Lodge** close to the modern bohemian neighborhoods of Silver Lake and Echo Park. And off hip Abbot Kinney Boulevard, the **Venice Beach Eco-Cottages** marry form with eco-friendly practices.

"There are some lovely B&Bs in the Pasadena area as well, including the Bissell House (⊕ *www.bissellhouse. com*), Artists' Inn (⊕ *www.artistsinn. com*) and Arroyo Vista Inn (⊕ *www. arroyovistainn.com*)." —Jean

---

great people-watching spot; free Wi-Fi. **Cons:** "vintage" bathrooms; some rooms have unremarkable views. $ *Rooms from: $289* ✉ *1415 Ocean Ave., Santa Monica* ☎ *310/395–9945, 800/538–8147* ⊕ *www. georgianhotel.com* 🛏 *56 rooms, 28 suites* ❑| *No meals* ✢ *3:F2.*

$$$$

HOTEL

🏨 **Hotel Casa del Mar.** In the 1920s it was a posh beach club catering to the city's elite; now the Casa del Mar is one of SoCal's most luxurious and pricey beachfront hotels, popular with celebrities and foreign dignitaries, with three extravagant two-story penthouses, a raised deck and pool, a newly reimagined spa, and an elegant ballroom facing the sand. **Pros:** excellent dining at Catch; free Wi-Fi; lobby socializing; gorgeous beachfront rooms. **Cons:** no room balconies; without a doubt, one of L.A.'s priciest beach stays. $ *Rooms from: $595* ✉ *1910 Ocean Way, Santa Monica* ☎ *310/581–5533, 800/898–6999* ⊕ *www. hotelcasadelmar.com* 🛏 *113 rooms, 16 suites* ❑| *No meals* ✢ *3:G2.*

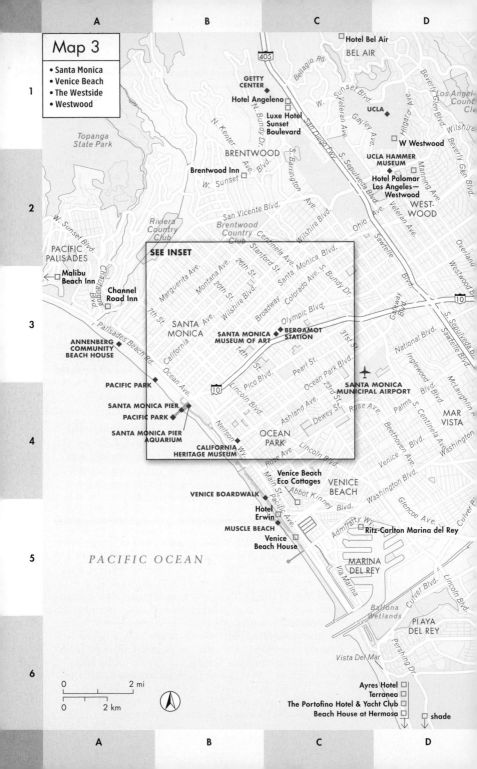

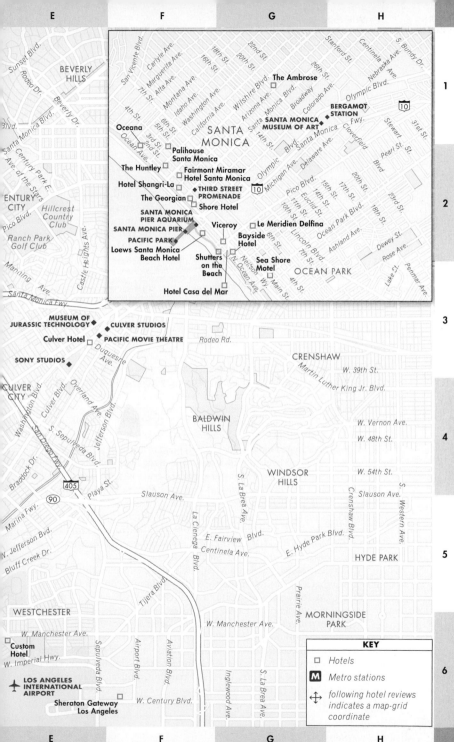

E   F   G   H

Sunset Blvd.

BEVERLY HILLS

Rodeo Dr.
Beverly Dr.
Santa Monica Blvd.
Ave. of the Stars

San Vicente Blvd.
Carlyle Ave.
Marguerita Ave.
Alta Ave.
7th St.
Montana Ave.
Idaho Ave.
Washington Ave.
California Ave.
4th St.
5th St.
6th St.
Wilshire Blvd.
Arizona Ave.
16th St.
18th St.
20th St.
22nd St.
26th St.
Stanford St.
Centinela Ave.
S. Bundy Dr.
Nebraska Ave.

The Ambrose

Broadway
Colorado Ave.
Olympic Blvd.
10

BERGAMOT STATION
Fwy.
Stewart St.
31st St.

SANTA MONICA
Oceana
3rd St.
5th St.
6th St.
Ocean Ave.
Palihouse Santa Monica
SANTA MONICA MUSEUM OF ART
Santa Monica Blvd.
Cloverfield
Pearl St. St.

The Huntley
Fairmont Miramar Hotel Santa Monica
Michigan Ave.
Delaware Ave.
Olympic
10
Pico Blvd.
Blvd.

Hotel Shangri-La
14th St.
15th St.
17th St.
20th St.
23rd St.
18th St.

The Georgian
THIRD STREET PROMENADE
Shore Hotel
11th St.
Euclid St.
10th St.
Lincoln Blvd.
Ocean Park Blvd.
Ashland Ave.
Dewey St.
Rose Ave.

SANTA MONICA PIER AQUARIUM
SANTA MONICA PIER
Viceroy
Le Meridien Delfina
Penmar Ave.

PACIFIC PARK
Bayside Hotel
5th St.
7th St.
Lake St.

Loews Santa Monica Beach Hotel
Shutters on the Beach
Neilson Wy.
N. Ocean Ave.
Sea Shore Motel
4th St.
Main St.
OCEAN PARK

Hotel Casa del Mar

CENTURY CITY
Pico Blvd.
Hillcrest Country Club
Ranch Park Golf Club
Castle Heights Ave.
Manning Ave.
Santa Monica Fwy.

MUSEUM OF JURASSIC TECHNOLOGY
CULVER STUDIOS
Rodeo Rd.
CRENSHAW
W. 39th St.
Martin Luther King Jr. Blvd.

Culver Hotel
PACIFIC MOVIE THEATRE
Duquesne Ave.

SONY STUDIOS
CULVER CITY
Washington Blvd.
Culver Blvd.
Overland Ave.
Jefferson Blvd.
S. Sepulveda Blvd.
Playa St.
405
90
Marina Fwy.
Braddock Dr.
San Diego Fwy.

Slauson Ave.
La Cienega Blvd.
S. La Brea Ave.
BALDWIN HILLS
WINDSOR HILLS
W. Vernon Ave.
W. 48th St.
W. 54th St.
Slauson Ave.
Crenshaw Blvd.
S. Western Ave.

E. Fairview Blvd.
Centinela Ave.
E. Hyde Park Blvd.
HYDE PARK

Tijera Blvd.
Prairie Ave.
MORNINGSIDE PARK

WESTCHESTER
W. Manchester Ave.
Custom Hotel
W. Imperial Hwy.
Sepulveda Blvd.
Airport Blvd.
Aviation Blvd.
W. Manchester Ave.
Inglewood Ave.
S. La Brea Ave.

LOS ANGELES INTERNATIONAL AIRPORT
Sheraton Gateway Los Angeles
W. Century Blvd.

W. Jefferson Blvd.
Bluff Creek Dr.

KEY

☐   *Hotels*

Ⓜ   *Metro stations*

✛   *following hotel reviews indicates a map-grid coordinate*

1

2

3

4

5

6

$$$$ ⊞ **Hotel Shangri-La.** Across from Santa Monica's oceanfront Palisades
HOTEL   Park, the 1939-built, art deco–style Hotel Shangri-La at the Ocean
is now in tune with the 21st century. **Pros:** admirable rehabilitation
of deco-style building now with up-to-date conveniences like soundproofing and iPod docks. **Cons:** some rooms are tight like cruise-ship
quarters. $ *Rooms from: $425* ⊠ *301 Ocean Ave., Santa Monica*
☎ *310/394–2791* ⊕ *www.shangrila-hotel.com* ↝ *36 rooms, 35 suites*
❘⊙❘ *No meals* ⊹ *3:F2.*

$$$ ⊞ **Huntley Santa Monica Beach.** A school of 300 ceramic fish crossing
HOTEL   a lobby wall sets the tone at this stylish property, two steep blocks
from the beach, near the Third Street Promenade, and chic Montana
Avenue. **Pros:** ocean views; fun social scene, and great views (and
drinks) at the Penthouse, the hotel's top floor restaurant. **Cons:** no pool;
Fodorites complain of noise from the restaurant and bar. $ *Rooms
from: $359* ⊠ *1111 2nd St., Santa Monica* ☎ *310/394–5454* ⊕ *www.
thehuntleyhotel.com* ↝ *188 rooms, 16 suites* ❘⊙❘ *No meals* ⊹ *3:F2.*

$$$$ ⊞ **Loews Santa Monica Beach Hotel.** Walk to the ocean side of the soaring
HOTEL   atrium here and you feel like you're on a cruise ship: massive windows
FAMILY   give way to the expansive sea below, sunny staff seems content to assist
with your needs, and the slashy mural behind reception intuits a sense
of place. **Pros:** resort vibe; walk to beach; pet- and kid-friendly. **Cons:**
small pool; Wi-Fi and parking are pricey. $ *Rooms from: $490* ⊠ *1700
Ocean Ave., Santa Monica* ☎ *310/458–6700, 800/235–6397* ⊕ *www.
loewshotels.com* ↝ *325 rooms, 17 suites* ❘⊙❘ *No meals* ⊹ *3:F2.*

$$$ ⊞ **Oceana.** Generous-size suites, soundproofed windows, an open-air
HOTEL   courtyard and pool, and ocean proximity add up to a delightful bou-
tique hotel. **Pros:** walk to prime shopping on Montana Avenue, the
Palisades park, or the beach. **Cons:** small pool. $ *Rooms from: $365*
⊠ *849 Ocean Ave., Santa Monica* ☎ *310/393–0486, 800/777–0758*
⊕ *www.hoteloceanasantamonica.com* ↝ *70 suites* ❘⊙❘ *No meals* ⊹ *3:F2.*

$$ ⊞ **Palihouse Santa Monica.** Tucked in a posh residential area three blocks
HOTEL   from the sea and lively Third Street Promenade, Palihouse Santa Monica
caters to design-minded world travelers craving spacious rooms and
suites decked out in whimsical antiques. **Pros:** design inspires artsy
types; walking distance to Santa Monica attractions; this is where the
cool kids hang out. **Cons:** no pool; decor might not appeal to more tra-
ditonal travelers. $ *Rooms from: $299* ⊠ *1001 3rd St., Santa Monica,
Santa Monica* ☎ *310/394–1279* ⊕ *www.palihousesantamonica.com*
↝ *8 rooms, 30 suites* ❘⊙❘ *No meals* ⊹ *3:F2.*

$ ⊞ **Sea Shore Motel.** On Santa Monica's busy Main Street, the Sea Shore is
HOTEL   a throwback to Route 66 and to '60s-style, family-run roadside motels.
Pros: close to beach and great restaurants; free Wi-Fi and parking; great
value for the location. **Cons:** street noise; motel-style decor and beds.
$ *Rooms from: $150* ⊠ *2637 Main St., Santa Monica* ☎ *310/392–2787*
⊕ *www.seashoremotel.com* ↝ *19 rooms, 5 suites* ❘⊙❘ *No meals* ⊹ *3:G3.*

$$$ ⊞ **Le Meridien Delfina Santa Monica.** Not far from I-10, this hotel appeals
HOTEL   to business types during the week and jet-setting leisure travelers who
fancy the sleek interiors, free self-parking, and close proximity to
Santa Monica's beaches and restaurants. **Pros:** four blocks from beach;
designer touches; free self-parking. **Cons:** a few blocks from Santa

Monica's main dining and shopping; Wi-Fi fee. $ *Rooms from: $300* ✉ *530 Pico Blvd., Santa Monica* ☎ *310/399–9344, 888/627–8532* ⊕ *www.starwoodhotels.com/lemeridien/property/overview/index. html?propertyID=1135* ⇆ *299 rooms, 11 suites* ⍩ *No meals* ✛ *3:G2.*

$$$
HOTEL
Fodor's Choice
★

Shore Hotel. With views of the Santa Monica Pier, this newly constructed hotel with a friendly staff offers eco-minded travelers stylish rooms with a modern design and scenic views steps from the sand and sea. **Pros:** excellent location near beach and Third Street Promenade; low carbon footprint hotel; free Wi-Fi. **Cons:** expensive rooms and parking fees; fronting the busy Ocean Avenue. $ *Rooms from: $389* ✉ *1515 Ocean Ave., Santa Monica* ☎ *310/458–1515* ⊕ *shorehotel.com* ⇆ *144 rooms, 20 suites* ⍩ *No meals* ✛ *3:F2.*

$$$$
HOTEL
FAMILY
Fodor's Choice
★

Shutters on the Beach. Set right on the sand, this gray-shingle inn has become synonymous with in-town escapism, and while the hotel's service gets mixed reviews from some readers, the beachfront location and show-house decor make this one of SoCal's most popular luxury hotels. **Pros:** romantic; discreet; residential vibe; steps to the sand. **Cons:** service not as good as it should be; very expensive. $ *Rooms from: $625* ✉ *1 Pico Blvd., Santa Monica* ☎ *310/458–0030, 800/334–9000* ⊕ *www.shuttersonthebeach.com* ⇆ *186 rooms, 12 suites* ⍩ *No meals* ✛ *3:G2.*

$$$$
HOTEL

Viceroy Santa Monica. Whimsy abounds at this stylized seaside escape— just look at the porcelain dogs as lamp bases and Spode china plates mounted on the walls—yet the compact rooms, which all have French balconies, and sexy mirrored walls draw quite the upscale clientele. **Pros:** eye-catching design; lobby social scene; pedestrian-friendly area. **Cons:** super-pricey bar and dining; pool for dipping, not laps. $ *Rooms from: $408* ✉ *1819 Ocean Ave., Santa Monica* ☎ *310/260–7500, 800/622–8711* ⊕ *www.viceroysantamonica.com* ⇆ *162 total rooms, 5 suites* ⍩ *No meals* ✛ *3:G2.*

LOS ANGELES INTERNATIONAL AIRPORT

$
HOTEL

Custom Hotel. Close enough to LAX to see the runways, the Custom Hotel is a playful and practical redo of a 12-story, midcentury modern tower by famed L.A. architect Welton Becket (of Hollywood's Capitol Records building and the Dorothy Chandler Pavilion). **Pros:** close to LAX and beach areas; designer interiors; and free Wi-Fi. **Cons:** at the desolate end of Lincoln Boulevard. $ *Rooms from: $179* ✉ *8639 Lincoln Blvd., Los Angeles International Airport* ☎ *310/645–0400, 877/287–8601* ⊕ *www.customhotel.com* ⇆ *248 rooms, 2 suites* ⍩ *No meals* ✛ *3:E6.*

$
HOTEL

Sheraton Gateway Los Angeles. LAX's swanky hotel just had some serious work done to her already sleek look, yet her appeal runs deeper than her style with in-transit visitors loving the around-the-clock room service, fitness center, and airport shuttle. **Pros:** plus for nonbusiness travelers: significantly lower weekend rates; free LAX shuttle. **Cons:** convenient to airport but not much else. $ *Rooms from: $199* ✉ *6101 W. Century Blvd., Los Angeles International Airport* ☎ *310/642–1111, 800/325–3535* ⊕ *www.sheratonlosangeles.com* ⇆ *714 rooms, 88 suites* ⍩ *No meals* ✛ *3:F6.*

VENICE

$$ HOTEL

Hotel Erwin. Formerly a Best Western, this now bona fide boutique hotel just a block off the Venice Beach boardwalk has a happening rooftop bar and lounge, appropriately named High, that even attracts locals (weather permitting). **Pros:** close to Santa Monica without hefty prices; staff is friendly and helpful; great food. **Cons:** some rooms face a noisy alley; no pool. [$] *Rooms from: $279* ✉ *1697 Pacific Ave., Venice* ☎ *310/452–1111, 800/786–7789* 🌐 *www.hotelerwin.com* *119 rooms* 🍴 *No meals* ✣ *3:C5.*

$$ RENTAL

Venice Beach Eco-Cottages. Husband and wife owners Ross and Lanii Chapman bring style and solar power together at these charming cottages in kitschy Venice, steps from Abbot Kinney's trendy restaurants and shops. **Pros:** charming cottage living; family-friendly; environmentally friendly practices. **Cons:** no restaurant, pool, or traditional hotel services; steep cleaning fee. [$] *Rooms from: $250* ✉ *447 Grand Blvd., Venice* ☎ *866/802–3110* 🌐 *www.venicebeachecocottages.com* *3 suites* 🍴 *No meals* ☞ *3-night minimum stay* ✣ *3:C5.*

$ HOTEL

Venice Beach House. A vestige of Venice's founding days, the Venice Beach House was one of the seaside enclave's first mansions, and many Craftsman-era details remain—dark woods, a glass-enclosed breakfast nook, a lattice-framed portico, and a fleet of stairs. **Pros:** historic home with many charms; steps from beach and bike bath; recently added air-conditioning. **Cons:** privacy and noise issues; parking $14; full prepayment required with cancellation penalties. [$] *Rooms from: $170* ✉ *15 30th Ave., Venice* ☎ *310/823–1966* 🌐 *www.venicebeachhouse.com* *4 rooms without baths, 5 suites* 🍴 *Breakfast* ✣ *3:C5.*

MARINA DEL REY

$$$$ HOTEL FAMILY Fodor's Choice ★

The Ritz-Carlton Marina del Rey. You might have a sense of déjà vu here since this resort, overlooking L.A.'s largest marina, is a favorite location of dozens of TV and film productions. **Pros:** sparkling gym and large pool; waterside location; helpful staff. **Cons:** formal dining only (poolside eatery, summers only); $40 valet parking. [$] *Rooms from: $459* ✉ *4375 Admiralty Way, Marina del Rey* ☎ *310/823–1700, 800/241–3333* 🌐 *www.ritzcarlton.com* *281 rooms, 23 suites* 🍴 *No meals* ✣ *3:C5.*

MALIBU

$$$ B&B/INN

Malibu Beach Inn. Set right on exclusive and private Carbon Beach, the hotel is home to all manner of the super-rich: the location doesn't get any better than this. **Pros:** live like a billionaire in designer-perfect interiors right on the beach. **Cons:** noise of PCH; no pool, gym, or hot tub; billionaire's travel budget also required. [$] *Rooms from: $385* ✉ *22878 Pacific Coast Hwy., Malibu* ☎ *310/456–6444* 🌐 *www.malibubeachinn.com* *41 rooms, 6 suites* 🍴 *No meals* ✣ *3:A3.*

MANHATTAN BEACH

$ HOTEL FAMILY

Ayres Hotel. The rates may be relatively modest, but the style here is grand, with the hotel resembling a stone-clad château, but don't let that "French countryside" feel fool you: it's close to I-405. **Pros:** free parking and Wi-Fi; lower weekend rates. **Cons:** on the edge of

Manhattan Beach but requires a drive to the ocean. $ *Rooms from: $149* ✉ *14400 Hindry Ave., Manhattan Beach* ☎ *310/536–0400, 800/675–3550* ⊕ *www.ayresmanhattanbeach.com* ↩ *173 rooms* ❍| *No meals* ✥ *3:D6.*

$$$ ⊞ **shade.** Super-contemporary design makes this place feel like an
HOTEL adults-only playground, and it's just a short walk to the shoreline, the local pier, and Manhattan Beach's lively, compact Downtown. **Pros:** lively bar scene at Zinc; a quick walk to the beach and dozens of restaurants; freebies including bikes, evening cake pops (made in house), expanded Continental breakfast, and Equinox gym passes. **Cons:** sharp-edged furniture; recommended for adults or older kids only; small dipping pool. $ *Rooms from: $359* ✉ *1221 N. Valley Dr., Manhattan Beach* ☎ *310/546–4995, 866/742–3377* ⊕ *www. shadehotel.com* ↩ *33 rooms, 5 suites* ❍| *Breakfast* ✥ *3:D6.*

HERMOSA BEACH

$$$ ⊞ **Beach House Hotel at Hermosa.** Sitting right on the sand, bordering
HOTEL the Strand (SoCal's famous beach bike and walk path), the Beach
Fodor'sChoice House looks like a New England sea cottage from a century ago. **Pros:**
★ on the beach; great outdoorsy activities; ample space. **Cons:** noise from the busy Strand; no pool; Continental breakfast only. $ *Rooms from: $369* ✉ *1300 The Strand, Hermosa Beach* ☎ *310/374–3001, 888/895–4559* ⊕ *www.beach-house.com* ↩ *96 suites* ❍| *Breakfast* ✥ *3:D6.*

REDONDO BEACH

$$ ⊞ **The Portofino Hotel & Yacht Club.** Open your balcony door and listen
HOTEL to the sounds of a naturally occurring Sea World at the Portofino: Ocean- and channel-side rooms echo with the calls of sea birds and sea lions; marina side rooms look over sailboats and docks. **Pros:** bike or walk to beach; relaxing stay; some ocean views. **Cons:** higher rates in summer and for ocean-view rooms. $ *Rooms from: $235* ✉ *260 Portofino Way, Redondo Beach* ☎ *310/379–8481, 800/468–4292* ⊕ *www.hotelportofino.com* ↩ *161 rooms, 5 suites* ❍| *No meals* ✥ *3:D6.*

RANCHO PALOS VERDES

$$$$ ⊞ **Terranea.** With the Pacific Ocean, Santa Monica Bay, and Cata-
RESORT lina Island all within view, L.A.'s only full-service oceanfront resort
FAMILY straddles 102 terraced acres at land's end on the scenic Palos Verdes
Fodor'sChoice Peninsula, making it popular with families and romance-seekers. **Pros:**
★ resort near town with faraway feel; blissful oceanfront spa; saline pools and hot tubs. **Cons:** pricey on-site dining; with resort fee and parking this luxury becomes very expensive. $ *Rooms from: $515* ✉ *100 Terranea Way Dr., Rancho Palos Verdes* ☎ *310/265–2800* ⊕ *www.terranea.com* ↩ *326 rooms, 34 suites, 20 bungalows, 50 casitas, 32 villas* ❍| *No meals* ✥ *3:D6.*

PASADENA

Pasadena is not only an easy detour from Los Angeles, but it is also a charming and historic city that can serve as your base while visiting the area. This small-town feel means a relaxing, slow pace, with the attractions of the city still nearby. It is more residential and conservative than the city. Nearby towns of Eagle Rock and Highland Park are some of the area's up-and-coming destinations populated with hip boutiques and fun restaurants.

$
HOTEL

⊞ **Hilton Pasadena Hotel.** Two blocks south of busy Colorado Boulevard, the Hilton Pasadena is still within walking distance of the city's vast convention center and close to the shops and plentiful restaurant choices of Old Town. **Pros:** amiable and helpful staff; central Downtown Pasadena location. **Cons:** compact bathrooms; so-so dining options; small pool. $ *Rooms from: $109* ⊠ *168 S. Los Robles Ave., Pasadena* ☎ *626/577–1000, 800/445–8667* ⊕ *www3.hilton.com/en/hotels/california/hilton-pasadena-pasphhf/index.html* ⇆ *285 rooms, 11 suites* ⦿*No meals* ✛ *4:D2.*

$$
HOTEL
FAMILY
Fodor'sChoice
★

⊞ **The Langham Huntington, Pasadena.** An azalea-filled Japanese garden and the unusual Picture Bridge, with murals celebrating California's history, are just two of the picturesque attributes of this grande dame that opened in 1907 and has long been a mainstay of Pasadena's social history. **Pros:** Great for romantic escape; excellent restaurant; top-notch spa. **Cons:** Set in a suburban neighborhood far from local shopping and dining. $ *Rooms from: $259* ⊠ *1401 S. Oak Knoll Ave., Pasadena* ☎ *626/568–3900* ⊕ *www.pasadena.langhamhotels.com* ⇆ *342 rooms, 38 suites* ⦿*No meals* ✛ *4:D2.*

ORANGE COUNTY AND CATALINA ISLAND

With Disneyland and Knott's Berry Farm

WELCOME TO ORANGE COUNTY AND CATALINA ISLAND

TOP REASONS TO GO

★ **Disney Magic:** Walking down Main Street, U.S.A., with Cinderella's Castle straight ahead, you really will feel like you're in one of the happiest places on Earth.

★ **Beautiful Beaches:** Surf, swim, paddleboard, or just relax on one of the state's most breathtaking stretches of coastline. Keep in mind, the water may be colder than you expect.

★ **Island Getaways:** Just a short high-speed catamaran ride away, Catalina Island feels 1,000 miles away from the mainland. Wander around charming Avalon, or explore the unspoiled beauty of the island's wild interior.

★ **The Fine Life:** Some of the state's wealthiest communities are in coastal Orange County, so spend at least part of your stay here experiencing how the other half lives.

★ **Family Fun:** Spend some quality time with the kids riding roller coasters, eating ice cream, fishing off ocean piers, and bodysurfing.

1 Disneyland Resort. Southern California's top family destination has expanded from the humble park of Walt Disney's vision to a megaresort with more attractions spilling over into Disney's California Adventure. But kids (and many adults) still consider it the happiest place on Earth.

2 Knott's Berry Farm. Amusement park lovers should check out this Buena Park attraction, with thrill rides, the *Peanuts* gang, and lots of fried chicken and boysenberry pie.

3 Coastal Orange County. The OC's beach communities may not be quite as glamorous as seen on TV, but coastal spots like Huntington Beach, Newport Harbor, and Laguna Beach are perfect for chilling out in a beachfront hotel.

12

0   5 mi

0   5 km

GETTING ORIENTED

Like Los Angeles, Orange County stretches over a large area, lacks a singular focal point, and has limited public transportation. You'll need a car and a sensible game plan to make the most of your visit. Anaheim, home of Disneyland, has every style of hotel imaginable, from family-friendly motels to luxurious high-rises. The coastal cities are more expensive but have cooler weather in summer marvelous beaches that you can enjoy throughout the year.

4 **Catalina Island.** This unspoiled island paradise—with its pocket-size town, Avalon, and large nature preserve—is just off the Orange County coast.

Updated
by Kathy A.
McDonald
With its tropical flowers and palm trees, the stretch of coast between Seal Beach and San Clemente is often called the California Riviera. Exclusive Newport Beach, artsy Laguna, and the surf town of Huntington Beach are the stars, but lesser-known gems on the glistening coast—such as Corona del Mar—are also worth visiting. Offshore, meanwhile, lies gorgeous Catalina Island, a terrific spot for diving, snorkeling, and hiking.

Few of the citrus groves that gave Orange County its name remain. This region south and east of Los Angeles is now ruled by tourism and high-tech business instead of farmers. Despite a building boom that began in the 1990s, the area is still a place to find wilderness trails, canyons, greenbelts, and natural environs. And just offshore, is a deep-water wilderness that's possible to explore via daily whale-watching excursions.

PLANNING

GETTING HERE AND AROUND
AIR TRAVEL
Orange County's main facility is John Wayne Airport Orange County (SNA), which is served by 10 major domestic airlines and two commuter lines. Long Beach Airport (LGB) is served by four airlines, including its major player, JetBlue. It's roughly 20 to 30 minutes by car from Anaheim.

Super Shuttle and Prime Time Airport Shuttle provide transportation from John Wayne and LAX to the Disneyland area of Anaheim. Round-trip fares average about $20 per person from John Wayne and $16 to $42 from LAX.

12

BUS TRAVEL

The Orange County Transportation Authority will take you virtually anywhere in the county, but it will take time; OCTA buses go from Knott's Berry Farm and Disneyland to Huntington Beach and Newport Beach. Bus 1 travels along the coast; buses 701 and 721 provide express service to Los Angeles.

Information Orange County Transportation Authority ☏ *714/636–7433* ⊕ *www.octa.net.*

CAR TRAVEL

The San Diego Freeway (Interstate 405), the coastal route, and the Santa Ana Freeway (Interstate 5), the inland route, run north–south through Orange County. South of Laguna, Interstate 405 merges into Interstate 5 (called the San Diego Freeway south from this point). A toll road, Highway 73, runs 15 miles from Newport Beach to San Juan Capistrano; it costs $5.25–$6.25 (lower rates are for weekends and off-peak hours) and is usually less jammed than the regular freeways. Do your best to avoid all Orange County freeways during rush hours (6–9 am and 3:30–6:30 pm). Highway 55 leads to Newport Beach. The Pacific Coast Highway (Highway 1) allows easy access to beach communities and is the most scenic route but expect it to be crowded, especially on summer weekends.

FERRY TRAVEL

There are two ferries that service Catalina Island; Catalina Express runs from Long Beach (about 90 minutes) and from Newport Beach (about 75 minutes). Reservations are advised for summers and weekends. During the winter months, ferry crossings are not as frequent as in the summer high season.

TRAIN TRAVEL

Amtrak makes daily stops in Orange County at all major towns. Metrolink is a weekday commuter train that runs to and from Los Angeles and Orange County.

Information Amtrak ☏ *800/872–7245* ⊕ *www.amtrak.com.*
Metrolink ☏ *800/371–5465* ⊕ *www.metrolinktrains.com.*

For more information on Getting Here and Around, see Travel Smart Los Angeles.

RESTAURANTS

Much like L.A., restaurants in Orange County are generally casual, and you'll rarely see men in jackets and ties. However, at top resort hotel dining rooms, many guests choose to dress up.

Of course, there's also a swath of casual places along the beachfronts— seafood takeout, taquerias, burger joints—that won't mind if you wear flip-flops. Reservations are recommended for the nicest restaurants.

Many places don't serve past 11 pm, and locals tend to eat early. Remember that according to California law, smoking is prohibited in all enclosed areas.

Prices in the restaurant reviews are the average cost of a main course at dinner or, if dinner is not served, at lunch (excluding sales tax).

HOTELS

Along the coast there are remarkable luxury resorts; if you can't afford a stay, pop in for the view at Laguna Beach's Montage or the always welcoming Ritz-Carlton at Dana Point. For a taste of the OC glam life, have lunch overlooking the yachts of Newport Bay at the Balboa Bay Resort.

As a rule, lodging prices tend to rise the closer the hotels are to the beach. If you're looking for value, consider a hotel that is inland along the Interstate 405 freeway corridor.

In most cases, you can take advantage of some of the facilities of the high-end resorts, such as restaurants and spas, even if you aren't an overnight guest.

Prices in the hotel reviews are the lowest cost of a standard double room in high season. Prices do not include taxes (as high as 15%, depending on the region).

VISITOR INFORMATION

The Anaheim-Orange County Visitor and Convention Bureau is an excellent resource for both leisure and business travelers and can provide materials on many area attractions. It's on the main floor of the Anaheim Convention Center.

The Orange County Tourism Council's website is also a useful source of information.

Information **Anaheim/Orange County Visitor & Convention Bureau** ✉ *Anaheim Convention Center, 800 W. Katella Ave., Anaheim* ☎ *714/765–8888* ⊕ *www.anaheimoc.org.* **Orange County Tourism Council** ⊕ *www.visittheoc.com.*

DISNEYLAND RESORT

26 miles southeast of Los Angeles, via I-5.

The snowcapped Matterhorn, the centerpiece of the Magic Kingdom, punctuates the skyline of Anaheim. Since 1955, when Walt Disney chose this once-quiet farming community for the site of his first amusement park, Disneyland has attracted more than 600 million visitors and tens of thousands of workers, and Anaheim has been their host.

To understand the symbiotic relationship between Disneyland and Anaheim, you need only look at the $4.2 billion spent in a combined effort to revitalize Anaheim's tourist center and run-down areas, and to expand and renovate the Disney properties into what is known now as Disneyland Resort.

The resort is a sprawling complex that includes Disney's two amusement parks; three hotels; and Downtown Disney, a shopping, dining, and entertainment promenade. Anaheim's tourist center includes Angel Stadium of Anaheim, home of baseball's 2002 World Series Champion Los Angeles Angels of Anaheim; the Honda Center (formerly the Arrowhead Pond), which hosts concerts and the Anaheim Ducks hockey team; and the enormous Anaheim Convention Center.

GETTING THERE

Disney is about a 30-mile drive from either LAX or Downtown. From LAX, follow Sepulveda Boulevard south to the Interstate 105 freeway and drive east 16 miles to the Interstate 605 north exit. Exit at the Santa Ana Freeway (Interstate 5) and continue south for 12 miles to the Disneyland Drive exit. Follow signs to the resort. From Downtown, follow Interstate 5 south 28 miles and exit at Disneyland Drive. **Disneyland Resort Express** (☎ *800/828–6699* ⊕ *graylineanaheim.com*) offers daily nonstop bus service between LAX, John Wayne Airport, and Anaheim. Reservations are not required. The cost is $30 one-way from LAX; and $20 from John Wayne Airport.

SAVING TIME AND MONEY

If you plan to visit for more than a day, you can save money by buying two- three-, four-, and five-day Park Hopper tickets that grant same-day "hopping" privileges between Disneyland and Disney's California Adventure. You get a discount on the multiple-day passes if you buy online through the Disneyland website.

A one-day Park Hopper pass costs $137 for anyone 10 or older, $131 for kids ages 3–9. Admission to either park (but not both) is $92 or $86 for kids 3–9; kids 2 and under are free.

In addition to tickets, parking is $16–$22 (unless your hotel has a shuttle or is within walking distance), and meals in the parks and at Downtown Disney range from $10 to $30 per person.

DISNEYLAND

FAMILY **Disneyland.** One of the biggest misconceptions people have about Disneyland is that they've "been there, done that" if they've visited either Florida's mammoth Walt Disney World or one of the Disney parks overseas. But Disneyland, which opened in 1955 and is the only one of the parks to be overseen by Walt himself, has a genuine historic feel and occupies a unique place in the Disney legend. Expertly run, with polite and helpful staff ("cast members" in the Disney lexicon), the park has plenty that you won't find anywhere else—such as the Indiana Jones Adventure ride and Storybook Land, with its miniature replicas of animated Disney scenes from classics such as *Pinocchio* and *Alice in Wonderland*. Characters appear for autographs and photos throughout the day; times and places are posted at the entrances. Live shows, parades, strolling musicians, nightly fireworks, and endless snack choices add to the carnival atmosphere. You can also meet some of the animated icons at one of the character meals served at the three Disney hotels (open to the public). Belongings can be stored in lockers just off Main Street; stroller rentals at the entrance gate are a convenient option for families with small tykes. ⊠ *1313 S. Disneyland Dr., between Ball Rd. and Katella Ave., Anaheim* ☎ *714/781–4636 Guest information* ⊕ *www. disneyland.com* ⊠ *$92; parking $16* ⊙ *Hrs vary.*

Fodor's Choice
★

PARK NEIGHBORHOODS

Neighborhoods for Disneyland are arranged in geographic order.

MAIN STREET, U.S.A. Walt's hometown of Marceline, Missouri, was the inspiration behind this romanticized image of small-town America, circa 1900. The sidewalks are lined with a penny arcade and shops that sell everything from tradable pins to Disney-theme clothing, an endless supply of sugar confections, and a photo shop that offers souvenirs created via Disney's PhotoPass (on-site photographers capture memorable moments digitally—you can access in person or online). Main Street opens a half hour before the rest of the park, so it's a good place to explore if you're getting an early start to beat the crowds (it's also open an hour after the other attractions close, so you may want to save your shopping for the end of the day). **Main Street Cinema** offers a cool respite from the crowds and six classic Disney animated shorts, including *Steamboat Willie*. There's rarely a wait to enter. Grab a cappuccino and fresh-made pastry at the Jolly Holiday bakery to jump-start your visit. Board the **Disneyland Railroad** here to save on walking; it tours all the lands plus offers unique views of Splash Mountain and the Grand Canyon and Primeval World dioramas.

NEW ORLEANS SQUARE This mini–French Quarter, with narrow streets, hidden courtyards, and live street performances, is home to two iconic attractions and the Cajun-inspired Blue Bayou restaurant. **Pirates of the Caribbean** now features Jack Sparrow and the cursed Captain Barbossa, in a nod to the blockbuster movies of the same name, plus enhanced special effects and battle scenes (complete with cannonball explosions). Nearby **Haunted Mansion** continues to spook guests with its stretching room and "doombuggy" rides (plus there's now an expanded storyline for the beating-heart bride). Its *Nightmare Before Christmas* holiday overlay is an annual tradition. This is a good area to get a casual bite to eat; the clam chowder in sourdough bread bowls, sold at the French Market Restaurant and Royal Street Veranda, is a popular choice. Food carts offer everything from just-popped popcorn to churros, and even fresh fruit.

FRONTIERLAND Between Adventureland and Fantasyland, Frontierland transports you to the wild, wild West with its rustic buildings, shooting gallery, mountain range, and foot-stompin' dance hall. The marquee attraction, **Big Thunder Mountain Railroad,** is a relatively tame roller coaster ride (no steep descents) that takes the form of a runaway mine car as it rumbles past desert canyons and an old mining town. Tour the Rivers of America on the **Mark Twain Riverboat** in the company of a grizzled old river pilot or circumnavigate the globe on the **Sailing Ship Columbia,** though its operating hours are usually limited to weekends. From here, you can raft over to Pirate's Lair on **Tom Sawyer Island,** which now features pirate-theme caves, treasure hunts, and music, along with plenty of caves and hills to climb and explore. If you don't mind tight seating, have a snack at the Golden Horseshoe Restaurant while enjoying the always-entertaining comedy and bluegrass show of Billy Hill and the Hillybillies. Children won't want to miss **Big Thunder Ranch,** a small petting zoo featuring pigs, goats, and cows, beyond Big Thunder Mountain.

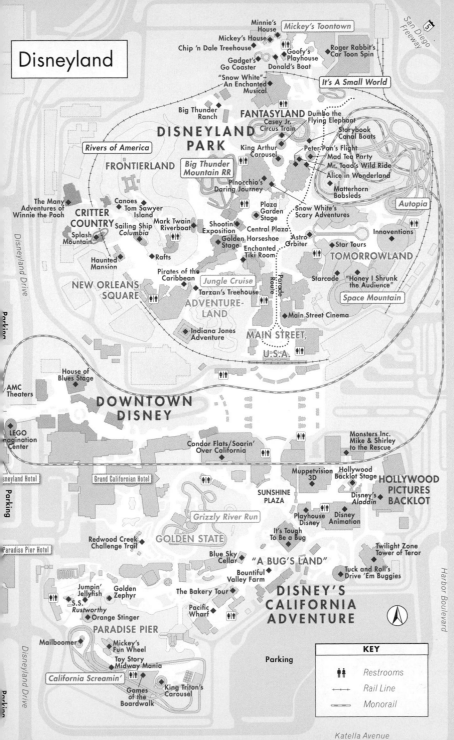

DID YOU KNOW?

Apparently, the plain purple teacup in Disneyland's Mad Tea Party ride spins the fastest—though no one knows why.

CRITTER COUNTRY Down-home country is the theme in this shady corner of the park, where Winnie the Pooh and Davy Crockett make their homes. Here you can find **Splash Mountain,** a classic flume ride accompanied by music and appearances by Brer Rabbit and other characters from *Song of the South.* Don't forget to check out your photo (the camera snaps close-ups of each car just before it plunges into the water) on the way out. The patio of the popular Hungry Bear Restaurant has great views of Tom Sawyer's Island and Davy Crockett's Explorer Canoes.

ADVEN-TURELAND Modeled after the lands of Africa, Polynesia, and Arabia, this tiny tropical paradise is worth braving the crowds that flock here for the ambience and better-than-average food. Sing along with the animatronic birds and tiki gods in the **Enchanted Tiki Room,** sail the rivers of the world with joke-cracking skippers on **Jungle Cruise,** and climb the *Disneyodendron semperflorens* (aka always-blooming Disney tree) to **Tarzan's Treehouse,** where you can walk through scenes, some interactive, from the 1999 animated film. Cap off the visit with a wild Jeep ride at **Indiana Jones Adventure,** where the special effects and decipherable hieroglyphics distract you while you're waiting in line. The skewers (some vegetarian options available) at Bengal Barbecue and pineapple whip at Tiki Juice Bar are some of the best fast-food options in the park.

FANTASYLAND Sleeping Beauty Castle marks the entrance to Fantasyland, a visual wonderland of princesses, spinning teacups, flying elephants, and other classic storybook characters. Rides and shops (such as the princess-theme Once Upon a Time and Gepetto's Toys and Gifts) take precedence over restaurants in this area of the park, but outdoor carts sell everything from churros to turkey legs. Tots love the **King Arthur Carousel, Casey Jr. Circus Train,** and **Storybook Land Canal Boats.** This is also home to **Mr. Toad's Wild Ride, Peter Pan's Flight,** and **Pinocchio's Daring Journey,** classic, movie-theater-dark rides that immerse riders in Disney fairy tales and appeal to adults and kids alike. The Abominable Snowman pops up on the **Matterhorn Bobsleds,** a roller coaster that twists and turns up and around on a made-to-scale model of the real Swiss mountain. Anchoring the east end of Fantasyland is **It's a Small World,** a smorgasbord of dancing animatronic dolls, cuckoo clock–covered walls, and variations of the song everyone knows, or soon *will* know, by heart. Beloved Disney characters like Ariel from *Under the Sea* are also part of the mix. Fantasy Faire is a fairy tale-style village that collects all the Disney princesses together. Each has her own reception nook in the Royal Hall. Condensed retellings of *Tangled* and *Beauty and the Beast* take place at the Royal Theatre.

DISNEY'S TOP ATTRACTIONS

Finding Nemo: Board a yellow submarine and view a 3-D animated adventure.

Haunted Mansion: A "doombuggy" takes you through a spooky old plantation mansion.

Matterhorn Bobsleds: At the center of the Magic Kingdom, this roller coaster simulates bobsleds.

Pirates of the Caribbean: Watch buccaneers wreak havoc as you float along in a rowboat.

Space Mountain: This scary-but-thrilling roller coaster is indoors—and mostly in the dark.

MICKEY'S
TOONTOWN

Geared toward small fries, this lopsided cartoonlike downtown, complete with cars and trolleys that invite exploring, is where Mickey, Donald, Goofy, and other classic Disney characters hang their hats. One of the most popular attractions is **Roger Rabbit's Car Toon Spin,** a twisting, turning cab ride through the Toontown of *Who Framed Roger Rabbit?* You can also walk through **Mickey's House** to meet and be photographed with the famous mouse, take a low-key ride on **Gadget's Go Coaster,** or bounce around the fenced-in playground in front of **Goofy's House.**

TOMOR-
ROWLAND

This popular section of the park continues to tinker with its future, adding and enhancing rides regularly. One of the newest attractions, Star Tours, is a 3-D immersive experience in the world of *Star Wars.* **Finding Nemo's Submarine Voyage** updates the old Submarine Voyage ride with the exploits of Nemo, Dory, Marlin, and other characters from the Disney Pixar film. Try to visit this popular ride early in the day if you can and be prepared for a wait. The interactive **Buzz Lightyear Astro Blasters** lets you zap your neighbors with laser beams and compete for the highest score. Hurtle through the cosmos on **Space Mountain** or check out mainstays like the futuristic **Astro Orbiter** rockets, **Innoventions,** a self-guided tour of the latest toys and gadgets of tomorrow, and **Caption EO,** a 3-D film featuring the music and talents of the late Michael Jackson. Disneyland Monorail and Disneyland Railroad both have stations here. There's also a video arcade and dancing water fountain that makes a perfect playground for kids on hot summer days. The Jedi Training Academy spotlights future Luke Skywalkers in the *Star Wars*–theme show's crowd.

Besides the eight lands, the daily live-action shows and parades are always crowd-pleasers. **Fantasmic!** is a musical, fireworks, and laser show in which Mickey and friends wage a spellbinding battle against Disneyland's darker characters. ■**TIP➜** Arrive early to secure a good view; if there are two shows scheduled for the day, the second one tends to be less crowded. A fireworks display sparks up most evenings. Brochures with maps, available at the entrance, list show and parade times.

DISNEY CALIFORNIA ADVENTURE

FAMILY
Fodor'sChoice
★

Disney California Adventure. The sprawling Disney California Adventure, adjacent to Disneyland (their entrances face each other), pays tribute to the Golden State with eight theme areas that re-create vintage architectural styles and embrace several hit Pixar films via engaging attractions. In 2012, the front gate was revamped—visitors now enter through the art deco–style Buena Vista Street—and the 12-acre Cars Land and Radiator Springs Racers, an immediate blockbuster hit (FASTPASS tickets for the ride run out early most days), was added. Other popular attractions include World of Color, a nighttime water-effects show, and Toy Story Mania!, an interactive adventure ride hosted by Woody and Buzz Lightyear. At night, the park takes on neon-color hues as glowing signs light up Route 66 in Cars Land and Mickey's Fun Wheel, a mega-size Ferris wheel on the Paradise

12

BEST TIPS FOR DISNEYLAND

Buy entry tickets in advance.
Many nearby hotels sell park admission tickets; you can also buy them through the Disney website. If you book a package deal, such as those offered through AAA, tickets are included, too.

The lines at the ticket booths can take more than an hour on busy days, so you'll definitely save time by buying in advance, especially if you're committed to going on a certain day regardless of the weather.

Come midweek. Weekends, especially in summer, are a mob scene. Holidays are crowded, too. A rainy winter weekday is often the least crowded time to visit.

Plan your times to hit the most popular rides. Fodorites recommend getting to the park as early as possible. If you're at the park when the gates open, make a beeline for the top rides before the crowds reach a critical mass. Another good time is the late evening, when the hordes thin out somewhat, and during a parade or other show. Save the quieter attractions for midafternoon.

Use FASTPASS. These passes allow you to reserve your place in line at some of the most crowded attractions (only one at a time). Distribution machines are posted near the entrances of each attraction. Feed in your park admission ticket, and you'll receive a pass with a printed time frame (generally up to 1–1½ hours later) during which you can return to wait in a much shorter line.

Plan your meals to avoid peak mealtime crowds. Start the day with a big breakfast so you won't be too hungry at noon, when restaurants and vendors get swarmed. Wait to have lunch until after 1.

If you want to eat at the **Blue Bayou** in New Orleans Square, you can make a reservation up to six months in advance online. Another (cheaper) option is to bring your own food. There are areas just outside the park gates with picnic tables set up for this. And it's always a good idea to bring water.

Check the daily events schedule online or at the park entrance. During parades, fireworks, and other special events, sections of the parks clog with crowds. This can work for you or against you. An event could make it difficult to get around a park—but if you plan ahead, you can take advantage of the distraction to hit popular rides.

Send the Teens Next Door. Disneyland's newer sister park, California Adventure, features more intense rides suitable for older kids (Park Hopper passes include admission to both parks).

Pier. Unlike at Disneyland, cocktails, beer, and wine are available, and there's even an outdoor dance spot, the Mad T Party. Live nightly entertainment also features a 1930s jazz troupe that arrives in a vintage jalopy. ⊠ *1313 S. Disneyland Dr., between Ball Rd. and Katella Ave., Anaheim* ☎ *714/781–4636* ⊕ *www.disneyland.com* ⊠ *$92; parking $16* ⊙ *Hrs vary.*

PARK NEIGHBORHOODS

BUENA VISTA STREET
California Adventure's grand entryway re-creates the lost 1920s of Los Angeles that Walt Disney encountered when he moved to the Golden State. There's a **Red Car trolley** (modeled after Los Angeles's bygone streetcar line); hop on for the brief ride to Hollywood Land. Buena Vista Street is also home to a Starbucks outlet—within the Fiddler, Fifer & Practical Café—and the upscale Carthay Circle Restaurant and Lounge, which serves modern craft cocktails and beer.

CONDOR FLATS
Dive into California's history and natural beauty with nature trails, a winery, and a tortilla factory (with free samples). Condor Flats has **Soarin' Over California,** a spectacular simulated hang-glider ride over California terrain.

GRIZZLY PEAK
Test your outdoorsman skills on the **Redwood Creek Challenge Trail,** a challenging trek across net ladders and suspension bridges. **Grizzly River Run** mimics the river rapids of the Sierra Nevadas; be prepared to get soaked.

HOLLYWOOD LAND
With a main street modeled after Hollywood Boulevard, a fake blue-sky backdrop, and real soundstages, this area celebrates California's most famous industry. **Disney Animation** gives you an insider's look at the work of animators and how they create characters. **Turtle Talk with Crush** lets kids have an unrehearsed talk with computer-animated Crush, a sea turtle from *Finding Nemo.* The Hyperion Theater hosts **Aladdin—A Musical Spectacular,** a 45-minute live performance with terrific visual effects. ■TIP➔ **Plan on getting in line about half an hour in advance: the show is worth the wait.** On the film-inspired ride, **Monsters, Inc. Mike & Sulley to the Rescue,** you climb into taxis and travel the streets of Monstropolis on a mission to safely return Boo to her bedroom. A major draw for older kids is the looming **Twilight Zone Tower of Terror,** which drops riders 13 floors. Their screams can be heard throughout the park!

A BUG'S LAND
Inspired by the 1998 film *A Bug's Life,* this section skews its attractions to an insect's point of view. Kids can spin around in giant takeout Chinese food boxes on **Flik's Flyers,** and hit the bug-shaped bumper cars on **Tuck and Roll's Drive 'Em Buggies.** The short show *It's Tough to Be a Bug!* gives a 3-D look at insect life.

CARS LAND
Amble down Route 66, the main thoroughfare of Cars Land, a pitch-perfect re-creation of the vintage highway. Quick eats are found at the Cozy Cone Motel (in a teepee-shape motor court) while Flo's V8 café serves hearty comfort food. Start your day at Radiator Springs Racers, the park's most popular attraction, where waits can be two hours or longer. Strap into a nifty sports car and meet the characters of Pixar's *Cars;* the ride ends in a speedy auto race through the red rocks and desert of Radiator Springs.

PACIFIC WHARF
The Wine Country Trattoria at the Golden Vine Winery is a great place for Italian specialties paired with California wine; relax outside on the restaurant's terrace for a casual bite. Mexican cuisine and potent margaritas are available at the Cocina Cucamonga Mexican Grill and Rita's Baja Blenders.

PARADISE PIER This section re-creates the glory days of California's seaside piers. If you're looking for thrills, the **California Screamin'** roller coaster takes its riders from 0 to 55 mph in about four seconds and proceeds through scream tunnels, steeply angled drops, and a 360-degree loop. **Goofy's Sky School** is a rollicking roller coaster ride that goes up three stories and covers more than 1,200 feet of track. **Mickey's Fun Wheel,** a giant Ferris wheel, provides a good view of the grounds at a more leisurely pace. There are also carnival games, a fish-theme carousel, and Ariel's Grotto, where future princesses can dine with the mermaid and her friends (reservations are a must). Get a close-up look of Ariel's world on the **Little Mermaid—Ariel's Undersea Adventure.** The best views of the nighttime music, water and light show, **World of Color,** are from the paths along Paradise Bay. Book a picnic dinner at the Golden Vine Winery that includes a ticket to a viewing area to catch all the show's stunning visuals.

OTHER ATTRACTIONS

FAMILY **Downtown Disney.** Downtown Disney is a 20-acre promenade of dining, shopping, and entertainment that connects the resort's hotels and theme parks. Restaurant-nightclub **House of Blues** spices up its Delta-inspired ribs and seafood with various live music acts on an intimate two-story stage. At **Ralph Brennan's Jazz Kitchen** you can dig into New Orleans–style food and music. Sports fans gravitate to **ESPN Zone,** with American grill food, interactive video games, and 175 video screens telecasting worldwide sports events. An **AMC** multiplex movie theater with stadium-style seating plays the latest blockbusters and, naturally, a couple of kid flicks. Shops sell everything from Disney goods to antique jewelry—don't miss **Vault 28,** a hip boutique that sells one-of-a-kind vintage and couture clothing and accessories. At the mega-sized **Lego Store,** there are hands-on demonstrations and space to play with the latest Lego creations. Parking is a deal: the first three hours are free, with two extra hours with validation. ✉ *1580 Disneyland Dr., Anaheim* ☎ *888/262–4386* 🌐 *disneyland.disney.go.com/downtown-disney* 🎟 *Free* 🕒 *Daily 7 am–2 am; hrs at shops and restaurants vary.*

WHERE TO EAT

$$$$ NORTHERN ITALIAN 🍴 **Anaheim White House.** Several small dining rooms are set with crisp linens and candles in this flower-filled 1909 mansion. The northern Italian menu includes steak, rack of lamb, and fresh seafood. Try the signature ravioli *arragosta*, lobster-filled pasta in a ginger-and-citrus sauce. A three-course prix-fixe low-calorie lunch, served weekdays, costs $23. [$] *Average main: $35* ✉ *887 S. Anaheim Blvd., Anaheim* ☎ *714/772–1381* 🌐 *www.anaheimwhitehouse.com* 🕒 *No lunch Sat.*

$$$ MEDITERRANEAN 🍴 **Catal Restaurant & Uva Bar.** Famed chef Joachim Splichal and his staff take a relaxed approach at this bi-level Mediterranean spot. People-watch at the colorful, outdoor Uva (Spanish for "grape") bar on the ground floor, where there are specialty cocktails, craft beers, and more than 40 wines by the glass. Burgers here are crowd-pleasers, as are appetizers from corn arepas to lemony hummus. Upstairs, Catal's menu has tapas, a variety of flavorful paellas (lobster is worth the splurge), and charcuterie. ■ **TIP→ Reserve a table on the outdoor terrace for an awesome view of the Disneyland fireworks.** [$] *Average main: $30* ✉ *Downtown Disney, 1580 S. Disneyland Dr., Suite 103, Anaheim* ☎ *714/774–4442* 🌐 *www.patinagroup.com.*

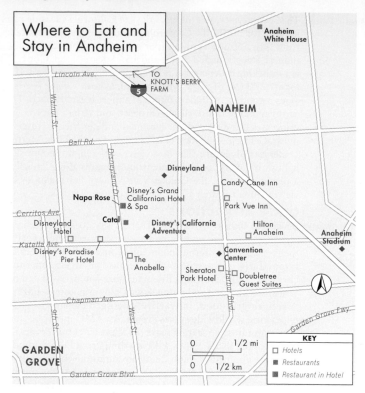

Where to Eat and Stay in Anaheim

$$$$ ✕ **Napa Rose.** Done up in a lovely arts and crafts style, this eatery
AMERICAN overlooks a woodsy corner of Disney's California Adventure park.
The contemporary cuisine is matched with an extensive wine list,
with 1,000 labels and 80 available by the glass. For a look into the
open kitchen, sit at the counter and watch the chefs as they whip up
such signature dishes as pan-roasted diver scallops in a sauce of lobster, lemon, and vanilla, and slowly braised beef short rib in a Cabernet jus. There's also a list of kid-friendly dishes. A cocktail on the
outdoor patio with a fire pit is a pleasant way to end the night. The
four-course, $95 prix-fixe menu changes weekly. ⑤ *Average main: $40*
✉ *Disney's Grand Californian Hotel, 1600 S. Disneyland Dr., Anaheim* ☎ *714/300–7170* ⊕ *disneyland.disney.go.com/grand-californian-
hotel/napa-rose* ⚓ *Reservations essential.*

WHERE TO STAY

$ ☷ **The Anabella.** At the Anaheim Convention Center, this hotel's Span-
HOTEL ish Mission–style exterior and leafy landscaping set it apart from other
budget properties. **Pros:** 15-minute walk to Disneyland and California Adventure entrance; extended happy hour at hotel bar; free Wi-Fi.
Cons: some complaints about thin walls. ⑤ *Rooms from: $120* ✉ *1030
W. Katella Ave., Anaheim* ☎ *714/905–1050, 800/863–4888* ⊕ *www.
anabellahotel.com* ⤴ *234 rooms, 124 suites* ⑩ *No meals.*

12

$$ 🛏 **Candy Cane Inn.** One of the Disneyland area's first hotels, the Candy
HOTEL Cane is one of Anaheim's most relaxing properties, with spacious
and understated rooms and an inviting palm-fringed pool. **Pros:**
proximity to everything Disney; friendly service; well-lighted prop-
erty. **Cons:** rooms and lobby are on the small side; all rooms face
parking lot. $ *Rooms from: $149* ✉ *1747 S. Harbor Blvd., Anaheim*
☎ *714/774–5284, 800/345–7057* ⊕ *www.candycaneinn.net* ⇌ *171
rooms* ❍❘ *Breakfast.*

$$$$ 🛏 **Disney's Grand Californian Hotel & Spa.** The most opulent of Disney-
RESORT land's three hotels, the Craftsman-style Grand Californian offers views
FAMILY of Disney California Adventure and Downtown Disney. **Pros:** gor-
Fodor'sChoice geous lobby; plenty for families; direct access to theme parks. **Cons:**
★ the self-parking lot is across the street; standard rooms are on the
small side. $ *Rooms from: $482* ✉ *1600 S. Disneyland Dr., Anaheim*
☎ *714/635–2300, 714/956–6425 reservations* ⊕ *disneyland.disney.
go.com/grand-californian-hotel* ⇌ *904 rooms, 44 suites, 50 villas*
❍❘ *No meals.*

$$ 🛏 **Doubletree Guest Suites Anaheim Resort-Convention Center.** This upscale
HOTEL hotel near the Anaheim Convention Center and a 20-minute walk from
Disneyland caters to business travelers and vacationers alike. **Pros:** huge
suites; elegant lobby; walking distance to a variety of restaurants. **Cons:**
a bit far from Disneyland; pool area is small. $ *Rooms from: $139*
✉ *2085 S. Harbor Blvd., Anaheim* ☎ *714/750–3000, 800/215–7316*
⊕ *doubletree3.hilton.com* ⇌ *50 rooms, 202 suites* ❍❘ *No meals.*

$$ 🛏 **Hilton Anaheim.** Next to the Anaheim Convention Center, this busy
HOTEL Hilton is one of the largest hotels in Southern California with a restau-
FAMILY rant and food court, cocktail lounges, a full-service gym, and its own
Starbucks. **Pros:** efficient service; great children's programs; some rooms
have views of the nightly fireworks. **Cons:** huge size can be daunting;
fee to use health club. $ *Rooms from: $159* ✉ *777 Convention Way,
Anaheim* ☎ *714/750–4321, 800/445–8667* ⊕ *www.anaheim.hilton.com*
⇌ *1,479 rooms, 93 suites* ❍❘ *No meals.*

$$ 🛏 **Park Vue Inn.** Watch the nightly fireworks from the rooftop sundeck at
HOTEL this bougainvillea-covered Spanish-style inn, one of the closest lodgings
to Disneyland main gate. **Pros:** easy walk to Disneyland, Downtown
Disney, and Disney California Adventure; good value; some rooms have
bunk beds. **Cons:** all rooms face the parking lot; some complain about
early-morning street noise. $ *Rooms from: $151* ✉ *1570 S. Harbor
Blvd., Anaheim* ☎ *714/772–3691, 800/334–7021* ⊕ *www.parkvueinn.
com* ⇌ *76 rooms, 8 suites* ❍❘ *Breakfast.*

SPORTS

Anaheim Ducks. The National Hockey League's Anaheim Ducks, winners
of the 2007 Stanley Cup, play at Honda Center. ✉ *Honda Center, 2695
E. Katella Ave., Anaheim* ☎ *877/945–3946* ⊕ *ducks.nhl.com.*

Los Angeles Angels of Anaheim. Professional baseball's Los Angeles Angels
of Anaheim play at Angel Stadium. An "Outfield Extravaganza" celebrates great plays on the field, with fireworks and a geyser exploding
over a model evoking the California coast. ✉ *Angel Stadium, 2000 E.
Gene Autry Way, Anaheim* ☎ *714/940–2000* ⊕ *www.angelsbaseball.
com* Ⓜ *Metrolink Angels Express.*

KNOTT'S BERRY FARM

25 miles south of Los Angeles, via I-5, in Buena Park.

FAMILY   **Knott's Berry Farm.** The land where the boysenberry was invented (by crossing raspberry, blackberry, and loganberry bushes) is now occupied by Knott's Berry Farm. In 1934 Cordelia Knott began serving chicken dinners on her wedding china to supplement her family's income—or so the story goes. The dinners and her boysenberry pies proved more profitable than husband Walter's farm, so the two moved first into the restaurant business and then into the entertainment business. The park is now a 160-acre complex with 40 rides, dozens of restaurants and shops, a brick-by-brick replica of Philadelphia's Independence Hall, and loads of Americana. Although it has plenty to keep small children occupied, the park is best known for its awesome rides. The boardwalk area was expanded in 2013, adding two coasters—the stomach-churning Rip Tide turns thrill seekers upside down and around several times—water features to cool things off on hot days, and a lighted promenade. And, yes, you can still get that boysenberry pie (and jam, juice—you name it). ⊠ *8039 Beach Blvd.* ✢ *Between La Palma Ave. and Crescent St., 2 blocks south of Hwy. 91* ☎ *714/220–5200* ⊕ *www.knotts.com* ✉ *$62.*

PARK NEIGHBORHOODS

THE   Not-for-the-squeamish thrill rides and skill-based games dominate the
BOARDWALK   scene at the **boardwalk.** New roller coasters—Coast Rider, Surfside Glider, and Pacific Scrambler—were added in 2013 and surround a pond that keeps things cooler on hot days. Go head over heels on the **Boomerang** roller coaster, then do it again—backward. The boardwalk is also home to a string of test-your-skill games that are fun to watch whether you're playing or not, and Johnny Rockets, the park's newest restaurant.

CAMP SNOOPY   It can be gridlock on weekends, but small fries love this miniature High Sierra wonderland where the *Peanuts* gang hangs out. Tykes can push and pump their own mini–mining cars on **Huff and Puff,** zip around a pint-size racetrack on **Charlie Brown Speedway,** and hop aboard **Woodstock's Airmail,** a kids' version of the park's Supreme Scream ride. Most of the rides here are geared toward kids only, leaving parents to cheer them on from the sidelines. **Sierra Sidewinder,** a roller coaster near the entrance of Camp Snoopy, is aimed at older children, with spinning saucer-type vehicles that go a maximum speed of 37 mph.

FIESTA   Over in **Fiesta Village** are two more musts for adrenaline junkies: **Mon-**
VILLAGE   **tezooma's Revenge,** a roller coaster that goes from 0 to 55 mph in less than five seconds, and **Jaguar!,** which simulates the motions of a cat stalking its prey, twisting, spiraling, and speeding up and slowing down as it takes you on its stomach-dropping course. There's also **Hat Dance,** a version of the spinning teacups but with sombreros, and a 100-year-old **Dentzel Carousel,** complete with an antique organ and menagerie of hand-carved animals.

GHOST TOWN   Clusters of authentic old buildings relocated from their original mining-town sites mark this section of the park. You can stroll down the street, stop and chat with a blacksmith, pan for gold (for a fee), crack open a geode, check out the chalkboard of a circa-1875 schoolhouse, and ride an original Butterfield stagecoach. Looming over it all is **GhostRider,** Orange County's first wooden roller coaster. Traveling up to 56 mph and reaching 118 feet at its highest point, the park's biggest attraction is riddled with sudden dips and curves, subjecting riders to forces up to three times that of gravity. On the Western-theme **Silver Bullet,** riders are sent to a height of 146 feet and then back down 109 feet. Riders spiral, corkscrew, fly into a cobra roll, and experience overbanked curves. The **Calico Mine** ride descends into a replica of a working gold mine. The **Timber Mountain Log Ride** is a visitor favorite—the flume ride underwent a complete renovation in 2013. Also found here is the park's newest thrill ride, the **Pony Express,** a roller coaster that lets riders saddle up on packs of "horses" tethered to platforms that take off on a series of hairpin turns and travel up to 38 mph. Don't miss the **Western Trails Museum,** a dusty old gem full of Old West memorabilia and rural Americana, plus menus from the original chicken restaurant, and an impressive antique button collection. **Calico Railroad** departs regularly from Ghost Town station for a round-trip tour of the park (bandit holdups notwithstanding).

This section is also home to **Big Foot Rapids,** a splash-fest of white-water river rafting over towering cliffs, cascading waterfalls, and wild rapids. Don't miss the visually stunning show at **Mystery Lodge,** which tells the story of Native Americans in the Pacific Northwest with lights, music, and beautiful images.

INDIAN TRAILS Celebrate Native American traditions through interactive exhibits like tepees and daily dance and storytelling performances.

Knott's Soak City Water Park is directly across from the main park on 13 acres next to Independence Hall. It has a dozen major water rides; the latest is **Pacific Spin,** an oversize waterslide that drops riders 75 feet into a catch pool. There's also a children's pool, 750,000-gallon wave pool, and funhouse. Soak City's season runs mid-May to mid-September. It's open daily after Memorial Day, weekends only after Labor Day, and then closes for the season.

WHERE TO EAT AND STAY

$$ AMERICAN FAMILY

🍴 **Mrs. Knott's Chicken Dinner Restaurant.** Cordelia Knott's fried chicken and boysenberry pies drew crowds so big that Knott's Berry Farm was built to keep the hungry customers occupied while they waited. The restaurant's current incarnation (outside the park's entrance) still serves crispy fried chicken, along with fluffy hand-made biscuits, mashed potatoes, and Mrs. Knott's signature chilled cherry-rhubarb compote. On a busy day the restaurant will cook up 1,200 chickens. The wait, unfortunately, can be an hour or more on weekends and longer on holidays (Mother's Day is crazy busy!). To beat the lines, order from the adjacent takeout counter and enjoy a picnic at the duck pond. Jump-start a visit to the park with a hearty breakfast here. There's three hours of free parking in the lot across from the restaurant. [$] *Average main: $17* ✉ *Knott's Berry Farm Marketplace, 8039 Beach Blvd.* ☎ *714/220–5080.*

$ RESORT FAMILY 🏨 **Knott's Berry Farm Hotel.** Knott's Berry Farm runs this convenient high-rise hotel, which sits on the park grounds surrounded by graceful palm trees. **Pros:** easy access to Knott's Berry Farm; plenty of family activities; basketball court. **Cons:** lobby and hallways can be noisy; public areas show significant wear-and-tear. [$] *Rooms from: $89* ✉ *7675 Crescent Ave.* ☎ *714/995–1111, 866/752–2444* 🌐 *www.knottshotel.com* 🛏 *320 rooms* 🍴 *No meals.*

THE COAST

Running along the Orange County coastline is scenic Pacific Coast Highway (Highway 1, known locally as the PCH). Older beachfront settlements, with their modest bungalow-style homes, are joined by posh gated communities. The pricey land between Newport Beach and Laguna Beach is where Laker Kobe Bryant, novelist Dean Koontz, and a slew of Internet and finance moguls live.

Though the coastline is rapidly being filled in, there are still a few stretches of beautiful, protected open land. And at many places along the way you can catch an idealized glimpse of the Southern California lifestyle: surfers hitting the beach, boards under their arms.

LONG BEACH AND SAN PEDRO

About 25 miles southeast of Los Angeles, via I-110 south.

EXPLORING

FAMILY **Aquarium of the Pacific.** Sea lions, nurse sharks, and penguins, oh my!—this aquarium focuses on creatures of the Pacific Ocean. The main exhibits include large tanks of sharks, stingrays, and ethereal sea dragons, which the aquarium has successfully bred in captivity. The Great Hall features the multimedia attraction *Penguins,* a panoramic film that captures the world of this endangered species. Be sure to say hello to Betty, one of the recent rescues at the engaging sea otter exhibit. For a nonaquatic experience, head to Lorikeet Forest, a walk-in aviary full of the friendliest parrots from Australia. Buy a cup of nectar and smile as you become a human bird perch. If you're a true tropical animal lover, book an up-close-and-personal Animal Encounters Tour ($109) to learn about and assist in the care and feeding of the animals; or find out how the aquarium functions with the extensive Behind the Scenes Tour ($42.95, including admission). Certified divers can book a supervised dive in the aquarium's Tropical Reef Habitat ($299). Twice daily whale-watching trips on the *Harbor Breeze* depart from the dock adjacent to the aquarium; summer sightings of blue whales are an unforgettable thrill. ✉ *100 Aquarium Way, Long Beach* ☎ *562/590–3100* 🌐 *www.aquariumofpacific.org* 🎟 *$28.95* 🕒 *Daily 9–6.*

Cabrillo Marine Aquarium. Dedicated to the marine life that flourishes off the Southern California coast, this Frank Gehry–designed center gives an intimate and instructive look at local sea creatures. Head to the Exploration Center and S. Mark Taper Foundation Courtyard for kid-friendly interactive exhibits and activity stations. Especially fun is the "Crawl In" aquarium, where you can be surrounded by fish without

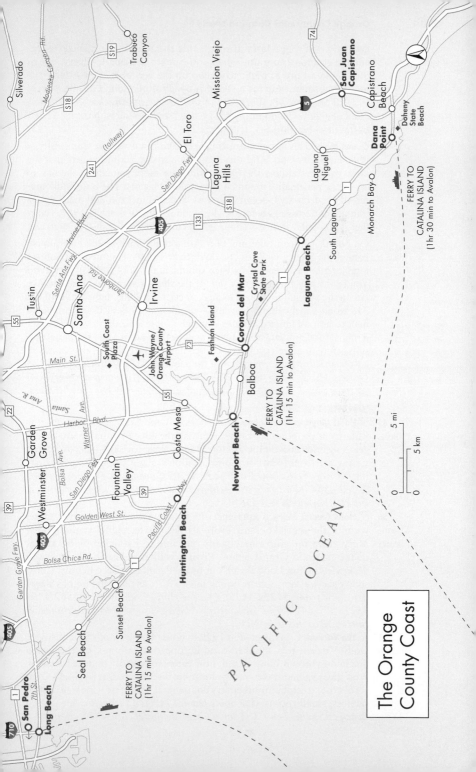

getting wet. From March through July the aquarium organizes a legendary grunion program, when you can see the small, silvery fish as they come ashore at night to spawn on the beach. ■ **TIP→ After visiting the museum, stop for a picnic or beach stroll along Cabrillo Beach.** ✉ *3720 Stephen M. White Dr., San Pedro, Los Angeles* ☎ *310/548–7562* 🌐 *www.cabrilloaq.org* 🎟 *$5 suggested donation, parking $1 per hr* ⏲ *Tues.–Fri. noon–5, weekends 10–5.*

FAMILY **Queen Mary.** This impressive example of 20th-century cruise ship opulence is the last of its kind. And there's a saying among staff members that the more you get to know the *Queen Mary,* the more you realize she has an endearing personality to match her wealth of history. The beautifully preserved art deco–style ocean liner was launched in 1936 and made 1,001 transatlantic crossings before finally berthing in Long Beach in 1967. Today there's a popular Princess Diana exhibit and a daily British-style high tea.

On board, you can take one of a dozen tours, such as the informative Behind the Scenes walk or the downright spooky Haunted Encounters tour. (Spirits have reportedly been spotted in the pool and engine room.) You could stay for dinner at one of the ship's restaurants, listen to live jazz in the original first-class lounge, or even spend the night in one of the 346 wood-panel cabins. The ship's neighbor, a geodesic dome originally built to house Howard Hughes's *Spruce Goose* aircraft, now serves as a terminal for Carnival Cruise Lines, making the *Queen Mary* the perfect pit stop before or after a cruise. Anchored next to the *Queen* is the *Scorpion,* a Russian submarine you can tour for a look at Cold War history. ✉ *1126 Queens Hwy., Long Beach* ☎ *877/342–0742* 🌐 *www.queenmary.com* 🎟 *Tours $28–$75, including a self-guided audio tour* ⏲ *Hrs vary for tours.*

WHERE TO STAY

$$ HOTEL 🏨 **Hotel Maya–a Doubletree Hotel.** Formerly the Coast Long Beach, this waterfront property set on 11 acres, on the edge of a manmade beach, gets a second lease on life as Hotel Maya. **Pros:** low-key vibe; dedicated staff; waterfront location. **Cons:** location is slightly confusing for first-time visitors. [$] *Rooms from: $129* ✉ *700 Queensway Dr., Long Beach* ☎ *562/435–7676* 🌐 *www.hotelmaya.doubletree.com* 🛏 *196 rooms, 1 suite* 🍴 *No meals* ✥ *3:D6.*

$$ HOTEL FAMILY 🏨 **Hotel Queen Mary.** Experience the golden age of transatlantic travel without the seasickness: a 1936–art deco style reigns on the *Queen Mary,* from the ship's mahogany paneling to its nickel-plated doors to the majestic Grand Salon. **Pros:** a walkable historic Promenade deck; views from Long Beach out to the Pacific; art deco details. **Cons:** spotty service; no soundproofing makes for a challenging night's sleep. [$] *Rooms from: $139* ✉ *1126 Queens Hwy., Long Beach* ☎ *562/435–3511, 877/342–0742* 🌐 *www.queenmary.com* 🛏 *346 staterooms, 9 suites* 🍴 *No meals* ✥ *3:D6.*

$ B&B/INN 🏨 **The Varden.** Constructed in 1929 to house Bixby Knolls Sr.'s mistress, Dolly Varden, this small historic European-style hotel, on the metro line in downtown Long Beach, now caters to worldly budget travelers. **Pros:** great value for downtown location; discount passes to Gold's Gym across the street; complimentary continental breakfast. **Cons:** no resort services; small rooms. [$] *Rooms from: $119* ✉ *335 Pacific Ave., Long Beach* ☎ *562/432–8950* 🌐 *www.thevardenhotel.com* 🛏 *35 rooms.*

A mural at Huntington Beach

HUNTINGTON BEACH

40 miles southeast of Los Angeles, I-5 south to I-605 south to I-405 south to Beach Blvd.

Once a sleepy residential town with little more than a string of rugged surf shops, Huntington Beach has transformed itself into a resort destination. The town's appeal is its broad white-sand beaches with often-towering waves, complemented by a lively pier, shops and restaurants on Main Street, and a growing collection of resort hotels.

A draw for sports fans and partiers of all stripes is the U.S. Open professional surf competition, which brings a festive atmosphere to town annually in late July. There's even a Surfing Walk of Fame, with plaques set in the sidewalk around the intersection of PCH and Main Street.

ESSENTIALS

Visit Huntington Beach ⊠ *301 Main St., Suite 212* ☎ *714/969–3492, 800/729–6232* ⊕ *www.surfcityusa.com.*

EXPLORING

Bolsa Chica Ecological Reserve. Wildlife lovers and bird-watchers flock to Bolsa Chica Ecological Reserve, which has a 1,180-acre salt marsh where 321 of Orange County's 420 bird species—including great blue herons, snowy and great egrets, and brown pelicans—have been spotted in the past decade. Throughout the reserve are trails for bird-watching, including a comfortable 1½-mile loop. Free, guided tours depart from the walking bridge on the second Saturday of each month at 10 am. There are two entrances off the Pacific Coast Highway: one close to the Interpretive Center and a second 1 mile south on Warner Avenue, opposite Bolsa Chica State Beach. ⊠ *Bolsa Chica Wetlands Interpretive Center, 3842 Warner Ave.* ☎ *714/846–1114* ⊕ *www.bolsachica.org* 🔄 *Free* ⊙ *Interpretive Center daily 9–4.*

Bolsa Chica State Beach. In the northern section of the city, Bolsa Chica State Beach is usually less crowded than its southern neighbors. The sand is somewhat gritty and not the cleanest, but swells make it a hot surfing spot. Picnic sites and barbecue pits can be reserved in advance. **Amenities:** food and drink; lifeguards; parking; showers; toilets. **Best for:** sunset; surfing; swimming; walking. ⊠ *Pacific Coast Hwy., between Seapoint St. and Warner Ave.* ☎ *714/846–3460* ⊕ *www.parks. ca.gov/?page_id=642* 🔄 *$15 parking.*

Huntington Pier. This pier stretches 1,800 feet out to sea, well past the powerful waves that gave Huntington Beach the title of "Surf City U.S.A." A farmers' market and arts fair is held on Friday afternoons; an informal car show sets up most weekends. ⊠ *Pacific Coast Hwy.* ⊕ *www.huntingtonbeachca.gov.*

NEED A BREAK?

Ruby's. At the end of Huntington Pier sits Ruby's, part of a California chain of 1940s-style burger joints. Try the Cobb, with bacon and slices of avocado. ⊠ *1 Main St.* ☎ *714/969-7829* ⊕ *www.rubys.com.*

Huntington City Beach. Stretching for 3½ miles from Bolsa Chica State Beach to Huntington State Beach, Huntington City Beach is most crowded around the pier; amateur and professional surfers brave the waves daily on its north side. Fire pits, numerous concession stands, an area for dogs, and well-raked white sand make this a popular beach come summertime. **Amenities:** food and drink; lifeguards; parking; showers; toilets. **Best for:** sunset; surfing; swimming; walking. ⊠ *Pacific Coast Hwy., from Beach Blvd. to Seapoint St.* ☎ *714/536–5281* ⊕ *www.ci.huntington-beach.ca.us* 🔄 *Parking $15 weekdays, $17 weekends, $20–$27 holidays.*

Huntington State Beach. This state beach also has 200 fire pits, so it's popular day and night. There are changing rooms, concession stands, lifeguards, Wi-Fi access, and ample parking. A 6-mile bike path connects to the area's other stretches of sand. Picnic areas can be reserved in advance for a $150 fee; otherwise it's first come, first served. On hot days, expect crowds at this broad, soft sandy beach. **Amenities:** food and drink; lifeguards; parking; showers; toilets. **Best for:** sunset; surfing; swimming; walking. ⊠ *Pacific Coast Hwy., from Beach Blvd. south to Santa Ana River* ☎ *714/536–1454* ⊕ *www.parks.ca.gov/?page_id=643* 🔄 *$15 parking.*

International Surfing Museum. Just up Main Street from Huntington Pier, the International Surfing Museum pays tribute to the sport's greats with an impressive collection of surfboards and related memorabilia. They've even got the Bolex camera used to shoot the 1966 surf documentary *Endless Summer.* ⊠ *411 Olive Ave.* ☎ *714/960-3483* ⊕ *www. surfingmuseum.org* 🔄 *$2* ⊙ *Sun. noon–5, Mon. and Wed.–Fri. noon–7, Tues. noon–9, Sat. 11–7.*

WHERE TO EAT

$$$$
SEAFOOD

✕ **Duke's.** Freshly caught seafood reigns supreme at this homage to surfing legend Duke Kahanamoku; it's also a prime people-watching spot right at the beginning of Huntington Pier. Choose from several fish-of-the-day selections—many with Hawaiian flavors—prepared in one of five ways. Or try the crispy coconut shrimp or tuna tacos with Maui onions. Duke's mai tai is not to be missed. $ *Average main: $34* ✉ *317 Pacific Coast Hwy.* ☎ *714/374–6446* ⊕ *www. dukeshuntington.com.*

12

$$ ✕ **Lou's Red Oak BBQ.** You won't find any frills at Lou's Red Oak BBQ—
AMERICAN just barbecue pork, grilled linguica, rotisserie chicken, and a lot of beef. Try the tri-tip (either as an entrée or on a toasted bun smothered with traditional Santa Maria-style salsa) or the smoked turkey plate for a hearty nosh. $ *Average main: $17* ✉ *21501 Brookhurst St.* ☎ *714/965–5200* ⊕ *www.lousbbq.com.*

$ ✕ **Wahoo's Fish Taco.** Proximity to the ocean makes this eatery's
MEXICAN mahimahi-filled tacos taste even better. This healthy fast-food chain—
FAMILY tagged with dozens of surf stickers—brought Baja's fish tacos north of the border to quick success. $ *Average main: $7* ✉ *120 Main St.* ☎ *714/536–2050* ⊕ *www.wahoos.com.*

WHERE TO STAY

$$$$ 🏨 **Shorebreak Hotel.** Across the street from the beach, this boutique
HOTEL hotel attracts a mix of couples, families, and the hipster-surfer crowd. **Pros:** proximity to beach and shops; comfortable beds; quiet rooms despite central location. **Cons:** steep valet parking fee; courtyard rooms have uninspiring alley views. $ *Rooms from: $289* ✉ *500 Pacific Coast Hwy.* ☎ *714/861–4470, 877/744–1117* ⊕ *www.shorebreakhotel.com* 🛏 *157 rooms* ⦿| *No meals.*

SPORTS AND THE OUTDOORS

SURFING

Corky Carroll's Surf School. This surf school organizes lessons, weeklong workshops, and international surf camps at Bolsa Chica State Beach. Private lessons are available year-round. ☎ *714/969–3959* ⊕ *www. surfschool.net.*

Dwight's. You can rent wet suits as well as surf and boogie boards at Dwight's, one block south of Huntington Pier. ✉ *201 Pacific Coast Hwy.* ☎ *714/536–8083.*

SHOPPING

HSS Pierside. The best surf-gear source is HSS Pierside, across from Huntington Pier. It's staffed by true surf enthusiasts. ✉ *300 Pacific Coast Hwy.* ☎ *714/841–4000* ⊕ *www.hsssurf.com.*

NEWPORT BEACH

6 miles south of Huntington Beach via the Pacific Coast Highway.

Newport Beach has evolved from a simple seaside village to an icon of chic coastal living. Its ritzy reputation comes from megayachts bobbing in the harbor, boutiques that rival those in Beverly Hills, and spectacular homes overlooking the ocean.

Newport is said to have the highest per-capita number of Mercedes-Benzes in the world; inland Newport Beach's concentration of high-rise office buildings, shopping centers, and luxury hotels drive the economy. But on the city's Balboa Peninsula, you can still catch a glimpse of a

Riding the waves at Newport Beach

more innocent, down-to-earth beach town scattered with taco spots, tackle shops, and sailor bars.

ESSENTIALS

Visitor and Tour Information Visit Newport Beach ✉ *401 Newport Center Dr.* ☎ *855/569–7678* ⊕ *www.visitnewportbeach.com.*

EXPLORING

Balboa Island. This sliver of terra firma in Newport Harbor boasts quaint streets tightly packed with impossibly charming multimillion-dollar cottages. The island's main drag, Marine Avenue, is lined with equally picturesque cafés and shops.

NEED A BREAK?

Sugar & Spice. Stop by ice cream parlor Sugar & Spice for a Balboa Bar—a slab of vanilla ice cream dipped first in chocolate and then in a topping of your choice such as hard candy or Oreo crumbs. Other parlors serve the concoction, but Sugar & Spice claims to have invented it back in 1945. ✉ *310 Marine Ave., Balboa Island* ☎ *949/673–8907.*

Balboa Peninsula. Newport's best beaches are on Balboa Peninsula, where many jetties pave the way to ideal swimming areas. The most intense bodysurfing place in Orange County and arguably on the West Coast, known as the **Wedge**, is at the south end of the peninsula. It was created by accident in the 1930s when the Federal Works Progress Administration built a jetty to protect Newport Harbor. ■**TIP**→ Rip currents mean it's strictly for the pros—but it sure is fun to watch an experienced local ride it. ⊕ *www.visitnewportbeach.com/vacations/balboa-peninsula.*

FAMILY **ExplorOcean.** This destination has exhibits on the history of the harbor, ocean explorers, and scientific aspects of the Pacific Ocean. There's a fleet of ship models: some date to 1798, and one is made entirely of gold and silver. Another fun feature is a touch tank holding local sea creatures. ✉ *600 E. Bay Ave.* ☎ *949/675–8915* 🌐 *www.explorocean.org* 🎟 *$5* 🕒 *Mon.–Thurs. 11–3:30, Fri. and Sat. 11–6, Sun. 11–5.*

Newport Harbor. Sheltering nearly 10,000 small boats, Newport Harbor may seduce even those who don't own a yacht. Spend an afternoon exploring the charming avenues and surrounding alleys. Several grassy areas on the primarily residential Lido Isle have views of the water. ✉ *Pacific Coast Hwy.*

Newport Pier. Jutting out into the ocean near 20th Street, Newport Pier is a popular fishing spot. Street parking is difficult, so grab the first space you find and be prepared to walk. On weekday mornings, you're likely to encounter dory fishermen hawking their predawn catches, as they've done for generations. On weekends the area is alive with kids of all ages on in-line skates, skateboards, and bikes dodging pedestrians and whizzing past fast-food joints and classic dive bars. ✉ *72 McFadden Pl.*

Orange County Museum of Art. The Orange County Museum of Art gathers a collection of modernist paintings and sculpture by California artists like Richard Diebenkorn, Ed Ruscha, Robert Irwin, and Chris Burden. There are also cutting-edge international works. ✉ *850 San Clemente Dr.* ☎ *949/759–1122* 🌐 *www.ocma.net* 🎟 *$12* 🕒 *Wed. and Fri.–Sun. 11–5, Thurs. 11–8.*

WHERE TO EAT

$$$ AMERICAN 🍴 **3-Thirty-3.** If there's a nightlife "scene" to be had in Newport Beach, this is it. This stylish eatery attracts a convivial crowd—both young and old—for midday, sunset, and late-night dining. A long list of small, shareable plates heightens the camaraderie. Pair a cocktail with charred lollipop lamb chops or chicken satay while you check out the scene, or settle in for a dinner of Kobe flatiron steak or sesame-topped ahi tuna. [$] *Average main: $25* ✉ *333 Bayside Dr.* ☎ *949/673–8464* 🌐 *www.3thirty3nb.com.*

$$$ BRASSERIE 🍴 **Basilic.** This intimate French-Swiss bistro adds a touch of old-world elegance to the island with its white linen and flower-topped tables. Chef Bernard Althaus grows the herbs used in his classic French dishes. Head here for charcuterie, steak au poivre, and a fine Bordeaux. [$] *Average main: $28* ✉ *217 Marine Ave., Balboa Island* ☎ *949/673–0570* 🌐 *www.basilicrestaurant.com* 🕒 *Closed Sun. and Mon. No lunch.*

$ SEAFOOD 🍴 **Bear Flag Fish Co.** Expect long lines in summer at this indoor/outdoor dining spot serving up the freshest local fish (swordfish, sea bass, halibut, and tuna) and a wide range of creative seafood dishes (the Hawaiian-style *poke* salad with ahi tuna is a local favorite). Order at the counter, which doubles as a seafood market, and sit at one of the many shared tables in the dining room or on the small patio. One of the few restaurants in Southern California with its own fishing boat, there's a good chance some line-caught local fish will be on the menu. Oysters are a great choice, and the fish tacos topped with the house-made hot sauce are not to be missed. [$] *Average main: $10* ✉ *407 31st St.* ☎ *949/673–3474* 🌐 *www.bearflagfishco.com.*

$$$$ SEAFOOD 🍴 **The Cannery.** This 1920s cannery building still teems with fish, but now they go into dishes on the eclectic Pacific Rim menu rather than being packed into crates. Settle in at the sushi bar, dining room, or patio before choosing between sashimi, seafood platters, or the upscale surf-and-turf with bone-in rib eye steaks and grilled Maine lobsters. The menu includes a selection of steaks, ribs, and seafood from the world's waters. Many diners arrive by boat, as there's a convenient dock off the front entrance. [$] *Average main: $35* ✉ *3010 Lafayette Rd.* ☎ *949/566–0060* 🌐 *www.cannerynewport.com.*

WHERE TO STAY

$$$$ RESORT 🏨 **Balboa Bay Resort.** Sharing the same frontage as the private Balboa Bay Club that once hosted Humphrey Bogart, Lauren Bacall, and the Reagans, this hotel has one of the best bay views around. **Pros:** exquisite bayfront views; comfortable beds; a raked beach for guests. **Cons:** not much within walking distance; high nightly hospitality fee. [$] *Rooms from: $309* ✉ *1221 W. Coast Hwy.* ☎ *949/645–5000* 🌐 *www.balboabayresort.com* 🛏 *149 rooms, 10 suites* 🍽 *No meals.*

$$$$ HOTEL 🏨 **The Island Hotel.** Across the street from stylish Fashion Island, this 20-story tower caters to business types during the week and luxury seekers weekends. **Pros:** 24-hour exercise facilities; first-class spa; great location. **Cons:** steep valet parking prices; some rooms have views of mall; pricey rates. [$] *Rooms from: $259* ✉ *690 Newport Center Dr.* ☎ *949/759–0808, 866/554–4620* 🌐 *www.theislandhotel.com* 🛏 *295 rooms, 83 suites* 🍽 *No meals.*

SPORTS AND THE OUTDOORS

BOAT RENTALS

Balboa Boat Rentals. You can tour Lido and Balboa isles with kayaks ($15 an hour), sailboats ($45 an hour), small motorboats ($70 an hour), and electric boats ($75 to $95 an hour) at Balboa Boat Rentals. ✉ *510 E. Edgewater Ave.* ☎ *949/673–7200* 🌐 *www.boats4rent.com.*

BOAT TOURS

Catalina Flyer. At Balboa Pavilion, the Catalina Flyer operates a 90-minute daily round-trip passage to Catalina Island for $70. Reservations are required. ✉ *400 Main St.* ☎ *800/830–7744* 🌐 *www.catalinainfo.com.*

Gondola Company of Newport. Try a one-hour Venetian-style gondola cruise with the Gondola Company of Newport. It costs $85 for two and is frequently voted as the best place to take a date in Orange County. ✉ *Lido Marine Village, 3400 Via Oporto* ☎ *949/675–1212* 🌐 *www.gondolas.com.*

Hornblower Cruises & Events. This operator books three-hour weekend dinner cruises with dancing for $82. The two-hour Sunday brunch cruise starts at $63. ✉ *2431 West Coast Hwy.* ☎ *949/631–2469* 🌐 *www.hornblower.com.*

FISHING

Davey's Locker. In addition to a complete tackle shop, Davey's Locker offers half-day sportfishing trips starting at $41.50. ✉ *Balboa Pavilion, 400 Main St.* ☎ *949/673–1434* 🌐 *www.daveyslocker.com.*

A whimbrel hunts for mussels at Crystal Cove State Park.

SHOPPING

Balboa Pavilion. On the bay side of the peninsula, Balboa Pavilion was built in 1905. Today it is home to a restaurant and shops and serves as a departure point for Catalina Island ferries and whale-watching cruises. In the blocks around the pavilion you can find restaurants, shops, and the small Balboa Fun Zone, a local kiddie hangout with a Ferris wheel. On the other side of the narrow peninsula is Balboa Pier. ⊠ *400 Main St.* ☎ *800/830–7744* ⊕ *www.balboapavilion.com.*

Fashion Island. Shake the sand out of your shoes to head inland to the ritzy Fashion Island outdoor mall, a cluster of arcades and courtyards complete with koi pond, fountains, and a family-friendly trolley—plus some awesome ocean views. It has the luxe department stores Neiman Marcus and Bloomingdale's plus expensive spots like Jonathan Adler, Kate Spade, and Michael Stars. ⊠ *401 Newport Center Dr., between Jamboree and MacArthur Blvds., off PCH* ☎ *949/721–2000, 855/658–8527* ⊕ *www.shopfashionisland.com.*

CORONA DEL MAR

2 miles south of Newport Beach, via PCH.

A small jewel on the Pacific Coast, Corona del Mar (known by locals as "CDM") has exceptional beaches that some say resemble their majestic Northern California counterparts. South of CDM is an area referred to as the Newport Coast or Crystal Cove—whatever you call it, it's another dazzling spot on the California Riviera.

EXPLORING

Corona del Mar State Beach. This beach is actually made up of two beaches, Little Corona and Big Corona, separated by a cliff. Both have soft, golden-hue sand. Facilities include fire pits and volleyball courts. Two colorful reefs (and the fact that it's off-limits to boats) make Corona del Mar great for snorkelers and for beachcombers. Parking in the lot is a steep $15 and $25 on holidays, but you can often find a spot on the street on weekdays. **Amenities:** lifeguards; parking; showers; toilets. **Best for:** snorkeling; sunset; swimming. ✉ *3100 Ocean Blvd., Newport Beach* ☎ *949/644–3151* 🌐 *www.parks.ca.gov.*

FAMILY
Fodor's Choice ★

Crystal Cove State Park. Midway between Corona del Mar and Laguna, Crystal Cove State Park is a favorite of local beachgoers and wilderness trekkers. It encompasses a 3.2-mile stretch of unspoiled beach and has some of the best tide pooling in Southern California. Here you can see starfish, crabs, and other sea life on the rocks. The park's 2,400 acres of backcountry are ideal for hiking, horseback riding, and mountain biking, but stay on the trails to preserve the beauty. **Crystal Cove Historic District** holds a collection of 46 handmade historic cottages (16 of which are available for overnight rental), decorated and furnished to reflect the 1935 to 1955 beach culture that flourished here. On the sand above the high tide line and on a bluff above the beach, the cottages offer a funky look at beach life 50 years ago. ✉ *8471 N. Coast Hwy., Laguna Beach* ☎ *949/494–3539* 🌐 *www.crystalcovestatepark.com* 🎟 *$15 parking* 🕒 *Daily 6–dusk.*

NEED A BREAK?

Beachcomber at Crystal Cove Café. Beach culture flourishes in the Crystal Cove Historic District's restaurant, the Beachcomber at Crystal Cove Café. The umbrella-laden deck is just a few steps above the white sand. ✉ *Crystal Cove, 15 Crystal Cove, Newport Coast* ☎ *949/376–6900* 🌐 *www.thebeachcombercafe.com.*

Sherman Library and Gardens. This 2½-acre botanical garden and library specializes in the history of the Pacific Southwest. You can wander among cactus gardens, rose gardens, a wheelchair-height touch-and-smell garden, and a tropical conservatory. There's a good gift shop, too. Café Jardin serves lunch on weekdays and Sunday brunch. ✉ *2647 E. Pacific Coast Hwy.* ☎ *949/673–0033* 🌐 *www.slgardens.org* 🎟 *$3* 🕒 *Daily 10:30–4.*

WHERE TO EAT AND STAY

$ AMERICAN

🍴 **Pacific Whey Cafe.** The ovens rarely get a break here; everything is made from scratch daily. Pick up a BLTA (a BLT with avocado) for a picnic across the street at Crystal Cove State Park. Or stay—at a communal table inside or in the courtyard, which has an ocean view—for organic buckwheat pancakes or grilled salmon with citrus sauce. [$] *Average main: $10* ✉ *Crystal Cove Promenade, 7962 E. Coast Hwy., Newport Coast* ☎ *949/715–2200* 🌐 *www.pacificwhey.com.*

$ MEDITERRANEAN

🍴 **Panini Cafe.** For reasonably priced food and outstanding espresso drinks, this link of a local chain packs a lot of punch for your dining dollars. Think straight-from-the-oven breads, pizzas, and pastas, as well as grilled panini stuffed with roast beef, onions, and provolone cheese. This is a breakfast favorite among locals; at dinner, entrées include Mediterranean classics like moussaka and kebabs. $ *Average main: $10* ✉ *2333 E. Coast Hwy.* ☎ *949/675–8101* ⊕ *www. mypaninicafe.com.*

$$$$
RESORT
FAMILY

🏨 **The Resort at Pelican Hill.** Adjacent to Crystal Cove State Park, this Mediterranean-style resort has spacious bungalow suites, each with Italian limestone fireplaces and marble baths, built into terraced hillsides overlooking the Pacific. **Pros:** paradise for golfers; gracious, attentive staff. **Cons:** sky-high prices; common areas can feel cold. $ *Rooms from: $595* ✉ *22701 Pelican Hill Rd. S, Newport Coast* ☎ *949/612–0332, 888/507–6427* ⊕ *www.pelicanhill.com* ⚲ *204 suites, 128 villas* ❏*No meals.*

SHOPPING

Crystal Cove Promenade. Adding to Orange County's overwhelming supply of high-end shopping and dining is Crystal Cove Promenade, which might be described as the toniest strip mall in America. The storefronts and restaurants of this Mediterranean–inspired center are lined up across the street from Crystal Cove State Park, with the shimmering Pacific waters in plain view. ✉ *7772–8112 E. Coast Hwy., Newport Beach* ⊕ *www.crystalcove.com/beach-living/shopping.*

LAGUNA BEACH

10 miles south of Newport Beach on PCH, 60 miles south of Los Angeles, I-5 south to Hwy. 133, which turns into Laguna Canyon Rd.

Fodor'sChoice
★

Even the approach tells you that Laguna Beach is exceptional. Driving in along Laguna Canyon Road from the Interstate 405 freeway gives you the chance to cruise through a gorgeous coastal canyon, large stretches of which remain undeveloped. You'll arrive at a glistening wedge of ocean.

Laguna's welcome mat is legendary. On the corner of Forest and Park avenues is a gate proclaiming, "This gate hangs well and hinders none, refresh and rest, then travel on." A gay community has long been established here. Art galleries dot the village streets, and there's usually someone daubing up in Heisler Park. Along the Pacific Coast Highway you'll find dozens of clothing boutiques, jewelry shops, and cafés.

ESSENTIALS

Visitor and Tour Information Laguna Beach Visitors Center ✉ *381 Forest Ave.* ☎ *949/497–9229, 800/877–1115* ⊕ *www.lagunabeachinfo.com.*

EXPLORING

1,000 Steps Beach. Off South Coast Highway at 9th Street, 1,000 Steps Beach is a hard-to-find spot tucked away in a neighborhood with great waves and hard-packed, white sand. There aren't really 1,000 steps down (but when you hike back up, it'll certainly feel like it). **Amenities:** parking. **Best for:** sunset; surfing; swimming. ✉ *South Coast Hwy., at 9th St.*

Looking for shells on Laguna Beach, one of the nicest stretches of sand in Southern California

Laguna Art Museum. The Laguna Art Museum displays American art, with an emphasis on California artists from all periods. Special exhibits change quarterly. ⊠ *307 Cliff Dr.* ☏ *949/494–8971* ⊕ *www. lagunaartmuseum.org* ⊠ *$7* ⊙ *Fri.–Tues. 11–5, Thurs. 11–9.*

Laguna Coast Wilderness Park. The Laguna Coast Wilderness Park is spread over 7,000 acres of fragile coastal territory, including the canyon. The 40 miles of trails are great for hiking and mountain biking and are open daily, weather permitting. Docent-led hikes are given regularly. ⊠ *18751 Laguna Canyon Rd.* ☏ *949/923–2235* ⊕ *www.ocparks.com/ parks/lagunac* ⊠ *$3 parking.*

FAMILY **Main Beach Park.** A stocky 1920s lifeguard tower marks Main Beach Park, where a wooden boardwalk separates the sand from a strip of lawn. Walk along this soft-sand beach, or grab a bench and watch people bodysurfing, playing volleyball, or scrambling around two half-basketball courts. The beach also has children's play equipment. Most of Laguna's hotels are within a short (but hilly) walk. **Amenities:** lifeguards; parking; showers; toilets. **Best for:** sunset; swimming; walking. ⊠ *Broadway at S. Coast Hwy.*

Wood's Cove. Off South Coast Highway, Wood's Cove is especially quiet during the week. Big rock formations hide lurking crabs. This is a prime scuba diving spot, and at high tide much of the beach is underwater. Climbing the steps to leave, you can see a Tudor-style mansion that was once home to Bette Davis. Street parking is limited. **Amenities:** none. **Best for:** snorkeling; scuba diving; sunset. ⊠ *Diamond St. and Ocean Way.*

12

WHERE TO EAT

$$$ INTERNATIONAL 🍴 **Sapphire Laguna.** This Laguna Beach establishment is part gourmet pantry (a must-stop for your every picnic need) and part global dining adventure. Iranian-born chef Azmin Ghahreman takes you on a journey through Europe and Asia with dishes ranging from a Korean monkfish hot pot to Spanish-style seafood paella. Nearly a dozen beers from around the world and a fittingly eclectic wine list round out the experience. The dining room is intimate and earthy but infused with local style. Brunch is a favorite with locals, as well—enjoy it on the patio in good weather. [$] *Average main: $27* ✉ *The Old Pottery Place, 1200 S. Coast Hwy.* ☎ *949/715–9888* 🌐 *www.sapphirellc.com.*

$$$$ MODERN AMERICAN Fodor's Choice ★ 🍴 **Studio.** In a nod to Laguna's art history, Studio has house-made specialties that entice the eye as well as the palate. You can't beat the location, atop a 50-foot bluff overlooking the Pacific Ocean. And because the restaurant occupies its own Craftsman-style bungalow, it doesn't feel like a hotel dining room. Under the deft direction of executive chef Craig Strong, the menu changes seasonally and features the finest seafood and the freshest locally grown produce (some herbs come from a small garden just outside the kitchen). You might begin with paper-thin charred shrimp carpaccio or black pepper seared hamachi before moving on to a perfectly cooked King salmon in subtle cardamom sauce or lamb chops on a bed of pomegranate quinoa. The wine list here is bursting with nearly 2,500 labels. Service is crisp and attentive. [$] *Average main: $55* ✉ *Montage Laguna Beach, 30801 S. Coast Hwy.* ☎ *949/715–6420* 🌐 *www.studiolagunabeach.com* ✍ *Reservations essential* ⏲ *Closed Mon. No lunch.*

$ VEGETARIAN 🍴 **Zinc Café & Market.** Families flock to this small Laguna Beach institution for reasonably priced breakfast and lunch options. Try the signature quiches or poached egg dishes in the morning, or swing by later in the day for healthy salads, house-made soups, quesadillas, or pizzettes. The café also has great artisanal cheeses and gourmet goodies you can take with you or savor on the outdoor patio. All the sweets are house-made, including the mega-size brownies. [$] *Average main: $12* ✉ *350 Ocean Ave.* ☎ *949/494–6302* 🌐 *www.zinccafe.com* ⏲ *No dinner Nov.–Apr.*

WHERE TO STAY

$$$ HOTEL 🏨 **La Casa del Camino.** This historic Spanish-style hotel opened in 1929 and was once a favorite of Hollywood stars. **Pros:** breathtaking views from rooftop lounge; personable service; close to beach. **Cons:** some rooms face the highway; frequent events can make hotel noisy; some rooms are very small. [$] *Rooms from: $229* ✉ *1289 S. Coast Hwy.* ☎ *949/497–2446, 888/367–5232* 🌐 *www.lacasadelcamino.com* 🛏 *26 rooms, 10 suites* 🍽 *No meals.*

$$$$ RESORT FAMILY Fodor's Choice ★ 🏨 **Montage Laguna Beach.** Laguna's connection to the Californian plein air artists is mined for inspiration at this head-turning, lavish hotel. **Pros:** top-notch, enthusiastic service; idyllic coastal location; special programs cover everything from art to marine biology. **Cons:** multinight stays required on weekends and holiday; expensive valet parking. [$] *Rooms from: $595* ✉ *30801 S. Coast Hwy.* ☎ *949/715–6000, 866/271–6953* 🌐 *www.montagelagunabeach.com* 🛏 *188 rooms, 60 suites* 🍽 *No meals.*

SPORTS AND THE OUTDOORS

WATER SPORTS

Hobie Sports. In summer, rent bodyboards at Hobie Sports. ✉ *294 Forest Ave.* ☎ *949/497–3304* 🌐 *www.hobiesurfshop.com.*

SHOPPING

Coast Highway, Forest and Ocean avenues, and Glenneyre Street are full of art galleries, fine jewelry stores, and clothing boutiques.

Candy Baron. Get your sugar fix at the time-warped Candy Baron, filled with old-fashioned goodies like gumdrops, bull's-eyes, and more than a dozen barrels of saltwater taffy. ✉ *231 Forest Ave.* ☎ *949/497–7508* 🌐 *www.thecandybaron.com.*

DANA POINT

10 miles south of Laguna Beach, via the Pacific Coast Highway.

Dana Point's claim to fame is its small-boat marina tucked into a dramatic natural harbor and surrounded by high bluffs. The early-March Dana Point Festival of the Whales celebrates the passing gray whale migration with two weekends full of activities.

EXPLORING

Dana Point Harbor. Dana Point Harbor was first described more than 100 years ago by its namesake, Richard Henry Dana, in his book *Two Years Before the Mast.* At the marina are docks for private boats and yachts, shops, restaurants, and boat, kayak, stand-up paddleboard, and bike rentals. ✉ *Dana Point Harbor Dr.* ☎ *949/923–2255* 🌐 *www.danapointharbor.com.*

Doheny State Beach. At the south end of Dana Point, Doheny State Beach is one of Southern California's top surfing destinations, but there's a lot more to do within this 61-acre area. There are five indoor tanks and an interpretive center devoted to the wildlife of the Doheny Marine Refuge, as well as food stands, picnic facilities, and volleyball courts. Divers and anglers hang out at the beach's western end, and during low tide, the tide pools beckon both young and old. The water quality ocassionally falls below state standards—signs are posted if that's the case. **Amenities:** food and drink; lifeguards; parking; showers; toilets. **Best for:** partiers; sunset; surfing; swimming; walking. ✉ *25300 Dana Point Harbor Dr.* ☎ *949/496–6172* 🌐 *www.dohenystatebeach.org* 🎫 *$15 parking.*

WHERE TO EAT

$$$ FRENCH 🍴 **Gemmell's.** Accomplished chef Byron Gemmell's moderately priced bistro is a welcome change from the fish houses that dominate this town, particularly around the harbor. In a laid-back but romantic setting, you can begin with escargots or French onion soup before moving on to rack of lamb with thyme demi-glace or roasted duck in a seductive rum-banana liquor reduction. Finish with a soufflé—either classic chocolate or Grand Marnier. The wine list includes some reasonably priced Bordeaux. The food is rich, but a meal here won't break the bank. [$] *Average main: $25* ✉ *34471 Golden Lantern St., Dana Point* ☎ *949/234–0063* 🌐 *www.gemmellsrestaurant.com.*

$$$ AMERICAN 🍴 **Wind & Sea.** Unobstructed marina views make this a particularly appealing place for lunch or a sunset dinner. On warm days, patio tables beckon you outside, and looking out on the Pacific might put you in the mood for a retro cocktail like a mai tai. Among the entrées, the macadamia-crusted mahimahi and the grilled teriyaki shrimp stand out. The Sunday breakfast buffet is good value at $15 per person. [$] *Average main: $25* ✉ *Dana Point Harbor, 34699 Golden Lantern St.* ☎ *949/496–6500* 🌐 *www.windandsearestaurants.com.*

WHERE TO STAY

$$$ B&B/INN 🏨 **Blue Lantern Inn.** Combining New England–style architecture with a Southern California setting, this white-clapboard B&B rests on a bluff overlooking the harbor and ocean. **Pros:** bikes to borrow; one room welcomes pets; free Wi-Fi and parking. **Cons:** nearby restaurant can be noisy. [$] *Rooms from: $235* ✉ *34343 St. of the Blue Lantern* ☎ *949/661–1304, 800/950–1236* 🌐 *www.bluelanterninn.com* 🛏 *29 rooms* 🍴 *Breakfast.*

$$$$ RESORT FAMILY Fodor's Choice ★ 🏨 **Ritz-Carlton, Laguna Niguel.** Combine the Ritz-Carlton's top-tier level of service with an unparalleled view of the Pacific and you're in the lap of luxury at this resort. **Pros:** beautiful grounds and views; luxurious bedding; seamless service. **Cons:** some rooms are small for the price; culinary program has room to grow. [$] *Rooms from: $475* ✉ *1 Ritz-Carlton Dr.* ☎ *949/240–2000, 800/542–8680* 🌐 *www.ritzcarlton.com* 🛏 *367 rooms, 29 suites* 🍴 *No meals.*

$$$$ RESORT 🏨 **St. Regis Monarch Beach Resort and Spa.** Grand and sprawling, the St. Regis can satisfy your every whim with its 172 acres of grounds, private beach club, 18-hole Robert Trent Jones Jr.– designed golf course, three swimming pools, and tennis courts. **Pros:** immaculate rooms; big bathrooms with deep tubs; beautiful spa. **Cons:** hotel layout is somewhat confusing; high resort fee. [$] *Rooms from: $495* ✉ *1 Monarch Beach Resort, off Niguel Rd.* ☎ *949/234–3200, 800/722–1543* 🌐 *www.stregismb.com* 🛏 *325 rooms, 75 suites.*

SPORTS AND THE OUTDOORS

Capt. Dave's Dolphin & Whale Watching Safari. You have a good chance of getting a water's-eye view of resident dolphins and migrating whales if you take one of these tours on three deluxe catamarans. Dave Anderson, a marine naturalist and filmmaker, and his wife run the safaris year-round. The endangered blue whale is sometimes spotted in summer. Reservations are required for the safaris, which last 2½ hours and cost $65. ✉ *24440 Dana Point Harbor Dr.* ☎ *949/488–2828* 🌐 *www.dolphinsafari.com.*

SAN JUAN CAPISTRANO

5 miles north of Dana Point, Hwy. 74, 60 miles north of San Diego, I-5.

San Juan Capistrano is best known for its historic mission, where the swallows traditionally return each year, migrating from their winter haven in Argentina, but these days they are more likely to choose other local sites for nesting. St. Joseph's Day, March 19, launches a week of fowl festivities. Charming antiques stores, which range from pricey to cheap, line Camino Capistrano.

Mission San Juan Capistrano

GETTING HERE AND AROUND

If you arrive by train, which is far more romantic and restful than battling freeway traffic, you'll be dropped off across from the mission at the San Juan Capistrano depot. With its appealing brick café and preserved Santa Fe cars, the depot retains much of the magic of early American railroads. If driving, park near Ortega and Camino Capistrano, the city's main streets.

EXPLORING

FAMILY

Fodor's Choice

★

Mission San Juan Capistrano. Founded in 1776 by Father Junípero Serra, Mission San Juan Capistrano was one of two Roman Catholic outposts between Los Angeles and San Diego. The Great Stone Church, begun in 1797, is the largest structure created by the Spanish in California. Many of the mission's adobe buildings have been preserved to illustrate mission life, with exhibits of an olive millstone, tallow ovens, tanning vats, metalworking furnaces, and the padres' living quarters. The gardens, with their fountains, are a lovely spot in which to wander. The bougainvillea-covered Serra Chapel is believed to be the oldest church still standing in California and is the only building remaining in which Fr. Serra actually led Mass. Mass takes place weekdays at 7 am in the chapel. Enter via a small gift shop in the gatehouse. ⊠ *Camino Capistrano and Ortega Hwy.* ☎ *949/234–1300* ⊕ *www.missionsjc.com* ⊠ *$9* ⊘ *Daily 9–5.*

WHERE TO EAT

$$

AMERICAN

✕ **The Ramos House Cafe.** It may be worth hopping the Amtrak to San Juan Capistrano just for the chance to have breakfast or lunch at one of Orange County's most beloved restaurants. Here's your chance to visit one of Los Rios Historic District's board-and-batten homes dating back to 1881. This café sits practically on the railroad tracks across from the depot—nab a table on the patio and dig into a hearty breakfast, such as the smoked bacon scramble. The weekend brunch includes champagne, memorable mac-and-cheese with wild mushrooms, and huckleberry coffee cake. Every item on the menu illustrates chef-owner John Q. Humphreys' creative hand. $ *Average main: $18* ⊠ *31752 Los Rios St.* ☏ *949/443–1342* ⊕ *www.ramoshouse.com* ⊗ *Closed Mon. No dinner.*

NIGHTLIFE
Swallow's Inn. Across the way from Mission San Juan Capistrano you'll spot a line of Harleys in front of the Swallow's Inn. Despite a somewhat tough look, it attracts all kinds—bikers, surfers, modern-day cowboys, grandparents—for a drink, a casual bite, and some rowdy live music. ⊠ *31786 Camino Capistrano* ☏ *949/493–3188* ⊕ *www.swallowsinn.com.*

CATALINA ISLAND

Fodor's Choice ★ Just 22 miles out from the L.A. coastline, across from Newport Beach and Long Beach, Catalina has virtually unspoiled mountains, canyons, coves, and beaches; best of all, it gives you a glimpse of what undeveloped Southern California once looked like.

Water sports are a big draw, as divers and snorkelers come for the exceptionally clear water surrounding the island. Kayakers are attracted to the calm cove waters and thrill seekers have made the eco-themed zip line so popular, there are nighttime tours via flashlight in summer. The main town, Avalon, is a charming, old-fashioned beach community, where yachts and pleasure boats bob in the crescent bay. Wander beyond the main drag and find brightly painted little bungalows fronting the sidewalks; golf carts are the preferred mode of transport.

In 1919, William Wrigley Jr., the chewing-gum magnate, purchased a controlling interest in the company developing Catalina Island, whose most famous landmark, the Casino, was built in 1929 under his orders. Because he owned the Chicago Cubs baseball team, Wrigley made Catalina the team's spring training site, an arrangement that lasted until 1951.

In 1975, the Catalina Island Conservancy, a nonprofit foundation, acquired about 88% of the island to help preserve the area's natural flora and fauna, including the bald eagle and the Catalina Island fox. These days the conservancy is restoring the rugged interior country with plantings of native grasses and trees. Along the coast you might spot oddities like electric perch, saltwater goldfish, and flying fish.

GETTING HERE AND AROUND
FERRY TRAVEL Two companies offer ferry service to Catalina Island. The boats have both indoor and outdoor seating and snack bars. Excessive baggage is not allowed, and there are extra fees for bicycles and surfboards. The waters around Santa Catalina can get rough, so if you're prone to seasickness, come prepared. Winter, holiday, and weekend schedules vary, so reservations are recommended.

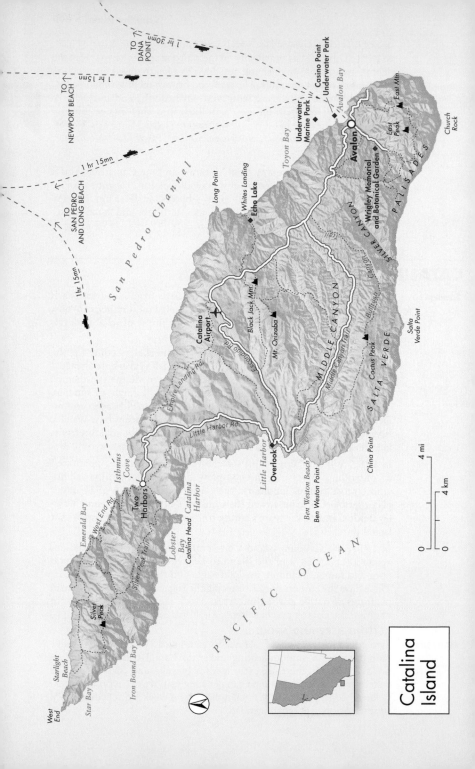

Catalina Island

12

Catalina Express makes an hour-long run from Long Beach or San Pedro to Avalon and a 90-minute run from Dana Point to Avalon with some stops at Two Harbors. Round-trip fares begin at $74.50, with discounts for seniors and kids. On busy days, a $15 upgrade to the Commodore Lounge, when available, is worth it. Service from Newport Beach to Avalon is available through the Catalina Flyer. Boats leave from Balboa Pavilion at 9 am (in season), take 75 minutes to reach the island, and cost $70 round-trip. Return boats leave Catalina at 4:30 pm. Reservations are required for the Catalina Flyer and recommended for all weekend and summer trips. ■TIP➔ Keep an eye out for dolphins, which sometimes swim alongside the ferries.

GOLF CARTS Golf carts constitute the island's main form of transportation for sightseeing in the area, however some parts of town are off limits as is the island's interior. You can rent them along Avalon's Crescent Avenue and Pebbly Beach Road for about $40 per hour with a $40 deposit, payable via cash or traveler's check only.

HELICOPTER TRAVEL Island Express helicopters depart hourly from San Pedro, Santa Ana, and Long Beach next to the Queen Mary (8 am–dusk). The trip from Long Beach takes about 15 minutes and costs $125 one-way, $250 round-trip (plus tax). Reservations a week in advance are recommended (☎ 800/228–2566).

TIMING

Although Catalina can be seen in one very hectic day, several inviting hotels make it worth extending your stay for one or more nights. A short itinerary might include breakfast on the pier, a tour of the interior, a snorkeling excursion at Casino Point, or beach day at the Descanso Beach Club and a romantic waterfront dinner in Avalon.

After late October, rooms are much easier to find on short notice, rates drop dramatically, and many hotels offer packages that include transportation from the mainland and/or sightseeing tours. January to March you have a good chance of spotting migrating gray whales on the ferry crossing.

TOURS

Santa Catalina Island Company runs 16 Discovery Tours, including the *Flying Fish* boat trip (summer evenings only); a comprehensive inland motor tour; a tour of Skyline Drive; several Casino tours; a scenic tour of Avalon; a glass-bottom-boat tour; an undersea tour on a semi-submersible vessel; an eco-themed zip line tour that traverses a scenic canyon; a speedy Dolphin Quest that searches for all manner of sea creatures. Reservations are highly recommended for the inland tours. Tours cost $10 to $178. There are ticket booths on the Green Pleasure Pier, at the Casino, in the plaza, and at the boat landing. Catalina Adventure Tours, which has booths at the boat landing and on the pier, arranges similar excursions at comparable prices.

The Catalina Island Conservancy organizes custom ecotours and hikes of the interior. Naturalist guides drive open Jeeps through some gorgeously untrammeled parts of the island. Tours start at $70 per person for a two-hour trip (two-person minimum); you can also book half- and full-day tours. The tours run year-round.

ESSENTIALS

Ferry Contacts Catalina Express ☎ *800/481–3470* ⊕ *www.catalinaexpress. com.* **Catalina Flyer** ☎ *949/673–5245, 800/830–7744* ⊕ *www.catalinainfo.com.*

Golf Cart Rentals Island Rentals ⊠ *125 Pebbly Beach Rd., Avalon* ☎ *310/510–1456* ⊕ *www.catalinagolfcartrentals.com.*

Helicopter Contacts Island Express ☎ *800/228–2566* ⊕ *www.islandexpress.com.*

Visitor and Tour Information Catalina Adventure Tours ☎ *877/510–2888* ⊕ *www.catalinaadventuretours.com.* **Catalina Island Chamber of Commerce & Visitors Bureau** ⊠ *#1 Green Pleasure Pier, Avalon* ☎ *310/510–1520* ⊕ *www.catalinachamber.com.* **Santa Catalina Island Company** ☎ *877/778– 8322* ⊕ *www.visitcatalinaisland.com.* **Catalina Island Conservancy** ⊠ *125 Claressa Ave., Avalon* ☎ *310/510–2595* ⊕ *www.catalinaconservancy.org.*

AVALON

A 1- to 2-hour ferry ride from Long Beach, Newport Beach, or San Pedro; a 15-minute helicopter ride from Long Beach or San Pedro, slightly longer from Santa Ana.

Avalon, Catalina's only real town, extends from the shore of its natural harbor to the surrounding hillsides. Its resident population is about 3,800, but it swells with tourists on summer weekends. Most of the city's activity, however, is centered on the pedestrian mall on Crescent Avenue, and most sights are easily reached on foot. Private cars are restricted and rental cars aren't allowed, but taxis, trams, and shuttles can take you anywhere you need to go. Bicycles, electric bikes, and golf carts can be rented from shops along Crescent Avenue.

EXPLORING

Fodor's Choice
★

Casino. This circular white structure is one of the finest examples of art deco architecture anywhere. Its Spanish-inspired floors and murals gleam with brilliant blue and green Catalina tiles. In this case, *casino,* the Italian word for "gathering place," has nothing to do with gambling. To the right of the theater's grand entrance is the quaint Catalina Island Museum, which examines and chronicles 7,000 years of island history. First-run movies are screened nightly at the Avalon Theatre, noteworthy for its classic 1929 theater pipe organ and art deco wall murals.

The Santa Catalina Island Company leads two tours of the Casino—the 30-minute basic tour ($10) and the 90-minute behind-the-scenes tour ($25), which leads visitors through the green room and into the Wrigleys' private lounge. ⊠ *1 Casino Way* ☎ *310/510–2414 museum, 310/510– 0179 theater* ⊕ *www.catalinamuseum.org* ⌨ *Museum $5* ☺ *Daily 10–5.*

Casino Point Dive Park. In front of the Casino are the crystal clear waters of the Casino Point Dive Park, a protected marine preserve where moray eels, bat rays, spiny lobsters, harbor seals, and other sea creatures cruise around kelp forests and along the sandy bottom. It's a terrific site for scuba diving, with some shallow areas suitable for snorkeling. Equipment can be rented on and near the pier. The shallow waters of Lover's Cove, east of the boat landing, are also good for snorkeling.

Green Pleasure Pier. Head to the Green Pleasure Pier for a good vantage point of Avalon. On the pier you can find the visitor information, snack stands, and scads of squawking seagulls. It's also the landing where visiting cruise ship passengers catch tenders back out to their ship. ✉ *End of Catalina Ave.*

Wrigley Memorial and Botanic Garden. Two miles south of the bay is Wrigley Memorial and Botanic Garden, home to plants native to Southern California. Several grow only on Catalina Island—Catalina ironwood, wild tomato, and rare Catalina mahogany. The Wrigley family commissioned the garden as well as the monument, which has a grand staircase and a Spanish-style mausoleum inlaid with colorful Catalina tile. The mausoleum was never used by the Wrigleys, who are buried in Pasadena. ✉ *Avalon Canyon Rd.* ☎ *310/510–2897* 🌐 *www.catalinaconservancy.org* 🎟 *$7* 🕒 *Daily 8–5.*

WHERE TO EAT

$$$ SEAFOOD 🍴 **Bluewater Avalon.** Overlooking the ferry landing and the entire harbor, the open-to-the-salt-air Bluewater Avalon offers freshly caught fish, savory chowders, and all manner of shellfish. If they're on the menu, don't miss the swordfish steak or the sandabs. Opened in 2013, the dining room has an understated nautical vibe. Fishing rods serve as room dividers, and plank floors lend a casual feel inside and out. Vintage black-and-white photos aknowledge the island's famed sports fishing legacy. The wraparound patio is the preferred spot to dine, but beware of aggressive seagulls that may try to snatch your food. Happy hour attracts a crowd for the craft beers, potent cocktails, and tasty bites like popcorn shrimp and oyster shooters. [$] *Average main: $25* ✉ *306 Crescent Ave.* ☎ *310/510–3474* 🌐 *www.bluewateravalon.com.*

$ AMERICAN FAMILY 🍴 **Descanso Beach Club.** Set on an expansive deck overlooking the water, Descanso Beach Club serves a wide range of favorites: peel-and-eat shrimp, hamburgers, salads, nachos, and wraps are all part of the selection. Watch the harbor seals frolic just offshore while sipping the island's super-sweet signature cocktail, the Buffalo Milk, a mix of fruit liqueurs, vodka, and whipped cream. Fire pits and colorful beach cabanas add to the scene, as does the sound of happy and terrified screams from the zip-liners in the canyon above the beach. [$] *Average main: $15* ✉ *Descanso Beach, 1 Descanso Ave.* ☎ *310/510-7410.*

$$$ SEAFOOD 🍴 **The Lobster Trap.** Seafood rules at the Lobster Trap—the restaurant's owner has his own boat and fishes for the catch of the day and, in season, spiny lobster. Ceviche is a great starter, always fresh and brightly flavored. Locals (you'll see many at the small counter) come for the relaxed atmosphere, large portions, draft beer, and live music on weekend nights. [$] *Average main: $24* ✉ *128 Catalina St.* ☎ *310/510–8585* 🌐 *catalinalobstertrap.com.*

WHERE TO STAY

$$$ HOTEL 🏨 **Aurora Hotel & Spa.** In a town dominated by historic properties, the Aurora is refreshingly contemporary, with a hip attitude and sleek furnishings. **Pros:** trendy design; quiet location off main drag; close to restaurants. **Cons:** standard rooms are small, even by Catalina

standards; no elevator. [$] *Rooms from: $219* ✉ *137 Marilla Ave., Avalon* ☎ *310/510–0454, 800/422–6836* 🌐 *www.auroracatalina.com* 🛏 *15 rooms, 3 suites* 🍴 *Breakfast.*

$$$ HOTEL 🏨 **Hotel Villa Portofino.** Steps from the Green Pleasure Pier, this European-style hotel creates an intimate feel with brick courtyards and walkways and suites named after Italian cities. **Pros:** romantic; close to beach; incredible sundeck. **Cons:** ground floor rooms can be noisy; some rooms are on small side; no elevator. [$] *Rooms from: $235* ✉ *111 Crescent Ave.* ☎ *310/510–0555, 888/510–0555* 🌐 *www.hotelvillaportofino.com* 🛏 *35 rooms* 🍴 *Breakfast.*

$$$ HOTEL 🏨 **Hotel Vista del Mar.** On the bay-facing Crescent Avenue, this third-floor property is steps from the beach, where complimentary towels, chairs, and umbrellas await guests. **Pros:** comfortable beds; central location; modern decor. **Cons:** no restaurant or spa facilities; few rooms with ocean views; no elevator. [$] *Rooms from: $250* ✉ *417 Crescent Ave.* ☎ *310/510–1452, 800/601–3836* 🌐 *www.hotel-vistadelmar.com* 🛏 *12 rooms, 2 suites* 🍴 *Breakfast.*

SPORTS AND THE OUTDOORS

BICYCLING

Brown's Bikes. Look for rentals on Crescent Avenue and Pebbly Beach Road, where Brown's Bikes is located. Beach cruisers and mountain bikes start at $20 per day. Electric bikes are also on offer. ✉ *107 Pebbly Beach Rd.* ☎ *310/510–0986* 🌐 *www.catalinabiking.com.*

DIVING AND SNORKELING

The Casino Point Underwater Park, with its handful of wrecks, is best suited for diving. Lover's Cove is better for snorkeling (but you'll share the area with glass-bottom boats). Both are protected marine preserves.

Catalina Divers Supply. Head to Catalina Divers Supply to rent equipment, sign up for guided scuba and snorkel tours, and attend certification classes. It also has an outpost at the Dive Park at Casino Point. ✉ *No. 7 Green Pleasure Pier* ☎ *310/510–0330* 🌐 *www.catalinadiverssupply.com.*

TRAVEL SMART
LOS ANGELES

GETTING HERE AND AROUND

The Los Angeles metro area has more than 12 million residents, so be prepared to rent a car and fight for space on the freeway (especially at rush hour) to make your way along the array of destinations that span from the carefree beaches of the coastline to the glitz and glamour of Beverly Hills shops, the nightlife of Hollywood, and the film studio action of the Valley. It's worth it. Nowhere else in the country can you spot celebrities over breakfast, sunbathe on the beach in the afternoon, and head out to the slopes for skiing within hours.

■ AIR TRAVEL

Nonstop flights from New York to Los Angeles take about six hours; with the three-hour time change, you can leave JFK by 8 am and be in L.A. by 11 am. Some flights may require a midway stop, making the total excursion between 7½ and 8½ hours. Flight times are 3 hours from Dallas, 4 hours from Chicago, and 11½ hours from London.

AIRPORTS

The sixth-largest airport in the world in terms of passenger traffic, Los Angeles International Airport (LAX) is served by more than 60 major airlines. Because of heavy traffic around the airport (not to mention the city's extended rush hours), you should allow yourself plenty of extra time. All departures are from the upper level, while arrivals are on the lower level.

Several secondary airports serve the city. Bob Hope Airport in Burbank is close to Downtown L.A., so it's definitely worth checking out. Long Beach Airport is equally convenient. Flights to Orange County's John Wayne Airport are often more expensive than those to the other secondary airports. Also check out Long Beach Airport and LA/Ontario International Airport.

Driving times from LAX to different parts of the city vary considerably: it will take you 20 minutes to get to Santa Monica, 30 minutes to Beverly Hills, and at least 45 minutes to get to Downtown L.A. In heavy traffic it can take much longer. From Bob Hope Airport, it's 30 minutes to Downtown. Plan on at least 45 minutes for the drive to Long Beach Airport, and an hour from John Wayne Airport or LA/Ontario International Airport.

Airport Information Bob Hope Airport (*BUR*). ⌧ *2627 N. Hollywood Way, Burbank* ☎ *818/840–8840* ⊕ *www.burbankairport.com.* **John Wayne Airport** (*SNA*). ⌧ *18601 Airport Way, Santa Ana* ☎ *949/252–5200* ⊕ *www. ocair.com.* **Long Beach Airport** (*LGB*). ⌧ *4100 Donald Douglas Dr., Long Beach* ☎ *562/570– 2600* ⊕ *www.lgb.org.* **Los Angeles International Airport** (*LAX*). ⌧ *1 World Way* ☎ *310/646–5252* ⊕ *www.lawa.org.* **LA/Ontario International Airport** (*ONT*). ⌧ *E. Airport Dr., Ontario* ☎ *909/937–2700* ⊕ *www.lawa.org/welcomeont.aspx.*

GROUND TRANSPORTATION

If you're not renting a car, a taxi is the most convenient way to get to and from the airport. The rates between Downtown and LAX start at $46.50, but can increase significantly if there's a backup on the freeway. Getting Downtown from Bob Hope Airport costs $40 to $50. Taxis to and from LA/Ontario International Airport run on a meter and cost $60 and $70, depending on traffic. From Long Beach Airport, trips to Downtown L.A. are metered and cost roughly $65.

For two or three passengers, shuttles can be an economical option at $16 to $22. These big vans typically circle the airport, departing when they're full. Your travel time depends on how many other travelers are dropped off before you. At LAX, SuperShuttle allows walk-on shuttle passengers without prior reservations; if you're headed to the airport, call at least 24 hours in advance.

Operated by Los Angeles World Airports, FlyAway buses travel between LAX and Van Nuys, Westwood, La Brea, and Union Station in Downtown L.A. The cost is $7 to $10, and is payable only by credit or debit card. With departure at least every hour, buses run 24 hours a day.

Airport Transportation FlyAway
☎ 866/435–9529 ⊕ www.lawa.org.
SuperShuttle ☎ 323/775–6600, 800/258–3826 ⊕ www.supershuttle.com.

FLIGHTS
Delta, United, Southwest, and American have the most nonstop flights to Los Angeles International Airport. Jet-Blue and Southwest also have numerous daily flights to airports in and around Los Angeles.

▌BUS TRAVEL

Inadequate public transportation has plagued L.A. for decades. That said, many local trips can be made, with time and patience, by buses run by the Los Angeles County Metropolitan Transit Authority. In certain cases—visiting the Getty Center, for instance, or Universal Studios—buses may be your best option. There's a special Dodger Stadium Express that shuttles passengers between Union Station and the world-famous ballpark for home games. It's free if you have a ticket in hand, and saves you parking-related stress.

Metro Buses cost $1.50, plus 35¢ for each transfer to another bus or to the subway. A one-day pass costs $5, and a weekly pass is $20 for unlimited travel on all buses and trains. Passes are valid from Sunday through Saturday. For the fastest service, look for the red-and-white Metro Rapid buses; these stop less frequently and are able to extend green lights. There are 25 Metro Rapid routes, including along Wilshire and Vermont boulevards.

Other bus services make it possible to explore the entire metropolitan area. DASH minibuses cover six different circular routes in Hollywood, Mid-Wilshire, and Downtown. You pay 50¢ every time you get on. The Santa Monica Municipal Bus Line, also known as the Big Blue Bus, is a pleasant and inexpensive way to move around the Westside. Trips cost $1, and transfers are free. An express bus to and from Downtown L.A., run by Culver CityBus, costs $1.

You can pay your fare in cash on MTA, Santa Monica, and Culver City buses, but you must have exact change. You can buy MTA passes at customer centers throughout the city, as well as at some convenience and grocery stores.

Bus Information Culver CityBus
☎ 310/253–6510 ⊕ www.culvercity.org.
DASH ☎ 310/808–2273 ⊕ www.ladottransit. com/dash. **Los Angeles County Metropolitan Transit Authority** ☎ 323/466–3876 ⊕ www. metro.net. **Santa Monica Municipal Bus Line** ☎ 310/451–5444 ⊕ www.bigbluebus.com.

▌CAR TRAVEL

If you're used to urban driving, you shouldn't have too much trouble navigating the streets of Los Angeles. If not, L.A. can be unnerving. However, the city has evolved with drivers in mind. Streets are wide and parking garages abound, so it's more car-friendly than many older big cities.

If you get discombobulated while on the freeway, remember this rule of thumb: even-numbered freeways run east and west, odd-numbered freeways run north and south.

GASOLINE
As of this writing, gasoline costs around $3.50 a gallon. Most stations are self-service; the few remaining full-service stations are mostly in and around the Westside. There are plenty of stations everywhere. Most stay open late, and many are open 24 hours.

GETTING AROUND

There are plenty of identical or similarly named streets in L.A. (Beverly Boulevard and Beverly Drive, for example), so be as specific as you can when asking directions. Expect sudden changes in addresses as streets pass through neighborhoods, then incorporated cities, then back into neighborhoods. This can be most bewildering on Robertson Boulevard, an otherwise useful north–south artery that, by crossing through L.A., West Hollywood, and Beverly Hills, dips in and out of several such numbering shifts in a matter of miles.

PARKING

Parking rules are strictly enforced in Los Angeles, so make sure you check for signs and read them carefully. Illegally parked cars are ticketed or towed quickly. Parking prices vary from 25¢ (in public lots and at meters) to $2 per half hour (in private lots). Downtown and Century City rates may be as high as $25 an hour, though prices tend to drop on weekends.

Parking in Downtown L.A. can be tough, especially on weekdays. Try the garage at the FIG at 7th retail complex (⊠ *725 S. Figueroa St.),* which is spacious, reasonably priced, and visitor-friendly. It's $13 before 9 am and $8 after 4 pm and on weekends.

In Hollywood, the underground facility at the Hollywood & Highland shopping complex (⊠ *6801 Hollywood Blvd.*) charges $2 for the first four hours. In Beverly Hills, the first two hours are free at several lots on or around Rodeo Drive. The Westside Pavilion (⊠ *10800 Pico Blvd.*) offers three hours of free parking at its garage.

At some shops, restaurants, and hotels in Los Angeles, valet parking is virtually assumed. The cost is usually $6 to $8. Keep small bills on hand to tip the valets.

ROAD CONDITIONS

Beware of weekday rush-hour traffic, which is heaviest from 7 am to 10 am and 3 pm to 7 pm. CommuteSmart offers real-time traffic information, and the California Highway Patrol has a road-conditions hotline. To encourage carpooling, some crowded freeways reserve an express lane for cars carrying more than one passenger.

Parallel streets can often provide viable alternatives to jam-packed freeways, notably Sepulveda Boulevard for I-405; Venice and Washington boulevards for I-10 from Mid-Wilshire west to the beach; and Ventura Boulevard, Moorpark Street, or Riverside Drive for U.S. 101 through the San Fernando Valley.

Information California Highway Patrol ☎ *800/427–7623 for road conditions* ⊕ *www.chp.ca.gov/index.php.* **CommuteSmart** ☎ *213/922–2811* ⊕ *www.commutesmart.info.*

ROADSIDE EMERGENCIES

For minor problems faced by motorists (running out of gas, blowing a tire, needing a tow to the nearest phone), California's Department of Transportation has a Metro Freeway Service Patrol. More than 145 tow trucks patrol the freeways offering free aid to stranded drivers. Reach them on your cell phone by calling 511.

If your car breaks down on an interstate, pull over onto the shoulder and call the state police from your cell phone or walk to the nearest emergency roadside phone. When calling for help, note your location according to the small green mileage markers posted along the highway.

Emergency Services Metro Freeway Service Patrol ☎ *323/982–4900 for break-downs* ⊕ *www.mta.net.*

RULES OF THE ROAD

Seat belts are required for all passengers in California, as is the use of federally approved car seats for children under nine or less than 4 feet 9 inches tall. California law requires that drivers use hands-free devices when talking on cell phones. Texting and driving is illegal and results in a hefty fine.

The speed limit is 25 to 35 mph on city streets and 65 mph on freeways unless otherwise posted. Some towns, including Beverly Hills and Culver City, use radar at traffic lights to reduce speeding.

Speeding can earn you fines starting at $266. It is illegal to drive in California with a blood alcohol content of 0.08% or above (0.01% if you're under 21). There are strict penalties for first offenders. Checkpoints are set up on weekends and holidays across the county.

Parking infractions can result in penalties starting at $68. Having your vehicle towed and impounded will cost nearly $300 even if you pay up immediately, and more if you don't. LAX is notorious for handing out tickets to drivers circling its busy terminals; avoid the no-parking zones and keep loading or unloading to a minimum.

Turning right on red after a complete stop is legal unless otherwise posted. Many streets in Downtown L.A. are one-way, and a left turn from one one-way street onto another is allowed. On some major arteries, left turns are illegal during rush hour. Certain car-pool lanes, designated by signage and a white diamond, are reserved for cars with more than one passenger. Freeway on-ramps often have stop-and-go signals to regulate the flow of traffic, but cars in high occupancy vehicle (HOV) lanes can pass the signal without stopping.

Keep in mind that pedestrians always have the right of way in California; not yielding to them, even if they're jaywalkers, may result in a $211 ticket.

CAR RENTAL

In Los Angeles, a car is a necessity. Keep in mind that you'll likely be spending a lot of time in it, and options like a plug for your cell phone could make a significant difference in your day-to-day comfort.

Major-chain rates in L.A. begin at $35 a day and $200 a week, plus sales tax. Luxury vehicles start at $69 a day. Open-top convertibles are a popular choice for visitors wanting to make the most of the sun. Note that the major agencies offer services for travelers with disabilities, such as hand-controls, for little or no extra cost.

In California you must be 21 and have a valid credit card to rent a car. Some agencies won't rent to those under 25, and those that may do charge extra.

Automobile Associations American Automobile Association (AAA). Most contact with the organization is through state and regional members. ☎ 315/797–5000 ⊕ www.aaa.com. **National Automobile Club.** Membership is open to California residents only. ☎ 650/294–7000 ⊕ www.thenac.com.

■ METRO TRAVEL

Metro Rail covers only a small part of L.A.'s vast expanse, but it's convenient, frequent, and inexpensive. Most popular with visitors is the underground Red Line, which runs from Downtown's Union Station through Mid-Wilshire, Hollywood, and Universal City on its way to North Hollywood, stopping at the most popular tourist destinations along the way.

The light-rail Green Line stretches from Redondo Beach to Norwalk, while the partially underground Blue Line travels from Downtown to the South Bay. The monorail-like Gold Line extends from Union Station to Pasadena and Sierra Madre. The Orange Line, a 14-mile bus corridor, connects the North Hollywood subway station with the western San Fernando Valley.

Most recently unveiled was the Expo Line, which connects Downtown to Culver City. When completed, it will reach nearly to the Pacific Ocean.

There's daily service from about 4:30 am to 12:30 am, with departures every 5 to 15 minutes. On weekends trains run until 2 am. Buy tickets from station vending machines; fares are $1.50, or $5 for an all-day pass. Bicycles are allowed on Metro Rail trains at all times.

Rail Information Los Angeles County Metropolitan Transit Authority ☎ 323/466–3876 ⊕ www.metro.net.

TAXI AND LIMO TRAVEL

Instead of trying to hail a taxi on the street, phone one of the many taxi companies. The metered rate is $2.70 per mile, plus a $2.85 per-fare charge. Taxi rides from LAX have an additional $4 surcharge. Be aware that distances are greater than they might appear on the map so fares add up quickly.

On the other end of the price spectrum, limousines come equipped with everything from full bars to nightclub-style sound-and-light systems. Most charge by the hour, with a three-hour minimum.

Limo Companies ABC Limo ☎ 818/637–2277 ⊕ www.abclimola.com. **American Executive** ☎ 800/927–2020 ⊕ www.americanexecutiveairportlimo.com. **Dav El Chauffeured Transportation Network** ☎ 800/922–0343 ⊕ www.davel.com. **First Class Limousine Service** ☎ 800/400–9771 ⊕ www.first-classlimo.com. **ITS** ☎ 800/487–4255 ⊕ www.itslimo.com.

Taxi Companies Beverly Hills Cab Co. ☎ 800/398–5221 ⊕ www.beverlyhillscabco.com. **Checker Cab** ☎ 800/300–5007 ⊕ www.ineedtaxi.com. **United Independent Taxi** ☎ 800/822–8294 ⊕ www.unitedtaxi.com. **Yellow Cab Los Angeles** ☎ 800/200–1085, 877/733–3305 ⊕ www.layellowcab.com. **Independent Cab Co.** ☎ 800/521–8294 ⊕ www.taxi4u.com.

TRAIN TRAVEL

Downtown's Union Station is one of the great American railroad terminals. The interior includes comfortable seating, a restaurant, and several snack bars. As the city's rail hub, it's the place to catch an Amtrak or Metrolink commuter train. Among Amtrak's Southern California routes are 22 daily trips to San Diego and five to Santa Barbara. Amtrak's luxury *Coast Starlight* travels along the spectacular coastline from Seattle to Los Angeles in just a day and a half (though it's often a little late). The *Sunset Limited* arrives from New Orleans, and the *Southwest Chief* comes from Chicago.

Information Amtrak ☎ 800/872–7245 ⊕ www.amtrak.com. **Metrolink** ☎ 800/371–5465 ⊕ www.metrolinktrains.com. **Union Station** ✉ 800 N. Alameda St. ☎ 213/683–6979 ⊕ www.amtrak.com.

ESSENTIALS

▌ HEALTH

The air pollution in L.A. may affect sensitive people in different ways. When pollution levels are high, it's a good idea to plan a day indoors or on a windy beach. The sun can burn even on overcast days, and the dry heat can dehydrate, so wear hats, sunglasses, and sunblock and carry water with you.

▌ HOURS OF OPERATION

Los Angeles is not a 24-hour city like New York, but in many places business hours extend well into the evening, especially for bigger stores and shopping centers. On Monday, many bars, restaurants, and shops (including outdoor sports outlets) remain closed.

Many L.A. museums are closed on Monday and major holidays. A few of the preeminent art museums, including the Norton Simon and Los Angeles County Museum of Art, stay open on Monday. Instead, the Norton Simon is closed Tuesday, the Los Angeles County museum on Wednesday. Most museums close around 5 pm or 6 pm, staying open late at least one night a week. Many museums, large and small, have weekly or monthly free days or hours when no admission is charged.

Most stores in Los Angeles are open 10 to 6, although many stay open until 9 pm or later, particularly those in trendy areas such as Melrose Avenue and in Santa Monica. Most shops are open on Sunday at least in the afternoon.

▌ MONEY

Although not inexpensive, costs in Los Angeles tend to be a bit lower than in other major cities such as New York and San Francisco. For instance, in a low-key local diner, a cup of coffee might cost around $1.50. In high-profile establishments, costs escalate; a cup of coffee in a trendy eatery can cost as much as $5.

ITEM	AVERAGE COST
Cup of Coffee	$2
Glass of Wine	$9
Glass of Beer	$7
Sandwich	$9
15-Minute Taxi Ride	$20
Museum Admission	$10

Prices throughout this guide are given for adults. Reduced fees are almost always available for children, students, and senior citizens.

▌ RESTROOMS

You can assume that gas stations along the highways outside of town will have a bathroom available, but this isn't true of every station in L.A. itself. Restrooms in parks can be sub-par. Restaurants and bars may have signs that read "For Patrons Only" so that you're obliged to buy something to use the facilities. Better bets for relatively clean, obligation-free restrooms are those in department stores, fast food outlets, and bookstores.

▌ SAFETY

Very minor earthquakes occur frequently in Southern California; most of the time they're so slight that you won't notice them. If you feel a stronger tremor, follow basic safety precautions. If you're indoors, take cover in a doorway or under a table or desk—whichever is closest. Protect your head with your arms. Stay clear of windows, mirrors, or anything that might fall from the walls. Do not use elevators. If you're in an open space, move away from buildings, trees, and power lines. If you're outdoors near buildings, duck into a doorway. If you're driving, pull over to the side of the road, avoiding overpasses, bridges, and power lines, and stay inside the car. Expect aftershocks, and take cover again if they are strong.

Of the Metro lines, the Red, Green, and Expo lines are the safest and are more regularly patrolled. The Blue Line can be sketchy after dark. Avoid riding in empty cars, and move with the crowd when going from the station to the street.

▍ TAXES

The sales tax in Los Angeles is 9.75%, one of the highest in California. There's none on most groceries, but there is on newspapers and magazines. The tax on hotel rooms ranges from 13% to 15.5%.

▍ TIME

Los Angeles is in the Pacific time zone, two hours behind Chicago, three hours behind New York, and eight hours behind London.

▍ TIPPING

The customary tip rate is 15%–20% for waiters and taxi drivers and 15% to 20% for hairdressers and barbers. Bellhops and baggage handlers receive $1 to $2 per bag; parking valets and hotel maids are usually tipped $2 to $3. Bartenders get about $1 per drink. In restaurants, a handy trick for estimating the tip is to move the decimal point of the total cost one space and then double that to get 20%.

▍ TOURS

You can explore L.A. from many vantage points and even more topical angles. Not surprisingly, lots of guides include dollops of celebrity history and gossip. Most tours run year-round, and most require advance reservations.

BUS AND VAN TOURS

Guideline Tours offers sightseeing trips all around L.A., including Downtown, Universal Studios, and Hollywood. L.A. Tours and Sightseeing has several tours by van and bus covering various parts of the city, including Downtown, Hollywood, and Beverly Hills. The company also operates tours to Disneyland, Universal Studios, and Six Flags Magic Mountain. Starline Tours of Hollywood picks up passengers from area hotels and from Grauman's Chinese Theatre. Universal Studios, Knott's Berry Farm, and a slightly tawdry TMZ tour of celebrity hot spots are some of the highlights on this popular tour company's agenda.

Fees and Schedules Guideline Tours
☎ 323/461–0156, 800/604–8433
⊕ www.tourslosangeles.com. **L.A. Tours and Sightseeing** ☎ 323/460–6490
⊕ www.latours.net. **Starline Tours of Hollywood** ☎ 323/463–3333, 800/959–3131
⊕ www.starlinetours.com.

HELICOPTER TOURS

If you want an aerial tour, lift off with Orbic Air. Based at Van Nuys Airport, the company has been flying its two- and four-passenger helicopters for more than a dozen years, and the pilots have years of experience. It's $84 per person for the basic 15-minute tour.

Fees and Schedules Orbic Air ☎ 818/988–6532 ⊕ www.orbicair.com.

SCOOTER TOURS

For an unusual perspective on L.A.'s attractions, you can take a tour of the city on a Segway electric scooter. The $89 tours might include the UCLA campus, Santa Monica, or Downtown. The guided rides last just over two hours.

Fees and Schedules Segway Tours
☎ 310/358–5900 ⊕ www.segwow.com.

SPECIAL-INTEREST TOURS

With Architecture Tours L.A., you can zip all over the city in a comfortable minivan on a private tour with a historian. Rates start at $70. Esotouric has an innovative take on the city; its weekend bus tours ($58 and up) explore the darker side of L.A. that Raymond Chandler revealed in books like *The Big Sleep* and *The Long Goodbye*.

Beverly Hills operates year-round trolley tours focused on art and architecture. They last 40 minutes and depart from 11 am to 4 pm every weekend throughout the year, as well as Tuesday to Friday in the summer. Tickets cost $5. Soak up the glow of classic neon signs from an open double decker bus on tours offered by the Museum of Neon Art. They cost $65 and are offered June through September.

Take My Mother Please will arrange lively, thematic combination walking and driving tours; for instance, you could explore sights associated with the film *L.A. Confidential*. Rates start at $450 for up to three people for a half day.

Fees and Schedules Architecture Tours L.A ☎ 323/464–7868 ⊕ www.architecturetoursla. com. **City of Beverly Hills Trolley Tours** ✉ Dayton Way and Rodeo Dr., Beverly Hills ☎ 310/285–2500 ⊕ www.beverlyhills.org/ exploring/trolleytours. **Esotouric** ☎ 213/373– 1947 ⊕ www.esotouric.com. **Neon Cruise** ☎ 213/489–9918 ⊕ www.neonmona.org. **Take My Mother Please** ☎ 323/737–2200 ⊕ www.takemymotherplease.com.

WALKING TOURS

Red Line Tours offers daily one- and two-hour walking tours of behind-the-scenes Hollywood. Tours, which cost $25, are led by docents and include headsets to block out street noise. The Los Angeles Conservancy's 2½-hour-long walking tours ($10) cover the Downtown area.

Fees and Schedules Los Angeles Conservancy ☎ 213/623–2489 ⊕ www.laconservancy.org. **Red Line Tours** ☎ 323/402–1074 ⊕ www.redlinetours.com.

▌ VISITOR INFORMATION

Discover Los Angeles publishes an annually updated general information packet with suggestions for entertainment, lodging, and dining, as well as a list of special events. There are two visitor information centers, both accessible to Metro stops: the Hollywood & Highland entertainment complex and Union Station.

The Santa Monica Convention and Visitors Bureau runs a drop-in visitor information center on Main Street that is open daily 9 to 5, as well as three kiosks at Palisades Park, the Santa Monica Pier, and the Third Street Promenade.

Contacts Beverly Hills Conference and Visitors Bureau ☎ 310/248–1000, 800/345– 2210 ⊕ www.lovebeverlyhills.com. **Discover Los Angeles** ☎ 213/624–7300, 800/228–2452 ⊕ www.discoverlosangeles.com. **Hollywood Chamber of Commerce** ☎ 323/469–8311 ⊕ www.hollywoodchamber.net. **Long Beach Area Convention and Visitors Bureau** ☎ 562/436–3645 ⊕ www.visitlongbeach.com. **Pasadena Convention and Visitors Bureau** ☎ 626/795–9311 ⊕ www.pasadenacal. com. **Santa Monica Convention & Visitors Bureau** ☎ 310/393–7593, 800/544–5319 ⊕ www.santamonica.com. **Visit California** ☎ 916/444–4429, 800/862–2543 ⊕ www.visitcalifornia.com. **Visit West Hollywood** ☎ 310/289–2525, 800/368–6020 ⊕ www.visitwesthollywood.com.

INDEX

A

A.O.C. ✕, 222
Abbot Kinney Boulevard, 105
Ace Hotel ☰, 243
Acorn (shop), 192–193
Adamson House and Malibu
   Lagoon Museum, 111–112
Ahmanson Theatre, 161
Air travel, 272, 312–313
All India Cafe ✕, 235
Ambrose, The ☰, 260
American Rag Cie (shop), 183
Ammo ✕, 207
Amoeba Records, 172
Anabella, The ☰, 284
Anaheim White House ✕, 283
ANdAZ West Hollywood ☰,
   256
Angelini Osteria ✕, 221
Angels Flight Railway, 42
Animal ✕, 207
Annenberg Community Beach
   House, 102
Annenberg Space for Photog-
   raphy, 86
Apartment rentals, 261
Apple Pan, The ✕, 227
Aquarium of the Pacific, 27,
   288
Architecture, 28
Architecture and Design
   Museum (A&D), 95
Arclight/Cinerama Dome, 160
Art galleries
Beverly Hills and the Westside,
   80, 92
Laguna Beach, 300
Pasadena, 120–121, 124, 129
Santa Monica, 102–104
Artisan Cheese Gallery ✕, 215
Asanebo ✕, 215
Aurora Hotel & Spa ☰,
   309–310
Avalon ☰, 251
Avalon (Catalina Island),
   308–310
Avila Adobe, 43
Ayres Hotel ☰, 266–267

B

Badmaash ✕, 203
Balboa Bay Resort ☰, 296
Balboa Island, 294
Balboa Peninsula, 294
Balboa Pavilion, 297
Bar Marmont, 144

Bar Pintxo ✕, 228
Barney Greengrass ✕, 217
Barnsdall Park, 76
Bars, 135–152
Baseball, 29, 285
Basilic ✕, 295
Basketball, 29
Bayside Hotel ☰, 260
Bazaar by José Andrés, The
   ✕, 217
Beachcomber at Crystal Cove
   Café ✕, 298
Beach House at Hermosa ☰,
   267
Beach house rentals, 261
Beaches
Malibu, 108, 112
Santa Monica, 99, 105, 108,
   112–116
South Coast and Catalina
   Island, 270, 291–292,
   298–300, 302
Bear Flag Fish Co. ✕, 295
Bed & Breakfasts, 257, 261
Bel Air, 221, 256
Belvedere, The ✕, 217–218
Bergamot Station (gallery), 102
Beso ✕, 210
Beverly Center, 181
Beverly Gardens Park, 83
Beverly Hills and the Westside,
   12–13, 77–96
children, activities for, 81, 88,
   94, 96
lodging, 251–256
restaurants, 81–83, 217–221
shopping, 176–182
sightseeing, 77–96
Beverly Hills Hotel & Bunga-
   lows ☰, 252
Beverly Hills Plaza Hotel ☰,
   252
Beverly Hilton ☰, 252
Beverly Wilshire, a Four Sea-
   sons Hotel ☰, 252
Bicycling, 18, 57, 102, 106–
   107, 310
Bistro 45 ✕, 235
BLD ✕, 222
Blue Lantern Inn ☰, 303
BOA Steakhouse ✕, 229
Boardner's (bar), 138
Boat and ferry travel, 305, 307
Boat rentals, 296
Bob's Big Boy ✕, 73

Bolsa Chica Ecological Reserve,
   291
Bolsa Chica State Beach, 292
Book Soup (shop), 183
Border Grill ✕, 229
Botanical gardens, 57
Bottega Louie ✕, 203
Bouchon Bistro ✕, 218
Breadbar ✕, 225
Brentwood, 224–225, 259
Brentwood Inn ☰, 259
Broad Contemporary Art
   Museum (BCAM), 92
Broadway (downtown Los
   Angeles), 38–39
Broadway Bar, 135
Bunker Hill Steps, 44
Burbank, 72–74
lodging, 250–251
restaurants, 213
Bus travel, 273, 313
Bus and van tours, 318
Business hours, 317
nightlife, 134
restaurants, 202

C

Cabaret and variety, 151–152
Cabrillo Marine Aquarium,
   288, 290
Café Zinc & Market ✕, 301
California African–American
   Museum, 44
California Heritage Museum,
   102
California Science Center,
   26–27, 39
Candy Cane Inn ☰, 285
Cannery, The ✕, 296
Canter's ✕, 222
Capitol Records Tower, 67
Car rentals, 14, 315
Car travel, 14–15, 20, 36,
   78–79, 273, 313–315
Casino, 308
Casino Point Underwater Park,
   308
Castle Green, 126
Catal Restaurant & Uva Bar
   ✕, 283
Catalina Island, 270–271,
   305–310
Catalina Island Museum, 308
Cathedral of Our Lady of the
   Angels, 38, 40

Celebrity sightings, 21, 42, 92, 96
Century City, 86, 225–226, 259
Cha Cha Cha ✕, 214
Cha Cha Lounge, 142
Cham ✕, 236
Chamberlain ⊞, 256
Channel Road Inn ⊞, 260
Chateau Marmont Hotel ⊞, 256
Cheemosphere House, 67
Chex Jay Restaurant (bar), 146, 151
Children's activities, 27. ⇨ See also under specific areas
Chinatown, 38, 44
Chinese American Museum, 46
Chinois on Main ✕, 229
Cicada ✕, 204
City Hall of Los Angeles, 46
Cleo ✕, 210
Climate, 14
Coast Anabelle Hotel ⊞, 250
Coffeehouses, 152
Cole's (bar), 146
Comedy clubs, 138–139, 149
Comme Ça ✕, 222
Concert halls, 156–158
Corona del Mar, 297–299
Corona del Mar State Beach, 298
Costs, 135. ⇨ See also Price categories
Counter, The ✕, 229
Craft and Folk Art Musuem (CAFAM), 95–96
Craft Los Angeles ✕, 225–226
Crescent Avenue (Catalina Island), 308
Crescent Beverly Hills, The ⊞, 252
Crustacean ✕, 218
Crystal Cove Promenade, 299
Crystal Cove State Park, 298
Cube Café & Marketplace ✕, 210
Culver City, 226–227, 259
Culver Hotel ⊞, 259
Currency. ⇨ see Money matters
Custom Hotel ⊞, 265
CUT ✕, 218

D

Da Pasquale ✕, 219
Dana Point, 302–303
Dana Point Harbor, 302
Dance, 158
Decades (shop), 185
Descanso Beach Club ✕, 309

Descanso Gardens, 120, 126–127
Dining. ⇨ See Restaurants and under specific areas
Disney Studios, 73
Disneyland, 275–280
Disneyland Resort, 16, 27, 270, 274–285
Disney's California Adventure, 280–285
Disney's Grand Californian Hotel & Spa ⊞, 285
Diving, 308, 310
Dockweiler State Beach, 111
Doheny State Beach, 302
Dolby Theatre, 61–62
Dolce Vita (bar), 148
Dolphin watching, 303
Don Blocker State Beach, 113
Dorothy Chandler Pavilion, 156
Doubletree Guest Suites (Anaheim) ⊞, 285
Downtown, 12, 35–52
bars, 135–136
children, activities for, 39, 40, 50
lodging, 243–247
restaurants, 203–217
shopping, 170–171
sightseeing, 38–52
Downtown Disney, 283
Downtown L.A. Standard ⊞, 135
Duke's (Huntington Beach) ✕, 292

E

Echo, The (bar), 143
Echo Park, 76
bars and clubs, 143
shopping, 176
Egyptian Theatre, 67–68
El Capitan Theatre, 61–62
El Cholo ✕, 210
El Floridita (Latin music club), 139, 141
El Pueblo de Los Angeles, 38, 40–41
Élan Hotel, The ⊞, 257
Emergencies, 314
Engine Co. No. 28 ✕, 204
Exposition Park, 46

F

Fairmont Miramar Hotel & Bungalows Santa Monica ⊞, 260

Farmer's Daughter Hotel ⊞, 240, 257
Farmers' Market and The Grove, 79, 92, 182, 188
Farmers' Markets
Beverly Hills and Westside, 79
Downtown, 38, 41–42
West Hollywood and Melrose Avenue, 182, 188
Farmshop ✕, 229, 232
Fashion Island, 297
Father's Office ✕, 232
Fenyes Mansion, 126
Ferry travel, 273, 305, 307
Figueroa Hotel ⊞, 243
Film, 159–160
Fishing, 296
Flea markets, 129, 194
Football, 29
Formosa Café (bar), 144, 146 147
Four Seasons Hotel, Los Angeles at Beverly Hills ⊞, 252
Fowler Museum at UCLA, 87
Fred Segal (shop), 185, 191
Fred 62 ✕, 214
Free activities, 25
Freeway driving, 15
Frolic Room (bar), 147

G

Gagosian Gallery, 80
Gamble House, 121
Garden Cottage Bed and Breakfast ⊞, 257
Gardens, 83, 298, 309
Geffen Contemporary at MOCA, 38, 41
Gemmell's ✕, 302
Georgian Hotel, The ⊞, 260–261
Getty Center, 17, 88, 90,
Getty Villa Malibu, 102–103
Gingergrass ✕, 216
Gjelina ✕, 236
Golf, 296
Gordon Ramsay at the London ✕, 223
Grafton on Sunset, The ⊞, 257
Grammy Museum, 41
Grand Central Market, 38, 41–42
Grauman's Chinese Theater, 16, 61, 67
Greek Theatre, 57, 158
Green Pleasure Pier, 309
Greystone Mansion, 83

Griffith Observatory and Planetarium, 57, 59, 74–75
Griffith Park, 27, 56–57, 75
Grill on the Alley, The ✕, 219
Groundling Theatre, 138
Grove, The, 92, 182, 188
Guelaguetza ✕, 211
Guided tours, 16–17
Guinness World of Records, 68
Gumbo Pot ✕, 223

H

H.D. Buttercup (mall), 190
Harvelle's (bar), 147, 151
Health, 317
Helicopter tours, 307–308, 318
Henri Bendel (department store), 179
Heritage Square Museum, 126
Hermosa Beach, 115, 152, 267
Hiking, 57
Hilton Anaheim ☲, 285
Hilton Checkers Los Angeles ☲, 243
Hilton Pasadena Hotel ☲, 268
Hockey, 29, 285
Hollyhock House, 76
Hollywood and the studios,12, 53–76
bars, 137–141
children, activities for, 57, 71
lodging, 247–248, 250
restaurants, 68, 71, 198–199, 207, 210–213
shopping, 172–173
sightseeing, 60–74
sports and outdoor activities, 57
Hollywood and Vine, 68
Hollywood Bowl, 63, 156–157
Hollywood Forever Cemetery, 62–63
Hollywood Heritage Museum, 70
Hollywood High School, 70
Hollywood Museum, 63, 65
Hollywood RockWalk, 70
Hollywood Roosevelt Hotel ☲, 247
Hollywood Sign, 70–71
Hollywood Walk of Fame, 16, 61, 65
Hollywood Wax Museum, 71
Honey's Kettle Fried Chicken ✕, 226
Horseback riding, 57, 75
Hotel Amarana Burbank ☲, 250–251
Hotel Angeleno ☲, 259

Hotel Bel Air ☲, 256
Hotel Erwin ☲, 266
Hotel Maya–a Doubletree Hotel ☲, 290
Hotel Palomar Los Angeles–Westwood ☲, 259, 267
Hotel Queen Mary ☲, 290
Hotel Shangri-La ☲, 264
Hotel Villa Portofino ☲, 310
Hotel Vista del Mar ☲, 310
Hotels. ⇨ See also Lodging under specific areas
price categories, 14, 242–268
Huntington Beach, 291–293
Huntington Gardens, 24
Huntington Library, Art Collections, and Botanical Gardens, 120–121, 124
Huntington Pier, 292
Huntley Santa Monica Beach ☲, 264
Hyatt Regency Century Plaza ☲, 259

I

Inn at 657 ☲, 245
International Surfing Museum, 292
Island Hotel, The ✕, 296
Italian Hall Building, 46
Itineraries, 22–24

J

Japanese American Cultural and Community Center, 46
Japanese American National Museum, 48
Jar ✕, 223
Jazz clubs, 139, 151
JiRaffe ✕, 232
Joe's Restaurant ✕, 236
Josie ✕, 232–233
JW Marriott Los Angeles at L.A. Live ☲, 245

K

Kate Mantilini ✕, 219
Katsuya ✕, 224–225
Kibitz Room at Canter's Deli (bar), 147
Kidspace Children's Museum, 27, 127
Kirk Douglas Theatre, 161
Kitson (shop), 185
Knott's Berry Farm (theme park), 270, 286–288
Knott's Berry Farm Hotel ☲, 288

L

L.A. Live, 42
La Brea Tar Pits, 94
La Casa del Camino Hotel ☲, 301
Laguna Art Museum, 300
Laguna Beach, 299–302
LAMILL Coffee Boutique ✕, 217
Langer's Deli ✕, 205
Langham Huntington, Pasadena ☲, 268
Las Tunas State Beach, 108, 113
Latin music clubs, 139–140
Laurel Tavern ✕, 216
Lazy Ox Canteen ✕, 205
Le Meridien Delfina Santa Monica ☲, 264
Le Parc Suite Hotel ☲, 257
L'Ermitage Beverly Hills Hotel ☲, 253
Lemonade ✕, 223
Legends Bike Tours, 104
Limousines, 316
Line, The (hotel) ☲, 245
Little Dom's ✕, 214
Little Flower Candy Company ✕, 236
Little Tokyo, 38, 49
Lobster, The ✕, 233
Lobster Trap, The ✕, 309
Lodging, 7, 14, 239–268, 274
alternatives, 261
amenities, 242
best bets, 244
children, 242, 247
Fodor's choice, 244
neighborhoods, 241
price categories, 14, 242–243, 275
reservations, 242
reviews, 243–268
Loews Hollywood Hotel ☲, 247
Loews Santa Monica Beach Hotel ☲, 264
London West Hollywood ☲, 257–258
Long Beach, 288–290
Los Angeles County Arboretum, 127
Los Angeles County Museum of Art (LACMA), 92–93
Los Angeles International Airport (LAX) area
lodging, 265

Los Angeles Museum of the Holocaust, 96
Los Angeles Theatre, 49
Los Angeles Zoo, 71
Los Feliz, 74–75
bars and clubs, 141
lodging, 251
restaurants, 198–199, 214–215
shopping, 174–175
Los Feliz Lodge 🏨, 251
Lotería! Grill Hollywood ✕, 211
Lou's Red Oak BBQ ✕, 293
Lucques ✕, 223
Luxe Hotel Sunset Boulevard 🏨, 256
Lynda and Stewart Resnick Exhibition Pavilion, 93

M

MAC on Robertson (shop), 176
Magic Castle Hotel 🏨, 247
Main Beach Park, 300
Main Street (Santa Monica), 100
Maison 140 🏨, 253
Malibu
Bars, 152
beaches, 108, 111–114
lodging, 266
restaurants, 114, 235
shopping, 193
sightseeing, 111–114
Malibu Beach Inn 🏨, 266
Malibu Lagoon State Beach, 108, 112
Malibu Lumberyard, 193
Malibu Pier, 112
Manhattan Beach
beaches, 114–115
lodging, 266–267
sightseeing, 114–115
Marina del Rey
beaches, 109
lodging, 266
sightseeing, 109
Matsuhisa ✕, 219
Maxfield (shop), 186
Meal plans, 7
Mélisse ✕, 233
Melrose Avenue, 80, 182–189
Melrose Place, 171, 182
Meltdown (shop), 172
Merry-go-round (Griffith Park), 57, 75
Metro Rail, 48, 315
MILK ✕, 82
Millenium Biltmore Hotel 🏨, 245

Million Dollar Theater, 50
Miracle Mile, 96
Mission San Gabriel Archangel, 129–130
Mission San Juan Capistrano, 304–305
MOCA Gallery, 92
MOCA Grand Avenue, 42
Mosaic Hotel 🏨, 253
Moment Hotel 🏨, 248
Money matters, 317
Montage Beverly Hills 🏨, 253
Montage Laguna Beach 🏨, 301
Monte Alban ✕, 227
Mori Sushi ✕, 227
Mosaic Hotel 🏨, 253
Moss at SLS Beverly Hills (shop), 181
Mount Hollywood, 57
Movie palaces, 160
Mr. Cecil's California Ribs ✕, 228
Mrs. Knott's Chicken Dinner Restaurant ✕, 287
Muscle Beach, 108–109
Museum of Contemporary Art (MOCA), 38, 41, 92
Museum of Tolerance, 81–82
Museums, 26–27
Adamson House and Malibu Lagoon Museum, 111–112
Annenberg Space for Photography, 86
Architecture and Design Museum (A&D), 93
Bergamot Station, 102
Broad Contemporary Art Museum (BCAM), 93
California African–American Museum, 44
California Heritage Museum, 102
California Science Center, 26–27, 39
Catalina Island Museum, 308
Chinese American Museum, 46
Craft and Folk Art Museum (CAFAM), 95–96
Fowler Museum at UCLA, 86
Geffen Contemporary, 26, 38, 41
Getty Center, 17, 88, 90, 124
Grammy Museum, 41
Heritage Square Museum, 126
Hollywood Heritage Museum, 70
Hollywood Wax Museum, 71

Huntington Library, Art Collections, and Botanical Gardens, 120–121, 124
International Surfing Museum, 292
Japanese American National Museum, 48
Kidspace Children's Museum, 27, 127
Laguna Art Museum, 300
Los Angeles County Museum of Art (LACMA), 92–93
Los Angeles Museum of the Holocaust, 96
Museum of Contemporary Art (MOCA), 38, 41, 92
Museum of Tolerance, 81–82
Natural History Museum of Los Angeles County, 40, 50
Newport Harbor, 295
Norton Simon Museum, 120, 124
Orange County Museum of Art, 295
Pacific Asia Museum, 127
Page Museum at the La Brea Tar Pits, 94
Paley Center for Media, 86
Pasadena Museum of California Art, 129
Petersen Automotive Museum, 96
Ripley's Believe It or Not, 71
Skirball Cultural Center, 90
UCLA Hammer Museum, 87
Will Rogers State Historic Park and Museum, 104–105
Music Center, 39
Musso & Frank Grill ✕, 137, 148

N

Napa Rose ✕, 284
Nate 'n' Al's ✕, 81
Natural History Museum of Los Angeles County, 26, 40, 50
Newport Beach, 293–297
Newport Harbor, 295
Newport Pier, 295
Nicholas Canyon County Beach, 114
Nick & Stef's Steakhouse ✕, 206
Nightlife, 131–152. ⇨ See also under specific areas
Nobu Malibu ✕, 235
NoHo Arts District, 74
Nokia Theater L.A. Live, 39, 157

North Hollywood, *74, 213*
Norton Simon Museum, *120, 124*

O

O Hotel ☷ , *245*
Oceana ☷ , *264*
Old Mill, The (El Molino Viejo), *127*
Old Town Pasadena, *120, 124*
Olvera Street, *171*
Oliverio ✕ , *219*
Omni Los Angeles Hotel at California Plaza ☷ , *245*
Orange County, *270*
Orange County Museum of Art, *295*
Orpheum Theatre, *50*

P

Pacific Asia Museum, *129*
Pacific Design Center, *92*
Pacific Park, *102*
Pacific Whey Cafe & Baking Company ✕ , *298*
Page Museum of the La Brea Tar Pits, *94*
Paley Center for Media, *86*
Palm, The ✕ , *224*
Palihotel ☷ , *248*
Palihouse Santa Monica ☷ , *264*
Panini Cafe ☷ , *298*
Pantages Theatre, *68*
Paramount Pictures, *65*
Park Vue Inn ☷ , *285*
Parking, *314*
Parkway Grill ✕ , *237*
Pasadena, *13, 117–130*
children, activities for, *127*
lodging, *268*
restaurants, *124, 235–237*
shopping, *129, 194*
sightseeing, *118–130*
Pasadena Museum of California Art, *129*
Pasadena Playhouse, *164*
Patina ✕ , *206*
Pecorino ✕ , *225*
Peninsula Beverly Hills ☷ , *253*
Performing arts, *153–166*
Pershing Square, *50*
Petersen Automotive Museum, *96*
Philippe the Original ✕ , *206*
Pie 'N Burger ✕ , *237*
Pig 'n Whistle ✕ , *68*
Pink's Hot Dogs ✕ , *211*

Pizzeria Mozza ✕ , *211*
Planet Blue (shop), *192*
Playa Del Ray, *112*
Portofino Hotel & Yacht Club ☷ , *267*
Porto's Bakery ✕ , *213*
Price categories, *317*
dining, *14, 203*
lodging, *14, 242–243*
Providence ✕ , *211–212*

Q

Queen Mary (ocean liner), *290*

R

Rainbow Bar & Grill, *144*
Ramos House Cafe ✕ , *304–305*
Rancho Palos Verdes, *267*
Red O ✕ , *224*
Redbury ☷ , *248*
Redondo Beach, *115–116, 266*
Resort at Pelican Hill ☷ , *299*
Restaurants, *7, 14, 18–19, 195–237, 273*. ⇨ See also under specific areas
best bets, *198–199*
children in, *202*
cuisine, *200–201*
dress, *202*
Fodor's choice, *198–199*
hours, *202*
local chains, *220*
price categories, *14, 203*
smoking in, *202*
reservations, *202*
reviews, *203–237*
taxes, *202*
tipping, *202*
Restrooms, *317*
Richard J. Riordan Central Library, *50, 52*
Ripley's Believe It or Not, *71*
Ritz–Carlton, Laguna Niguel ☷ , *303*
Ritz Carlton, Los Angeles ☷ , *246*
Ritz–Carlton Marina del Rey, The ☷ , *266*
Robert H. Meyer Memorial State Beach, *112*
Robertson Boulevard, *182*
Rock music clubs, *142–143*
Rodeo Drive, *17, 80, 82, 171, 182*
Rose Bowl, *129*

Rose Bowl Flea Market, *129, 194*

S

Safety, *317*
St. Regis Monarch Beach Resort anad Spa ☷ , *303*
Saladang Song ✕ , *237*
San Juan Capistrano, *304–305*
San Pedro, *288–290*
Santa Monica and the beaches, *13, 97–108*
bars, *101, 151–152*
children, activities for, *100–101*
lodging, *260–267*
restaurants, *101, 109, 114, 198–199, 228–234*
shopping, *191–194*
sightseeing, *100–108*
Santa Monica Aquarium, *101*
Santa Monica Beach, *27, 101*
Santa Monica Boulevard, *86*
Santa Monica Pier, *17, 101*
Santa Monica Place, *101*
Santa Monica Seafood ✕ , *233*
Santa Monica State Beach, *103*
Sapphire Laguna ✕ , *301*
Scenic views, *19*
Scooter tours, *318*
shade ☷ , *267*
Sheraton Gateway Los Angeles Hotel ☷ , *265*
Sheraton Universal ☷ , *251*
Sherman Library and Gardens, *298*
Shopping, *167–194*. ⇨ See also under specific areas
Shore Hotel ☷ , *265*
Shorebreak Hotel ☷ , *293*
Shrine Auditorium, *157*
Shutters on the Beach ☷ , *265*
Sightseeing tours, *16–17, 104*
Silent Movie Theater, *159*
Silver Lake, *76*
bars and clubs, *142–143*
lodging, *261*
shopping, *175–176*
restaurants, *198–199, 216–217*
Sirtage Hotel ☷ , *253*
Skateboarding, *104, 110*
Skirball Cultural Center, *90*
SLS Hotel at Beverly Hills ☷ , *253, 256*
Smoking, *202*
Snorkeling, *308, 310*
Snow White café ✕ , *71*
Soap Plant Wacko/La Luz de Jesus Gallery, *174–175*
Sofi ✕ , *226*

South Coast and Catalina Island, 288–305
beaches, 291–292, 298–300, 302
children, activities for, 288, 295, 298, 300
dining and lodging, 290, 292–293, 295–296, 298–299, 301–305
nightlife and the arts, 305
shopping, 297, 299, 302
sports and outdoor activities, 293, 296, 302–303
visitor invormtion, 294
Spago Beverly Hills ✕, 221
Spas, 249
Special–interest tours, 319
Sports and the outdoors, 18–20, 29, 104, 106–107. ⇨ *See also* under specific sports
Sportsmen's Lodge ⊠, 251
Sprinkles Cupcakes, 82
Standard Downtown L.A., The ⊠, 246
Standard Hollywood, The ⊠, 149, 258
Staples Center, 39, 52, 158
Star sightings, 21, 42, 92, 96
Strand bike path, 106–107
Strip, 30–34
Studio ✕, 301
Studio City, 72, 173, 215–216, 251
Subway travel, 48
Sugar & Spice ✕, 294
Sunset Boulevard, 94
Sunset Marquis Hotel and Villas ⊠, 258
Sunset Plaza, 96
Sunset Restaurant and Bar ✕, 114
Sunset Tower Hotel, The ⊠, 258
Surfas (shop), 189
Surfing, 293
Susina Bakery, 82
Swallow's Inn (club), 305
Symbols, 7

T

Taxes, 202, 318
Taxis and limousines, 316
TCL Chinese Theatre, 67
Tender Greens ✕, 226
Terranea ⊠, 267
Theater, 161–166
Third Street Promenade, 101, 192

Three Clubs (bar), 138
3–Thirty–3 ✕, 295
Ticket sources, 155
Tiki Ti (bar), 142
Time, 318
Tipping, 202, 318
Topanga State Beach, 114
Topanga State Park, 112
Torrance Beach, 116
Tournament House, 130
Tours and packages, 16–17, 307, 318–319
Tra di Noi ✕, 235
Train travel, 273, 316
Transportation, 14, 321–315
Trapeze School of New York, 104
Tutti Gelati ✕, 124
25 Degrees ✕, 68, 207

U

UCLA Hammer Museum, 87
Umami Burger ✕, 214
Union Station, 52
Universal City, 72, 251
Universal Studios Hollywood, 62, 72
University of California, Los Angeles (UCLA), 87–88
Urasawa ✕, 221
Urth Café ✕, 81

V

Vacation rentals, 261
Valentino ✕, 236
Varden, The ✕, 290
Venice, 105, 109–110, 152, 193, 236, 266
Venice Beach, 17, 109, 105, 109
Venice Beach Boardwalk, 109
Venice Beach Eco–Cottages ⊠, 266
Venice Beach House ⊠, 266
Venice Beach Oceanfront Walk, 109
Venice Beach Skate Plaza, 104
Versailles ✕, 228
Vibrato Grill, Jazz, etc. ✕, 221
Viceroy Santa Monica ⊠, 264
Visitor information, 15, 274, 319. ⇨ *See also* under specific areas

W

W Hollywood ⊠, 250
W Westwood ⊠, 259
Wa Sushi & Bistro ✕, 226
Wahoo's Fish Taco ✕, 293

Walking tours, 319
Wallis Annenberg Center for the Performing Arts, 82
Wally's (shop), 190
Walt Disney Concert Hall, 16, 38, 42–43, 158
Warner Bros. Studios, 62, 73–74
Water Grill ✕, 206–207
Water sports, 302
Waterloo & City ✕, 237
Watts Tower, 53
Weather, 14
West Hollywood
bars, 143–144, 149–150
lodging, 256–258
restaurants, 221–224
shopping, 182–189
West Hollywood Design District, 95
West Hollywood Library, 94–95
West Los Angeles, 227–228
Westin Bonaventure Hotel & Suites ⊠, 246
Westside. ⇨ *see* Beverly Hills and the Westside
Westside Tavern ✕, 228
Westward Beach– Point Dune, 114
Westwood, 189–190, 259–260
Whale–watching, 303
Will Rogers State Beach, 105
Will Rogers State Historic Park and Museum, 104–105
Wilshire ✕, 236
Wilshire Boulevard, 92
Wiltern LG Theater, 158
Wind & Sea ✕, 303
Wrigley Mansion, 130
Wrigley Memorial and Botanical Garden, 309

Y

Yamashiro ✕, 138
Yolk (shop), 176
Yuca's Hut ✕, 215

Z

Zankou Chicken ✕, 212–213
Zoo, 57

PHOTO CREDITS

Front cover: Walter Bibikow / age fotostock [Description: Los Angeles International Airport (LAX)]. Back cover (from left to right): Karin Lau/iStockphoto; Kinetic Imagery/Shutterstock; Scott Vickers/ iStockphoto. Spine: JingleBeeZ Photo Gallery/Shutterstock. 1,Walter Bibikoe/age footstock. 2, Paul Fisher/iStockphoto. 5, ames sf/Flickr. Chapter 1: Experience Los Angeles: 8–9, Jose Gil/iStockphoto. 10, Christopher Hudson/iStockphoto. 11(left), Jose Gil/Shutterstock. 11 right), Andrea Wyner. 12, Kinetic Imagery/Shutterstock. 13 (left), scoutingstock/Shutterstock. 13 (right), Michel Stevelmans/Shutterstock. 16 (left), Ted Chi/Flickr. 16 (top center), Boomer/ LACVB. 16 (top right), Diana Lundin/Shutterstock. 16 (bottom right), Joe Shlabotnik/Flickr. 17 (left), Lee Pettet/iStockphoto. 17 (top right), S. Greg Panosian/iStockphoto. 17 (bottom right), Famke Backx/ iStockphoto. 18, Douglas H. Kim/iStockphoto. 19 (left), pointnshoot/Flickr. 19 (right), Sean Goebel/ iStockphoto. 20, Kristen_a Meringue Bake Shop. 21 (left), scoutingstock/Shutterstock. 21 (right), Michael Stevelmans. 22, Stanislave Kharapov/Shutterstock. 23(left), Jay Spooner/iStockfoto. 23(right), Adan Garcia/Flickr. 24, La Citta Vita/Flickr. 25, vmiramontes/Flickr. 26, UCLA Hammer Museum. 27, Ted Chi/Flickr. 28, Nickolay Stanev/Shutterstock. 29, Yogma/Flickr. 30, Heeb Christian/age fotostock. 31 (top right), Neil Emmerson/age fotostock. 31 (bottom right), stevelyan/Flickr. 32 (top), IK's World trip/Flickr. 32 (bottom), Kjetil Ree/Wikimedia Commons. 33(top left), Stepan Mazurov/Flicker. 33 (bottom left), 33(top right), The Key Club. 34(top), Mike Simpson/Stockphoto. 34(bottom),**viv**/Flickr. Chapter 2: Downtown Los Angeles: 35, Robert Holmes. 37, Luis Lopez/Flickr. 38, Larry Brownstein/PhotoDisc/Getty Images. 39, adamsofen/Flickr. 41, Adrian Miles/Flickr. 43, S. Greg Panosian/iStockphoto. 45, Epic Stock/Shutterstock. 47, Brett Shoaf/Artistic Visuals. 49, Ned Raggett/Flickr. 51, Omar Omar/Flickr. Chapter 3: Hollywood and the Studios: 53, Robert Holmes. 55, Byron W.Moore/Shutterstock. 56, David Livingston/iStockphoto. 57 (top), Clinton Steeds/Flickr. 57 (bottom), wolfsavard/Flickr. 58, Clinton Steeds/Flickr. 59, David Liu/iStockphoto. 61, Robert Holmes. 63, Andy Z/Shutterstock. 64, Brett Shoaf/Artistic Visuals. 66, Universal Studios, Hollywood. 69, Kayte Deioma/Alamy. 73, Universal Studios, Hollywood. Chapter 4: Beverly Hills and the Westside: 77, David Liu/iStockphoto. 79, Lee Pettet/iStockphoto. 80, Andy Hwang/iStockphoto. 81, Brett Shoaf/Artistic Visuals. 83, Karin Lau/iStockphoto. 84–85, Scott Leigh/ iStockphoto. 87, Brett Shoaf/ Artistic Visuals. 89, Lee Pettet/iStockphoto. 91, Karin Lau/iStockphoto. 93, prayitno/Flickr. 95, Robert Holmes. Chapter 5: Santa Monica and the Beaches: 97, thelastminute/ Flickr. 99, Jose Gil/Shutterstock. 100, SIME/Giovanni Simeone/ eStock Photo. 103, jonrawlinson/Flickr. 110, NOIZE Photography/Flickr. 113, Naki Kouyioumtzis / age fotostock. 106, Naki Kouyioumtzis/ age fotostock. 107 (left), Pygmy Warrior/Flickr, 107 (top right), alonozoD/Flicker. 107 (center right), Anton J. Geisser/age fotostock. 107 (bottom right), ames sf/Flckr. 110, NOIZE Photography/Flickr. 113, Richard Ross with the courtesy of the J. Paul Getty Trust. Chapter 6: Pasadena: 117, prayitno/ Flickr. 119, The Huntington Library, Art Collections, and Botanical Gardens. 120, maveric2003/Flickr. 122–123, Brett Shoaf/Artistic Visuals. 125, wikipedia.org. 128, Lowe Llaguno/Shutterstock. Chapter 7: Nightlife: 131, sunny_J/Flickr. 132, Epic Stock/Shutterstock. 140, Heeb Christian/age fotostock. 145 (top), Trujillo Paumie. 145 (bottom), michael balderas/iStockphoto. 146 (top left), Tamsin Slater/ Flickr. 146 (top right), tannazie/Flickr. 146 (bottom center), Trujillo Paumie. 146 (bottom right), CV Photography / Alamy. 146 (bottom), Trujillo Paumie. 147 (top left), Chez Jay. 147 (bottom left), Kibitz Room. 147 (bottom center), stevendamron/Flickr. 147 (top right), bORjAmATiC/Flickr. 147 (bottom right), wikipedia.org. 147 (bottom), Never Cool in School / Leslie Kalohi/Flickr. 148 (top left), Musso & Frank Grill. 148 (bottom left), Howard Wise. 148 (top center), Never Cool in School / Leslie Kalohi/ Flickr. 148 (top right), rawkblog.blogspot.com/fl ickr. 148 (bottom right), arnold l inuyaki/ fl ickr. 148 (bottom), Musso & Frank Grill. Chapter 8: Performing Arts: 153, WDCH, Music Center of Los Angeles County. Photo by Alex Pitt. 154, Monika Rittershaus. 157, Steve Cohn. 162, Craig Schwartz Photography. Chapter 9: Shopping: 167, Ian Cumming/age fotostock. 168, M. Ariano. 177, prayitno/Flickr. 180, Stella Levy/iStockphoto. 184, Philippe Renault/age fotostock. 193, Brett Mulcahy/ Shutterstock. Chapter 10: Where to Eat: 195, Aaron Cook. 196, Noe Montes, noemontes.com. 198, courtesy of Cicada. 199 (top left), Ethan Pines. 199 (top right), courtesy of Cicada. 199 (bottom), Elizabeth Eastman, J. Paul Getty Trust. 200, wisely/Flickr. 201(bottom left), Gonzalo Rivero/Wikipedia.org. 201(top right), Ron Diggity/Flickr.220, David Berkowitz/Flickr. Chapter 11: Where to Stay: 239, Dean Dimascio. 240, Renaissance Hollywood Hotel & Spa. 248, Jonathan Rouse. Chapter 12: Disneyland and Knott's Berry Farm: 269, Robert Holmes. 270, Marc Pagani Photography/Shutterstock. 271 (top), berned_you, Fodors.com member. 271 (bottom), Brent Reeves/Shutterstock. 272, Robert Holmes. 278, www.ericcastro.biz/Flickr. 291, Robert Holmes. 294, Scott Vickers/iStockphoto. 297, www.rwongphoto/Alamy. 300, Brett Shoal/Artistic Visuals Photography. 304, Lowe Llaguno/Shutterstock.

NOTES

NOTES

NOTES

NOTES

NOTES

NOTES

NOTES

NOTES

NOTES

ABOUT OUR WRITERS

Sarah Amandolare is a Los Angeles-based freelance journalist whose work has appeared in the *New York Times, Los Angeles Times, BBC Travel,* and *Salon,* among others. Her preferred city escapes: hikes in Topanga Canyon and whale watching at Point Dume in Malibu. She used her expertise for our Pasadena, Santa Monica, and Shopping chapters.

An award-winning novelist and filmmaker, **Jim Arnold** has worked as a freelance writer for *Frontiers* and *Variety.* He's currently recovering from a long career as an entertainment industry public relations executive. A fourth-generation California native, Jim has lived and loved in Los Angeles, San Francisco, Palm Springs, and Sacramento. His favorite place to chill in L.A. is Griffith Park. He updated our Hollywood and the Studios chapter.

Cindy Arora is a Los Angeles–based freelance journalist whose work has appeared in *Saveur, Orange Coast Magazine, Edible Los Angeles, Pasadena Weekly,* and the *Orange County Register.* She is a native Angeleno who grew up eating Tijuana-style tacos in East L.A., bacon-wrapped hot dogs in Hollywood, and some of the best dim sum—outside of Hong Kong—in the San Gabriel Valley. She updated Where to Eat.

Our Where to Stay updater **Michele Bigley** has contributed to more than two dozen guidebooks. She grew up in Los Angeles and has since spent her time bouncing between L.A., San Francisco, and Hawaii. Her work has appeared in the *Los Angeles Times, Boston Globe, Islands,* CNN, and many more. When in L.A., you can find her trying to surf at Topanga State Beach.

Alene Dawson is a *Los Angeles Times* contributor and has written for numerous other print and online outlets, including *Town & Country, Elle,* and *Marie Claire.* She also writes essays and fiction, including short stories and screenplays. Road-tripping up California's Pacific Coast Highway is only one of many gifts that come from living in the Golden State, and she highly recommends the experience. She updated Beverly Hills.

Dianne de Guzman is a writer and videographer whose work appears in the *Los Angeles Times, Business Insider,* and *SFist.* She is always looking for the next adventure, whether that means finding the best burger or bar in town or researching scuba diving spots for her next trip. She updated our Performing Arts and Nightlife chapters.

Finding the unexpected is Los Angeles freelance writer and frequent traveler **Kathy A. McDonald**'s favorite assignment. A writer with peripatetic beats, she covers film business, design, and destinations, and is a frequent contributor to *Variety, Los Angeles Confidential,* and other publications. Art galleries, modern architecture, and thrift stores entice her; she rarely passes an open house or yard sale without stopping. She updated Orange County.

Clarissa Wei is a Los Angeles writer whose works have appeared on CNN, CBS Los Angeles, the *Los Angeles Times, L.A. Weekly, The Village Voice, USA Today, The New York Times, Serious Eats,* and KCET. Clarissa is known for her Chinese food expertise and has appeared on *Bizarre Foods with Andrew Zimmern.* She's the founder of Curated Gnomes, a food tour company in Los Angeles. She covered Downtown for this edition.